Theories for decolonial social
work practice
in South Africa

T0347006

OXFORD
UNIVERSITY PRESS

Oxford University Press is a department of the University of Oxford.
It furthers the University's objective of excellence in research, scholarship,
and education by publishing worldwide. Oxford is a registered trade mark of
Oxford University Press in the UK and in certain other countries.

Published in South Africa by
Oxford University Press Southern Africa (Pty) Limited

Vasco Boulevard, Goodwood, N1 City, Cape Town, South Africa, 7460
P O Box 12119, N1 City, Cape Town, South Africa, 7463

Oxford University Press Southern Africa (Pty) Ltd 2019

Theories for decolonial social work practice in South Africa

ISBN 978 0 19 072135 0

First impression 2019

Typeset in Utopia Std 9,5pt on 12pt
Printed on 70 gsm woodfree paper

Acknowledgements
Publishing Manager: Alida Terblanche
Publisher: Marisa Montemarano
Development Editor: Jeanne Maclay-Mayers
Project Manager: Gugulethu Baloyi
Editor: Revenia Abrahams
Indexer: Michel Cozien
Art Director: Judith Cross
Cover Designer: Yaseen Baker
Spec Designer: Danielle Nieuwenhuis
Typesetter: Tella Publishing
Printed and bound by: ABC Press
10119

Abridged Table of Contents

Chapter 1   Introduction to social work theory – *Adrian van Breda*.. 1

Chapter 2   Decoloniality in social work – *Rinie Schenck*..20

Chapter 3   Developmental social work – *Antoinette Lombard*..47

Chapter 4   Social constructionism – *Rinie Schenck*..67

Chapter 5   Ecosystems – *Paul Mbedzi*..86

Chapter 6   *Ubuntu – Johannah Sekudu*...105

Chapter 7   Resilience – *Adrian van Breda*...120

Chapter 8   Attachment – *Johannah Sekudu*...140

Chapter 9   Feminisms – *Shahana Rasool*...157

Chapter 10 Sustainable livelihoods – *Antoinette Lombard*...178

Chapter 11 Person-centred – *Paul Mbedzi*...198

Chapter 12 Spirituality – *Glynnis Dykes and Shernaaz Carelse*...222

Chapter 13 Strengths-based – *Adrian van Breda*...243

Chapter 14 Circle of Courage – *Glynnis Dykes*...262

Chapter 15 Mapping the way forward in decolonising social work theory
             in South Africa – *Johannah Sekudu*..280

Table of Contents

Abridged Table of Contents iii
Table of Contents iv
Preface.. ix
Foreword.. xi
About the authors xii
Acknowledgements.. xiv

Chapter 1   **Introduction to social work theory** – *Adrian van Breda*................. 1
            1.1   Introduction 2
            1.2   Relevance of theory for social work 3
            1.3   Eclectic use of theory..6
            1.4   Definition of terms 7
            1.5   Deconstructing social work theory...8
            1.6   Decolonising social work theory 10
            1.7   Constructing indigenous theory..11
                  1.7.1   Developmental social work...13
                  1.7.2   *Ubuntu*-based practice 14
            1.8   Overview of the book...14
            1.9   Conclusion 16
Chapter 2   **Decoloniality in social work** – *Rinie Schenck*................................20
            2.1   Introduction...21
            2.2   Definition of terms 23
                  2.2.1   Colony 23
                  2.2.2   Colonialism..24
                  2.2.3   Colonisation...24
                  2.2.4   Coloniality..24
                  2.2.5   Decolonisation 25
                  2.2.6   Decoloniality 26
            2.3   Historical background to colonisation globally and in Africa 26
                  2.3.1   Colonisation of Africa..27
                  2.3.2   Colonisation of the rest of the world 28
            2.4   Process of colonisation of the person..29
            2.5   Historical process of decolonisation...30
            2.6   Social work and coloniality...31
            2.7   Summary of the premises of decoloniality..................................34
                  2.7.1   Critical consciousness and conscientisation.....................34
                  2.7.2   Reconstructing power and hierarchies...............................36
                  2.7.3   Reconstructing knowledge..38
                  2.7.4   Reconstructing the self (person and community)................38
                  2.7.5   Decoloniality is the process of creating a humanity 39
                  2.7.6   Decoloniality requires a search for wholeness thinking............41
                  2.7.7   Change through dialogue, participation and collective action.......41
                  2.7.8   Facilitating decoloniality is an action-reflection process............42
            2.8   Conclusion 42
Chapter 3   **Developmental social work** – *Antoinette Lombard*........................47
            3.1   Introduction 48
            3.2   Context for developmental social work..48
            3.3   Definitions of developmental social work 50
                  3.3.1   Key definitions..50
                  3.3.2   Critical reflections on the definitions 51
            3.4   Developmental social work and sustainable development 53
            3.5   Features of developmental social work 56

		3.5.1	Promote human rights and human development	56
		3.5.2	Integrate social and economic development	57
		3.5.3	Integrate micro and macro practice	58
		3.5.4	Facilitate people participation	59
		3.5.5	Collaborate in partnerships	59
	3.6	Relevance of developmental social work for decolonial social work	60
	3.7	Conclusion	62
Chapter 4	**Social constructionism – *Rinie Schenck***	**67**
	4.1	Introduction	68
	4.2	Epistemology	68
		4.2.1	Positivistic thinking	70
		4.2.2	Constructivism and social constructionism	71
	4.3	So what is social constructionism?	72
	4.4	Examples of social constructionism	74
		4.4.1	Example 1: Religious beliefs	74
		4.4.2	Example 2: Waste pickers	74
		4.4.3	Example 3: Trauma	75
	4.5	Social constructionism's assumptions about people	76
		4.5.1	Ideas about the self	76
		4.5.2	People or the system is closed to information	76
		4.5.3	Realities are constructed collectively	77
		4.5.4	A process of meaning making through language	77
		4.5.5	Social constructionism's view of change	78
	4.6	Applying the social constructionist approach	78
		4.6.1	Importance of the relationship in social constructionism	79
		4.6.2	Dialogue	79
	4.7	Relevance of social constructionism for decolonised social work	81
	4.8	Conclusion	82
Chapter 5	**Ecosystems – *Paul Mbedzi***	**86**
	5.1	Introduction	87
	5.2	Historical background and overview of ecosystems theory	88
	5.3	Key concepts in the ecological perspective	90
		5.3.1	Social environment	91
		5.3.2	Transactions	91
		5.3.3	Energy	91
		5.3.4	Interface	92
		5.3.5	Adaptation	92
		5.3.6	Coping	92
		5.3.7	Interdependence	92
	5.4	Key concepts in general systems theory	93
		5.4.1	Boundaries	93
		5.4.2	Subsystems	93
		5.4.3	Homeostasis	94
		5.4.4	Differentiation	94
		5.4.5	Entropy	94
		5.4.6	Negative entropy	95
		5.4.7	Equifinality	95
	5.5	Levels of the ecological system	95
		5.5.1	Microsystem	96
		5.5.2	Mesosystem	96
		5.5.3	Exosystem	97
		5.5.4	Macrosystem	97

5.6	Ecosystems theory in social work practice	98
5.7	Ecosystems theory for decolonial social work practice	100
5.8	Conclusion	101

Chapter 6 **Ubuntu – Johannah Sekudu** **105**
6.1	Introduction	106
6.2	The origin of *Ubuntu*	106
6.3	What *Ubuntu* means	107
	6.3.1 *Ubuntu* as a foundation for practical mutual existence	109
	6.3.2 Principles and values that guide *Ubuntu*	110
6.4	Relevance of *Ubuntu* for decolonial social work practice	113
	6.4.1 Using *Ubuntu* in social work with individuals	114
	6.4.2 Using *Ubuntu* in social work with communities	116
6.5	Conclusion	117

Chapter 7 **Resilience – Adrian van Breda** **120**
7.1	Introduction	121
7.2	Two approaches to social work thinking and practice	121
	7.2.1 Pathogenic approach	121
	7.2.2 Salutogenic approach	122
7.3	Conceptual building blocks of resilience theory	124
	7.3.1 Adversity	125
	7.3.2 Outcomes	126
	7.3.3 Protective factors	126
7.4	Definitions of resilience	127
7.5	Individualised versus ecological approaches to resilience	130
	7.5.1 Individualised approach	130
	7.5.2 Ecological approach	132
7.6	Relevance of resilience theory for decolonial social work	134
7.7	Conclusion	136

Chapter 8 **Attachment – Johannah Sekudu** **140**
8.1	Introduction	141
8.2	Overview of attachment theory	142
	8.2.1 Stages of attachment	142
	8.2.2 Role of attachment	143
	8.2.3 Styles of attachment	144
8.3	Attachment theory for decolonial practice	147
8.4	Application of attachment theory in social work practice	149
	8.4.1 Intervention at micro level	150
	8.4.2 Intervention at macro level	154
8.5	Conclusion	154

Chapter 9 **Feminisms – Shahana Rasool** **157**
9.1	Introduction	158
9.2	Strands of feminism	159
9.3	Pre-, post-, anti- and de-colonial feminisms	161
	9.3.1 Theory	161
	9.3.2 Decolonial social work practice	165
	9.3.3 Application	165
9.4	Liberal feminism	165
	9.4.1 Theory	165
	9.4.2 Practice	166
	9.4.3 Application	166
9.5	Socialist and Marxist feminisms	167
	9.5.1 Theory	167

9.5.2 Practice 168
9.5.3 Application..168
9.6 Radical feminisms 169
9.6.1 Theory..169
9.6.2 Practice 170
9.6.3 Application..170
9.7 Commonalities among feminist strands 171
9.8 Conclusion 173
Chapter 10 Sustainable livelihoods – *Antoinette Lombard*................................**178**
10.1 Introduction..179
10.2 Sustainable livelihoods, poverty and development 180
10.3 Defining sustainable livelihoods 182
10.4 Sustainable livelihoods frameworks..187
10.4.1 Livelihood assets 188
10.4.2 Vulnerability context..191
10.4.3 Transforming structures and processes............................191
10.4.4 Livelihood strategies..191
10.4.5 Livelihood outcomes..192
10.5 Relevance of the SLA for decolonial social work practice...............193
10.6 Conclusion 194
Chapter 11 Person-centred – *Paul Mbedzi* **198**
11.1 Introduction..199
11.2 Historical background of the person-centred approach 199
11.3 Rogers' 19 propositions 201
11.4 Core conditions for facilitation 206
11.4.1 Genuineness/congruency..207
11.4.2 Unconditional positive regard 207
11.4.3 Empathy 208
11.5 Values inherent in the person-centred approach 208
11.5.1 Respect...209
11.5.2 Individualisation 209
11.5.3 Self-determination 209
11.5.4 Confidentiality 210
11.6 The person-centred facilitation process..211
11.6.1 Phase 1: Creating a safe space for facilitation....................211
11.6.2 Phase 2: Exploring unsymbolised experiences 212
11.6.3 Phase 3: Reconstruction of the self 212
11.6.4 Phase 4: Ending the process...213
11.7 Basic communication skills...213
11.8 Advanced communication skills..213
11.8.1 Advanced empathy 214
11.8.2 Exploring distortions or discrepancies 215
11.8.3 Immediacy 217
11.9 Decolonial person-centred practice..218
11.10 Conclusion 219
Chapter 12 Spirituality – *Glynnis Dykes and Shernaaz Carelse* **222**
12.1 Introduction..223
12.2 Defining spirituality and religion..223
12.2.1 What is spirituality? 224
12.2.2 What is religion? 225
12.3 History of spirituality and religion in social work 227
12.3.1 Stage 1: Sectarian origins...227

12.3.2 Stage 2: Secularisation and professionalisation 228
12.3.3 Stage 3: Resurgence of interest in S&R in social work 230
12.4 Decoloniality and spirituality 230
12.5 Spiritual assessment and intervention...231
12.5.1 Starting the helping process..231
12.5.2 A biopsychosocial-spiritual approach as assessment tool.......233
12.5.3 Macro assessment and intervention 235
12.6 Self-awareness and professional identity in spirituality and religion.....236
12.7 Conclusion 237
Chapter 13 Strengths-based – *Adrian van Breda* **243**
13.1 Introduction...244
13.2 Strengths perspective 244
13.3 Asset-based community development..246
13.3.1 ABCD methods..246
13.3.2 Appreciative inquiry 248
13.3.3 Sustainable livelihoods 250
13.3.4 ABCD's contribution to decolonial social work practice 252
13.4 Narrative therapy 253
13.4.1 Narrative practice 253
13.4.2 Solution-focused brief therapy 255
13.4.3 Narrative therapy for decolonial social work practice 256
13.5 Conclusion 258
Chapter 14 Circle of Courage – *Glynnis Dykes* **262**
14.1 Introduction...263
14.2 Origins and foundations of the Circle of Courage 263
14.2.1 The philosophical base for the Circle of Courage....................264
14.2.2 Embedded theoretical frameworks 265
14.3 Four quadrants of the Circle of Courage...266
14.3.1 Belonging..266
14.3.2 Mastery...267
14.3.3 Independence 268
14.3.4 Generosity 269
14.4 Circle of Courage in the South African context.................................269
14.4.1 The CoC in decolonial practice...270
14.4.2 The South African child: Status and care 270
14.5 Social work use of the Circle of Courage..271
14.5.1 Micro and mezzo practice...272
14.5.2 Macro practice 275
14.6 Conclusion 276
Chapter 15 Mapping the way forward in decolonising social work theory
in South Africa – *Johannah Sekudu* **280**
15.1 Introduction...280
15.2 Aspects to consider in mapping the way forward..............................280
15.2.1 Decentring Global North theory...280
15.2.2 Doing research on indigenous African practices 281
15.2.3 Developing African values and techniques 282
15.2.4 Theorising change processes 283
15.2.5 Developing African approaches to macro change.....................284
15.2.6 Developing skills of researchers, theorists and authors 285
15.3 Conclusion 285

Index..287

Theories for decolonial social work practice in South Africa emerged within a particularly volatile social context in South Africa in the 2015–2019 period of higher education and social work. In post-1994 democratic South Africa, 2015 was arguably a watershed moment in higher education in which students reached a tipping point regarding the continued colonisation of higher education. This manifested most publicly in the #FeesMustFall and #RhodesMustFall movements. Students demanded a financially accessible education that is not the preserve of the wealthy elite. They further demanded an education that is rooted in Africa and that addresses the postcolonial era in which we now live, study and work. The call was, and remains, for a fundamental reimagining of higher education that deliberately rejects colonial hegemonies, and that seeks to embody African history, values and aspirations.

Social work, as one of the disciplines in higher education, heeded this call and began working in purposeful and collective ways towards decolonising its educational programme. In 2016, the Association of South African Social Work Education Institutions (ASASWEI) facilitated a series of regional dialogues with social work academics on decolonising social work education. In 2017, ASASWEI hosted an international conference on decolonial social work education and practice, in partnership with the Association of Schools of Social Work in Africa and the National Department of Social Development. In 2018, ASASWEI partnered with the *Southern African Journal of Social Work and Social Development* to produce a themed journal issue on decolonising social work education in South Africa.

This book, while not commissioned by ASASWEI, is written by members of ASASWEI and is a response by the editors and authors to some of the themes that have emerged through these various conversations. First, it is a response to the recognition that social work education relies inadequately on local (South African, African or Global South) literature. All too often, educators prescribe books from the USA and UK. While social work scholars in South Africa do publish research, few scholarly books have emerged that can also be used in the classroom. Second, it is a response to the need for practice theories that are rooted in Africa generally and the South African context particularly, and that address the challenges communities continue to face post-apartheid. And third, it responds to the need for practice theory that contributes to the liberation of people and structures from the tenacious bonds of colonialism.

We have used the term 'decolonial' in our title. Terms like these are contested and there does not appear to be universal agreement on their exact meanings. In this book, we understand *colonisation* to mean the socio-historical period in which a country is ruled by a foreign power (the coloniser), and *decolonisation* to refer primarily to the historical process of the withdrawal or expulsion of that power, and the work to undo the structural impositions of the coloniser (e.g., through changing legislation and instituting employment equity policies). We understand *coloniality* to refer to the ways in which the coloniser infiltrates the minds of people – both colonised and coloniser – to shape thinking, believing, feeling and valuing in ways that align with and perpetuate the colonial agenda. Thus, for example, the belief that white is good and black is bad is a result of coloniality.

Decoloniality, then, is about undoing colonial ways of being, thinking, relating, acting and structuring. In part, decoloniality is about redeeming the mind from the bondage of coloniality. In South Africa, this involves, for example, white people recognising and rejecting white privilege and black people embracing black heritage and power. In addition, decoloniality is, in part, social, calling for new ways of relating between black and white that are rooted in mutual respect and responsiveness to historical woundedness. Finally, decoloniality is structural, involving a redesign of social institutions and systems that embody our Africanness. Decoloniality is not about discarding Global North knowledge systems; it is about decentring them, and about placing African knowledge systems on at least the same footing as other knowledge systems. That is, it seeks a plurality of knowledge systems that interact as equals.

Ideally, this book would present a range of indigenous (African) theories of social work practice. But, in fact, at this time, little social work practice theory has emerged from within South Africa. This remains an ongoing project for social work in South Africa. This book therefore presents a range of indigenised theories of social work practice, mostly drawn from the Global North, but adapted for and embodied within the African context. Some chapters (e.g., decoloniality, developmental social work and *Ubuntu*) draw almost entirely on African knowledge systems; some chapters (e.g., feminisms) draw on both African and Global North knowledge systems, while other chapters (e.g., social constructionism, resilience and strengths-based practices) draw on Global North knowledge systems modified through extensive research and practice experience in Africa.

We selected the theories for this book based on their potential contribution to the decolonial agenda. The selected theories needed to have more than only clinical application at the micro level of practice – they needed to be able to address personal, social and structural issues at mezzo or macro levels as well. Theories also needed to have the potential not only to address problems that people face, but also to facilitate transformation and liberation, particularly in the wake of generations of colonisation, institutionalised racism and violence.

The first three chapters of the book lay a contextual foundation for social work practice theories in South Africa. The first chapter introduces theory itself, the political and situated nature of theory, how it is constructed, and what constitutes indigenised and indigenous theories. The second chapter addresses the topic of decoloniality, not so much from a conceptual and theoretical perspective, but rather in relation to what decolonial social work processes might look like. The third chapter provides an overview of developmental social work – one of the approaches to social work practice that is indigenous to South Africa, which is also the bedrock of social welfare and social work in South Africa.

The remaining chapters of the book present 11 practice theories, sequenced from more epistemological towards more practical. The chapters on *Ubuntu*, spirituality, and the circle of courage have special resonance in Africa – *Ubuntu* and spirituality are central to African ways of being, while the circle of courage is the central conceptual model for child welfare services in South Africa. Social constructionism aligns well with decoloniality's concern for a plurality of knowledge systems; ecosystems theory champions the centrality of the social environment; resilience theory and strengths-based practices work to identify and promote indigenous knowledge and practice systems; the chapter on feminisms addresses an ongoing point of conflict in society, regarding women and gender relations; and attachment theory and the person-centred and sustainable livelihoods approaches speak to the micro-macro continuum of developmental social work practice.

The book concludes with a reflection on the way forward for theories for decolonial social work theory and practice in South Africa. It maps out the agenda for work yet to be done in decolonising social work education and practice in this part of Africa.

The editors and authors hope that this book will provide a thoughtful and useful resource for social workers in South Africa, but also further afield in Africa and the Global South, about theories that inform and guide practice. And ultimately, we hope that this book will contribute towards the decolonial agenda and the liberation of South Africa.

Foreword

Since the end of apartheid in the early 1990s, South African social work educators and practitioners have pioneered the deconstruction and reconstruction of social work education in the southern African region and beyond. Such efforts have included discourses on developmental social work, indigenisation of social work practice and education, and culturally relevant social work. The current book, *Theories for decolonial social work practice in South Africa*, edited by Prof Adrian D. van Breda of the University of Johannesburg and Dr Johannah Sekudu of the University of South Africa (UNISA), is the latest in the series of efforts aimed at decolonising social work theory, education and practice, and setting them free from their colonial past.

The debates and discussions on the relationship between social work in Africa and social work in the West (particularly North America and Europe) are about the structure, content, and direction of social work education and practice. The end of apartheid energised the efforts to make the social work profession culturally relevant. Whereas the goal has been clear, there have been difficulties with new theoretical foundations of the profession consistent with weaning the profession from its past and from theories and processes that are not entirely applicable in the African context.

This work, with its central themes of decolonial social work and developmental social work, is the first of its kind that attempts to develop theoretical frameworks for social work designed to free the profession in South Africa from some of its foreign 'entanglements'. This volume provides the foundation for the search for cultural relevance or appropriateness in African social work, which has not been clearly defined before. The concept of decoloniality is given prominence, becoming the theoretical basis for tackling some of the challenges that are associated with the profession. The decolonial discourse is a fresh attempt to recreate a profession underpinned by indigenous concepts. It emphasises the rediscovery and recreation of principles, values, knowledge and skills that are the basis of life of the South African.

Decolonial social work is conceptualised and perceived in relation to developmental social work. This edited work takes the reader through a theoretical construct focusing on reshaping thinking and behaviour that does not reinforce the colonial agenda of social work education and practice in South Africa. Placing African value systems at the centre of the profession also supports the idea of social work becoming developmental. This in effect supports the welfare system South Africa adopted after the demise of apartheid.

The theories presented give insight into the range of possible theories that may drive decolonial and developmental social work practice in South Africa. Theories such as *Ubuntu* and spirituality, which are core to African value systems and behaviours, are emphasised. Other theories – social constructionism, ecosystems, resilience, attachment, feminisms, sustainable livelihoods, person-centred approach, strength-based practice and Circle of Courage – are all treated in the context of their contribution to both the conceptual and the practical elements of decolonial and developmental social work practice and education in Southern Africa. The work outlines some of the challenges faced by the process of rethinking social work education in South Africa and gives insight into the difficulties associated with theoretical frameworks that must drive the decolonial agenda in social work and social development.

This is an interesting volume, a useful resource for social workers not only in South Africa but in Africa generally and beyond. Social work academics, researchers, practitioners and all those involved in interrogating social work with respect to its place in South Africa's development in particular, and that of Africa and the developing world in general, must read the book. It is a valuable addition to the search for social work education and practice that is befitting for Africa.

Prof Kwaku Osei-Hwedie
Dean, Faculty of Academic Affairs and Research
Kofi Annan International Peacekeeping Training Centre; Accra, Ghana

About the authors

Prof Adrian D. van Breda is Professor of social work at the University of Johannesburg, where he has taught for 12 years. Prior to that, he was a social worker, social work researcher and health research manager with the Department of Defence for 17 years. Adrian is a leading scholar in the area of resilience theory, serving as Vice President of Resilio, an international association that advances transdisciplinary resilience scholarship. He is also the leading African scholar on leaving care, serving as co-founder of an African network of care-leaving scholars (ANCR) and an Executive member of the global network (INTRAC). He is President of the Association of South African Social Work Education Institutions (ASASWEI) and is particularly interested in promoting African scholars and scholarship.

Dr Johannah Sekudu is a Senior Lecturer at the University of South Africa. She holds a DPhil degree from the University of Pretoria, where she also obtained her MSD (Health Care). She obtained her Bachelor of Social Work at the then University of the North, currently known as the University of Limpopo. Previously she taught at the North West University (Mafikeng Campus) and the University of Pretoria, where she worked for most of her career. Her career as a social worker started at Pretoria Child Welfare and GaRankuwa Hospital. She published several peer-reviewed articles and authored chapters to a book titled *Introduction to social work in the South African context* (2015), wherein social work theories are made applicable to the South African context.

Dr Shernaaz Carelse is a Lecturer in the Department of Social Work at the University of the Western Cape (UWC). Before joining UWC, she worked as a child and youth care worker and later as a social worker in different settings across the Western Cape. Her research interests are learning and teaching in academia, child and family well-being, and substance use disorders. She is involved in several research projects relating to scholarship of learning and teaching, youth in gangs, psychosocial well-being and empowerment of out-of-school youth, and gender-based violence. In addition, she has a key interest in the spirituality discourse in substance use disorders.

Dr Glynnis Dykes is a Senior Lecturer in the Department of Social Work at the University of the Western Cape. She completed her PhD in social work learning and teaching at Stellenbosch University. She is published in learning and teaching and the adverse childhood experiences of social work students, and specifically the effects on how students are able to learn within their individual contexts and own personal experiences. Her research interests include family well-being and parenting, and youth in gangs – especially the learning and teaching of these topics in social work, which are context-driven.

Prof Antoinette Lombard is a Professor in the Department of Social Work at the University of Pretoria and serves on several professional and academic bodies. Her research interests include developmental social work, social development, sustainable development and social change. She received the James Billups International Consortium for Social Development Leadership Award in 2013, a national award from the Minister of Science and Technology as the second runner up for the 2015 Distinguished Women in Science Award in the category Humanities and Social Sciences, and the Distinguish Educator of the Year Award from the Association for South African Social Work Education Institutions (ASASWEI) in 2017.

Dr Paul (Rembuluwani) Mbedzi is a Senior Lecturer in the Department of Social Work at the University of South Africa (UNISA). He obtained his PhD from UNISA and his research interests include marriage and couple counselling, family functioning and working with children. Prior to joining UNISA, he practised as a social worker in the public service and in diverse non-governmental organisations for many years. He co-authored several books including *Person-centred facilitation* (2013) and *Introduction to social work in the South African context* (2015).

Prof Shahana Rasool, a Rhodes Scholar, obtained her MA and PhD from the Department of Social Policy at the University of Oxford (UK). She is currently Associate Professor and Head of the social work department at the University of Johannesburg (UJ). Prior to coming to UJ, she lectured at the University of the Witwatersrand (WITS). She has a keen interest in social transformation, which began as an anti-apartheid activist in South Africa and continued through her work in the NGO sector in South Africa and Australia. Her research is primarily focused on gender-based violence. She is Vice President of the Association for Schools of Social Work in Africa (ASSWA) and the African representative on the International Association of Schools of Social Work (IASSW). She is chair of the International conference on Gender, which was held in Thailand in 2018 and will be held in Malaysia in 2019. She is also chair of the *Southern African Journal for Social Work and Social Development*.

Prof Rinie Schenck is the DST/NRF/CSIR Chair in Waste and Society at the University of the Western Cape (UWC). She was previously the Head of the Department of Social Work at UWC, and taught at the University of South Africa (UNISA) and the University of Pretoria. She published extensively in peer-reviewed journals, authored several book chapters, and was the co-editor for a few books.

Acknowledgements

The authors and publishers gratefully acknowledge permission to reproduce the following copyright material:

Chapter 1

p. 13. Source: Patel, L. 2015. *Social welfare and social development*. 2nd ed. Cape Town: Oxford University Press Southern Africa, p. 82. Reprinted by permission of Oxford University Press Southern Africa.

p. 14. Source: Nyaumwe, LJ & Mkabela, Q. 2007. Revisiting the traditional African cultural framework of ubuntuism: A theoretical perspective. *Indilinga: African Journal of Indigenous Knowledge Systems*, 6:2:152. Reprinted by permission of the editor, *Indilinga: African Journal of Indigenous Knowledge Systems*.

Chapter 2

p. 20. Source: wa Thiong'o, Ngũgĩ, "Ngũgĩ wa Thiong'o" (2009). *Meaningful Work 2009–2010*. 2. Available at http://thekeep.eiu.edu/humanitiescenter_meaningfulwork0910/2 Creative Commons License. This work is licensed under a Creative Commons Attribution-Noncommercial-No Derivative Works 3.0 License.

p. 22. **Figure 2.1 Development and progress of thought processes towards transformation**. Source: Harms Smith, LH & Nathane, M. 2017. #notdomestication #notindigenisation: Decoloniality in Social Work education. *Southern African Journal of Social Work and Social development*, 30(1), p 4. Reprinted by permission of the editor, *Southern African Journal of Social Work and Social Development*.

p. 24. Source: Maldonado-Torres, N (2007) On the coloniality of being. *Cultural Studies*, 21:2–3, 243. Reprinted by permission of the publisher (Taylor & Francis Ltd, http://www.tandfonline.com).

p.24. Definition of *colonialism* in English. Source: https://en.oxforddictionaries.com/definition/colonialism. Reproduced with permission of **Oxford Publishing Limited** through **PLSclear**.

p. 24. Source: Ndlovu-Gatsheni, SJ. 2015b. Decoloniality in Africa: A continuing search for a new world order. *Australasian Review of African Studies* (*ARAS*), 36(2):30. Reprinted by permission of *ARAS*.

p. 33. Source: Olson, JJ. 2007. Social Work's professional and social justice projects: Discourses in conflict. *Journal of progressive human services* 2007, 184(1):47, Taylor & Francis Ltd. Reprinted by permission of the publisher (Taylor & Francis Ltd, http://www.tandfonline.com).

p. 37. **Case study 2.2 Dealing with cultural mindsets**. Source: Akujobi, R. 2009. "Yesterday you were divorced. Today I am a widow": An appraisal of widowhood practices and the effects on the psyche of the women in Africa. *Gender and Behaviour*, 7(2):2460–2461.

p. 37. Source: Hugo, S. 2018. An empowerment programme for African young widows in Mangaung Metro, Free State. Unpublished survey data. Reprinted by permission of Ms Shirley Nozipo Hugo.

Chapter 3

p. 49. Source: Ahmad, M & Jariwala, HV. 2016. *Living in a global society*. Part One of a Two-Part Special Issue, 42(5):573–575. Reprinted by permission of the publisher (Taylor & Francis Ltd, http://www.tandfonline.com).

p. 51. Source: Gray, M. et al. (2018) 'The expansion of developmental social work in Southern and East Africa: Opportunities and challenges for social work field programmes', *International Social Work*, 61(6):974–987.

p. 51. Source: Patel, L. 2015. *Social welfare and social development*. 2nd ed. Cape Town: Oxford University Press Southern Africa, p. 127. Reprinted by permission of Oxford University Press Southern Africa.

p. 53. Text: Sustainable development, … 'planet from … future generations' (UN, 2015:5). Source: United Nations. 2015. *Transforming our world, the 2030 Agenda for Sustainable Development*. [Online]. Available: https://sustainabledevelopment.un.org/content/ documents/21252030%20Agenda%20for%20Sustainable%20Development%20web.pdf [Accessed 6 June 2019].

p. 53. Text: … 'eradicating poverty … sustainable development' (UN, 2015:5). Source: United Nations. 2015. *Transforming our world, the 2030 Agenda for Sustainable Development*. [Online]. Available: https://sustainabledevelopment.un.org/content/ documents/21252030%20Agenda%20for%20Sustainable%20Development%20web.pdf [Accessed 6 June 2019].

p. 54. Source: Hawkins, CA. 2010. Sustainability, human rights, and environmental justice: Critical connections for contemporary social work. *Critical Social Work*, 11(3):68. Reprinted by permission of the managing editor, *Critical Social Work*.

p. 57. Text: Integrated social and economic development … 'ensure that … in harmony with nature' (UN, 2015:5). Source: United Nations. 2015. *Transforming our world, the 2030 Agenda for Sustainable Development*. [Online]. Available: https://sustainabledevelopment.un.org/ content/documents/21252030%20Agenda%20for%20Sustainable%20Development%20web. pdf [Accessed 6 June 2019].

p. 58. Source: Reisch, M. 2016. Why macro practice matters. *Journal of Social Work Education*, 52(3):261. Reprinted by permission of the publisher (Taylor & Francis Ltd, http:// www.tandfonline.com).

p. 58. Source: Harrison, J, Van Deusen, K & Way, I. 2016. Embedding social justice within micro social work curricula. *Smith College Studies in Social Work*, 86(3):269. Reprinted by permission of the publisher (Taylor & Francis Ltd, http://www.tandfonline.com).

p. 58. Source: Sewpaul, V. © 2016. The West and the rest divide: Human rights, culture and social work. *Journal of Human Rights Social Work*, 1, p. 37. Reprinted by permission of Springer Nature.

Chapter 4

p. 70. **The following is a local example from Van der Watt (2016:4)** … . Source: Van der Watt, P. 2016. Engaging with the 'soil and the soul' of a community: Rethinking development, healing and transformation in South Africa. PhD thesis. University of the Free State, Bloemfontein, p. 4. Reprinted by permission of the Centre for Development Support, University of the Free State.

p. 72. Source: Saleebey, D.1994. Culture, theory and narrative: The intersection of meanings in practice. *Social Work*, 39(4):351–359. p. 352. Reprinted by permission of Oxford University Press.

p. 76. **Van der Watt (2016:179) provides an example of identities** … . Source: Van der Watt, P. 2016. Engaging with the 'soil and the soul' of a community: Rethinking development, healing and transformation in South Africa. PhD thesis. University of the Free State, Bloemfontein. p. 179. Reprinted by permission of the Centre for Development Support, University of the Free State.

p. 80. Case study adapted from: Van der Watt, P. 2016. *Engaging with the 'soil and the soul' of a community: Rethinking development, healing and transformation in South Africa*. PhD thesis. University of the Free State, Bloemfontein. p. 210.

p. 82. The next quotation by Bawden and Macadam (1990:139) concludes this chapter:

"Think about things" in a quite different way: for what we do ... about thinking. Bawden, R & Macadam, RD. 1990. Towards a university for people-centred development: A case history of reform. *Australian Journal of Adult and Community Education*, 30(3):138–53. Reprinted by permission of Adult Learning Australia(ALA).

Chapter 5

p. 89. Source: Weiss-Gal, I. 2008. The person-in-environment approach: Professional ideology and practice of social workers in Israel. *Social Work*, 53:65–75, p. 65. Reprinted by permission of Oxford University Press.

p. 89. Source: Strean, Herbert S (1979), 'The contemporary family and the responsibilities of the social worker in direct practice', *Journal of Jewish Communal Service*, 56(1):40–49. Reprinted by permission of the JPRO Network.

Chapter 6

p. 107. Source: Marston, JM. 2015. The spirit of "Ubuntu" in children's palliative care. *Journal of Pain and Symptom Management*, 50(3):424–427, p. 424. Copyright © 2015 American Academy of Hospice and Palliative Medicine. Reprinted by permission of Elsevier Inc.

p. 109. Nussbaum, B. 2003. African culture and Ubuntu: Reflections of a South African in America. *Perspectives*, 17(1):1–12, p. 2. Reprinted by permission of Barbara Nussbaum.

pp. 111–112. Nussbaum, B. 2003. African culture and Ubuntu: Reflections of a South African in America. *Perspectives*, 17(1):1–12. Reprinted by permission of Barbara Nussbaum.

p. 112. Source: Shonhiwa, S. 2006. *The effective cross-cultural manager: A guide for business leaders in Africa*. Cape Town: Zebra, 2006. Reprinted by permission of Shepherd Shonhiwa.

Chapter 7

p. 128. Masten, AS. 2015. *Ordinary magic: Resilience in development*. New York: Guilford Publications, p. 10.

p. 129. Van Breda, AD. 2018a. A critical review of resilience theory and its relevance for social work. *Social Work/Maatskaplike Werk*, 54, p. 4. Reprinted by permission of *Social Work/Maatskaplike Werk*.

p. 129. **Figure 7.1: Resilience as process and outcome**. Source: Van Breda, 2018:4 Van Breda, AD. 2018. A critical review of resilience theory and its relevance for social work. *Social Work/Maatskaplike Werk*, 54, p. 4. Reprinted by permission of *Social Work/ Maatskaplike Werk*.

p. 131. Source: Kobasa, SC. 1979. Stressful life events, personality, and health: An inquiry into hardiness. *Journal of Personality and Social Psychology*, 37, p. 1.

p. 134. Source: Weiss-Gal, I. 2008. The person-in-environment approach: Professional ideology and practice of social workers in Israel. *Social Work*, 53(1):65. Reprinted by permission of Oxford University Press.

p. 134. **Figure 7.2: Person-in-environment framework**. Source: Van Breda, 2017 (2):250. The Youth Ecological-Resilience Scale: A partial validation. *Research on Social Work Practice*, 27(2):248–257.

Chapter 9

p. 169. Source: Hassim, S. 1991. Gender, social location and feminist politics in South Africa. *Transformation*, 15, p. 1. Reprinted by permission of the managing editor, *Transformation*.

pp. 171–172. Source: Hassim, S. 1991. Gender, social location and feminist politics in South Africa. *Transformation*, 15, p. 72. Reprinted by permission of the managing editor, *Transformation*.

Chapter 10

pp. 181 & 183. Source: Chambers, R & Conway, G. 1992. *Sustainable rural livelihoods: Practical concepts for the 21st century*. IDS Discussion Paper 296. UK, Brighton: IDS, pp. 3, 5 & 6.

p. 184. Source: Scoones, I. 1998. *Sustainable rural livelihoods. A framework for analysis*. IDS Working Paper 72. UK, Brighton: IDS, pp. 5 & 6.

pp. 194–195: Source: Reprinted from *The Lancet*, Vol. 379, Sachs, J, From Millennium Development Goals to Sustainable Development Goals. 2206–2211, (2209). Copyright 2012, with permission from Elsevier.

p. 194. Text: The mix of assets ... 'If the potential ... would be reduced' (UNDP, 2015:iii). Source: United Nations Development Programme. 2015. *Human development report 2015: Work for human development*. [Online]. Available: http://hdr.undp.org/sites/default/files/2015_human_development_report.pdf [Accessed 1 May 2018].

p. 195. Text: The sustainable livelihoods ... 'the true aim ... lives' (UNDP, 2015:1). Source: United Nations Development Programme. 2015. *Human development report 2015: Work for human development*. [Online]. Available: http://hdr.undp.org/sites/default/files/2015_human_development_report.pdf [Accessed 1 May 2018].

Chapter 11

p. 200. Source: Joseph, S & Murphy, D. 2013. Person-centred approach, positive psychology, and relational helping: Building bridges. *Journal of Humanistic Psychology*, 53(1):26–51, p. 27. Copyright © 2013, © SAGE Publications.

p. 211. Text Source: (IASSW, 2018: Section 6.5). IASSW. 2018. *Global social work statement of ethical principles*. International Association of Schools of Social Work. Available [Online] https://www.iassw-aiets.org/wp-content/uploads/2018/04/Global-Social-Work-Statement-of-Ethical-Principles-IASSW-27-April-2018-1.pdf [Accessed 06 June 2019].

Chapter 12

p. 224. Definition of *religiosity* in English. Source: https://en.oxforddictionaries.com/definition/religiosity. Reproduced with permission of **Oxford Publishing Limited** through **PLSclear**.

p. 224. Definition of *theology* in English. Source: https://en.oxforddictionaries.com/definition/theology. Reproduced with permission of **Oxford Publishing Limited** through **PLSclear**.

p. 226. Definition of *religion* in English. Source: https://en.oxforddictionaries.com/definition/religion. Reproduced with permission of **Oxford Publishing Limited** through **PLSclear**.

p. 231. Source: Mekada J. Graham, The African-centred worldview: Developing a paradigm for social work, *The British Journal of Social Work* 1999; 29(2):251–267, doi:10.1093/oxfordjournals.bjsw.a011445. Reprinted by permission of Oxford University Press on behalf of the British Association of Social Workers.

p. 232. Source: Knitter, P. 2010. Social work religious diversity: Problems and possibilities. *Journal of Religion and Spirituality in Social Work: Social Thought*, 29(3):256–270, p. 260. Reprinted by permission of the publisher (Taylor & Francis Ltd, http://www.tandfonline.com).

p. 233. Source: Republic of South Africa. Council on Higher Education (CHE). 2015. Higher Education Qualifications Sub-Framework. Qualifications Standard for Bachelor of Social Work, South Africa. ©Council on Higher Education, 2013. Reprinted with permission of the Council Higher Education.

p. 234. Figure 12.1: Biopsychosocial and spiritual framework (BPSS) Ch 13. Hipwell, WT. 2009. An asset-based approach to indigenous development in Taiwan. *Asia Pacific Viewpoint*, 50, 289–306, p. 297. Adapted from: Sulmasy, D. 2002. A bio-psychosocial-spiritual model for the care of patients at the end of life. *The Gerontologist*, 42(3):24–33, Figure 2. Reprinted by permission of Oxford University Press.

p. 236. Source: Reprinted by permission from Springer Nature: *Clinical Social Work Journal*, Reupert, A. 2007. Social worker's use of self. *Clinical Social Work Journal*, 35(2):107–116, p. 108. © 2007.

Chapter 13

p. 244. Source: Weick, A, Rapp, C, Sullivan, WP & Kisthardt, W. 1989. A strengths perspective for social work practice. *Social Work*, 34(4):350–54, p. 352. Reprinted by permission of Oxford University Press.

p. 247. Source: Mathie, A & Cunningham, G. 2003. From clients to citizens: Asset-based community development as a strategy for community-driven development. *Development in Practice*, 13(5):474–486, p. 477. Reprinted by permission of the publisher (Taylor & Francis Ltd, http://www.tandfonline.com).

p. 251. Source: Nel (2015:514) Nel, H. 2015. An integration of the livelihoods and asset-based community development approaches: A South African case study. *Development Southern Africa*, 3(2):511–525, p. 514. Reprinted by permission of the publisher (Taylor & Francis Ltd, http://www.tandfonline.com).

p. 251. **Activity 13.2: Sustainable livelihoods framework**. Adapted from: United Kingdom. DFID. 1999. *Sustainable livelihoods guidance sheets*. London: Department for International Development.

p. 252. Source: Macleod, MA & Emejulu, A. 2014. Neoliberalism with a community face? A critical analysis of asset-based community development in Scotland. *Journal of Community Practice*, 22(4):430–450, pp. 431 & 437. Reprinted by permission of the publisher (Taylor & Francis Ltd, http://www.tandfonline.com).

p. 252. Source: Hipwell, WT. 2009. An asset-based approach to indigenous development in Taiwan. *Asia Pacific Viewpoint*, 50:289–306, p. 297.

pp. 257–258. Source: Butler, J. 2017. Who's your mob? Aboriginal mapping: Beginning with the strong story. *International Journal of Narrative Therapy and Community Work*, 3:22–26, pp. 23 & 24. Reprinted by permission of The Dulwich Centre.

Chapter 14

p. 268. Source: Gilgun, J. 2002. Completing the Circle: American Indian medicine wheels and the promotion of resilience of children and youth in care. *Journal of Human Behavior in the Social Environment*, 6(2):65–84, p. 73. Reprinted by permission of the publisher (Taylor & Francis Ltd, http://www.tandfonline.com).

p. 269. '**Generosity**' Source: Brokenleg, M. 1999. Native American perspectives on generosity. *Reclaiming Children and Youth*, 8(2):66–68, (p.67). Reprinted by permission of the author.

p. 273. **Figure 14.2 Assessment essentials**. Compiled from information in: Jackson, W. 2014. *The Circle of Courage: Childhood socialization in the 21st century*. Doctoral thesis in partial fulfilment of the degree of Doctor in Philosophy. Wayne State University, Detroit, Michigan USA; Lee, B & Perales, K. 2007. Circle of Courage: Reaching youth in residential care. *Residential Treatment for Children and Youth*, 22(4):1–16.

Introduction to social work theory

Adrian van Breda

 Case Study 1 The need for theory to inform social work practice

Sibongile is a social worker working at an organisation that provides comprehensive social welfare services to families. She is really committed to making family life better for people. This is partly motivated by her own family experiences as a child, where she felt neglected and caught between parents who often fought and eventually got divorced.

Many of the couples that Sibongile works with at this organisation present with domestic violence; usually it is the husband who beats on the wife, though occasionally it's the other way around, and sometimes they beat on each other. It really upsets Sibongile, because it brings back painful memories from her childhood. She wishes she could rescue these couples from themselves.

When she works with these couples, Sibongile finds herself working intuitively. She doesn't really know how to make sense of their violence. And she doesn't really know what she can do to help them. Sometimes she feels threatened by the husbands; they're aggressive and intimidating, reminding her of her own father and making her feel like a child again. At other times, though, she gets angry at these husbands and reprimands them, even threatens them with legal action. And on occasion she gets very frustrated with the wives, because some of them are so passive and helpless; she wants to shake them by the shoulders and tell them to stand up for themselves, like she wished her mother would have done.

Reflective questions
- According to what framework is Sibongile making sense of the dynamics of the couples with whom she works? Is it a theoretical framework, or a personal framework?
- How helpful is the framework she's using in helping her understand what is happening in the marriages of these couples?
- How helpful is the framework in guiding her practice?
- How would reading theory about domestic violence benefit Sibongile's work?

1.1 Introduction

This chapter sets the stage for the rest of the book. It introduces the concept of 'theory', explaining what it is and why it is important for social workers. Sometimes social workers think that theory is abstract and not particularly useful for helping people. Sometimes this is indeed true! But, this book aims to show that theory can be extremely useful, often absolutely essential, for us to provide effective, useful and ethical social work services to people. Often the people we work with are extremely vulnerable; thus, we need to offer a service that is based on sound principles and theories, drawn from a recognised body of literature, rather than just making it up as we go along. In many ways, it is our use of theory that makes social work a profession, and not lay counselling or being a supportive friend.

Practical case studies are used throughout this chapter to illustrate how theory provides a valuable framework that enables the social worker to provide transformative social welfare services in line with the rights and values provided in the South African Constitution.

The reflective questions on the case study are intended to show how, in the absence of such theory, Sibongile's ability to work with domestic violence was weakened. As a result, she worked intuitively. And because of her own painful childhood experiences, she often worked in unhelpful and even unethical ways with these couples. Mastering theory relevant to working with domestic violence would have empowered her to understand these couples and given her a map for intervening with them.

However, with so many theories around, it can be hard to know which theory to use. Often theories conflict with one another, so that when you adopt one theory to guide your practice, you find your work criticised by someone using another theory. Perhaps the multitude of theories overwhelms and confuses us, rather than enabling and empowering us. In this book, we present theories in 14 chapters, some of which present multiple theories that have a common theme. We hope that this will provide you with a range of theoretical options from which to choose, like a menu at a restaurant. This chapter will orientate you to this menu, so that you understand the options available to you.

For us who practise social work in South Africa, or other parts of Africa, an additional challenge is that the theories that are available to us are mostly American or European. In the past, given the colonial history of the African content, these theories mostly served the interests of colonialism. As a result, there is a serious absence of African theory that feels 'local' and that addresses the contextual realities of who we are, where we work, and the people with whom we work. Some aspects of existing theories may prove to be irrelevant and inappropriate to our context of developmental social work. Therefore, the challenge is to draw not only from existing theories but also from our own experiences, transformative legislation and policies, and constitutional values to develop African theory that is appropriate to our context. In this book, we endeavour to translate theory into our contexts, showing where and how they could be useful. We aim to adjust them to be more relevant to us, particularly as we practise developmental social work. We're calling this a process of 'decolonising theory'. Chapter 2 of this book focuses on this aspect in more detail.

In this chapter, I explain what it means to decolonise theory. It involves critically engaging with theories that we import from the Global North (particularly America and Europe), bringing to light their taken-for-granted assumptions, and recognising that all theory is situated, contextual and political. In this way, we can discard those aspects of theory that do not align with our contexts and goals and keep those that do.

But I hope to take you a bit further in this chapter towards developing our own indigenous theory. In truth, we have not made much headway in developing South African social work theory. So, I will map out some of the approaches that we could take to develop our own theory and illustrate this with a couple of examples of projects to develop indigenous social work theories in Africa.

1.2 Relevance of theory for social work

What is theory? Payne (2016:5) defines theory as 'a generalized set of ideas that describes and explains our knowledge of the world around us in an organized way. A social work theory is one that helps us to do or to understand social work'.

According to this definition, theory has two main purposes for social workers:

1. **Theory helps us to understand or make sense of the world**. Generally, theory helps us to make sense of belief and value systems, gender relations, and the socio-cultural and economic contexts of society, among others. For Sibongile (in the case study), that means theory would help her understand the patterns of violence in the couples she works with. Instead of only making sense of their violence according to her own experiences as a child, she would also be able to make sense of them according to theories. These theories are often rooted in other theories and in evidence, making them more trustworthy than her personal experiences and intuition. In Sibongile's case, theory would also help her think more clearly about her clients, to take a step back from her personal experiences, and to engage with her clients on their own terms.

2. **Theory guides our interventions**. For Sibongile, instead of reacting to the couples she worked with, as if they were her own parents, her professional behaviour would be guided by procedures, processes and skills that are rooted in theory and that have been tested through research and practice. She would feel more empowered to provide a professional and helpful service to these couples, rather than being overwhelmed by her powerful feelings.

Different theories make sense of the world in different ways. Also, different theories are based on different values, and they are applied through different procedures and skills. Thus, the theory you read will influence how you understand and make sense of the world (knowledge), what is important to you (values), and how you practise social work (skills). Theory, therefore, can have an enormous impact on your work as a social worker.

Let's imagine that Sibongile speaks with her supervisor about her difficulties, and that her supervisor suggests that she reads up social work theory about domestic violence. How would her choice of theory influence her work? I'm going to present three different theories that Sibongile could use and show how these would influence her work. As you work through these sections, consider the following four questions:

1. What knowledge, values and skills are embedded in each theory?
2. What are the strengths and limitations of each theory?
3. To what extent is each theory aligned with an African worldview?
4. To what extent does each theory appeal personally to you as a practice approach?

Let us imagine that Sibongile's supervisor advises her to read **feminist** social work literature (see Chapter 9 for details), such as Allen (2013), Dominelli (2002), Eyal-Lubling and Krumer-Nevo (2016), Fawcett et al. (2005), Todd (2016), and Valentich (2011), as well as chapters on feminist practice in books by Payne (2016) and Sharf (2012).

Feminist theory

While reading the feminist social work literature, Sibongile quickly realised that there are numerous feminist theories available, and that they have a wide range of differences between them (see Chapter 9). Nevertheless, feminist theory helped Sibongile to understand domestic violence as an expression of male power over women, which is called patriarchy. It explained that society is structured at the widest and deepest levels to favour and advantage men, while subordinating women. Thus, men enjoy a sense of entitlement and authority, both in the private sphere of the home and in public places like the workplace, community and politics. Feminist theory helped her to recognise how the power of men over women and children is institutionalised in social and political systems, and how these patterns have been handed down from generation to generation.

Furthermore, according to feminist theories, patriarchy legitimates men's use of violence to control and subordinate women. In a patriarchal society, women must be submissive and obedient to men, and men should use whatever means they have to remind women of this. There are marked power differences between women and men, with men enjoying far more power than women. Domestic violence is thus, according to feminist theory, an expression of power; violence is a tool to maintain male power over women in the home.

Drawing on feminist theories, particularly radical feminist theory (see Chapter 9), Sibongile adopts a strong stance against patriarchy, arguing that men and women should be equal in power. She informs the couples she works with that there is no place for violence by men against women. She is strongly pro-woman and concerned to challenge the social structures and domestic patterns that reinforce male dominance, which are sometimes even legally permitted. She is thus attentive to the ways her female clients are blocked in their career progression, the ways the burden of caring for children keeps her clients economically dependent on their husbands, and the ways the local magistrate discourages women who seek the court's protection from abusive husbands.

Sibongile begins to advise wives to leave their husbands and to move into a shelter for battered women. She educates women on the cycle of battering (Walker, 2009), helping them to recognise the repeated pattern of violence in their marriages and to realise that this pattern is not going to change. She helps these women consider that returning to the marriage is a return to a life of abuse and terror, and that they would be better off setting up a life on their own, where they have control over their own future. She begins to engage in social action to advocate for broader structural changes and to dismantle patriarchal ways of thinking and relating. To do this, Sibongile speaks to some of the women she works with and they decide to participate in the 16 Days of Activism Against Women and Child Abuse campaign.

In the next case study, rather than feminist theory, Sibongile's supervisor advises her to read **family systems** literature, such as Gurman and Kniskern (2014), Nichols and Schwartz (2008), and Rasheed et al. (2011), as well as literature on the use of family systems interventions with cases of domestic violence, such as Gelles and Maynard (1987), Hamel (2006), and Murray (2006).

 Family systems theory

After reading up on family systems theory, which includes a wide range of family therapy models, such as narrative therapy (see Chapter 13), Sibongile began to understand domestic violence as a form of communication between partners in a marriage. The literature explained that in most cases both husband and wife engage in violence (slapping, pushing, etc.), and that this behaviour forms part of a larger pattern of interaction between them.

Using the family systems concepts of circular causation and feedback loops, Sibongile understood that in a system one thing does not 'cause' another thing. Rather, multiple things cause another thing, which in turn helps to cause something else, often contributing to the first things in this cycle. This is called 'circular causation' – quite different from feminist theory's belief that patriarchy causes domestic violence ('linear causation'). For example, Sibongile understood that a wife's irritation about her husband's emotional disengagement might cause frustration to a husband, leading him to withdraw into silence, which might increase her annoyance with him, which might lead to him hitting her, which might result in her becoming quiet and submissive, which might create space for him to engage with her more closely, which might result in an experience of emotional intimacy. Family systems theory helped her recognise these complex and apparently contradictory circles of cause and effect.

Drawing on family systems theory, Sibongile begins to meet with her couples conjointly, and to give close attention to the patterns of interaction between them. She uses a range of circular questions, which are central to family therapy interviewing, like triangulatory questions, which involve one person in the family commenting on the interaction between two others, and tracking of interaction sequences, which involves carefully identifying patterns of interactions between people over time. These techniques help Sibongile to recognise that even the negative aspects of marriage, including violence, serve a function in the family, and have at least some positive benefits.

Recognising, however, that violence is unacceptable in marriages, she helps couples critically reflect on the advantages and disadvantages of using violence as a way of achieving these positive benefits. Focusing on the here and now, she helps them develop alternative patterns of communication that lead to these benefits in more satisfying and nonviolent ways. In so doing, she helps not only to reduce the levels of violence in these couples, but also to put in place healthier and more respectful underlying patterns of interaction that contribute to a happier marriage.

Now, let us imagine that, rather than feminist or family systems theories, Sibongile's supervisor advises her to read **Ubuntu** literature (see Chapter 6 for details), such as Kumalo (2017), Nussbaum (2003), Nyaumwe and Mkabela (2007), Sarra and Berman (2017), and Shokane and Masoga (2018), as well as texts on African social work, such as Osei-Hwedie (2014) and Mogorosi and Thabede (2018).

 ### Ubuntu

After reading the *Ubuntu* literature, Sibongile quickly realised that none of these texts provided her with a model of social work practice. Nevertheless, she learned how *Ubuntu* is a foundational philosophy of life across diverse African groups that explains the nature of being human as being in relationship with others. Thus, *Ubuntu* emphasised for her the centrality of human dignity and respect, the interconnectedness of people with one another in community, and the need for compassion, fairness and protection. This literature also emphasised for her the importance of collective decision-making that promotes communal harmony and well-being.

Considering *Ubuntu*, Sibongile begins to explore with her clients their basic beliefs about the nature of humanity and personhood, with the hope that they would touch on the concept of *Ubuntu*. In fact, they do, and tapping into this cultural topic generates useful and interesting conversation. She picks up a disconnect in many of the couples between their idealisation of *Ubuntu* as an African value, and the way they are engaging with each other. She begins gently confronting them with the reality that their relationship is not characterised by *Ubuntu*.

Taking her cue from *Ubuntu*'s emphasis on collective decision-making, Sibongile encourages couples to include their families in the discussions. In some cases, the parents or uncles of her clients are living nearby and come into the office for a larger family meeting. In other cases, Sibongile gets permission from her supervisor to travel to the family homes to meet with the elders. Mindful that her gender and age might make engaging with families difficult, Sibongile works to conduct herself appropriately, and to win over the families through her respect and politeness.

Sibongile finds that in many cases, the couples had not consulted with the elders, and that her efforts to facilitate this consultation lead to the family taking a firm stand for *Ubuntu* values in the marriage. In other cases, the family draws on culture to support the right of the husband to use violence as a means of control. When this happens, Sibongile becomes almost an advocate for *Ubuntu*, helping the family to recover this value system and apply it in the marital context. In most cases, the families can see how violence in the marriage is at odds with the *Ubuntu* philosophy and they work with the couple to eliminate the patterns of violence.

Reflective questions

- What are your views on these three theoretical approaches to understanding and working with domestic violence? What are the strengths and limitations of each approach?
- Comparing these three approaches, do you think any one of them is the 'right' or 'wrong' approach? Why do you think so?
- Which approach fits best with your own views of the world and with your own values? What is it about this approach that appeals to you?
- How well does each of these approaches fit with social work values and principles?
- Do you think there is a useful way to integrate these theoretical approaches? If so, how will you do this?

1.3 **Eclectic use of theory**

One's choice of theory can generate radically different understandings of people's challenges and ways of working with them. In the case studies discussed above, you might see both strengths and limitations in each theory and feel that some combination of the theories might be useful. And you would probably be right. We call this approach 'eclectic' (Payne, 2016).

Eclectic approach, means drawing together aspects of two or more theories and integrating them to fit the mission and expectations of the social work organisation and your own ways of making sense of the world.

There are risks for working eclectically, however. It can easily degenerate into a naïve and haphazard throwing together of a couple of ideas from here and there. Instead of having to explain the theoretical foundation of one's work, one can get away with saying 'I work eclectically', which seems to mean you can do anything. An additional risk is that social workers might combine apparently incompatible or contradictory theories without careful thought.

This is sloppy and unprofessional practice and is not what eclectic means. Rather, when you work eclectically, as most of us do, you must be able to articulate the various theories or theoretical strands that you have selected and argue how they work together as a whole. The advantage of working this way is that you can draw on the best and most useful of a range of theories that address different facets of people's experiences and that provide a multidimensional service to them.

Case Study 5   **Using an eclectic approach in social work practice**

In the case study, for example, Sibongile could integrate all three of the theories used above into a coherent approach to domestic violence. She could draw on feminism's firm commitment to nonviolence and to taking a stand against gender-based violence. But she could frame that commitment within the African value system of *Ubuntu*, which emphasises mutual coexistence and dignity. She could then draw on the insights and techniques of family systems therapies to work with couples to translate into practice the feminist-*Ubuntu* commitment to nonviolent communitarianism in the marriage. In this way, Sibongile would be drawing on three different theories and weaving them together in a coherent approach, which we call eclectic practice.

1.4   Definition of terms

There are a multitude of different terms related to the word 'theory' that you may encounter in the literature on social work theory. They can be quite confusing, as the differences between them are subtle. There is, moreover, often debate between academics over whether a particular 'theory' (such as social development) is a theory, an approach, a perspective, a paradigm, a framework, and so on.

Payne (2016) suggests that there are three main categories of 'theory' in social work, namely:
1. theories about the lives of people, which explain the world around us;
2. theories that explain what social work is; and
3. theories of how to do social work, which he refers to as 'practice theory'.

This book is focused primarily on the third category. We aim in this book to provide theories that guide your thoughts on practice. The theories we are interested in are not primarily about explaining the world around you (such as explaining poverty, sexuality or disability), though we believe that these theories are very important. Instead, we are interested here in theories that help to inform and guide the way you work with people who need your assistance.

> **Theory**, 'a generalized set of ideas that describes and explains our knowledge of the world around us in an organized way. A social work theory is one that helps us to do or to understand social work' (Payne, 2016:5).

This then provides the first distinction in definitions:
- 'Theory' (specifically, 'explanatory theory') provides a systematic and (usually) evidence-based explanation about human and social behaviour (Payne, 2016).
- 'Practice theory' provides a systematic and (usually) evidence-based description and explanation for how to facilitate human and social change.

For example, cognitive-behaviourism is an explanatory theory that explains how thoughts and behaviours influence each other, while cognitive-behavioural therapy is a practice theory that guides your practice in influencing thoughts and behaviours.

A 'perspective' is a broader term, which refers to 'ways of thinking about the world based on consistent values and principles. Perspectives help you to apply a coherent set of ideas to what is happening' (Payne, 2016:9). A perspective is like a pair of coloured sunglasses; you see what everyone else sees, but with a specific colour. Payne cites feminism (see Chapter 9) as an example of a perspective, because it has a clear set of views related to the place of gender in the lives of people. The strengths perspective (Saleebey, 2013) (see Chapter 13) is similarly (and explicitly) a perspective, because it filters its view of the world through consistent assumptions about the presence of strengths and capabilities in people.

An 'approach' is a similarly broad term, but while perspective emphasises the way we perceive and make sense of the world, approach suggests the way we consequently work in the world. It is thus more practice oriented than perspective. However, approach suggests a broad approach to practice, rather than the technical details of the practice, which is better captured in the term 'model'.

A 'model' is thus a more structured term, referring to a sequence of activities that a social worker should follow in working with people. A model is often presented as a diagram, is often based on research, and is often intended to guide professional behaviour. The steps of the 4D model of Appreciative Inquiry (see Chapter 13) are an example of a model. The Circle of Courage (see Chapter 14) is also a model, but less a model of steps and more a model of assessment.

However, it is advisable to not get too stuck in trying to define these terms. There is, in fact, no absolute consensus on these definitions. Increasingly, scholars recognise that the boundaries between them are blurry and that there is not a great deal of practical value in arguing over these distinctions. Thus, Nash et al. (2005b:22) write:

> The postmodern view is more inclusive in its definition of theory, which is not limited to an explanatory function but which also includes models and perspectives as theory. In the postmodern sense, theory is understood as one or more of the following:
> - provable explanations as to why something happens (explanatory theory)
> - organized descriptions of an activity in a structured form (models)
> - ways of conceptualizing the world or a particular subject (perspectives).

In this book, therefore, we use the term 'theory' inclusively to refer to explanatory theory, perspectives, approaches and practice models, all of which can be used by social workers to inform and guide practice.

1.5   Deconstructing social work theory

There is a popular tendency among people, including social workers, to think of theory as something pristine, pure and objective. It is as if people assume that those who write theory do so in the abstract, without being influenced by their context, assumptions and preferences. Most of the theory that we use in social work has been generated in the Global North, particularly in America, but also the United Kingdom and Europe. The developers of theories in these countries may tend to assume that their world, with its culture, values, socioeconomic status and so on, is the same as everyone else's world.

But, in fact, theory is always situated in a local context. In other words, theory never exists in the abstract, as a pure idea. It is always located within time, space and person, and therefore influenced by the time in which it was written, by its location in the world, and by the demographic, personality and life experiences of the person who wrote it.

In more theoretical terms, we can say that theory is a social construct (see Chapter 4 on social constructionism). Theory is not something we discover, in the way that we might discover a diamond – the diamond already exists in the ground waiting to be found. Rather, theory is constructed by people. Theory is something people imagined in their mind, something they thought up, something they wrote, and something they created or constructed. And these thoughts gain credibility when they are discussed with other people and when other people agree with the theory or contribute to shaping it. Thus, theory is socially constructed and situated.

> **Social construct**, something that exists, not because it is actually there for us to see and touch, but because people have agreed that it exists and described what it is.

 Deconstructing psychoanalysis

Psychoanalysis was developed by Freud. His theories were strongly influenced by the post-Victorian interests in sexuality, particularly the sexuality of women and children (Shaw, 2013). These interests were even more pronounced in Austria, where Freud lived and worked. His theory of psychosexual development was developed based on his work with mostly female clients who were expressing the culture of the times. It is therefore no surprise that sexuality (libido) is central to Freud's theories and psychoanalytic technique. Even if Freud's theories could be empirically proven to be an objectively true reflection of his clients, it does not necessarily mean his theories were true of other people in his time, people in Austria today, or people living in South Africa today.

Consequently, an important task for us who use theory is to deconstruct theory, a term most associated with the French philosopher, Jacques Derrida (White, 1992).

> **Deconstruction**, a process of looking behind the apparent objective truth of something – something that has become so accepted that it is taken for granted as being 'obviously true' – to reveal its underlying assumptions.

These assumptions, typically, are not articulated, and even the author of the theory may not have been aware of them. Thus, all theory is based on assumptions and situated in contexts. Deconstruction is about making these assumptions and contexts visible.

It is also important for us to recognise that theory is political. Even when theory was not developed for political reasons, it is often used towards political ends. For example, some theories have been taken up in the service of a neoliberal agenda. The neoliberal agenda seeks to absolve the state of its responsibility for taking care of its citizens, and to make individual citizens responsible to take care of themselves. This includes individuals taking responsibility for macro issues, such as poverty, inequality, race and gender. One such theory is resilience (discussed in Chapter 7), which neoliberals are increasingly using because it is perceived to champion the individual as the primary agent of human development (Van Breda, 2019).

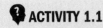 **ACTIVITY 1.1**

Select one of the theories that you have learnt in your studies so far. It could be something from psychology (e.g., Erickson's psychosocial theory), sociology (e.g., Marxism) or social work (e.g., social development).
- Investigate the socio-historical context in which this theory was developed. How has the theory been influenced by its context?
- Can you identify any hidden assumptions in this theory? What influence do those assumptions have on the theory and how we use it?
- If you are not aware of this theory's context and assumptions, how might that compromise your work?

 Underlying assumptions of theories

Let us briefly return to the three theories that Sibongile used in her work with domestic violence, and identify and critique a couple of the underlying assumptions of each:
- **Feminist theory.** Feminism (particularly radical feminism) divides the world along gender lines, and attributes most of the problems of the world to patriarchy (male power over women). But this does not adequately consider the role of race and class in determining the experiences of people, nor does it consider the role of poverty in shaping people's lives, both in society and in the home. Feminist theory's assumptions can lead to polarisation of men and women, rather than finding constructive ways to coexist. Post-conflict and African models of feminism (see Chapter 9) give more consideration to these critiques.
- **Family systems theory.** Family systems theories tend to avoid any focus on the forces outside of the (usually nuclear) family that may contribute to the family's challenges. The family is often seen as a closed system; thus, all the work is done within the family. More recent family therapy models, e.g., narrative therapy (see Chapter 13), are far more attentive to issues of power and justice in society.
- *Ubuntu*. *Ubuntu* emerged within a communalistic society, where personhood is located not so much in the self as in the community, in stark contrast to America, for example, which is highly individualistic. As a result, *Ubuntu* may not be of global relevance, but rather a locally relevant and situated value system. There is, however, an idealisation of *Ubuntu* as being lived out in African society, when the facts strongly indicate that *Ubuntu* currently reflects our aspirations more than our reality. It also neglects the reality that African communities have become increasingly individualistic, in response to both colonialism and globalisation.

1.6 Decolonising social work theory

There are many excellent text books on social work theory and particularly practice theory (e.g., Healy, 2005; Nash et al., 2005a; Nichols & Schwartz, 2008; Howe, 2009; Walsh, 2010; Rasheed et al., 2011; Sharf, 2012; Gurman & Kniskern, 2014; Coady & Lehmann, 2016; and Payne, 2016). So, what is different about this book? Is it just another text on social work theory?

No, we hope not!

We have written this book with the deliberate intent of selecting and presenting theories that we believe will be helpful for decolonial social work practice in a post-1994 South Africa (see Chapter 2 on decoloniality). We have endeavoured to deconstruct our own agenda, by explicitly stating our context, purpose and assumptions as indicated below:
- The context of this book is postcolonial Africa. We live in a period following centuries of colonisation and half a century of institutionalised racism.
- The purpose of this book is to present theories that help us to continue our transition out of colonisation and coloniality towards an inclusive South African future.

- This book assumes that some theories may be more useful and relevant for this purpose than others.

In light of this, we decided not to include some theories, even though we know that they are widely used by social workers in South Africa, and even though we ourselves might use them. We excluded these theories because we felt they were not adequately relevant to African cultures, not sufficiently useful for transforming our society, or not adequately aligned (or alignable) with a decolonial agenda. (We also excluded some theories because of the page limits of the book.)

Most obvious in the theories we have excluded are psychodynamic theory and cognitive-behavioural theory. While we believe these may be useful theories for individual change, we concluded that they were too focused on changing the individual, and not adequately usable to effect social and structural change. We are not saying that South African social workers should not be using these theories (indeed, my own practice and teaching is strongly influenced by psychodynamic theory), but rather that they are not particularly useful in facilitating South Africa's liberation from coloniality.

Having selected the theories we thought were important for decolonial social work practice, we then had to acknowledge that almost all these theories had been developed in the Global North, in contexts very different from our own. Thus began the process of decolonising or indigenising these theories. By this we mean deconstructing the theory, by examining its underlying assumptions and contexts, and revising them to be more suitable and relevant to our current context and assumptions. The theories, therefore, remain Global North theories, but we have endeavoured to make them relevant to the South African postcolonial context.

An example of this is narrative therapy, which is presented in Chapter 13. This therapy, influenced by European theories, was developed in Australia. It is not an African theory. However, we selected it because it has strong roots in the principles of deconstruction and has been used with indigenous groups in Australia. In the presentation of this theory in Chapter 13, I endeavour to show how it can be useful in our own context to facilitate decoloniality and liberation.

At a practical level, the section above, where Sibongile integrated three practice theories into a thoughtful eclectic practice model, is an example of decolonial social work theory. Sibongile repurposed the theories imported from the Global North (feminism and family systems theory) to fit the African context by weaving them together with African paradigms (notably *Ubuntu*).

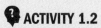 **ACTIVITY 1.2**

Return to the theory you selected in Activity 1.1.
- How can you revise that theory to make it more relevant to your own context?
- Are there different ways of explaining the theory that would give it an African flavour?
- How might this theory be useful for the continued liberation and transformation of South African communities?

1.7 Constructing indigenous theory

Adapting theories from the Global North for use in South Africa is all well and good, but, ideally, we would like practice theories that have been developed in South Africa. These would be indigenous theories that draw on the wealth of our cultural and social heritage.

Collectively in this country, we have numerous experiences of overcoming oppression, poverty and conflict. It feels like we should easily be able to generate our own theory.

But the truth is, we have not done very much. Why might this be?

Perhaps it is partly because of the convenience of using existing theories, even if they don't fit very well with our context, and partly because developing theory sounds very difficult. Those of us who do and publish research are familiar with the various qualitative and quantitative research methods and can implement these with relative ease. But when it comes to developing theory, we are uncertain of what procedures need to be followed. In addition, the idea of 'theory' seems exalted and daunting, something beyond us. One of the things I hope that this book will accomplish is to excite new social workers to be bold enough to venture into the terrain of theory development.

What methodologies can be used to develop theory? Sadly, little has been written on the methodology of theory building, particularly in the applied sciences, and particularly concerning practice theory building. Some of the methods available are complex and appear to have limited utility for developing practice theory. Two examples of theory building methods are the following:

1. Swanson and Chermack (2013) present a multiphase, circular process of developing theory for applied disciplines like social work, involving both deductive and inductive activities. It starts (a) with an initial abstract conceptualisation of the theory, based on the theory builder's current insight into the phenomenon, (b) followed by the operationalisation of that theory into detailed propositions, (c) which are then empirically tested in one or more studies to confirm the propositions, and (d) then applied into practice, (e) leading to refinements of the conceptualisation, and so on.

2. Eisenhardt and Graebner (2007) present an argument for using multiple case studies to inductively construct theory. A case is a single and in-depth view of a single example of the phenomenon being studied. The case is usually studied from multiple angles or perspectives, e.g., by getting different people's views on it or using multiple methods of data collection, such as both interviews and an analysis of written documents. Multiple in-depth case studies permit theory to evolve and be tested and refined on each new case, in a process similar to grounded theory.

Grounded theory (Glaser & Strauss, 1999; Charmaz, 2012; Oliver, 2012; Charmaz, 2014; and Corbin & Strauss, 2015) is the main qualitative research method for inductive theory building. Grounded theory is a methodology for engaging closely with the dynamics in human living, through in-depth interviews and close analysis of the transcripts, to generate theory. It uses an iterative cycle of collecting data, analysing it, formulating key questions that require more focused attention, theoretically sampling additional participants who can shed light on those questions, collecting more data, analysing it, constantly comparing the data from the new interviews with the previous interviews, resolving earlier questions, refining the emerging theory, formulating additional questions that require yet more focused attention, and so on.

Grounded theory, 'systematic, yet flexible guidelines for collecting and analysing qualitative data to construct theories from the data themselves ... Grounded theory begins with inductive data, invokes iterative strategies of going back and forth between data and analysis, uses comparative methods, and keeps you interacting and involved with your data and emerging analysis' (Charmaz, 2014:1).

Case Study 7 **Developing an indigenous theory**

After testing out her eclectic approach to work with domestic violence, Sibongile decides to develop an indigenous theory of marital counselling, including a focus on domestic violence. To do so, she uses grounded theory methods to generate indigenous practice theory by focusing on the ways people use indigenous resources to address the challenges they face in life. Following the iterative processes described above, she constructs an indigenous theory of problem solving, which she then repurposes into a practice theory for social workers:

- She starts by interviewing multiple couples who had used traditional ways (or non-professional ways) to work on their marital difficulties.
- Through the grounded theory methods, Sibongile begins to recognise recurring patterns of problem-solving interactions between the marital partners and between the couple and other people and resources in their social environment, as well as cultural concepts that inform and influence their actions, including *Ubuntu*.
- She theoretically samples additional couples, to clarify certain aspects of these patterns, and to test how consistent they are.
- Once she has a clear picture of these indigenous practices, Sibongile proceduralises them and formalises the role of the social worker in facilitating them. In so doing, Sibongile constructs an indigenous practice theory for marital counselling.

There is much need for indigenous practice theory for South African social workers. Such theory would tap into indigenous healing processes that have worked in past generations, be rooted in a cultural value framework that emphasises interdependence and mutual respect, and modernise indigenous healing processes for our contemporary society. Sadly, we have little such theory. The key example of a well-developed indigenous social work theory is the developmental social work approach. Additionally, *Ubuntu*-based social work practice is a concept that has potential to be developed into a theory. These indigenous social work theories are briefly discussed below.

1.7.1 Developmental social work

Developmental social work, as conceptualised by Patel (2015), is arguably the best example of an indigenous South African social work practice approach (see Chapter 3 for a fuller discussion on developmental social work). It is based on international developmental theory (e.g., Midgley, 1995), but has been expanded in important ways to fit the South African socio-political history and present context. It is, thus, not a decolonisation (or indigenisation) of an existing theory, because it is not merely an adaptation or adjustment of existing theory to fit the local context. Rather, developmental social welfare includes entirely new components that are unique to Patel's conceptualisation of developmental social work, such as the human rights approach and the bridging of the micro-macro divide. Patel (2015:82) thus writes:

> *South Africa's developmental approach to social welfare evolved from the country's unique history of inequality and the violation of human rights as a result of colonialism and apartheid. This history, experience and meaning of oppression for the majority of South Africans, together with a long tradition of human agency and social action to change these conditions, shaped the construction of the new society. Consequently, social welfare*

thinking and practice were infused with notions of transformation and human emancipation and an acknowledgement that reconciliation and healing the divisions of the past were critical to building a united South Africa based on democratic values, social justice, gender equality and human rights.

1.7.2   *Ubuntu*-based practice

Ubuntu is probably the most widely touted and known African culture concept (see Chapter 6 for an in-depth discussion on *Ubuntu*). It refers to 'the reciprocal belief that an individual's humanity is expressed through personal relationships with others in a community and in turn other people in that community recognize the individual's humanity' (Nyaumwe & Mkabela, 2007:152). While this concept has been much romanticised and, some argue, is rarely apparent in contemporary communities, it continues to resonate with Africans. In other words, we continue to think of *Ubuntu* as something important for our society, even if we do not practise it and do not see much evidence of it. This dissonance suggests that *Ubuntu* is a cultural construct that has much potential to be developed into a social work practice theory.

While Chapter 6 of this book provides a solid grounding in *Ubuntu* and some innovative recommendations for its application in social work practice, it is not yet a fully conceptualised practice model. To develop it to the status of a practice theory, it would need to follow a process similar to that of Swanson and Chermack (2013), whereby the initial conceptualisation, as presented in Chapter 6, is operationalised, confirmed and applied. This process can be done through multiple studies, by multiple individuals, creating a valuable opportunity for collaborative theory building by emerging social work scholars. In addition, theory can also be developed and validated through use. Thus, when social workers (including undergraduate students) begin to implement an emerging practice theory, it gets tested and refined through use, and in that way begins to gain the stature of 'theory'.

1.8   Overview of the book

The rationale for this book was set out in section 1.6. We identified the need for a book on social work practice theories that are rooted in the African context, thus, for example, drawing on case examples that are appropriate to our context. In addition, given our place in history, there is a need for a book of theories that will be useful for decolonial social work practice. This implies that these theories should contribute to the transformation and liberation of all peoples and should help to redress the harm caused by generations of colonisation and institutionalised racism. And, thirdly, given our commitment to developmental social welfare and social work, these practice theories need to be aligned with the principles of developmental practice. For example, the theories need to speak to the continuum of micro-mezzo-macro practice.

In consultation with social work academics around the country, we decided on the theories that we believed would be most aligned with these needs, resulting in 15 chapters:

1.   This first chapter introduces theory and its place in social work practice. The chapter also addresses the decoloniality of theory and the construction of indigenous theories, which are central to the purpose of this book. Finally, Chapter 1 provides an orientation to and overview of the book.

2. Chapters 2 and 3 provide the two-layered foundation of the book. Chapter 2 focuses on decoloniality, a term that appears in the title of the book. The chapter provides the socio-political history of colonisation and definitions of the range of terms used in decolonial literature. The chapter leads towards an outline of decolonial practice, so that decoloniality is not merely an ideal, but also a practice.

3. Chapter 3 provides a second layer of foundation, by focusing on developmental social work, which is the nationally accepted approach to social work in South Africa. This chapter provides the context and definitions of developmental social work, and unpacks the central themes underpinning developmental practice. The contribution of developmental social work to decolonial practice is set out.

4. Chapters 4 to 14 provide the detail on 11 theories for decolonial social work practice, from a developmental approach. The chapters are sequenced to start with those that are higher-order conceptual theories and move towards theories that are increasingly practice oriented. Chapter 4 presents social constructionism, which is argued to be an epistemology – a way of making sense of the world. Constructionism has already been apparent in this chapter and continues to manifest throughout the book. Chapter 4 explains what social constructionism is, presents a constructionist approach to practice, and discusses how it contributes to decolonial social work.

5. Chapter 5 addresses a central social work perspective, viz. ecosystems. This chapter explains the ecological perspective and systems theory, shows how it is applied in social work practice, and discusses its link to decolonial social work.

6. Chapter 6 advances insights into *Ubuntu* as a particularly African value system that has significant implications for social work in Africa and for decolonial practice. It maps the precolonial history of *Ubuntu* and explicates the underlying values and humanitarian implications of *Ubuntu*. The chapter also applies *Ubuntu* to micro and macro social work practice.

7. Chapter 7 discusses resilience theory, which has become increasingly popular in recent years. It gives attention to the theoretical building blocks of resilience, leading towards a critical comparison of individual and ecological approaches to resilience. The relevance of resilience for decolonial social work practice is explored.

8. Chapter 8 explains attachment theory, arguably the most 'micro' of all the theories in the book. The stages and styles of attachment are set out, showing how these early patterns of relations continue to manifest in adult life. The relevance of attachment theory for decolonial practice is discussed, and it is applied to both micro and macro social work practice.

9. Chapter 9 addresses feminist theory. The historical development of feminism is comprehensively reviewed, with a focus on postcolonial feminisms that have emerged in Africa. Throughout, the chapter applies feminist thinking to social work practice, and shows the contribution feminism makes to decolonial practice.

10. Chapter 10 shows the relevance of sustainable livelihoods theory for addressing poverty, one of the major challenges facing South Africa and much of the Global South. The conceptual components of sustainable livelihoods are rigorously discussed, and their relevance for decolonial social work explored.

11. Chapter 11 covers the person-centred approach, which underpins the relational basis of much social work practice. The conceptual and practice dimensions of this approach are set out, and its application to micro and macro decolonial social work practice is discussed.

12. Chapter 12 explores the topic of spirituality. This topic was chosen because of the deep spirituality that underlies much of African society. The terms spirituality and religion

are defined, and the history of spirituality in social work is set out. The chapter shows how spirituality contributes to decolonial practice and presents an approach to working with spirituality across the micro-mezzo-macro continuum.

13. Chapter 13 discusses several approaches to strengths-based practices, including the strengths perspective, asset-based community development at macro level, and narrative therapy at micro-mezzo levels. The relevance of these approaches for both indigenous and decolonial practice is explained.

14. Chapter 14 presents the last practice theory: the Circle of Courage. This theory underpins all social service practice with children in South Africa. The origins and conceptual foundation of the Circle of Courage are explained, its relevance for South African social work is discussed, and its application to micro, mezzo and macro practice is set out.

15. The final chapter of the book, Chapter 15, reflects on where we have come to in the development of theory for decolonial social work practice in South Africa, and maps out key areas for further work in the future.

1.9 Conclusion

This chapter set out to introduce the topic of theory, and, in particular, to critique the imposition of Western theories on African society. The need for theory was argued as a way of contributing to a coherent and professional service to the individuals and communities that social work serves. But these theories must be critically engaged and deconstructed, by identifying their underlying assumptions and values. Not all theories are equally relevant, useful and appropriate for our context, particularly in the postcolonial period that we are presently in.

Two main approaches for ensuring contextually relevant theory are advanced in this chapter:

1. Decolonising existing theory, which involves adapting, enculturating and indigenising existing (typically Global North) theory for use in our context and which forms the basis of most of this book.

2. Constructing indigenous theories that emerge from within our Global South context, which forms the basis particularly of Chapters 2, 3 and 6.

Finally, the chapter provides an overview of the book. The authors and editors hope that you will find the book stimulating and relevant to your social work practice. Furthermore, we hope that this book will prompt at least some of you to work on developing new indigenous theories for decolonial social work practice in South Africa and elsewhere in the Global South.

Chapter activity

1. **Reflective question**. Reflecting back on your education and practice so far, which theories have been most useful to you? With which have you felt the most connection personally? And which do you think will continue to influence your practice going forward? What is it about these theories that you connect with?

2. **Personal context**. Think of a problem that you, your family or your community are facing. What theory or theories help explain the problem and what to do about it? What insights does this theory provide you?

3. **Critical question**. Identify a theory that you have learnt about that you think is not only poorly aligned with our social context, but may even be negatively aligned (i.e., could

undermine our efforts to transform and liberate society). What is it about this theory that is so poorly aligned?

References

Allen, M. 2013. *Social work and intimate partner violence.* Abingdon, UK: Routledge.

Charmaz, K. 2012. The power and potential of grounded theory. *Medical Sociology online,* 6:3:1–15.

Charmaz, K. 2014. *Constructing grounded theory.* 2nd ed. London, UK: Sage.

Coady, N & Lehmann, P (eds.). 2016. *Theoretical perspectives for direct social work practice: A generalist-eclectic approach.* New York: Springer.

Corbin, J & Strauss, AL. 2015. *Basics of qualitative research: Techniques and procedures for developing grounded theory.* 4th ed. Thousand Oaks, CA: Sage.

Dominelli, L. 2002. *Feminist social work theory and practice.* Houndmills, UK: Palgrave Macmillan.

Eisenhardt, KM & Graebner, ME. 2007. Theory building from cases: Opportunities and challenges. *Academy of Management Journal,* 50(1):25–32.

Eyal-Lubling, R & Krumer-Nevo, M. 2016. Feminist social work: Practice and theory of practice. *Social Work,* 61(3):245–254.

Fawcett, B, Featherstone, B, Fook, J & Rossiter, A (eds.). 2005. *Practice and research in social work: Postmodern feminist perspectives.* London, UK: Routledge.

Gelles, RJ & Maynard, PE. 1987. A structural family systems approach to intervention in cases of family violence. *Family Relations,* 36(3):270–275.

Glaser, BG & Strauss, AL. 1999. *The discovery of grounded theory: Strategies for qualitative research.* New Brunswick, USA: Aldine Transaction.

Gurman, AS & Kniskern, DP (eds.). 2014. *Handbook of family therapy.* London, UK: Routledge.

Hamel, J: 'Domestic violence: A gender-inclusive concept'. *In*: Hamel, J & Nicholls, TL (eds.). 2006. *Family interventions in domestic violence: A handbook of gender-inclusive theory and treatment.* pp. 3–26. New York: Springer.

Healy, K. 2005. *Social work theories in context: Creating frameworks for practice.* New York: Palgrave Macmillan.

Howe, D. 2009. *A brief introduction to social work theory.* Basingstoke, UK: Palgrave Macmillan.

Kumalo, RS: 'The challenging landscape of South Africa and implications for practicing *ubuntu'. In*: Dreyer, J, Dreyer, Y, Foley, E & Nel, M (eds.). 2017. *Practicing ubuntu: Practical theological perspectives on injustice, personhood and human dignity.* pp. 22–33. Zurich, Switzerland: Lit Verlag.

Midgley, J. 1995. *Social development: The developmental perspective in social welfare.* London, UK: Sage.

Mogorosi, LD & Thabede, DG. 2018. Social work and indigenisation: A South African perspective. *Southern African Journal of Social Work and Social Development,* 30(1):1–18.

Murray, CE. 2006. Controversy, constraints, and context: Understanding family violence through family systems theory. *The Family Journal,* 14(3):234–239.

Nash, M, Munford, R & O'Donoghue, K (eds.). 2005a. *Social work theories in action.* London: Jessica Kingsley Publishers.

Nash, M, O'Donoghue, K & Munford, R: 'Introduction: Integrating theory and practice'. *In*: Nash, M, Munford, R & O'Donoghue, K (eds.). 2005b. *Social work theories in action.* pp. 15–28. London: Jessica Kingsley Publishers.

Nichols, MP & Schwartz, RC. 2008. *Family therapy: Concepts and methods*. 8th ed. Boston, MA: Pearson.

Nussbaum, B. 2003. African culture and ubuntu. *Perspectives*, 17(1):1–12.

Nyaumwe, LJ & Mkabela, Q. 2007. Revisiting the traditional African cultural framework of ubuntuism: A theoretical perspective. *Indilinga: African Journal of Indigenous Knowledge Systems*, 6(2):152–163.

Oliver, C. 2012. Critical realist grounded theory: A new approach for social work research. *The British Journal of Social Work*, 42:371–387.

Osei-Hwedie, K. 2014. Afro-centrism: The challenge of social development. *Social Work/ Maatskaplike Werk*, 43(2):106–116.

Patel, L. 2015. *Social welfare and social development*. 2nd ed. Cape Town: Oxford University Press Southern Africa.

Payne, M. 2016. *Modern social work theory*. 4th ed. New York: Oxford University Press.

Rasheed, JM, Rasheed, MN & Marley, JA. 2011. *Family therapy: Models and techniques*. Los Angeles, CA: Sage.

Saleebey, D (ed.). 2013. *The strengths perspective in social work practice*. Boston, MA: Allyn & Bacon.

Sarra, J & Berman, K. 2017. Ubuntu as a tool for resilience: Arts, microbusiness, and social justice in South Africa. *Conflict Resolution Quarterly*, 34(4):455–490.

Sharf, RS. 2012. *Theories of psychotherapy and counseling: Concepts and cases*. 5th ed. Belmont, CA: Brooks/Cole, Cengage Learning.

Shaw, B. 2013. *Historical context for the writings of Sigmund Freud*. [Online]. Available: https://www.college.columbia.edu/core/content/writings-sigmund-freud/context [Accessed 26 April 2018].

Shokane, AL & Masoga, MA. 2018. African indigenous knowledge and social work practice: Towards an Afro-sensed perspective. *Southern African Journal of Social Work and Social Development*, 30(1):1–18.

Swanson, RA & Chermack, TJ. 2013. *Theory building in applied disciplines*. San Francisco, CA: Berrett-Koehler.

Todd, S: 'Feminist theories'. *In*: Coady, N & Lehmann, P (eds.). 2016. *Theoretical perspectives for direct social work practice: A generalist-eclectic approach*. 3rd ed. pp. 357–372. New York: Springer.

Valentich, M: 'Feminist theory and social work practice'. *In*: Turner, FJ (ed.). 2011. *Social work treatment: Interlocking theoretical approaches*. 5th ed. pp. 205–224. New York: Oxford University Press.

Van Breda, AD. 2019. Reclaiming resilience for social work: A reply to Garrett. *British Journal of Social Work*, 49(1):272–276.

Walker, LEA. 2009. *The battered woman syndrome*. 3rd ed. New York: Springer.

Walsh, J. 2010. *Theories for direct social work practice*. 2nd ed. Belmont, CA: Cengage.

White, M: 'Deconstruction and therapy'. *In*: Epston, D & White, M (eds.). 1992. *Experience, contradiction, narrative and imagination*. pp. 109–151. Adelaide, Australia: Dulwich Centre.

Annotated websites and activities

https://www.youtube.com/results?search_query=social+work+theory
YouTube has lots of videos on various social work theories. Have a look at what is on offer. You'll notice a lot of CBT and ecosystems videos. Watch one or two on theories that you have heard of, and also one or two on theories that you have not heard of or know little about.

http://www.communitycare.co.uk/2017/12/13/wont-need-theory-nonsense-students-experience-social-work-placement/
This a blog written by a student social worker in England, reporting that his experience of theory has been dismissed or trivialised during his field placements. Read not only his blog, but also the comments in response.

http://www.podsocs.com/podcast/social-work-theory/
Malcolm Payne is a key author on social work theories. This is a podcast (an audio recording) of an interview with him, where he talks about theories and paradigms, and their importance for social work practice.

Annotated websites and activities are also available on Learning Zone.

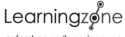

oxford.co.za/learningzone

Decoloniality in social work

Rinie Schenck

By the end of this chapter, you should be able to:

✓ Define and distinguish between the concepts colony, colonisation, coloniality, decolonisation and decoloniality
✓ Describe the background to colonisation globally and in Africa
✓ Explain the process of colonisation of the person
✓ Develop an overview of the history of decolonisation
✓ Demonstrate knowledge of the role social work played in the process of coloniality
✓ Demonstrate knowledge and understanding of the premises of decoloniality for social work.

> The colonial process dislocates the traveler's mind from the place he or she already knows to a foreign starting point even with the body still remaining in his or her homeland. It is a process of continuous alienation from the base, a continuous process of looking at oneself from outside of self or with the lenses of a stranger. One may end up identifying with the foreign base as the starting point toward self, that is from another self towards one self, rather than the local being the starting point, from self to other selves (Ngũgĩ wa Thiong'o, 2014:39).

2.1 Introduction

Currently, it is argued that schools, universities and churches are sites for reproducing coloniality (hence, the emergence of the #FeesMustFall and #RhodesMustFall movements in 2015 and 2016). Ndlovu-Gatsheni (2013) states clearly that we do not have African universities, but we have universities in Africa. He argues that these universities are currently offering programmes to maintain coloniality. Harms Smith and Nathane (2017) also emphasise that South African social work education is situated in Western modernism.

> **Modernism**, a school of thought advocating rational thinking and the use of science, reason and universal truth.

Harms Smith and Nathane (2017:2) state that if social justice, empowerment and dignity form the basis of social work, as formulated by the global definition for social work in 2014, 'then it should engage with issues of ideology, power relations, oppression and decolonisation'. But, they argue, social work typically is not engaged with these themes. Harms Smith and Nathane (2017) further argue that social justice, as social work's core value, is impossible to be achieved if ideologies of inequality and oppression are accepted (Mullaly, 2002; Harms Smith & Nathane, 2017). The implication of this statement is not only that social work should break free from European domination and find its own intellectual space, but also that it should critically reflect and break free from any form of ideology, theory, relationship, and institution which supports inequality and oppression.

Challenging inequality and oppression

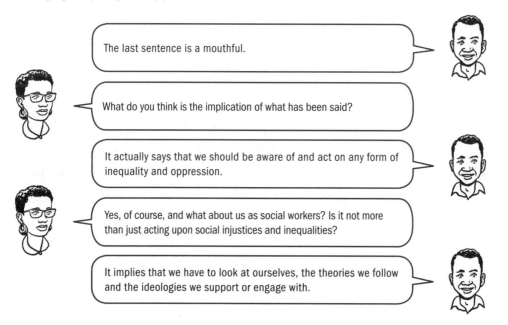

The last sentence is a mouthful.

What do you think is the implication of what has been said?

It actually says that we should be aware of and act on any form of inequality and oppression.

Yes, of course, and what about us as social workers? Is it not more than just acting upon social injustices and inequalities?

It implies that we have to look at ourselves, the theories we follow and the ideologies we support or engage with.

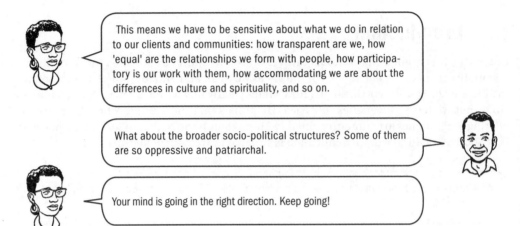

You may wonder why we discuss decolonisation and decoloniality in the social work theory book as it is not a social work theory per say. This chapter interrogates and investigates decoloniality in order to assist and guide us in 'choosing', developing and constructing transformational social work theories relevant for practice in South Africa (see Chapter 1). These theories should be aimed at guiding social service practitioners (including social workers) to assist their clients and themselves in facilitating the process of becoming free of oppression and social injustices in all its varieties in our societies. It is an attempt to provide a framework for thinking and acting (theory and practice) to enable social workers to identify their core functions as enhancers of social justice, freedom and the well-being of people. And, above all, to address structural injustices that keep this country and its people back from all they can become.

Harms Smith and Nathane (2017:4) provide us with a very helpful figure that describes the continuum of social work knowledge, theory and practice towards decolonisation and social justice. Figure 2.1 below provides an indication of the development and progress of theoretical and ideological thought processes towards transformation.

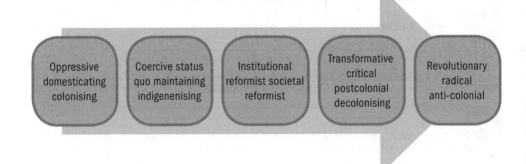

Figure 2.1 Development and progress of thought processes towards transformation
Source: *Harms Smith & Nathane* (2017:4)

This chapter starts by explaining decolonial terminologies. It will then give a very brief overview of the history of colonisation globally and in South Africa. We will then look at the history of social work in South Africa and the facilitation of the process of decolonisation. This chapter is a working document and one of the first attempts towards describing decolonisation and decoloniality in social work. We hope it will guide your thinking processes when you 'select' theories for socially just social work practice. We conclude the chapter by attending to the principles and practices that should underscore our thinking of decoloniality, and express some thoughts on the way forward.

2.2   Definition of terms

There are numerous terms used to describe various facets of decoloniality. These terms have contested meanings to such an extent that debates over terminology can impede our ability to work in response to these issues. In this section, an accessible overview of these terms and their meanings is provided.

2.2.1   Colony

So, what does the word colony mean? When people from one country (e.g., Britain, Germany, France) move to another (e.g., South Africa, Namibia, Nigeria) and seize control of and settle in the host country (therefore these people are referred to as settlers), while keeping ties with their homeland, the host country is known as a colony. This is different from migration, where you adopt the new country as your own. When a country is colonised, the coloniser takes partial or full control of the colonised country. The British, for example, raised the Union Jack (their flag) to indicate that another country is now under British control and governance. It means that the land they colonised became part of or a colony of the motherland (in this case Britain). Up to this date, despite independence, the former British colonised countries are still linked to the United Kingdom through their membership of the Commonwealth. South Africa, Kenya, Zimbabwe, Australia, New Zealand, and Canada were among the colonies of Britain. (To read more about the Commonwealth, you can visit their website at http://the-commonwealth.org/member-countries.)

> *Colony*, a country or area that is fully or partially under the political control of another country and occupied by settlers from that country.

2.2.2 Colonialism

Building on the previous definition, colonialism occurs when one country seizes control of another country.

> **Colonialism**, 'a political and economic relation in which the sovereignty of a nation or a people rests on the power of another nation' (Maldonado-Torres, 2007:243).

This implies that the people of the colonised country do not have the power to govern themselves (Ndlovu-Gatsheni, 2015b; Maldonado-Torres, 2007). The online English Oxford *Living* Dictionaries describes colonialism as '[t]he policy or practice of acquiring full or partial political control over another country, occupying it with settlers, and exploiting it economically' (https://en.oxforddictionaries.com/definition/colonialism). Colonialism involves the process of losing your sovereignty (for those being colonised) or gaining control over others (for the coloniser).

2.2.3 Colonisation

Colonisation is seen as an *event* that happened in the past when the colonial powers took over power and the administration of the countries they have colonised (Maldonado-Torres, 2016). In the South African context, the British had already colonised the then Cape Colony by 1795, but only gained power over the rest of South Africa after the Anglo-Boer War in 1902. In 1910, the whole of South Africa was declared the Union of South Africa and South Africa was under full British rule (see the history later in the chapter). In 1961, South Africa became the independent Republic of South Africa (under apartheid rule).

Though South Africa was no longer a colony of Britain, many refer to the apartheid system as another form of colonialism – *internal colonialism* – which refers to the subjugation of one group by another group within the same country.

2.2.4 Coloniality

The concept coloniality was introduced by the Peruvian sociologist Anibal Quijano, and Argentinians Mignolo and Maldonado-Torres (Ndlovu-Gatsheni, 2015a). While colonialism refers to the event of political control of one country by another, coloniality focuses on the process of this control, which extends long after the withdrawal of the colonial power.

> **Coloniality**, a *process* of 'control, domination, and exploitation disguised in the language of salvation [often Christianity], progress, modernisation and being good for every one' (Mignolo as cited in Ndlovu-Gatsheni, 2015b:30).

Coloniality does not stop the moment the colonisers leave the country or hand over the ruling stick. In the process of coloniality, the mindset and identity of the colonised people change and the presence of the colonisers is still felt everywhere. Until today, according to

Maldonado-Torres (2016), the effect of colonisation is that the world is still going through globalisation and solidification of a civilisation system that has coloniality as its basis. The world is still dominated by the West.

Coloniality, therefore, refers to long-standing patterns of power that emerge as a result of colonialism. It survives colonialism and is maintained in the books, academic performance, cultural patterns, mindset, self-image and aspirations of people. According to Maldonado-Torres (2007:243), 'we breathe coloniality all the time and every day'.

Ngũgĩ wa Thiong'o (2009:2) further describes coloniality as being:

> [d]ismembered from the land, from labour, from power and from memory. The result is destruction of the base from which people launch themselves into the world.

Frantz Fanon (1968:2) views the process of coloniality as holding the people in a grip and emptying their brains of all forms and content. It turns to the past of oppressed people and distorts, disfigures and destroys it.

From an academic viewpoint, coloniality can be seen as a *process* that had an epistemological, psychological, cultural, spiritual and linguistic impact, with the result that the oppressed may have adopted an identity that is furthest away from themselves (Freire, 1998). An 'extended' view of coloniality is seen as all forms of oppressions or colonialism where a person is oppressed or invaded (on different levels) by another. An abuser 'invades' the abused. As Harms Smith and Nathane (2017) clearly state, the chronological ending of the geopolitical arrangements does not mean that coloniality has ended. We have to recognise the enduring nature of the impact of colonialism.

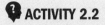

ACTIVITY 2.2

1 Make a list of all the hierarchical, oppressed and invaded relationships you can think of.
   • Choose one of the relationships and indicate why you see this relationship as oppressive and/or 'colonised'.
   • What are the power relations?
   • What is the effect of the relationship on the person who is 'colonised'?
2 Make time to watch the 1986 film *The Mission* in class or at home.
   • Describe the colonisation processes that took place between the missionaries and the local people.
   • What were the effects or consequences of these relationships?

2.2.5   Decolonisation

Decolonisation is the *events* that took place after World War II when, among others, the colonised African countries agitated for independence from the colonial powers and demanded that colonial powers withdraw their administration from Africa. The important Pan-African movement rose during this time and is seen as the major driving force behind the start of the decolonisation of Africa. During this process, due to mounting pressure from inside and outside African colonies, the colonial powers had to relinquish control of these countries. Ghana was the first sub-Saharan African country to gain independence from European colonisers in 1957.

> *Decolonisation*, the withdrawal of a colonial power from a host country, and the handing back of political power and autonomy to the host country.

2.2.6 Decoloniality

Decoloniality, according to Ndlovu-Gatsheni (2015a), is a process of regaining identity and epistemology, and a liberating political movement. An *epistemology* refers to how we think, decide and act (see Chapter 4 on social constructionism). Ndlovu-Gatsheni (2015a) further sees the process of decoloniality as one that seeks to unmask and unveil coloniality (the oppression and the power relations), while Maldonado-Torres (2016:10) refers to decoloniality as a process of 're-humanising the world', 'breaking hierarchies', opening up 'other forms of being in the world', and (re)constructing our identities and how we think about who and what we are. Maldonado-Torres (2016:23) refers to this process as 'building the world of the you'. Steve Biko (1978) claims decoloniality implies developing an attitude of the mind (identity) and a way of life (epistemology).

> *Decoloniality*, a *process* of colonised people remembering who they are, reclaiming their identity, voice, knowledge and power, and re-establishing themselves in the world (Ndlovu-Gatsheni, 2015b).

To be able to grasp the above concepts more clearly, some historical background may be helpful, which will be discussed in the next section.

 ACTIVITY 2.3

Now that you have an understanding of decoloniality, jot down some thoughts on why you think it is important to engage with the process of decoloniality in:
1 general (you yourself, your community and South Africa); and
2 social work (in South Africa).

2.3 Historical background to colonisation globally and in Africa

It can be debated when the process of colonisation started. Did it start with Chistopher Columbus in the sixteenth century when he crossed the Atlantic Ocean towards the Americas? Or when the Portuguese Bartolomeu Diaz sailed around Africa in the fifteenth century? Or did it start when the Dutch and Portuguese erected trading stations along the African coast in the seventeenth century on their way to the East to be able access the sought-after spices and porcelain? There were also the Spanish missionaries in the 1600s invading the South Americas, and those missionaries who followed the traders to the African countries.

2.3.1 Colonisation of Africa

According to Schenck (2017), there are many traces of interaction between people in Zimbabwe and those from other parts of the world, in fact, as early as the sixth to ninth centuries. The political units such as Mapungubwe (in South Africa) and Great Zimbabwe already had visitors during the eleventh to sixteenth centuries. In an archaeological study, it was found that the Portuguese ventured much further inland into Zimbabwe than only visiting the coastal trading stations of Mozambique. Evidence shows that these interactions were complex and involved more than the trading of goods. Africa was not as 'dark' as the imperialists and colonisers of the nineteenth century thought it to be.

However, none of the above was as impactful as the nineteenth century's 'scramble for Africa' (Pakenham, 1991:xv; Hart, 2018). Pakenham (1991:xv) says that the scramble for Africa 'bewildered everyone'. For many years, according to Pakenham (1991), Europe nibbled at the mysterious African continent. This continent was regarded by the Europeans as 'dark Africa' and a 'no man's land'. The rulers were African and 'the treasures were buried in African soil'. There was no reason to intervene or venture into the 'dark' continent except for the coastal trading stations, although the British, by that time, have already established themselves in South Africa. The Berlin conference in 1885 is seen as the turning event when Otto von Bismarck, the then Chancellor of Germany, invited the European countries to decide the fate of the 'irrational people of Africa' (Plaatje, 2013:123). Between 1884 and the end of the nineteenth century, the 'scramble' resulted in Europe occupying the whole African continent. There were now 30 new colonies (including Zimbabwe, South Africa and Namibia), and protectorates (e.g., Botswana), 10 million square miles of new territory, and 110 million 'dazed new subjects' (Pakenham, 1991:xv). According to Plaatje (2013), the 'scramble for Africa' was about control over Africa's resources (minerals) and people (labour). Exploitation and domination followed. Pakenham (1991:xv) explains that 'Africa, was sliced up like a cake, the pieces swallowed by five rival nations – Germany, Italy, Portugal, France, and Britain (with Spain taking some scraps) – and Britain and France were at each other's throats'. The result was that the colonial world became a replica of Europe, politically, structurally, administratively but, above all, epistemologically and spiritually (Plaatje, 2013).

The reasons given for the colonisation were described as the four Cs, namely Commerce, Civilisation, Conquest, wrapped in Christianity (Pakenham, 1991). The reasons could not have been better phrased as the following remark from Cecil John Rhodes, who was the flag-bearer for colonising South Africa and Zimbabwe (then called Rhodesia – named after Rhodes):

> *I contend that we (the British) are the first race in the world and that the more of the world we inhabit the better it is for human race. Just fancy those parts that are at present inhabited by the most despicable specimen of human being, what an alteration there would be in them if they were brought under Anglo Saxon influence ... if there be a God, I think that what he would like me to do is to paint as much of the map of Africa British Red as possible* (Flint, 1974:248).

It was also this grabbing and colonisation of South Africa and its resources that led to the Anglo-Boer War between 1899 and 1902. The 'Boers' attempted to resist the colonisation of the Free State and Transvaal Provinces during what is known as the Anglo-Boer War. Increased recognition is now being given to the role that black people played in this war. At the time, the Cape Colony and Natal were already under British rule. British teachers and ministers of religion were brought to South Africa to 'anglicise' the people under British rule, as Rhodes indicated in the quote above – painting Africa red and bringing its inhabitants under Anglo Saxon influence.

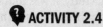 **ACTIVITY 2.4**

The chapter provides a glimpse of the history of colonisation. Authors like Ndlovu–Gatsheni (2015b) urge us to take note of the history to be able to understand colonisation and coloniality. There are several historical and political books which can be read in this regard. Identify at least one source and share it with your fellow students. Pakenham's (1991) *The scramble for Africa: White man's conquest of the dark continent from 1876 to 1912* is worth reading and informative.

2.3.2 Colonisation of the rest of the world

Similar processes of colonisation happened in Australia, India, Canada, New Zealand, and the South Americas. For example, read the article by Boulton (2018) regarding New Zealand's history of colonisation. Similar to South African history, the Dutchman, Abel Tasman, was said to have 'discovered' New Zealand in 1642 (10 years before another Dutchman, Jan van Riebeeck, set foot in Cape Town). New Zealand was colonised by the British Captain James Cook, who reached New Zealand in 1769. Boulton (2018) further explains that oral Māori history has it that Māoris were already in New Zealand 1 000 years before the British came. Similar colonisation processes took place during which Māori autonomy, family life, and their economic base and political authority were eroded.

Colonisation and empire building, throughout Africa, Australia, New Zealand, the South Americas, Canada and Asia, according to Hart (2018), resulted in Europe controlling 80% of the world's land by 1900.

Ndlovu-Gatsheni (2015a) indicated further that, during the colonisation period, the colonised countries were incorporated into the world economy through, among others, the slave trade and use of (cheap) labour in the capitalist system. This contributed to the European and North American commerce and wealth. Colonisation further incorporated Africa into the European and North American culture, languages, legal systems, technology, Christianity/religions, moral order, and political, educational and administrative structures. The end result, according to Ndlovu-Gatsheni (2015b), is that what these countries currently know about themselves was influenced by the West (Boulton, 2018).

Section 2.3 provided an historical overview of colonisation. In the next section, a brief description is provided of the process of colonisation of people.

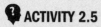 **ACTIVITY 2.5**

1 It might be of interest to read some of the colonising histories of our neighbouring countries such as:
 • Namibia by the Germans: http://www.sahistory.org.za/place/namibia.
 • Mozambique by the Portuguese: https://en.wikipedia.org/wiki/History_of_Mozambique.
2 Also visit the map in the following link which shows the colonisation of Africa: https://cs.wikipedia.org/wiki/Soubor:Scramble-for-Africa-1880-1913.png.

2.4   Process of colonisation of the person

It is of great value to briefly discuss the process of colonisation to help us to understand colonisation. Mathebane and Sekudu (2018) describe the process in South Africa as follows:

- **Stage 1: Denial and withdrawal**. Colonisation reduces the 'colonised' to the inferior and the 'other' (us and them). The colonised are denied equal rights and access with the result that they withdraw to being marginalised. Although these processes started long before 1948 (as you could see in Rhodes' quote earlier), they were formalised when the apartheid policies were introduced in 1948.
- **Stage 2: Destruction and eradication**. During this stage, destruction of culture and social systems (like family, spiritual and cultural systems) is witnessed (Matahbane & Sekudu, 2018). Biko (1978:60) quotes Fanon by saying that this stage is not only a matter of disempowering people regarding power and independence, but it is also about 'emptying the native's brain'. In South Africa, African culture became 'barbarism', Africa was referred to as the 'dark continent', religion and spiritual practices were referred to as 'superstition', and so forth. The person's identity is questioned and even stripped (Biko, 1978:60). Hoosein (2018) describes a similar process of how the removal of the so-called coloured people from District Six in Cape Town destroyed their identity, culture and community resulting in intergenerational trauma.

> **❓ ACTIVITY 2.6**
>
> To understand what happened in District Six, you can watch the following YouTube video: https://www.youtube.com/watch?v=b67yryzEeag. Similar actions happened in places like Sophiatown in Johannesburg.

- **Stage 3: Denigration/belittlement and insult**. In this stage, according to Mathebane and Sekudu (2018), indigenous practices (such as culture, religion, language) are denigrated and replaced by those of the coloniser. This was demonstrated by the British, who had a clear policy to anglicise indigenous people in South Africa and convert them to Christianity, and therefore English-speaking teachers and religious ministers were brought in. After 1948, Afrikaans (a minority language) was made a compulsory subject in schools by the Afrikaner nationalist government. Furthermore, in South Africa, black people were denigrated and excluded from equal economic, political and social participation in society. Biko (1978) explains that black people suffered from an inferiority complex due to 300 years of oppression and denigration. Biko started the Black Consciousness Movement to make black people aware of their value and the need to reclaim their identity and humanity.
- **Stage 4: Surface accommodation/tokenism**. In the South African context, we know the process of tokenism very well. It superficially pretends to accommodate the oppressed.

> **❓ ACTIVITY 2.7**
>
> 1 Provide some examples of tokenism that you, or your family members or friends, have perceived or experienced in matters such as sport, politics, business, and education.
> 2 What are the possible effects of tokenism on the person who is the token appointee?

- **Stage 5: Transformation/exploitation.** During the last stage of colonisation, according to Biko (1978), the oppressed and their belief systems and practices are so disfigured that they turn against themselves. The people now become subservient.

By this time, you should have a clear idea that decolonisation is much more than gaining political control. Starting with some historical processes again, this will be discussed in the next section.

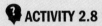

ACTIVITY 2.8

1   Let us stop and think for a moment. If colonisation resulted in transforming the colonised, what should be the decolonisation process?
2   Why, do you think, is decolonisation important for social work practice?
3   What decolonisation process should take place in social work?

2.5   Historical process of decolonisation

It was towards the mid-twentieth century that the process of decolonisation started, with African states politically dismantling the colonial administrations. Pakenham (1991:671) refers to this process as the 'scramble out of Africa'. In this regard, it seems that World War II (1939–1945) was the turning point. Meredith (2006) explains that during WWII, Africans were recruited to fight in the war. In total, 374,000 African people (black and white) fought in the British army, and 80,000 African troops were shipped to France to fight the Germans. In addition, in Africa, it was mainly during this period that infrastructure, such as airports and harbours, was built and expanded to provide the minerals European countries needed to be able to fight the war.

The aftermath of the war, says Meredith (2006), brought frustration and restlessness among the African countries and the decolonisation process started. Hart (2018) regards the first gathering of the Pan-African movement in Manchester (UK) in 1944 as the starting point of the anti-colonial revolution or Pan-African movement. The Pan-African movement, according to Hart (2018), was the most radical movement of the twentieth century, when people, forced into the world society as part of the European empires in the nineteenth century, sought to establish their independence. Hart (2018) identifies the intellectuals whose ideas drove the Pan-African movement as people such as:

- Frantz Fanon;
- WEB Du Bois; and
- Mahatma K Gandhi.

(For more information, see annotated websites at the end of this chapter.)

Harms Smith and Nathane (2017) highlight intellectuals whose ideas are the basis for decolonisation and most valuable for guiding social work as including:

- Frantz Fanon;
- Steve Biko;
- Aimé Césaire; and
- Paulo Freire.

(For more information, see annotated websites at the end of this chapter.)

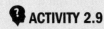 **ACTIVITY 2.9**

It would be worthwhile creating a group to read about the intellectuals mentioned above and summarise their ideas on decolonisation. A discussion in class on each of these authors might be informative. You can:
1 Identify the themes, similarities and differences in their thoughts.
2 Choose one of the authors and write a short essay on him or her to share with your class mates.
3 Highlight the significance of his or her thought regarding the decolonisation process.

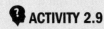 **ACTIVITY 2.10**

1 Watch the following videos, which provide the background of the Pan-African movement:
   • https://www.youtube.com/watch?v=mn12bNvt1sY; and
   • https://www.youtube.com/watch?v=OjgJ2KpyJ5w.
2 Also visit the Centre of Pan-African Thought at https://www.panafricanthought.com/papers/.

The main aims of the Pan-African movement were to promote the well-being and unity of African people and people of African descent throughout the world and to demand their self-determination and independence. The Pan-African movement was further striving towards securing civil rights, ending racial discrimination, and facilitating co-operation between African people and others who shared their aspirations.

Despite the Pan-African movement and the process of decolonisation of Africa, we did not enter the postcolonial world, according to Plaatje (2013) and Verster (2018). Mostly, the colonial rulers were just replaced with corrupt African leaders (Plaatje, 2013; Meredith, 2006). The (political and administrative) events of decolonisation took place, but the long-term effects of colonisation are still present within the people, and the corrupt leaders maintain the status quo to their own benefit.

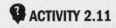 **ACTIVITY 2.11**

One of the books about the independence of African states that is readily available in bookshops is *The State of Africa: A history of fifty years of independence* by M Meredith (2006). If you want more light reading in this regard, you may try Sihle Khumalo's (2007) *Dark Continent: My Black Arse*.

2.6 Social work and coloniality

Before we can discuss the process and premises/framework of decoloniality in social work, we have to reflect on the historical roots of social work and why decoloniality is of importance for a book on social work theory. Chapter 1 has already shown how theories are situated and contextualised – they are political and can be used or misused for political ends. The same is true of social work practice, and thus of the profession itself.

Despite the fact that social workers are doing good work, the history and current practice of social work also show that we do not always work towards removing social injustices. When social work is embedded in hierarchical structures of inequality, with many levels of people having power over other people, social workers do not have the power to work towards social justice (Dominelli, 2010; Mullaly, 2002; Sewpaul, 2015).

The history of social work globally and in South Africa will help us to understand the predicament social work is in.

Dominelli (2010:28) outlines the history of social work in Europe as a response to the industrial revolution:

> Social work developed as a profession to deal with the social problems emanating from the process of industrialization. It relied heavily on philanthropic initiatives to begin with, but it soon became an outlet for the energies of middle-class women, who were instrumental in challenging definitions of what constituted professional social work, developing its scientific elements and eventually staffing the welfare state. Consequently, social work became a **'handmaiden' of the nation-state**, especially in Europe, where it became active in colonizing ventures that sought to spread messages about the superiority of Western culture. Its dependency on state funding also meant that social work was unable to finance its own autonomous development.

Harms Smith and Nathane (2017) remind us that social work has its origins in the prejudices of the Victorian middle and upper classes in the guise of philanthropic actions. The philanthropic movements were based on judgements of the poor by the middle and upper classes (us and them).

As in Europe, social work in South Africa also became the handmaiden or an extension of the government (Nicholas, Rautenbach & Maistry, 2010; Harms Smith & Nathane, 2017; Sewpaul, 2015). The welfare system in South Africa can be traced back to different times in the country's history, but the 'formal' welfare system in South Africa started after the Anglo-Boer War left thousands of orphans and women destitute. It is estimated that in total more than 40,000 women and children died in separate concentration camps where the British kept the South Africans after the implementation of the scorched earth policy. Welfare organisations, such as women's organisations (for example, the SAVF and ACVV) and the churches, established children's homes and support services primarily for white women and children. It was after the 1932 Carnegie Commission investigated the 'poor white problem' that the first Department of Welfare was established. Social work was formalised and the first social workers were trained by the University of South Africa, Stellenbosch University and the University of Pretoria to attend to the 'poor white problem'.

Much later, social work training was extended to the universities for black and so-called coloured people by the then apartheid government. These historical facts already emphasise the injustices of the system social work was 'born' into. In addition, social work services were also provided to the different racial groups by separate and different welfare departments.

Even though government departments and NGOs were rendering services to all people on an equal basis since 1994, authors such as Harms Smith and Nathane (2017), Olson (2007), Harlingten (2013) and Dominelli (2010) are of the opinion that worldwide social work is not living up to the ethics it should stand for. It is not free to address social injustices, and it is still the 'handmaiden of the state' and still not decolonised.

According to Olson (2007:47), social work is focusing more on gaining status as a profession rather than focusing on social justice and attending to the values and ethics it should stand for and facilitate:

> *More narrowly, social work's professional project consists of standardizing and codifying methods of intervention into 'evidence-based practices' so that they form a professional standard of care in all of the various venues in which social work is conducted.*

This is a far cry from a social justice paradigm that is constructionist in nature and starts in reflection and incorporates dialogue-action with others (see Chapter 4 for more on social constructionism).

Harlingten (2013:45) is of the opinion that social work has thus far 'mainly played the role of mediating between the state and the oppressed'. She argues that social work can no longer afford to sustain a practice model based on helping clients cope or adjust to unjust circumstances. For social work practice to remain credible, it cannot be content with 'systems tinkering' (Harlingten, 2013:45). Social work is most at home ameliorating suffering, advocating on behalf of clients, and asking the government to make changes to policies. Working for improvement in policies, taxation, political representation and other areas that impact the options and opportunities of individuals is a significant area of social work attention. Neutrality in the face of injustice is an ethical blunder, says Harlingten (2013:46): 'To do nothing [about injustices], supports the status quo and therefore is complicit with systems of injustice'.

To be able to understand injustices, it is helpful to take a look at the description of 'oppression'. Oppression is not new to society, but it is regarded as one of the major effects of colonisation in all its forms. We will therefore take a close look at what we refer to as oppression in this book.

> **Oppression,** relations of domination that divide people into dominant and superior groups over submissive and inferior groups.

Oppression involves dominance, which can be expressed by race (black/white), gender (male/female), sexuality (homosexual/heterosexual), religion (Muslim/Christian), age (parent/children), wealth (rich/poor), education (educated/uneducated), rank (employer/employee) and status (caste system). The opportunities for and examples of dominance and oppression are endless.

Dominelli (2010) explains that oppression touches all aspects of a person's life, which include: psychological; social; economic; and political. It targets first and foremost the person's sense of self and identity. Oppression is divisive and splitting (us and them), exclusionary, and socially unjust (Freire, 1998).

Case Study 1 | **Thinking about oppression**

A young girl told the social worker that she was raped by her cousin. She informed her parents about what happened. She described her experience of the incident as '... *he violated my inner being*'. The way the family then dealt with the *ishlazo* (disgrace) was that the cousin had to perform a ritual (offering a goat to the ancestors) as the ancestors were now angered by him. After the offender slaughtered the goat, he was allowed to continue with his life. The girl felt very hurt by this since she had to continue with her life without being heard or without receiving some support. The offender/oppressor was still in the community, laughing at and harassing her, and she was offered no support.

Reflective questions
- Share your ideas of how you think the social worker needs to assist the young girl, taking into consideration the context of the girl as well.
- What will be 'systems tinkering' in this case and what will be structural and social justice change?
- Reflect on the description of oppression. What is the implication for using theories that put us in a dominant/expert/powerful position over the people we work with?
- If we critically select theories, what should the theory enable us to do?

2.7 Summary of the premises of decoloniality

In this section, the premises of the process of decoloniality will be discussed, which can guide our thought processes when we discuss the theories for social work.

According to Mullaly (2002) and Dominelli (2010), decoloniality aims for a decolonised epistemic turn which enables professionals to question, think critically about, theorise, write and communicate a new epistemology (language) that can empower people, facilitate social justice (removing structural injustices), and facilitate remembered or newly co-constructed identities in the person, families and communities.

The premises deduced from different authors are discussed below.

2.7.1 Critical consciousness and conscientisation

For Freire (1998), Dominelli (2010), Maldonado-Torres (2007), Harms Smith and Nathane (2017) and Small (in Lombard & Schenck, 2017), the first stage of decoloniality is that oppression should be unveiled and addressed through the process of conscientisation with *both* the oppressed and the oppressor. Please note that the process of conscientisation is not equal to 'awareness-raising' (e.g., condom use to prevent sexually transmitted infections). Freire refers to levels of awareness or consciousness, and Hope and Timmel (1995:78-79) summarise Freire's levels of consciousness as follows:
- The *first or lowest level* of consciousness is referred to as *closed or broken consciousness*. People believe they cannot change their lives and that fate is out of their hands ('government should ...', 'schools should ...', 'the church should ...') Religious people will believe that only the god/s they believe in can make changes in their lives or they expect the government or other institutions or people such as leaders to make the changes. On this level, the person is not conscious of the socioeconomic contradictions within society. They don't question injustices and what it is doing to their lives. They are silent and docile (the colonised/oppressed person). Freire refers to this as the 'culture of silence' (Hope & Timmel, 1995:78).

- The *second level* of consciousness is referred to as *awakening consciousness*. People will start to gain insight into and become aware of their problems, but they still focus on symptoms and not root causes. They have the mind and will to change things, but they deal with problems that arise one at a time. They also naively follow strong leaders who they hope will bring about change so that they don't have to. Local actions to meet immediate needs will start.
- The *third level* is referred to as *reforming consciousness* where the people have the desire for self-determination and to share power. They start to question inequalities and injustices (on micro and macro levels). 'Why am I still in this abusive relationship?' 'Why is there so much inequality in the country?'
- On the *fourth level* of consciousness people develop a deep consciousness, the highest level of thought, and start seeing problems in context and as structural. Critical consciousness involves making connections between socioeconomic contradictions and injustices in society. People question old values and develop new values. They believe that they themselves can make changes and take agency. New relationships and structures are formed.

Hope and Timmel (1995) then also emphasise that using theories and methods which are top-down will maintain the status quo, while only democratic, participatory and empowering ways of working with people will enable them to move through the levels of critical consciousness.

❓ ACTIVITY 2.12

Adam Small, a poet, playwright and social worker, used his poems and plays/dramas to facilitate critical consciousness about political and socioeconomic issues in South Africa.

1 It is recommended that you read some of his work, e.g., *What about de lo* (law).
2 Listen to the poem at the link (there are English transcripts) https://www.youtube.com/watch?v=-j6ndtZYRKk. What awareness was made in this poem? What values were questioned?

Freire believes real change cannot take place or even start to take place if the oppressed (colonised) do not develop a deep critical awareness or consciousness (process of conscientisation). If this does not happen, then change is superficial and not structural. It is also at the point of critical consciousness that people are taking responsibility for the change process and collectively making the changes. If the oppressors also develop critical consciousness, then changes can be made peacefully. If the oppressors do not develop critical consciousness, it will probably result in conflict. Real critical consciousness takes time and is a process.

Conscientisation, a process aimed at awakening 'in the oppressed the knowledge, creativity, and constant critical reflexive capacities necessary to demystify and understand the power relations responsible for their marginalization and, through this recognition, begin a project of liberation' (Darder, 2018:xix).

Critical consciousness is important on two levels:

1. On one level social workers should be able to facilitate the process of critical consciousness with their clients (and the oppressors) to be able to deal with the root causes of their problems.

2. On another level social workers should develop critical awareness/consciousness about their own position as social workers in the local and global context.

In principle, unless social work addresses the root and structural causes of oppression and works towards the actual transformation of society, it cannot claim that it is facilitating social justice. It requires that we as social workers need to critically reflect on our epistemologies, ideologies and theories we are using as they determine the lenses through which we view the world.

 ACTIVITY 2.13

It is important that you develop a good understanding of Freire's concepts of conscientisation or critical consciousness and some techniques to facilitate it. The following link might be of value: http://www.train-ingfortransformation.co.za/wp-content/uploads/2016/04/impactstudy_2015_FACETOFACE.pdf.

1 One of the important techniques Freire used to assist people to develop deep consciousness is the 'why' technique. You can work in groups or pairs to practise this technique. Choose any issue and ask the 'why' question, similar to the example below:

Community: *We don't have food.*
Social worker: *Why don't you have food?*
Community: *We are poor.*
Social worker: *Why is there poverty?*
Community: *There are no jobs and income.*
Social worker: *Why are there no jobs and income?*
Community: *We are uneducated and too far from the cities. Here are no jobs in this town,* and so on.

2 This technique helps people to start making connections. Try this with other examples that may be linked to issues such as abuse, cultural practices, religion, and even some aspects we are not allowed to speak about usually. What power and oppression emerge?

2.7.2 Reconstructing power and hierarchies

At the heart of oppression are inequalities and unequal power relations. The first and foremost premise of decoloniality is to analyse, investigate, question and reconstruct power relations and hierarchies. We have to recognise oppression as the major source of social problems and change the dominant order. These power relations between the oppressor and the oppressed have many forms, e.g., male/female, rapist/raped, abuser/abused, heterosexual/LGBTIQ+, black/white, employer/employee, and social worker/client.

Social workers should understand oppression; its root causes and sources; how it is exerted (e.g., through culture and policies); its dynamics; its effect on the oppressed person, including its internalisation; and the social function it carries out in the interest of the dominant group.

Oppression also occurs when a person is blocked from opportunities to self-development, or excluded from full participation in society, or is denigrated to second-class citizenship because he or she belongs to a certain group.

ACTIVITY 2.14

1   Read *Training for Transformation* by Hope and Timmel (1995) on Freire's techniques to get to the root causes of oppression, which include the 'why' technique, the use of codes, and other participatory techniques. Available for download at http://edepot.wur.nl/429472.
2   Also read Augusto Boal's (1995) *Rainbow of desire: The Boal method of theatre and therapy.*

 Dealing with cultural mindsets

The following quote from Akujobi (2009:2460–2461) describes the position of some African widows in Nigeria:

> *In Afemai land of Edo State for ... widows are treated as outcast[s] she is often humiliated, she is not allowed having a bath, or washing her hands after eating. She is not to change her clothes or underwear for days; they are shaved seven days after their husbands' death. The widow will have to sit and sleep on the bare floor during her period of confinement ... Widows are also made to drink the water used to bathe the corpses of their deceased husbands; they are shaved and kept in seclusion for months while consultations are on as to the real cause of death of the man. The widow is not expected to receive condolence visits from sympathisers during the period of mourning, she is to be re-married by a relative of the late husband ... In most cases, she must vacate the matrimonial home for the relatives of the man.*

Similar situations are prevalent in South Africa where the family of the deceased husband will come and take his belongings and, in some instances, leave the widow and her children with nothing – even without a place to stay if the house belonged to the deceased husband – which is called property grabbing. One of the women in a study by Hugo (2018) explained:

> *Let us say the husband die through a car accident. You find that they (the family of the husband) blame the wife, saying that she bewitched him. They will be thinking she killed him so that she can be rich – but if it is the wife who is dead, the man are [sic] not blamed at all.*

This is a difficult situation as it is dealing with the cultural mindset of the community.

 ACTIVITY 2.15

1   Use the above example to role-play and interview the woman/women/family and or community using the 'why' question.
2   Reflect on the experiences of the interviewees and the facilitator.
3   Consider how and whether these inequalities can be dealt with. Take into consideration Freire's levels of consciousness or awareness. Should cultural practices be dealt with by social workers?

2.7.3 Reconstructing knowledge

The process of reflection and developing critical awareness includes critical reflection on the existing knowledge and the facilitation of reconstructing, re-membering of knowledge production, epistemologies, and politics. We have to look towards constructing knowledge that *empowers and liberates (rather than domesticates)* (Freire, 1998), *enables, capacitates* and *frees* us and others (Sen, 1999), however spiritually and culturally sensitive. For social service professions, this implies that we must create or use enabling and empowering theories and language based on the knowledge of the people or what they already know and are familiar to them. Theories that enable or empower *both* the social service professional as well as the clients (the oppressor and the oppressed) should be used. It requires changing mindsets towards inclusion and appreciating and valuing differences.

The reconstruction of knowledge includes the appreciation and development of indigenous knowledge systems (e.g., *Ubuntu*, Afrocentric theories and practices) and participatory practices that involve all those who are and will be affected.

 Reclaiming traditional knowledge

A social worker in the Limpopo province realised that parents experience many problems with their children for many (structural) reasons. The social worker then tried to assist the parents with parenting skills and a parenting programme, which were developed for the Western context.

Realising that she will not be able to impose these Western models of parenting on the community, the social worker decided to listen to the parents' experiences. She explored the skills they have used in the past and identified the ones that they value. In so doing, they developed and recreated the skills they value with which they can assist one another. One (of the many) of the aspects, which parents mentioned had become lost, that they wanted to bring back was the belief that 'every child is everyone's business'.

The parents then started planning to co-create an environment where they could collectively take responsibility for one another's children. This would create a safety net for children and a sense of belonging. In this case, the social worker listened and learnt and co-created more valued ways of parenting with the parents.

Generating and creating knowledge includes the appreciation and respect for differences and creating context within which we can learn from one another.

2.7.4 Reconstructing the self (person and community)

One of the main themes discussed under the process of coloniality refers to the impact colonialism has on the self and the identity of the individual and the collective. Under colonialism/oppression, the person and community 'lose' their identity and voice and may aspire to take on the identity of the 'superior'. They internalise the knowledge, values and language of the oppressor or dominant culture (Grobler et al., 2013; Freire, 1998; Ndlovu-Gatsheni, 2015a; Maldonado-Torres, 2016). Theories used towards or to facilitate decoloniality have to focus on self-discovery, self-reflection, (re)construction and re-appreciation of the self and regaining self-pride: Who are we? or Who am I?.

For Plaatje (2013) and Freire (1998), the struggle of the oppressed is located in the self and requires a psychological approach. Plaatje also emphasises that decolonising the mind of the oppressed (e.g., the black person, woman, LGBTIQ+ community) is not as complex as it is made out to be. It is more difficult to decolonise the mind of the oppressor (e.g., white person, male, homophobe) from a false sense of superiority and self-importance, and to decolonise homophobes from their sexual insecurities and white people from their privileges, etc. The process of decolonisation needs to focus on both the oppressor and the oppressed, and on reconstructing the self of *both* parties.

For Biko (1978), decoloniality is the facilitation of processes of regaining individual and collective identity and overcoming inferiority.

🔎 ACTIVITY 2.16

Let us look at ourselves for a moment.

We are often in both positions as oppressor and oppressed. A person may be an oppressed person in his or her work environment, while taking on the role of oppressor in a relationship with his or her partner, domestic worker/cleaner, car guard, etc.

1 Reflect on the different power relationships you are in and identify one in which you experience oppression (why?) and one in which you may be or potentially can be the oppressor (e.g., a parent/ employer).
2 As (potential) oppressor, what can we do to prevent us from acting in an oppressive manner towards others?
3 As the oppressed, how could we address this unequal oppressive relationship?
4 What is the effect of the oppressive relationship on you as a person?

An important aspect to emphasise is that for the social worker to be able to attend to social justice and oppression issues, self-knowledge is a prerequisite. We have to know why we do this and what theories and ideologies are driving our actions (Freire, 1998; Lombard & Schenck, 2017).

2.7.5 Decoloniality is the process of creating a humanity

One of the main contributions of Freire (1998), Small (in Lombard & Schenck, 2017) and Carl Rogers (Grobler et al., 2013) is the process of humanisation. Oppression and coloniality are seen as dehumanising, exclusionary and marginalising. Therefore, Freire (1998), Maldonado-Torres (2016) and Plaatje (2013) refer to the process of decoloniality as a humanising process based on respect for the person, love, empathy, care, social justice, and upholding human rights. It should be inclusive, appreciative and participatory/collective.

 Case Study 4 **Championing the humanity of all peoples**

Policy makers tend to make decisions or have discussions without consulting the people affected by such decisions and those who are regarded as experts. Some time ago, a conference was held about the development of guidelines for waste pickers in the formal waste system (not necessarily employing them but acknowledging their value and contributions). The facilitator invited all involved with the waste system, including the Director-General of the Department of Environmental Affairs as well as the waste pickers. The waste pickers also delivered their papers and contributions equal to the 'experts'. They were respected for their knowledge and skills.

Another element in the humanisation process is what Mathebane and Sekudu (2018) refer to as the mourning phase. Expression of anger is important before the healing process can start. Three hundred years of subjugation and trauma should be dealt with. Clients often experienced years of oppression in relationships of abuse, marital problems, or years of superiority, privilege, and having control over others. Dealing with anger and experiences of loss, and regaining humanity are critical. This process is supported by Hoosein (2018), which refers to the intergenerational trauma that are carried over from one generation to the other. This type of trauma, according to Hoosein (2018), does not fit into the traditional trauma narratives and needs to be dealt with differently.

> **Intergenerational trauma,** trauma carried over from generation to generation. The later generations might not always be consciously aware of it. It includes the transmission of oppression and its traumatic consequences from one generation to subsequent generations.

 ## Promoting humanness through interrupting intergenerational trauma

Van der Watt (2016) provides an example of healing and attending to trauma.

In her research, the black rural women with whom she worked, expressed concern about the behaviour of their children and their parenting practices. They told her (Van der Watt) that they do not know how to discipline and communicate with their children other than giving them a hiding and shouting at them. She explored their experiences as children and asked them to express how they wanted to be treated by their own parents. They indicated that they would have loved their parents to do certain things with them such as picking them up, comforting them when hurt, making time to talk, etc. In the process they realised how much anger they have about what their parents did to them and that they are doing the same to their children.

They noted how well they still remember everything that happened to them:

> *This means that our children will always remember what is happening to them now* (Van der Watt, 2016:197).

For these parents, the process of conscientisation has started and they worked on different ways of interacting with their children to build positive memories.

This premise resonates closely with Rogers' person-centred or people-centred approach (see Chapter 11). It requires us to work with people's strengths (see Chapter 13) and to enhance their well-being and increase their freedoms and capabilities (Sen, 1999). Theories to facilitate decoloniality should be people-centred, participatory and inclusive, and should facilitate empowerment, strengths, opportunities and capabilities.

The change process should be facilitated within equal and trusting relationships – in other words, an anti-oppressive, non-discriminatory, equal environment, and non-oppressive relationships should be created with the 'oppressed' to address the issues at hand collaboratively.

This premise requires the facilitator to be self-reflexive in terms of his or her value systems and power relations. The critical question to be asked is 'Can I work alongside people?' instead of 'with', 'for' or 'on behalf of' people.

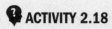 **ACTIVITY 2.17**

Working alongside people has certain implications for the social worker.

1 What in your opinion are the implications for the social worker to work 'alongside' the client instead of 'with', 'for' or 'on behalf of' the client? Take note of the change in language.

2 'You are studying social work to be educated, to help people, to be more powerful and have some status in your family and community, and now you are urged to let go of power and to be equal to the "uneducated".' Share your thoughts on this statement.

2.7.6 Decoloniality requires a search for wholeness thinking

Colonisation is divisive, fragmented, oppressive and punitive. The premise of wholeness views the link between body, spirit, and culture as well as between the person's perceptions, experiences, emotions and actions within his or her contexts (Dominelli, 2010). A change in experiences will bring about a change in perceptions and behaviour. Social workers therefore must view the community, service delivery, and systems holistically (see Chapter 5 on ecosystems theory) and be able to work with the complexity of clients' contexts. Changing one aspect of a system will influence the other parts of the system. It requires us to be sensitive to systems, including the environment, and not to intervene against the 'organism'. Growth should be organic, enhancing and empowering the system, strengthening the capacity of the person, groups and community and building on the knowledge they already have.

2.7.7 Change through dialogue, participation and collective action

Dialogue is central to decolonial change processes. You may ask: 'But what else do we use in the change process other than talking to and with our client?' Dialogue is seen by Freire as much more than communication. He used the term in the educational context to explain that education should not be 'talking to', 'telling' or 'teaching', but it should be a dialogue between the facilitator and the people. Together they create new knowledge, based on what the people know and understand, both experts in an equal relationship. Freire (1998) and Hope and Timmel (1995) use codes or problem-posing material to facilitate dialogue.

ACTIVITY 2.18

1 See handbooks with plenty of exercises based on the work of Freire at:
   • http://edepot.wur.nl/429472 (Hope & Timmel, 1995); and
   • http://www.trainingfortransformation.co.za/wp-content/uploads/2016/04/impactstudy_2015_FACETOFACE.pdf.

2 See also *Paulo Freire: Handbook for community youth workers* by D Soliar (2005).

3 Study these handbooks and choose one exercise to be applied in your class or group.

2.7.8 Facilitating decoloniality is an action-reflection process

Decoloniality – getting rid of oppression and social injustices – will not happen overnight. Colonisation and oppression have been with us for generations. Oppressed colonised communities may be in these contexts for generations (see Hoosein, 2018). Likewise, their oppressors may be in their privileged positions for generations. Changing mindsets, identities, behaviours and injustices do not happen after just one intervention. It is a process whereby people plan, act on their planning and then reflect on their actions and its effects – depending on the outcome, they then resort to replanning or further planning (see Figure 2.2). The reflection also includes the person and his or her own learning and awareness processes.

> **Action-reflection process**, a process of cycling between doing and thinking (reflecting critically on the doing, on what works and what doesn't, and why that is).

Freire (1998) and Hope and Timmel (1995), therefore, see change as an action-reflection-planning process. After each session with a client – be it a person, a group or community – the social worker needs to reflect on the way forward, the growth and change within him or herself and, if the process fits the purpose, on the person and the context. Is it relevant and sensitive to what is important for the people? Can they relate to the changes? Change is then ethical and incremental and builds on previous experiences.

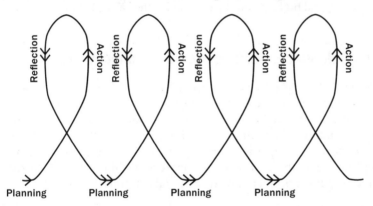

Figure 2.2 Action-reflection cycle

Source: Diagram created by author *Schenck* based on text by *Freire* (1998) and *Hope & Timmel* (1995)

2.8 Conclusion

Our epistemology determines how we act and respond to people. The social work theories we integrate into our thought processes determine the way we will act towards the people with whom we interact. Not all theories support and facilitate the process of decoloniality, anti-oppression, liberation and social justice. We took great care in choosing the theories in this book to assist us to: enhance critical thinking; think holistically; be respectful; enhance inclusion; embrace differences; be emancipatory; take an anti-oppressive stance; enhance empowerment and freedoms; and, above all, ensure social justice and the unveiling of injustices.

Freire (1998) clearly states that thinking alone does not change the world – we must have strategies for change as theory without action is worthless. The explanatory and practice theories should therefore be reflected on to ensure that they facilitate social justice and liberate our own minds and those of the people with whom we are working – the oppressor and the oppressed.

Chapter activity

1. **Reflective questions**.
   1.1 Reflecting on the chapter on decolonisation, what content/information stood out for you?
   1.2 What is your opinion of the fact that social work may be seen as maintaining social injustices? Can you identify possible examples?
   1.3 Should social work become a transformational/radical profession (see Figure 2.1)? If so, why and how should the profession change to make this happen?
2. **Personal context**.
   2.1 Can you identify situations or relationships where you have experienced oppression?
   2.2 Can you identify relationships in which you are/were (or potentially could be) the oppressor?
   2.3 In both instances, what is/was the effect of both relationships on you?
   2.4 What did you personally gain from this chapter?
3. **Critical questions**.
   3.1 What will you as a social worker have to do to:
      - Identify oppressive relationships and social injustices?
      - Change/address these relationships and social injustices?
   3.2 Identify a theory in the book that you think:
      - can assist us to transform and liberate people/society; and
      - may hamper our efforts to transform and liberate people and society.
   3.3 To address social injustices can be risky and messy.
      - Identify injustices where you think social workers will not be able to 'intervene', and substantiate your answers.
      - Identify injustices where social workers will be able to assist in making a difference, and substantiate your answers.

References

Akujobi, R. 2009. 'Yesterday you were divorced. Today I am a widow': An appraisal of widowhood practices and the effects on the psyche of the women in Africa. *Gender and Behaviour*, 7(2):2457–2468.

Biko, S. 1978. *I write what I like*. Johannesburg: Heinemann.

Boal, A. 1995. *Rainbow of desire: The Boal method of theatre and therapy*. New York: Routledge.

Boulton, A. 2018. Decolonising ethics: Considerations of power, politics and privilege in Aotearoa/New Zealand. *Southern Africa Journal of Social Work and Social Development*, 30(1):1–15.

Cesaire, A. 1972. *Discourse and colonialism: A poetics of anti-colonialism*. New York: Monthly Review Press.

Darder, A. 2018. *The student guide to Freire's 'pedagogy of the oppressed'*. London, UK: Bloomsbury.

Dominelli, L. 2010. *Social work in a globalizing world*. Cambridge: Polity.

English Oxford *Living* Dictionaries. 2019. [Online]. Available: https://en.oxforddictionaries.com [Accessed 4 June 2019].

Fanon, F. 1968. *The wretched of the earth*. New York: Grove Press.

Flint, JE. 1974. *Cecil Rhodes*. Boston: Little Brown.

Freire, P. 1998. *Pedagogy of freedom: Ethics, democracy and civic courage*. Lanham: Rowman & Littlefield.

Grobler, H, Schenck, R & Mbedzi, P. 2013. *Person-centred facilitation: Process, theory and practice*. 4th ed. Cape Town: Oxford University Press.

Harlingten, L. 2013. *Social work and social justice: Conversations with activists*. DPhil thesis. University of South Africa, Pretoria.

Harms Smith, LH & Nathane, M. 2017. #notdomestication #notindigenisation: Decoloniality in social work education. *Southern Africa Journal of Social Work and Social Development*, 30(1):1–18.

Hart, K. 2018. *Thinking new worlds: the anti-colonial intellectuals*. [Online]. Available: https://www.academia.edu/36912987/Thinking_new_worlds_the_anti-colonial_intellectuals [Accessed 13 July 2018].

Hoosein, S. 2018. Decolonising social work research with families experiencing intergenerational trauma. *Southern Africa Journal of Social Work and Social Development*, 30(1):1–18.

Hope, A & Timmel, S. 1995. *Training for transformation*. Gweru: The Grail.

Hugo, S. 2018. *An empowerment programme for African young widows in Mangaung Metro, Free State*. Unpublished survey data.

International Association of Schools of Social Work (IASSW). 2018. *Global social work statement of ethical principles*. [Online]. Available: https://tinyurl.com/iasswethics [Accessed 8 March 2019].

International Federation of Social Workers (IFSW). 2014. *Global definition of social work*. [Online]. Available: https://www.ifsw.org/what-is-social-work/global-definition-of-social-work/ [Accessed 13 July 2018].

Lombard, A and Schenck, R: 'Adam Small en sy pleidooi vir geregtigheid: 'n Gevallestudie' [Adam Small and his plea for justice: A case study]. *In*: Van der Elst, J (ed.). 2017. *Adam Small, denker, digter, dramaturg* [*Adam Small, thinker, poet, dramatist*]. Pretoria: Protea Boekehuis.

Maldonado-Torres, N. 2007. On the coloniality of being. *Cultural studies*, 21:240–270.

Maldonado-Torres, N. 2016. *Outline of ten theses on coloniality and decoloniality*. Frantz Fanon Foundation. [Online]. Available: http://foundation-frantzfanon.com/wp-content/uploads/2018/10/maldonado-torres outline of ten theses-10.23.16.pdf [Accessed 12 July 2018].

Maschi, T, Baer, J & Turner, SG. 2011. The psychological goods on clinical social work: A content analysis of the clinical social work and social justice literature. *Journal of Social Work Practice*, 25(2):233–253.

Mathebane, MS & Sekudu, J. 2018. Decolonising the curriculum that underpins social work education in South Africa. *Southern Africa Journal of Social Work and Social Development*, 30(1):1–19.

Meredith, M. 2006. *The state of Africa: A history of fifty years of independence*. London, UK: The Free Press.

Mullaly, B. 2002. *Challenging oppression: A critical social work approach*. New York: Oxford University Press.

Ndlovu-Gatsheni, SJ. 2013. Why decoloniality in the 21st century? *The Thinker: For thought leaders*, 48:10–15.

Ndlovu-Gatsheni, SJ. 2015a. Decoloniality as the future of South Africa. *History Compass*. Doi-10.1111/hic3.12264.

Ndlovu-Gatsheni, SJ. 2015b. Decoloniality in Africa: A continuing search for a new world order. *Australasian Review of African Studies* (ARAS), 36(2):22–50.

Ngũgĩ wa Thiong'o. 2009. *Meaningful work 2009-2010* [Online]. Available: http://thekeep.eiu.edu/cgi/viewcontent.cgi?article=1002&context=humanitiescenter_meaningfulwork0910 [Accessed 13 July 2018].

Ngũgĩ wa Thiong'o. 2014. *Globalectics: Theory and the politics of knowing*. New York: Columbia University Press.

Nicholas, L, Rautenbach, J & Maistry, M (eds.). 2010. *Introduction to social work*. Cape Town: Juta.

Olson, JJ. 2007. Social work's professional and social justice projects: Discourses in conflict. *Journal of Progressive Human Services*, 184(1):45–69.

Pakenham, T. 1991. *The scramble for Africa: White man's conquest of the dark continent from 1876 to 1912*. London: Random House.

Plaatje, SR. 2013. Beyond Western-centric and Eurocentric development: A case for decolonizing development. *Africanus*, 43(2):118–130.

Schenck, C. 2017. *Interaction, integration and innovation at the 17th century feira of Dambarare, northern Zimbabwe*. Unpublished MSc dissertation in Archaeology. University of Cape Town, Cape Town.

Sen, A. 1999. *Development as freedom*. Oxford: Oxford University Press.

Sewpaul, V. 2015. Politics with soul: Social work and the legacy of Nelson Mandela. *International Social Work*, 59(6):697–708.

Smith, L. 2014. Historiography of South African social work: Challenging dominant discourses. *Social Work/Maatskaplike Werk*, 50(3):305–331.

Soliar, D. 2005. *Paulo Freire: Handbook for community youth workers*. Durban, RSA: Anumtapo centre production. [Online]. Available: http://www.umtapocentre.org.za/getmodule.php?id=load_document_asset.php&assets_id=166 [Accessed 12 July 2018].

Van der Watt, P. 2016. *Engaging with the soil and the soul of a community: Rethinking development, healing and transformation in South Africa*. Unpublished PhD thesis. University of the Free State, Bloemfontein.

Verster, P. 2018. Postkoloniale teologie en die sending: Uitdagings en bedreigings [Postcolonial theology and mission: Challenges and threats]. *Tydskrif vir Geesteswetenskappe* [*Journal of Humanities*], 58(1):96–108.

Annotated websites and activities

http://www.differencebetween.net/miscellaneous/politics/ideology-politics/difference-between-modernism-and-postmodernism/#ixzz5KHmdFKM6
Read more about the difference between modernism and postmodernism at this link.

https://www.youtube.com/watch?v=0dXpAVE3frk
https://www.youtube.com/watch?v=_WBEmEhseoU
These two links on YouTube explain the scramble for Africa. You may also find more if you search on YouTube.

http://www.sahistory.org.za/people/frantz-fanon
https://en.wikipedia.org/wiki/W._E._B._Du_Bois#Pan-Africanism_and_Marcus_Garvey
https://www.biography.com/search?query=mahatma%20gandhi
http://www.sahistory.org.za/people/stephen-bantu-biko
http://www.sahistory.org.za/archive/discourse-colonialism-aime-cesaire
http://infed.org/mobi/paulo-freire-dialogue-praxis-and-education/
These are some of the websites where you can access more reading on decolonisation and the Pan-African intellectuals, including Frantz Fanon, WEB Du Bois, Mahatma K Ghandi, Steve Biko, Aimé Césaire and Paulo Freire.

http://www.trainingfortransformation.co.za/wp-content/uploads/2016/04/impact-study_2015_FACETOFACE.pdf
It is important that you develop a good understanding of Freire's concepts of conscientisation or critical consciousness and some techniques to facilitate it. The link above might be of value.

Annotated websites and activities are also available on Learning Zone.

oxford.co.za/learningzone

Developmental social work

CHAPTER

3

Antoinette Lombard

CHAPTER OUTCOMES

By the end of this chapter, you should be able to:

✓ *Define the term developmental social work*
✓ *Explain the rationale for developmental social work in the historical context of social welfare policy in South Africa*
✓ *Explain the context in which developmental social work is practised*
✓ *Discuss how developmental social work links with sustainable development*
✓ *Identify and describe the features of developmental social work*
✓ *Critically assess the relevance of developmental social work for decolonial social work practice in South Africa.*

 Case Study 1   Resilience of people

You work for an NGO that renders social services to a township in an urban area. The NGO's vision is a better future for children and families through an engaged and integrated community. The community profile shows high levels of poverty and unemployment. In many sections of the community, the environment is polluted with rubbish dumps. Many households consist of children where grandmothers or single mothers are the primary caregivers. For many families, their household income is dependent on one or more grants, specifically an old age pension, child support or foster care grants. The NGO supports some families on a monthly basis with food parcels.

In your engagement with the community you notice how much hope and resilience there are among the people, despite the many adversities that they face. You find the local school to be very supportive in providing you with a platform to reach out to children, families and the broader community. Through the school, you could identify a range of role players in the community, including people from within the community who are eager to volunteer their time and strengths. It reminds you of what you have learned about developmental social work. People have strengths and know best what they want and what they can contribute. What they need is support in strengthening their capabilities and having opportunities for a better future. You recognise why developmental social work is embedded in a human rights-based approach.

Reflective questions
- What human rights do you see violated in this community?
- What inspires you to work in this community?
- What social change do you envisage for the community?

3.1 Introduction

The colonial and apartheid history of South Africa determined the social welfare policy framework in which social services were historically delivered. When South Africa became a democracy in 1994, a new era dawned for social welfare in shifting from a discriminatory and human rights abusive social welfare policy to a policy framework that is non-racist and inclusive. This was achieved by adopting a developmental approach to social welfare and services. In 1997, South Africa's first democratic social welfare policy framework was adopted in the form of the *White Paper for Social Welfare* (RSA, 1997). This was informed by the social development approach which was advocated by the United Nations World Summit for Social Development in 1995 (RSA, 1997). Within this mandate, developmental social work evolved as a platform for social work to contribute to a more just and fair society for all.

Developmental social work, also referred to as the developmental approach to social work, is indigenous to South Africa from where it spread to other countries in Africa, and increasingly to countries in the Global North. Developmental social work has paved the way for social workers to be social change agents on all intervention levels, that is, individual, family, group and community. Developmental social work draws on approaches and theories that are person-centred and guided by empowerment, strengths, resilience, sustainable livelihoods, and social constructionism, among others. As you familiarise yourself with these and other approaches and theories discussed in this book, analyse them in relation to how they apply to developmental social work in micro and macro practice as is described in this chapter. Furthermore, developmental social work is aligned with the commitments of the Global Agenda for Social Work and Social Development (2012) (hereafter Global Agenda) and positioned to contribute to the 2030 Agenda for Sustainable Development (UN, 2015) (hereafter 2030 Agenda) and in doing so shows the profession's relevance in both local and global contexts.

> **Social change**, targets structural injustices such as poverty and inequality, and promotes people's well-being (Midgley, 2010) and human development.

This chapter provides the context and overarching framework for developmental social work. It helps lay the foundation for subsequent chapters in the book that discuss theories and approaches of relevance for developmental social work. We begin by discussing the context in which we practice developmental social work. This includes finding the rationale for developmental social work that evolved from the social welfare policy adopted when South Africa became a democracy. Next, developmental social work is defined from various authors' perspectives. In the following section, we debate how developmental social work links with sustainable development and enables us to contribute to the Global Agenda and the 2030 Agenda. We then engage with the features of developmental social work. Finally, we critically reflect on the relevance of developmental social work for decolonial social work practice, and then end the chapter with a conclusion.

3.2 Context for developmental social work

The developmental approach requires that social workers look at the world from a broader political, socioeconomic, and cultural perspective. This will help them understand what makes societies unequal and how social ills – e.g., poverty, hunger, homelessness, and lack of access to education, health and income – contribute to discrimination, exclusion and unjust societies. This broader context helps us to understand how decisions by nations and politicians and macroeconomic policies can hinder or promote human development and influence who are included and excluded and why. As our country's history shows, social workers are often restricted by government policies in the way that they are allowed to speak out on human rights abuses, which means they can also be oppressed in practising social work. However, this is the situation across the globe, which emphasises that social workers have to unite their efforts in making the world a better place.

Political turmoil and violence pose new challenges for the provision of social services to thousands of internally displaced people, especially women, children and the elderly fleeing from conflict areas (Mwansa, 2012). These marginalised and vulnerable people who we work with are exposed to conflict and violence. Ledwith (2016:105) refers to poverty as 'a crime against humanity'. For Green (2012:229), '[c]onflict both feeds and is fed by inequality'. Ahmad and Jariwala (2016:575) observe that 'efficient and effective social work services in a global society need to take a broad perspective, where peace and social justice, human rights, and social development must always be at the forefront'.

In developmental social work we need to understand the 'global dimensions of seemingly local problems' (Ife, 2012:119). Globalisation has made social problems international, which emphasises the interconnectedness between the global and the local (Dominelli, 2010). Sewpaul (2014a:33) argues that globalisation and its concomitant neoliberal capitalism have filtered into every facet of our lives and the world has become a global market 'where anything including human beings can be bought and sold'. People 'move across different parts of the world to escape poverty, wars, famine, and environmental degradation' (Dominelli, 2010:599).

Globalisation impacts on social work practice in the way it changes service delivery and creates social problems across the borders that practitioners have to address, 'such as people-trafficking and environmental issues'; it also emphasises the need for indigenisation, 'or the development of local-specific forms of theory and practice', which highlights the positive aspects of globalisation (Dominelli, 2010:599). Local and international contexts give us the opportunity to learn to 'appreciate differences, within and across groups, countries and regions', however, on condition that 'such differences are not harmful to any group of persons' (Sewpaul, 2016a:34). Kreitzer (2012) affirms the global-local context and remarks that international social work is also about the development of practices that are relevant in local contexts.

However, social work is globally and locally influenced by neoliberal, capitalist macro-economic policies, which South Africa has also adopted (Spolander et al. 2016:634, 642). These authors maintain that neoliberalism shapes and structures social welfare policy and services, and their implementation, and erodes critical social work voices.

Globalisation, 'a process of international exchange and integration involving increased economic activities, social interactions, political cooperation and improved communication' (Midgley, 2014:232).

Neoliberalism, 'an ideology that prioritises a free market principle that elevates profit above human or planetary wellbeing'. It justifies policies that increase social inequalities (Ledwith, 2016:xv).

Capitalism, an economic and political theory that stresses the role of markets (Midgley, 2014).

In summary, developmental social work is contextualised in the local-global interconnectedness of social problems across borders and the challenges associated with globalisation and neoliberalism. It is also contextualised in the contribution that developmental social work can make to the commitments of the Global Agenda and the 2030 Agenda.

Reflective questions
Look back at Case study 1 above and then answer the following questions:
- What impact of neoliberalism is visible in the community?
- What possible local-global links do you observe in the social problems that are prevalent in the community? How may this influence your practice approach?
- What are your observations on social workers having a role in peace-building, social justice and human rights in the community?

3.3 Definitions of developmental social work

There is no universal definition for developmental social work. With developmental social work being indigenous to South Africa, it is of significance that the authors below, who have contributed to defining it, all have their roots in South Africa. It gives the descriptions an authentic flavour with regard to having a deep understanding of our colonial and apartheid history.

3.3.1 Key definitions

James Midgley, Professor of the Graduate School and Harry and Riva Specht Professor Emeritus, University of California, Berkeley, is an authority in international social welfare and social development. His seminal book *Social development: The developmental perspective in social welfare* (1995) paved the way for many to follow, which further informed the study field.

Developmental social work, transcends conventional remedial and maintenance practice approaches by 'adopting social investment strategies that build on people's capabilities to be productive citizens and lead normal and fulfilling lives' (Midgley, 2010:xvi).

Midgley recognises common themes of developmental social work that provide a basis for a systematic conceptual perspective on developmental social work, including social change as a central theme, 'the use of strengths, empowerment and capacity enhancement, the notion of self-determination and client participation, and a commitment to equality and social justice', social investment and social rights (Midgley, 2010:13).

Leila Patel is the SARCHi Chair in Welfare and Social Development at the University of Johannesburg. She was appointed to manage and lead the process and the drafting of the White Paper for Social Welfare (RSA, 1997), which informed her seminal formulation of development practice in social welfare in her book *Social welfare and social development in South Africa*, second edition (2015), and comprehensive publication on the theme.

> **Developmental social work,** 'is informed by the social development approach to social welfare and involves the practical and appropriate application of knowledge, skills and values to enhance the well-being of individuals, families, groups, and communities in their social context. It also involves the implementation of research and the development and implementation of social policies that contribute to social justice and human development in a changing national and global context. Developmental social work aims to promote social change through a dual focus on the person and the environment and the interaction between the two' (Patel, 2015:127).

Mel Gray is a Professor Emeritus in social work at the School of Humanities and Social Services (Social Work), University of Newcastle, Australia. While still living in South Africa at the time, she wrote the first book publication on developmental social work in South Africa in 1998, *Developmental social work: Theory and practice in social work*. She has contributed extensively to the knowledge field of developmental social work. For the purpose of this chapter, see below a recent definition in an article on developmental social work in Southern and East Africa, which she co-authored.

> **Developmental social work,** 'affirms the social work profession's commitment to the eradication of poverty, recognises the link between welfare and economic development, and construes welfare as an investment in human capital rather than a drain on limited government resources' (Gray et al., 2018:975). It is an indigenous form of practice which is best positioned to intervene in situations of poverty, and focuses on community development, rather than casework, as a method of intervention.

Antoinette Lombard is a Professor in social work at the University of Pretoria. Her publications over the past twenty years contributed to conceptualising and applying developmental social work to various specialised fields and practice settings. She presents the following definition:

> **Developmental social work,** reaffirms social work's commitment to social justice and poverty eradication by promoting social change and human development for sustainable (social, economic and environment) development outcomes. It recognises the local-global link of social problems and is relevant to all social work fields, service levels and methods through the lens of human rights, ecological justice, micro and macro practice, and people participation. It is aligned with the commitments of the Global Agenda, and the 2030 Agenda.

3.3.2 Critical reflections on the definitions

Over the years, these authors' writings have developed and contributed new insights. It therefore does not do justice to the richness of their contributions to select just one of their publications to share their views on developmental social work. However, being familiar with their work, I will extend my comments wider.

All the definitions emphasise the importance of social change and thus embody a focus on structural injustices, poverty and inequality in particular, and human well-being and development. Developmental social work emphasises people participation, and strength-based and social investment strategies.

Patel and Lombard are more specific in referring to the interconnection between the local and the global. However, both Midgley and Gray write extensively on international social work and the link between the local and the global.

Although Gray gives preference to community development, she does not discard a role for casework. According to Midgley (2010), it is an oversimplification to strictly classify individualised casework as being remedial and community work as being developmental. Lombard and Kleijn (2006) make a strong case for casework and statutory work in relation to developmental social services. Van Breda (2018) presents a process model for casework in developmental social work.

All the authors see a pertinent role for government in developmental social work. Gray et al.'s (2018:975) reference to 'a drain on limited government resources' is true in the sense that resources are limited. However, from a social rights perspective, government's role as duty bearer must be questioned in relation to how the limited resources are influenced by the neoliberal macroeconomic policy.

The authors agree that developmental social work applies to both micro and macro practice. In this chapter, Lombard emphasises the interconnectedness between micro and macro practice as a strong argument in promoting social justice.

There is recognition among the authors that developmental social work includes conventional fields of practice such as child welfare, mental health, social work with disability, gerontology social work, social assistance, corrections, substance abuse, restorative justice and statutory work (Lombard & Kleijn, 2006; Midgley & Conley, 2010; Patel, 2015).

There is consensus that developmental social work is informed and inspired by social development as a social welfare policy, amongst other approaches to social welfare policy (Midgley, 1995; Patel, 2015).

The terms developmental social welfare and social development are often used interchangeably (Midgley, 2010; Patel, 2015). This is acceptable in the context that social development and social welfare are both multidisciplinary concepts. However, it is confusing to argue that developmental social work is social development. Although developmental social work and social development are 'closely associated', social development comprises a broader set of activities than those of developmental social work; furthermore, developmental social work is a 'distinctive form of practice', while social development is 'a broader interdisciplinary field closely associated with economic development projects and programs in the Global South' (Midgely, 2010:xiv). It is thus clearly not accurate to say that developmental social work is social development. If social development is a policy approach to social welfare, then that is what it is; social development 'informs and inspires developmental social work' (Midgley, 2010:xv). As a discipline, social work can contribute to social development as an end goal, while it can also use social development as a social investment strategy to integrate social and economic activities (Lombard, 2007). According to Lombard (2008:159), the conceptual confusion has an impact on South Africa's progress with developmental social welfare and social work.

📍 ACTIVITY 3.1

1 What is your view on the above definitions of developmental social work?
2 How does these definitions resonate with the understanding of developmental social work that you have obtained thus far in your studies and practice?
3 What would you exclude and what would you include if you were to write your own definition?

3.4 Developmental social work and sustainable development

In 2015, South Africa was among the 193 countries whose world leaders signed the Declaration of the 2030 Agenda, and in doing so committed to achieve the 17 Sustainable Development Goals (SDGs) and its 169 targets by 2030. Countries and stakeholders were called to work together in a collaborative partnership to implement the 2030 Agenda, which is an action plan for people, planet and prosperity (UN, 2015). This call also applies to social work. Social work is embedded in the value of social justice and upholding of human rights and as such committed to leaving no one behind as stated in the 2030 Agenda. This commitment is underpinned by the four themes of the Global Agenda.

Sustainable development, an approach to development (Midgley, 2014) that protects the 'planet from degradation, including through sustainable consumption and production … so that it can support the needs of the present and future generations' (UN, 2015:5). It has three dimensions – social, economic and environmental. It focuses on interventions that eradicate poverty and combat inequality while preserving the planet (UN, 2015).

 **ACTIVITY 3.2**

Locate a copy of the 17 SDGs and its 169 targets (UN, 2015) on the internet. Identify how they connect with social work and explain why you say so.

If we identify with the aim of the 2030 Agenda that none of the 17 SDGs should be met 'unless it is met for everyone' (Melamed, 2015:1), it means we commit social work to contribute to all the SDGs. This seems logical as they are integrated and indivisible and represent the three dimensions of sustainable development in a balanced manner (UN, 2015). Lombard (2015) shows how the 17 SDGs link with the four themes of the Global Agenda, namely:
1. promoting social and economic equality;
2. promoting the dignity and worth of all peoples;
3. promoting environmental and community sustainability; and
4. strengthening recognition of the importance of human relationships.

However, social workers represent one of many stakeholders in the 2030 Agenda partnership and contribute to the SDGs directly and indirectly. Social work's irrevocable link with the 2030 Agenda is embedded in the envisaged outcomes to end poverty and hunger and achieve gender equality and empower all women and girls. Within a normative or humanistic discourse, the link between rights and poverty is associated with a discourse that regards poverty as a violation of human rights (Dean, 2015). As Sewpaul (2014a:39) states, poverty is more than an economic issue, and, in a broader sense, 'it reflects the denial of human capabilities, an assault on human dignity and integrity, lack of opportunities for development and a denial of fundamental rights'. Dominelli (2014) adds that poverty is a human-made disaster and its impact aggravates all types of disasters. The 2030 Agenda recognises that 'eradicating poverty in all its forms and dimensions is the greatest global challenge and an indispensable requirement for sustainable development' (UN, 2015:5).

As social workers, we contribute to the three dimensions of sustainable development through our commitment to human rights and justice. Isbister (2001:4) captures the link between justice and human rights: 'Justice is the bedrock social virtue ... We have a right to justice'. Therefore, if social justice is part of the human rights discourse (Staub-Bernasconi, 2012), and human rights are indivisible and interconnected (Ife, 2012), as in the case of the SDGs (UN, 2015), we cannot argue for social justice without including economic and environmental justice. For Erickson (2012), social workers are compelled to act on environmental injustices because of their ethical mandate to address social injustice. This commitment is reflected in the four themes of the Global Agenda (2012) and as such affirms that we have a role in the 2030 Agenda's action plan for people (social), planet (environment) and prosperity (economic) (UN, 2015). The interrelatedness of social, economic and environmental justice is illustrated by Erickson (2012), stating that if ecosystems are degraded, communities face a loss of food systems and economic opportunities, resulting in severe poverty. Moreover, Ledwith (2016) aptly states that poverty is a human rights issue and peace can only be achieved from a social justice perspective, while social justice can only be understood by paying attention to economic justice and ecological sustainability.

Social justice, has three components: equality, freedom, and efficiency. 'People deserve to be treated as equals, they deserve to be free, and they deserve to get the best they can out of their limited resources ... Justice requires equality of opportunity, not equality of outcomes' (Isbister, 2001:4, 14).

Economic justice, applies to the individual person as well as the social order. It includes the moral principles that guide us in the design of our economic institutions which determine how a person earns a living. Economic freedom enables a person to engage creatively in 'the unlimited work beyond economics, that of the mind and the spirit' (Center for Economic and Social Justice, n.d.).

Environmental justice, ensuring that the human right to live in a clean, safe, and healthy environment is enjoyed by all people, given that '[t]he world's most poor, vulnerable, and oppressed people often live in the most degraded environments and have no control over resources' (Hawkins, 2010:68).

Social workers must expand the person-in-environment's long-standing focus on only the *social* environment, to include also the *physical* environment, which is important to sustain human life (Erickson, 2012). It means that we have to broaden our notion of the environment to include the natural world. This is largely an expansion from an anthropocentric to an ecocentric focus (Gray et al., 2013).

Ecocentric, a nature-centred system of values (versus human-centred) that sees all things as interconnected and the human as inseparable from nature. All life forms have intrinsic value, and human needs are not seen as superior to those of other life forms (Gray et al., 2013).

Anthropocentrism, the belief that human interests are central in environmental matters, specifically the inclination of the human species to regard itself as the dominant and most important entity in the universe. It is the evaluation of all reality and all action through an exclusively human perspective (Gray et al., 2013).

An ecocentric view emphasises that both people and planet (earth) are important for sustainable environments and communities. This view stimulated debate for social work to redefine justice, which led Besthorn (2013:38) to conclude that, '[i]n a practical sense, no matter how social work languages its idea of justice, in the end all justice is ecological'. Gray et al. (2013:298) echo this by stating that '[t]here is no doubt that ecological justice is firmly on the social work agenda'.

> **Ecological justice**, acknowledges the responsibilities to and the inalienable rights that non-human entities have in the natural world as opposed to only the extent these impinge upon human well-being. It embraces both environmental and social justice (Besthorn, 2013:37).

Environmental justice

I had a very interesting class today which rocks my understanding of social work and what I am supposed to do. From first year we learn that social justice is the core value of social work. Today I heard about environmental justice and that we should take note of the physical environment. Apparently, some social work scholars have started to write about this some years ago, but it was just a few.

That is weird. I cannot see how the planet is relevant to poor people who need an income to have a decent living. The only thing I know about the environment is that 'person-in-environment' thing where we look at the relationships and interaction that people have with others in the various systems that they function in.

That seems to be the issue. Now we have to look beyond that and see people and the planet.

Does the talking about climate change have something to do with this newness? It makes me think about the shocking droughts and floods that we see today.

Yes, and you know what, it is always the poor people who are the hardest hit. They are more at risk because they don't have the means.

But, you know, it strikes me in the drought that plants and animals also suffer. I read about a drought study where people depend on their land for survival. If the soil turns to sand, even the animals die as they have nothing to eat. Many families and communities then survive on drought relief and they feel hopeless.

It reminds me, when I drive in the township, I see children playing on rubbish dumps and animals sniffling for food around them. That must put their health at risk.

It seems that humans contribute to degrading the planet that they expect to care for them. It makes kind of sense that if people look after the planet, the planet will look after them.

Now you make me think. It makes sense that there is no social justice without environmental justice.

3.5 Features of developmental social work

Social work is a profession and academic discipline that we refer to as developmental social work in South Africa (Patel, 2015). According to Patel (2015:82), the themes that informed the policy framework of the White Paper for Social Welfare (RSA, 1997) in the South African context included a rights-based approach, economic and social development, democracy and participation, partnerships, and bridging the macro and micro practice divide. These themes of developmental social welfare are included in the features of developmental social work and are aligned with the five pillars of sustainable development known as the 5Ps: people; planet; prosperity; peace; and partnerships (UN, 2015).

3.5.1 Promote human rights and human development

Human rights are the key for human development and social inclusion. Article 1 of the Universal Declaration of Human Rights (UN, 1948) states that 'all human beings are born free and are equal in their dignity and rights'. Human dignity forms 'the value base of human rights' (Staub-Bernasconi, 2012:32).

The three-generation typology of human rights provides a conceptual framework for developmental social work practice (Lombard & Twikirize, 2014). First generation human rights are civil and political rights, which are fundamental freedoms and rights that are essential for democracy and civil society (Ife, 2012). Second generation human rights are known as economic, social and cultural rights and include rights that are provided in various forms of social provision or services in order for people to realise their full potential, such as the right to: employment; an adequate wage; housing; adequate food; education; adequate health care; and social security (Ife, 2012). Third generation human rights are collective rights that belong to the community and society and include 'the right to economic development, the right to benefit from world trade and economic growth, the right to live in a cohesive and harmonious society, and environmental rights such as the right to breathe unpolluted air, the right to access clean water, and the right to experience "nature"' (Ife, 2012:47).

For social work, first generation rights are relevant to build a just society; however, to achieve social equality and social justice goals, second and third generation rights are also important

(Ife, 2012). Dean (2015) refers to second generation rights as social rights. He asserts that, because they may be understood as expressions of human need, we can assume that they are essential to human development. In South Africa, the Constitution and the Bill of Rights (Chapter 1 of the Constitution) make provision for legally enforceable economic and social rights (Patel, 2015). However, because second generation rights are more complex and require more than legal guarantees, they involve policy development, political change, and the design and delivery of effective human services, which Ife (2012:51) indicates as being more the 'natural territory of the social worker and other human service workers'.

For Dean (2015:137), the capabilities approach of Amartya Sen (1999), which is encapsulated in the slogan 'development as freedom', promotes a holistic approach where the right to development is prioritised in order to transcend the distinction between first and second generation human rights. As Dean (2015) alludes, for Sen (1999), freedom is constituted through human development, not rights. Human rights create the space in which human capabilities may be realised and are only the means to an end, namely to guarantee basic human freedoms (Dean, 2015). South Africa's National Development Plan aims to 'eliminate poverty and reduce inequality by 2030' by focusing on the key capabilities that individuals need to live the life that they desire, of which education and skills and the opportunity to work are mostly prioritised (RSA, 2012:28).

> **Capabilities**, '[t]he ability of individuals and households to achieve desirable functionings and goals' (Midgley, 2014:230). 'If reading is a functioning, then literacy and being educated are the capabilities necessary for that functioning' (Shlosberg, 2007:31).

Building capabilities relates to the target of 'leaving no one behind', which in theory 'means ensuring that every individual achieves the full package of rights and opportunities' that the SDGs express (Melamed, 2015:1). Fighting the war on poverty and inequality 'includes standing up against injustices, and challenging violent state responses to people's actions to defend their rights' (Lombard, 2015:486). By advocating for and promoting human rights, social workers contribute to peace, prosperity, tranquillity and security, which, in the words of Nelson Mandela, 'are only possible if they are enjoyed by all without discrimination' (Crwys-Williams, 1910:90).

3.5.2   Integrate social and economic development

Integrated social and economic development promotes sustainable development as it will 'ensure that all human beings can enjoy prosperous and fulfilling lives and that economic, social and technological progress occurs in harmony with nature' (UN, 2015:5). The true aim of development is not only to increase incomes, but also to maximize people's choices to live long, healthy and creative lives by promoting human rights, freedoms, capabilities and opportunities (UNDP, 2015). Social and economic development are both important for human development, which explains why the UNDP 'takes a broad view of work, going beyond jobs' (UNDP, 2015:iii). It includes such activities as unpaid care work, voluntary work and creative work, which all contribute to the richness of human lives. It is the poorest people who are most severely affected by job losses, and 'low-paid work that is insufficient to provide a decent standard of living' (Dominelli, 2010:599). Therefore, whatever work people do, including voluntary work, it should be decent work that provides them with a sense of dignity and an opportunity to engage fully in society (UNDP, 2015). To end poverty, we have to develop socioeconomic models that do justice to low-income people who cannot overcome poverty or participate in markets to sell their products (Dominelli, 2014).

Social investment strategies, also known as the productivist approach to social welfare, involve a cluster of interventions that promotes economic participation and raises incomes and assets (Midgley, 2010). This includes human capital programmes, such as formal and informal education; other human capabilities, such as nutritional and health status; adult literacy; job training; preschool childcare centres; and women's educational programmes (Midgley, 2010). Social investment strategies should not be used in isolation from broader, community-based interventions, but in conjunction with national policies that promote sustainable development for all (Midgley, 2010).

Social protection is now regarded as a social investment strategy due to a greater recognition of its role in poverty alleviation and because it links economic and social policies, and enhances participation (Midgley, 2014). There is also growing evidence that social grants promote school attendance and raise standards of health and nutrition, fostering economic development and promoting long-term economic stability (Midgley, 2014).

3.5.3 Integrate micro and macro practice

While there is certainly greater emphasis in developmental social work to use intervention strategies that target the masses to ensure greater impact on ending poverty, hunger and inequality, a people-centred focus never loses sight of the vulnerabilities of individuals. As Rothman and Mizrahi (2017:91) say, social problems require 'complex and sustained intervention at all levels of social work practice'. Therefore, both micro and macro practice are important and we have to be open to both ends when and where we practice developmental social work. Furthermore, we should not see work for social justice occurring only on a macro level; it is equally relevant on a micro level. Reisch (2016:261) helps us understand this, saying that contrary to what is often thought, 'macro social work is not indirect practice'. He explains, '[a]ll social work practice occurs in a community context, and virtually all social workers work in organizations that are affected by social policies'. Extending this argument, Harrison, Van Deusen and Way (2016:269) elaborate that '[t]hroughout social work's history, a false dichotomy has been presented of either working toward social justice or working in micro practice'. They argue that social workers 'are uniquely situated to practice justly and ameliorate injustice through micro practice when enhancing individuals' economic (e.g., employment), psychological (e.g., self-esteem, social skills), and social (e.g., equality)' conditions.

What emerges from this discussion is that both micro and macro practice are important in developmental social work. It is thus a dual approach, which focuses particularly on the intersection of the two. Kiselica and Robinson (2001) also stress the interconnectedness between micro interventions and social justice when they say that social justice work calls for unconventional approaches to counselling, such as 'advocacy counselling'. They foresee a role for counsellors engaging in social action, but add a caution that they do not believe that this will be possible without 'a personal moral imperative' driving our work (Kiselica & Robinson, 2001:396). Sewpaul (2016b:706) affirms and argues that 'lifting micro levels of analyses and interventions into broader public issues brings social work into the realm of the political'.

All human interaction and endeavour involve power and resources and the struggle for these (Sheedy, 2013), which make social work political. This argument can be linked to the reasoning of Isbister (2001:166) that, if we defend the care that we give to our family as being compatible with justice, we do so in the distinctive way that matters to most of us, by emphasising that 'the personal is political'. He gives an example that we can draw from. If family and other relationships are marked by 'exploitation, subordination, and the unjustified use of power', he argues, it is important for all involved to understand the system in which they operate, how it relates to the wider society, and how it can be reformulated.

Applied to developmental social work, Midgley (2010:17) states that developmental social workers believe that 'political action is needed to challenge discrimination, racism, sexism, and other impediments to progress'. To this end, '[t]hey have recognized that improvements in material welfare are not only the result of economic progress, education, and similar interventions but of wider social and political changes that produce peaceful, democratic, egalitarian, and just societies'.

3.5.4 Facilitate people participation

Developmental social work emphasises giving a voice to people to engage in and influence their own development (Lombard, 2014). The importance of people participation is evident in the SDGs and its targets that are 'the result of over two years of intensive public consultation and engagement with civil society and other stakeholders around the world' where the voices of the poorest and the most vulnerable in particular received attention (UN, 2015:5). It is important for developmental social work to include peoples' voices in a democracy that embraces human rights. Furthermore, development is context-specific, and, as Mwansa (2012) suggests, our social work practice will benefit from people sharing their indigenous knowledge.

Being committed to justice for all and subscribing to a human rights framework in developmental social work, we have to be very attentive to ensure that clients who 'face exclusion, marginalisation and oppression' in their personal lived experiences, as well as in the wider societal contexts, have a voice (Sheedy, 2013:6). We can concur with Green (2012) that a rights-based approach rejects the idea that people who are poor are passive recipients of charity and that they have no other means of meeting their needs. We rather see clients as possessing the capabilities to take charge of their own development to realise their rights. Therefore, while we challenge structural injustices on macro and policy levels, we must also prepare and mobilise previously marginalised people and groups who have the 'power within' to demand their rights 'by challenging elites with "power over" them, and assert their rights by acquiring the "power to" do the things they need to improve their lives' (Green, 2012:26).

3.5.5 Collaborate in partnerships

Partnerships are important on global, regional, national and local levels to achieve sustainable development. The 2030 Agenda refers to a Global Partnership for Sustainable Development, based on a spirit of global solidarity, in which all countries, stakeholders and people participate and focus on the needs of the poorest and most vulnerable (UN, 2015). In alignment with the 2030 Agenda, the Global Agenda indicates the international organisations, including the UN, and the communities and organisations that should collaborate in achieving its commitments (Lombard, 2015).

It is on national level that governments are responsible to develop relevant policies and legislation and oversee the implementation thereof (UN, 2015). Patel (2015) indicates that in South Africa, the state is expected to play a leading role in promoting social development in a collaborative partnership model in service delivery. This happens in the context of a mixed economy of social welfare, also referred to as welfare pluralism, consisting of four sectors, namely government, voluntary (e.g., NGOs), informal (e.g., informal support by family, friends or other social networks), and commercial sectors (Gilbert, 2000).

The need for a global platform is stressed by Isbister (2001:173), who argues that:

> If our obligations to provide justice [are] based upon our connections with people, it cannot be the case that we have no international obligations of justice, since we are closely connected as foreigners.

However, in alignment with the 2030 Agenda being an '[a]genda of the people, by the people, and for the people' (UN, 2015:10), we have to make sure that we include clients as partners by giving them opportunities to develop their capabilities that will strengthen their dignity and self-agency to participate.

🎙 ACTIVITY 3.3

Look back at Case study 1 and do the following:
1 Analyse the community in relation to the features in developmental social work.
2 Reflect on how you will:
   a. promote human rights and human development;
   b. integrate social and economic development;
   c. integrate micro and macro practice;
   d. facilitate people participation; and
   e. collaborate in partnerships.
3 Take the five features of developmental social work addressed in section 3.5 and translate them into your home language. Use terminology that someone who is not familiar with social work subject language would understand.
4 Create a mind map, poster or flier that illustrates what developmental social work is in a way that a non-social worker will understand.

3.6 Relevance of developmental social work for decolonial social work

The strong emphasis on people participation in developmental social work helps us to remain sensitive to facilitate rather than control. In so doing, we respect and engage peoples' views rather than impose ours on them. It positions us to engage critically with perspectives that may be imposed from the Global North onto the Global South.

However, although developmental social work is meant to be decolonial, this does not mean it is truly so in all practice and education settings. More needs to be done on an ongoing basis, and we should remain mindful of the following:

- Decoloniality asks for a sensitive look at ourselves as social workers and educators – our worldviews, attitudes, and prejudices – and how we possibly keep systems in place that restrict clients' freedom. We should also identify our own oppressors in facilitating social change.
- To be prepared for local-global and micro-macro practice, we should be aware and appreciative of issues of diversity and multiculturalism; social, economic and environmental justice and human rights; empathy and compassion; and sustainable development, which will enable us to act responsibly (Sherman, 2016). We should be

equipped with technologies, information, paradigms, and practice knowledge that will enable us to work with communities for social change (Mwansa, 2012). This includes being trained to practise in the local context, but at the same time being prepared to follow the global trends that impact peoples' lives and influence them collectively. This understanding will, on the one hand, assist us to know and respect different worldviews and how they may impose on our thinking and approaches, and, on the other hand, assist us to embrace diversity and respect alternative ways of thinking and doing while we practise social work in a cosmos of different cultures and contexts.

- We need to become active and skilled advocates in policy-making and advocacy to promote social justice on micro, mezzo, and macro levels (Hoefer, 2012). To do this, we must adopt a critical stance that will enable us to question and analyse the forces that maintain injustice, discrimination and oppression (Sheedy, 2013). We have to 'explore the bigger political picture about power and disadvantage in society, and to consider different aspects of social work interventions and the methods' that we use (Higgs, 2015:121).

Because social work is grounded 'in the world of day-to-day practice, it cannot afford theoretical formulations that are not similarly grounded in [people's] lived reality' (Ife, 2012:216). Furthermore, social work practice can only occur in an environment of ongoing learning, and therefore social workers should be 'constantly learning and reformulating their world-views and approaches to practice, as a direct consequence of their day-to-day work' (Ife, 2012:217).

Sherman (2016) suggests that we can get committed to social justice at the local and international levels by encouraging students to engage in self-reflection by critically examining their own beliefs and attitudes, as well as their cultural and family traditions and views of social justice. This will help us to respond in a professional manner to social conditions that have an impact on individuals, families and communities.

Social problems emerge from the lived experiences of individuals who, on the one hand, need healing through psychosocial services, and, on the other hand, need freedom at a societal level from the consequences of injustices. We must address both personal action (agency) and structural changes in practising social work (Sheedy, 2013). Furthermore, 'social workers need to be able to critically analyse themselves and their practice and be prepared to be openly accountable through being critically analysed by others' (Sheedy, 2013:6). Ife (2012) concurs that a critical pedagogy approach to social work education will reinforce a human rights approach to social work. Paulo Freire's critical pedagogy can help us with this (Ledwith, 2016).

Critical pedagogy, an empowerment-based form of education that involves the active participation of the learner and incorporates conscientisation of the social and political context (Ife, 2012). It is a form of popular education based on people's life experiences, and can assist social workers, educators and students to question 'everyday life's taken-for-grantedness to see the contradictions we live by more clearly in order to act for change' (Ledwith, 2016:xi).

Conscientisation, 'a process of critical consciousness that starts with creating the context for people to question their everyday experience in order to recognise oppression as a political injustice rather than a personal failing' (Ledwith, 2016:xi).

Empowerment, 'a process of collective liberation from oppression by becoming critical' (Ledwith, 2016:xiii).

If we, as social workers, want to assist clients to challenge systemic injustices that impact their lives, we must first understand our own oppression and/or privileges and how these influence our behaviour personally and professionally. Zufferey (2012:661) reflects on her own case, indicating how 'unearned power and privilege is systematically attributed to ... [her] ... as a member of the dominant cultural group'. She argues that being aware 'of the negative effects of professional power can enable us to challenge systemic racism, to promote a social justice and human rights perspective and to respectfully consult with individuals and communities affected by this power' (Zufferey 2012:670–671).

In summary, Ledwith (2016:43–44) states that:

> ... [the] simple act of discovering some control over life's circumstances is empowering, energising and brings with it a sense of self-belief. It restores dignity. It also comes with a sense of identity, affirming who we are.

This approach will go a long way in reversing the effect of colonial invasion, where a loss of identity and culture greatly affected the psyche of the people of Africa (Kreitzer, 2012).

📍 ACTIVITY 3.4

Look back at Case study 1 and do the following:
1 How do you see the relevance of developmental social work for decolonial social work practice?
2 How do you see the relevance of the presented suggestions to shape the thinking and behaviour of practitioners, educators and students to better prepare them for decolonial practice?
3 How do you value using critical pedagogy yourself to better understand other peoples' worldviews?
4 How could your experience assist clients to use critical pedagogy to attain their voice and agency?

3.7 Conclusion

The socioeconomic and political context, and local-global interconnectedness of structural challenges such as poverty and inequality, influence the context in which social welfare and social work is practised. Informed by a developmental social welfare policy, developmental social work seeks to shift us from the traditional social control and maintaining functions of social work to 'greater system de-stabilising and social change efforts' (Sewpaul, 2014b:23) where people's participation and voices are central.

Developmental social work's emphasis on the interconnectedness of micro and macro practice foregrounds its role on both individual and structural/political levels. It affirms social work's position and role in human development, social change and sustainable development in contributing to a just and fair society.

Chapter activity

1. **Reflective question.** Think about where you come from, your education, opportunities, hardships, oppression or privileges, and vision of the future. How do your own life experiences relate to the issues that we have discussed? Think about structural injustices, social justice, human rights, and prejudices that shaped your thinking and behaviour. What do you discover about yourself if you use critical pedagogy to unblock your thinking?

What do you want to change in your life that will assist you in being a developmental social worker?

2. **Personal context**. Think about the community where you come from. What shapes the peoples' lives there? How do they respond to life's challenges? How do you see your community through the lens of human rights, social justice, and sustainable development? What challenges you to engage in the community to bring about change?

3. **Advocacy**. Identify any contemporary social issue that challenges you to respond. Think how you will use both micro and macro practice to advocate for and with the people.

4. **Critical questions**. Think about South Africa's longstanding history of discrimination, exclusion and oppression. How are social workers helping (or not helping) to build a more just and fair society? Do you see any possible red flags within yourself or colleagues that remind you of exercising control over clients that may keep them oppressed? What are they not doing, or doing wrong, that may question social workers' role and capabilities to contribute to social change? In what way are you oppressed or possibly oppressing colleagues in respect of how you are practising social work?

References

Ahmad, M & Jariwala, HV. 2016. Living in a global society. Part one of a two-part special issue, *Journal of Social Service Research*, 42(5):573–575.

Besthorn, FH: 'Radical equalitarian ecological justice'. *In*: Gray, M, Coates, J & Hetherington, T (eds.). 2013. *Environmental social work*. pp. 31–45. New York: Routledge.

Center for Economic and Social Justice. [Online]. Available: https://www.investopedia.com/terms/e/economic-justice.asp [Accessed 2 April 2018].

Crwys-Williams, J (ed.). 2010. *In the words of Nelson Mandela*. 2nd ed. Johannesburg: Penguin Books.

Dean, H. 2015. *Social rights and human welfare*. New York: Routledge.

Dominelli, L. 2010. Globalization, contemporary challenges and social work practice. *International Social Work*, 53(5):599–612.

Dominelli, L: 'Environmental justice at the heart of social work practice: Greening the profession'. *In*: Hessle, S (ed.). 2014. *Environmental change and sustainable social development*. pp. 133–149. Surrey: Ashgate.

Erickson, CL: 'Environmental degradation and preservation'. *In*: Healy, LM & Link, RJ (eds.). 2012. *Handbook of international social work, human rights, development, and the global profession*. pp. 184–189. Oxford: Oxford University Press.

Gilbert, N: 'Welfare pluralism and social policy'. *In*: Midgley, J, Tracy, MB & Livermore, M (eds.). 2000. *The handbook of social policy*. pp. 411–434. Thousand Oaks, CA: Sage.

Global Agenda for Social Work and Social Development. 2012. *Collaboration between IASSW, IFSW, ICSW*. [Online]. Available: http://www.globalsocialagenda.org [Accessed 15 September 2017].

Gray, M. 1998. *Developmental social work: Theory and practice in social work*. Cape Town: David Phillip.

Gray, M, Coates, J & Hetherington, T (eds.). 2013. *Environmental social work*. New York: Routledge.

Gray, M, Agillias, K, Mupedziswa, R & Mugumbate, J. 2018. The expansion of developmental social work in Southern and East Africa: Opportunities and challenges for social work field programmes. *International Social Work*, 61(6):974–987.

Green, D. 2012. *From poverty to power: How active citizens and effective states can change the world*. 2nd ed. Rugby, UP: Practical Action Publishing and Oxford: Oxfam International.

Harrison, J, Van Deusen, K & Way, I. 2016. Embedding social justice within micro social work curricula. *Smith College Studies in Social Work*, 86(3):258–273.

Hawkins, CA. 2010. Sustainability, human rights, and environmental justice: Critical connections for contemporary social work. *Critical Social Work*, 11(3):68–81.

Higgs, A: 'Social justice'. *In*: Bell, L & Hafford-Letchfield, T. 2015. *Ethics, values and social work practice*. pp. 112–121. New York: McGraw Hill Education.

Hoefer, R. 2012. *Advocacy practice for social justice*. Illinois: Lyceum Books.

Ife, J. 2012. *Human rights and social work. Towards rights-based practice*. 3rd ed. London: Cambridge University Press.

Isbister, J. 2001. *Capitalism and justice, envisioning social and economic fairness*. Bloomfield: Kumarian Press.

Kiselica, MS & Robinson, M. 2001. Bringing advocacy counseling to life: The history, issues, and human dramas of social justice work in counseling. *Journal of Counseling and Development*, 79:387–397.

Kreitzer. L. 2012. *Social work in Africa: Exploring culturally relevant education and practice in Ghana*. Calgary: University of Calgary Press.

Ledwith, M. 2016. *Community development in action: Putting Freire into practice*. Bristol: Policy Press.

Lombard, A. 2007. The impact of social welfare policies on social development in South Africa: An NGO perspective. *Social Work/Maatskaplike Werk*, 43(4):295–316.

Lombard, A. 2008. The implementation of the *White Paper for Social Welfare*: A ten-year review. *The Social Work Practitioner-Researcher/Die Maatskaplike Werk Navorser-Praktisyn*, 20(2):154–173.

Lombard, A. 2015. Global agenda for social work and social development. *Social Work/Maatskaplike Werk*, 52(4):482–499.

Lombard, A: 'A developmental perspective in social work theory and practice'. *In*: Spitzer, H, Twikirize, JM & Wairire, GG (eds.). 2014. *Professional social work in East Africa: Towards social development, poverty reduction and gender equality*. pp. 43–55. Kampala: Fountain Publishers.

Lombard, A & Kleijn, WC. 2006. Statutory social services: An integrated part of developmental social welfare service delivery. *Social Work/Maatskaplike Werk*, 42(3/4):213–233.

Lombard, A & Twikirize, JM. 2014. Promoting social and economic equality: Social workers' contribution to social justice and social development in South Africa and Uganda. *International Social Work*, 57(4):313–325.

Melamed, C. 2015. *Leaving no one behind: How the SDGs can bring real change*. London: Development Progress. [Online]. Available: https://www.odi.org/sites/odi.org.uk/files/odi-assets/publications-opinion-files/9534.pdf [Accessed 14 February 2019].

Midgley, J. 1995. *The developmental perspective in social welfare*. London, UK: Sage.

Midgley, J. 2014. *Social development: Theory and practice*. London, UK: Sage.

Midgley, J: 'The theory and practice of developmental social work'. *In*: Midgley, J & Conley, A (eds.). 2010. *Social work and social development, theories and skills for developmental social work*. pp. 3–28. New York: Oxford University Press.

Midgley, J & Conley, A: 'Introduction'. *In*: Midgley, J & Conley, A (eds.). 2010. *Social work and social development, theories and skills for developmental social work*. pp. xiii–xx. New York: Oxford University Press.

Mwansa, LK: 'Social work in Africa'. *In*: Healy, LM & Link, RJ (eds.). 2012. *Handbook of international social work*. pp. 365–371. New York: Oxford University Press.

Patel, L. 2015. *Social welfare and social development*. 2nd ed. Cape Town: Oxford University Press Southern Africa.

Reisch, M. 2016. Why macro practice matters. *Journal of Social Work Education*, 52(3):258–268.

Republic of South Africa. Ministry for Welfare and Population Development. 1997. *White Paper for Social Welfare*. GN 1108 in *GG* 386(18166) of 8 August 1997. Pretoria: Government Printer.

Republic of South Africa. The Presidency: National Planning Commission. 2012. *National Development Plan 2030. Our future - make it work*. Executive Summary. [Online]. Available: http://www.dac.gov.za/sites/default/files/NDP%202030%20-%20Our%20future%20-%20make%20it%20work 0.pdf.

Rothman, J & Mizrahi, T. 2014. Balancing micro and macro practice: A challenge for social work. *Social Work*, 59(1):91–93.

Sen, A. 1999. *Development as freedom*. Oxford: Oxford University Press.

Sewpaul, V: 'Social work and poverty reduction in Africa: The indelible reality'. *In*: Spitzer, H, Twikirize, JM & Wairire, GG (eds.). 2014a. *Professional social work in East Africa: Towards social development, poverty reduction and gender equality*. pp. 29–42. Kampala: Fountain Publishers.

Sewpaul, V: 'Social work and human rights: An African perspective'. *In*: Hessle, S (ed.). 2014b. *Human rights and social equality: Challenges for social work*. pp. 13–27. Surrey: Ashgate.

Sewpaul, V. 2016a. The West and the rest divide: Human rights, culture and social work. *Journal of Human Rights Social Work*, 1:30–39.

Sewpaul, V. 2016b. Politics with soul: Social work and the legacy of Nelson Mandela. *International Social Work*, 59(6):697–708.

Sheedy, M. 2013. *Core themes in social work: Power, poverty, politics and values*. Berkshire: McGraw Hill, Open University Press.

Sherman, P. 2016. Preparing social workers for global gaze: Locating global citizenship within social work curricula. *Social Work Education*, 35(60):632–642.

Shlosberg, D. 2007. *Defining environmental justice: Theories, movements, and nature*. New York: Oxford University Press.

Spolander, G, Engelbrecht, L & Sansfaçon, DAP. 2016. Social work and macro-economic neoliberalism: Beyond the social justice rhetoric. *European Journal of Social Work*, 19(5):634–649.

Staub-Bernasconi, SM: 'Human rights and their relevance for social work as theory and practice'. *In*: Healy, LM & Link, RJ (eds.). 2012. *Handbook of international social work*. pp. 30–36. New York: Oxford University Press.

United Nations Development Programme. 2015. *Human development report 2015: Work for human development*. [Online]. Available: http://hdr.undp.org/sites/default/files/2015_human_development_report_1.pdf [Accessed 9 June 2017].

United Nations. 1948. *Human Rights Declaration*. [Online]. Available: http://www.un.org/en/universal-declaration-human-rights/ [Accessed 1 August 2015].

United Nations. 2015. *Transforming our world, the 2030 Agenda for Sustainable Development*. [Online]. Available: https://sustainabledevelopment.un.org/content/documents/21252030%20Agenda%20for%20Sustainable%20Development%20web.pdf [Accessed 6 June 2019].

Van Breda, AD. 2018. Developmental social case work: A process model. *International Social Work*, 61(1):66–78.

Zufferey, C. 2012. 'Not knowing that I do not know and not wanting to know': Reflections of a white Australian social worker. *International Social Work*, 56(5):659–673.

Annotated websites and activities

The websites below can be helpful resources in developmental social work.

http://www.chr.up.ac.za/
This is the website of the Centre for Human Rights at the University of Pretoria, which is both an academic department and a non-governmental organisation working towards human rights education in Africa, a greater awareness of human rights, the wide dissemination of publications on human rights in Africa, and the improvement of the rights of women, people living with HIV, indigenous peoples, sexual minorities and other disadvantaged or marginalised persons or groups across the continent.

http://sdgcafrica.org/
This is the website of the Sustainable Development Goals Centre for Africa, which is an international organisation that supports governments, civil society, businesses and academic institutions in achieving the SDGs in Africa. They build upon Africa's existing successes by bringing together people, ideas, and innovation to collectively reach a more sustainable future.

https://www.uj.ac.za/faculties/humanities/csda
This is the website of the Centre for Social Development in Africa, located at the University of Johannesburg.

Look at the research that is done on social development and developmental welfare at the centre. Identify the topics that would assist you to contribute to a better understanding of developmental social work. What research areas would you like to engage in to promote developmental social work?

https://www.humanrightscareers.com/magazine/unicef-launches-free-online-course-on-social-change/
Visit the UNICEF website to see the free open online course on social norms and social change, which are jointly presented by the University of Pennsylvania and the United Nations Children's Fund (UNICEF). How could you benefit from this course?

Annotated websites and activities are also available on Learning Zone.

oxford.co.za/learningzone

Social constructionism

Rinie Schenck

> *The story I tell in these chapters is necessarily my story, grounded in my intuitions, influenced by my reading of the writers in whom I have delighted and on whose ideas I have drawn, and woven in with the texture of my life experience* (Reason, 1994:Chapter 2).

CHAPTER OUTCOMES

By the end of this chapter, you should be able to:

✓ *Describe the concept epistemology*

✓ *Contrast positivistic and constructionist epistemologies*

✓ *Identify and illustrate the assumptions underlying constructionist thinking*

✓ *Describe the values underlying constructionist thinking*

✓ *Identify and illustrate the skills when applying social constructionism*

✓ *Critically assess the relevance of social constructionism for decolonial social work practice in South Africa.*

 Case Study 1

How words construct reality

A child is told by his teacher that he is 'dom' or stupid and that he cannot do maths. The child starts to believe that he will not be able to pass school and is framed as 'lazy and naughty' by the teachers and parents.

What is important from this example is that problems are constructed in relationships and in language. The teacher perceives the child as struggling with maths and then calls him 'stupid'. In this instance, the teacher is in a powerful position as the 'knower' and the child will most likely believe the teacher.

In 2008, the author Antjie Krog wrote on her experiences of the Truth and Reconciliation Commission that 'in order to start this process of healing one needs to find words for one's experiences' (Krog, 2008:226). Finding or creating these words is the construction of our realities. Some of these realities leave us with options and opportunities, and others immobilise or oppress us as illustrated above.

Similarly, in South Africa, we have many stories of partners being abused and told they are ugly and not good enough. We have communities and groups of people being labelled and treated as less worthy.

Reflective activity: Telling our own story

Write down or think about a painful experience you have encountered. You do not need to share this with others. It is important to tell the story to yourself.

• Who said or did something to you that was very painful/traumatic?

• What power did the person/people have over you?

• How did this experience construct the perception you or others have about you?

• How did you respond then? Or how are you responding to it currently?

In this chapter, traumatic and painful incidents are used to illustrate social constructionism. At some point in their lives, all individuals and communities experience some form of trauma, loss and pain. These incidents can be the loss of parents or children, being involved in an accident, being robbed or raped, experiencing oppression, being abused, being forcefully removed, fleeing your country or community, living in poverty, or being exposed to gang-related activities.

4.1   Introduction

Two authors who I admire and from whom I have learnt through the years are Bradford Keeney (1983, *Aesthetics of change*) and Gregory Bateson (1979, *Mind and nature*). In a communication with Keeney, Bateson made the comment that 'differences are the "food for perception"' (Keeney, 1983:153). Here he made reference to the fact that knowledge and information lies in difference. We know what is high when we see low; we perceive silence after we have switched of the noisy air conditioner; we perceive light after darkness (or vice versa). So, to understand social constructionism, I will start with a quick reference to two different epistemologies, viz. positivism and modernism (Western thought processes), and then move on to explain what social constructionism is. My interpretation of social constructionism is also coloured by the work of American psychologist Carl Rogers (1951, *Client-centered therapy*), Brazilian pedagogue Paulo Freire (1972, *Pedagogy of the oppressed*), and the narrative approaches of Australian social worker Michael White (1995, *Re-authoring lives*). Lastly, an attempt will be made to relate social constructionism to decolonisation and the process of decoloniality.

Before the discussion of positivistic and constructionist thought processes, it is important to elaborate on epistemology as a concept.

4.2   Epistemology

According to Bateson (1979:228), the word epistemology refers to how we *think, know, decide and act* or the process of knowing. He further explains that it is impossible for a person *not* to have an epistemology. This implies that every person has a way of thinking, knowing and deciding – a way of how we view, perceive, experience (meaning making) and name the world. We all have different backgrounds, cultures, experiences and families. We have grown up in different contexts, and we have interacted with different people. Furthermore, we express our experiences in words and languages available to us.

> *Epistemology*, the study of knowledge; what it is and how we get it.

If we were to ask people to provide a reason for the drought in the Western Cape during 2016 and 2017, for example, we might get a variety of explanations ranging from it being the result of global warming and climate change to it being the result of the gods being angry. The explanations that people will give for the drought will relate to their epistemologies and will influence their thoughts and actions. They may pray for rain, do some rituals, or engage in actions to protest against global warming and to save the environment.

A wonderful case study is given by Matose and Mukamari (1994:69) where they described the different belief systems about trees in a certain part of Zimbabwe. In this case study, one of the reasons provided by people for protecting the trees is that they believe the trees bring rainfall by stopping the clouds; others believe the trees are the resting place of the cuckoo who sings for the rain. They further believe that ancestral spirits rest in the trees where they attend rainmaking ceremonies. This helps us to understand why they believe that they are not allowed to cut down the trees as they will be punished and the rain will stop. These belief systems are part of people's epistemology (how they think, know and decide) and will determine their actions towards trees in this instance.

Each social worker, just like each person, has her or his own epistemology. We all have ways of thinking, knowing and deciding based on our own personal experiences and belief systems, as well as the social work theories and knowledge we have obtained when we studied social work at a particular university in a particular country at a particular time in history. When I was at university, we focused on 'problem-solving' and 'psychodynamics'. Social constructionism, strengths-based and resilience theories were not known to us at that time; therefore, they could not be part of our epistemologies. Our epistemologies are further influenced by the books we read, our cultural, religious and spiritual beliefs, and the people we interact with. According to Keeney (1983:13), it is important to become aware of our epistemologies: 'Having no conscious awareness of one's epistemology ... may be risky'. These thought processes are the basis for our decisions and actions that may affect people's lives.

The implication of Keeney's statement is that the people (individuals, groups and communities) we interact with also have their own unique ways of viewing the world that may, in some respects, overlap with ours or they may be vastly different from ours. Our age, gender, race, sexual orientation and socioeconomic background experiences also play a role in the way we view the world.

 **ACTIVITY 4.1**

Write down how your age, gender, race, sexual orientation and socioeconomic background play a role in how you think, perceive, decide and act?

This explanation of the concept epistemology helps us to understand why social workers should engage in reflective practice. We need to start our social work journey by reflecting on our own epistemologies. We are frequently unaware of our epistemologies because we take them for granted. They are so deeply rooted in how we think that they are usually invisible to us. Epistemologies also change all the time and therefore reflective practice should be a deliberate, conscious, continuous process.

Hopefully, this chapter will assist you as a social worker/student to become aware of your epistemology, what is meaningful and make sense to you, and what will be included as it will in the end influence the people's lives with whom you interact. It will determine the way you interact with people, be it your family, friends, clients or community.

Discussing social constructionism as different from positivism or modernism will hopefully assist you to become aware of whether you are a linear (positivistic) or non-linear (circular, reflexive) thinker, or if you are in transition from the one to the other. It is not wrong or right to be either the one or the other (or a bit of both).

> *Linear thinking*, when we think in a straight line – step by step progressions, one thing causes another thing in clean and one-directional ways and neutral objectivity. For example, if a person is showing symptoms of sleeplessness and negativity then he or she is depressed.
>
> *Non-linear thinking*, implies that we can think in different directions and also start from different points. For example, depression and sleeplessness may both be related to problems in the family, which might be connected to stresses at work.
>
> *Circular/reflective thinking*, the idea that we try to understand our own thinking and practice to learn from it and improve on it (Leitch & Day, 2001).

You will now understand why this chapter starts with the quote from Reason (1994:Chapter 2). No one author or text can provide you with all the knowledge about social constructionism. They can only share knowledge the way they understand it in the context of social work.

4.2.1   Positivistic thinking

Positivism or modernism is an epistemology nested or embedded in modernism. The core of positivistic thinking refers to the belief that there is a reality 'out there' that can be scientifically and objectively discovered. Positivistic thinking believes that knowledge can be certain, established, and subjected to value judgement or speculative interpretations (Winter, 1989). It contains reductionistic thought processes, belief in linear causality, and neutral objectivity.

> *Modernism*, a school of thought that developed towards the end of the nineteenth century into the twentieth century. It is based on rational thinking, logic, scientific processes, and objectivity to provide clear and rational views of the world.

Positivism provides security, certainty and power to the people (e.g., social workers) who have the knowledge. For social workers, adopting a positivistic epistemology will assist them to have knowledge and power over the clients who do not know about scientific processes, psychopathologies and treatment methods. The clients will become the passive recipients of the 'care/protection/treatment' process (Epstein, 1994:6). The client or community will, for example, not know how to diagnose or assess trauma or PTSD. Positivistic epistemology does not necessarily make room for collaborative or participatory ways of working. The social worker will tend to *advise, guide, teach* and *instruct* the clients or community about how they should change. It is a top-down approach to treatment and development programmes and projects. One of the main reasons social workers have moved away from a positivistic way of thinking is that it may cause hurt more than healing.

There are many stories of top-down interventions with individuals, groups and communities that left the people more wounded than before. The following is a local example from Van der Watt (2016:4):

> *From 2006 to 2008, I participated in an evaluation process of projects by the National Department of Social Development, initiated as part of a*

presidential programme in 21 nodal districts in South Africa. This involved qualitative research on district and provincial level, followed by a support phase and a final evaluation. I was struck by the damage done through funded projects driven by pre-determined objectives … growing, chicken farming, beadwork, bakeries, sewing and more and the financial skills to facilitate the establishment of profitable businesses. Physical results were scant: a bunch of spinach, three heads of cabbage and a pig to show for an investment of R1.5 million. A group of grannies was in trouble because they were supposed to make a profit with a few chickens and sewing in a desolated area with no market. Project members were defeated by their 'flagship' chicken project in a semi-desert area. It was a sorry sight: barely alive chickens pecking about amidst the dead ones. Project members could not tell when last a chicken was slaughtered in their state-of-the-art abattoir.

Van der Watt's (2016) argument is that these projects were predetermined by the 'knowers' and left the women more scarred, more oppressed, and more wounded than was intended. Their failure labels became even bigger and heavier to carry.

 ACTIVITY 4.2

If you think about the case study by Van der Watt, what do you think could have been done differently? Now that you have read what positivism is, jot down what you think the opposite will be of positivism or positivistic thinking. Make some guesses.

4.2.2 Constructivism and social constructionism

You have now been introduced to positivistic thinking which claims that reality is objective. This section will introduce you to quite the opposite way of thinking referred to as post-modern thinking, which is based on the premise that knowledge and reality is subjective.

Constructivism and social constructionism have their roots in post-modern thinking but differ in respect of *where* the knowledge and reality are created or constructed.

Constructivism, the view that knowledge and realities are created within the individual.

Social constructionism, the view that realities and knowledge are created among people and in relationships.

It is said that a constructivist epistemology was already introduced in the eighteenth century by the philosopher Vico, when he pronounced that 'the human mind could know only what the human mind itself had constructed' and 'what is true is precisely what is made' (Van der Watt, 1993:9). Other Western philosophers, like Kant (who lived from 1724–1804), already took the eighteenth-century position against positivistic epistemology. Constructivist thinking has been around for quite a long time, but it was dominated by modern logical reasoning!

It is only since the 1960s in the Western world that the Western psychology and practice theorists started to give prominence to constructivist thoughts by founding their theories on constructivist philosophies. One example is Carl Rogers who in his seminal book

Client-centered therapy (1951) already indicated that people's realities are different and unique and that they perceive the world uniquely. He developed his person-centred or client-centred approach (see Chapter 11) in reaction to the positivistic approaches of the theories at the time. He wanted to bring the focus to the unique person, group and community (Grobler et al., 2013).

Berger and Luckman wrote their groundbreaking work *The social construction of reality* in 1966. It was during the 1990s that a variety of authors such as Kenneth Gergen (1991), Neimeyer (1995), and Anderson and Goolishian (1992) published extensively (and still are) on social constructionism. David Fisher, a social worker, published his *Introduction to constructivism for social workers* in 1991. In Australia, a social worker from the Dulwich Centre, Michael White, developed a narrative approach, based on constructionist principles (see Chapter 13). In the USA, Dennis Saleebey, a social worker, published his book *The strengths perspective in social work practice* in 1992, now in its sixth edition (see Chapter 13). You will find that many of the references made in this chapter are from the social constructionist thinkers of that time, because it was in this period that the main constructionist concepts were well formulated.

Carl Rogers emphasised that each person perceives and experiences his or her world and reality differently (Grobler et al., 2013), while Saleebey (1992:352) made the comment that 'the dream of discovering truth or reality apart from a people's and culture's interpretation may be just that – a dream'. Other authors (and pedagogists and community activists) such as Paulo Freire (1972, 1998) and Robert Chambers (1983), a development practitioner, proposed constructionist thoughts by highlighting that people are knowledgeable and can be trusted, and that we have to find ways in collaboration with them. The therapist, helper or development practitioner is not the only expert and we need to work alongside (collaboratively) the person or people. Carr and Kemmis (1991:71) went so far as to criticise positivism and the search for the truth as 'a pretentious and contemptible waste of time'.

As time went by, post-modern and social constructionists' thoughts matured, and theorists became more tolerant of positivist thoughts as just another way of looking at the world. It is every person's choice how to make sense of the world. According to the social constructionist, positivistic thinking is one additional valid way of viewing and perceiving the world.

4.3   So what is social constructionism?

As mentioned, social constructionists believe that no single objective perception or explanation of the world or reality is possible. Rather, there are multiple belief systems and perspectives, which are multiple ways of viewing and explaining the world. All our explanations are interpreted and constructed by the observer/ourselves in language. That is, we use words to tell stories that make sense of the world, and these stories actually construct or create the world as we perceive and experience it. Each of us constructs the world uniquely. We construct stories and give meaning and make sense of the world around us through the language available to us.

Although there might be an objective reality 'out there', we only have access to our constructions based on our perceptions, values, cultures, contexts and experiences. We cannot objectively and truly know that reality. All we really have access to are how we perceive and make sense of that 'reality'. Because we cannot truly know reality, each construction of reality is, more or less, a valid reflection of reality.

Talking with a social constructionist about rock concerts and social work

Okay, so what I see and describe as reality is the way I see it and not necessarily how you will see the same situation?

Yes, we can look at the same event and we may perceive and experience it differently. For instance, we go to a rock concert. Then, when we come back, I (who prefer classical music) may tell people that I hated every minute of it as it was loud, disorganised and the rock stars were screaming. You, on the other hand, may tell people it was great, well organised with the way they managed the thousands of people, and the sound and singers were great so that you could dance and shout. The experience was 'awesome'.

Oh, I get it! So, my explanation of the rock concert actually says more about me than about the event.

Interesting way of seeing things, is it not? To think that what you say, tells me more about you than about the event. It is about your experiences and perceptions of the event.

So how does this relate to me as a social worker?

Your description of clients (whether an individual or a community) will inevitably explain how you experience and view them and what theory you use to explain behaviour or circumstances. If both of us work from the same premise – for example, the strengths perspective – our descriptions may overlap, because we share a common way of theorising the world around us.

To take the concept of social constructionism further, it is believed that we construct realities collectively and in interaction with others through interchange (Gergen, 1994). We are constantly in interaction with others, and collectively constructing realities in the process of making sense of the world. We use language to describe our socially constructed realities. These constructions are also made within political, economic and social contexts. It is for this reason that we call this epistemology *'social constructionism'*. It is not so much about how you or I as an individual make sense of the world, but rather about how we as groups or collectives, as social systems, reach agreement on how we make sense of the world and understand the so-called 'reality out there'.

4.4 Examples of social constructionism

Social constructionism sounds quite abstract and philosophical. A few examples may help us understand it better. These examples show the usefulness of social constructionism in relation to how we make sense of the world, how we define ourselves, and how to explain our life experiences.

4.4.1 Example 1: Religious beliefs

The ways we construct realities can be illustrated with religion and our different belief systems, for example, in ancestors, a variety of gods (with different names), theological systems, and patterns of worship. Buddhists, Muslims, Christians, Rastafarians, and African traditional religions all have different religious beliefs. In Namibia, for example, the Herero refer to God as the *Njambi Karunga* (the giver of all blessings). In truth, none of us really knows God or how the world came into being. Our religions (or non-religious theories) are ways of making sense of the world around us; they provide narratives or stories that explain our origins and our relationship with the Divine. Religious communities are groups of people who share similar beliefs about these matters. In epistemological terms, these communities of faith have constructed an explanation of the world that they share, thus a social construction. These social constructions then shape our values, our behaviour, and our relationships. Also, in our families, cultures and communities we have learnt to conform to the norms and values that are commonly accepted in these contexts.

4.4.2 Example 2: Waste pickers

In addition to religious ways of making sense of the world, social constructionism also has implications for what names we use to describe things. For example, when I started with my own research on the waste pickers, my co-researchers and I did not know what we should call people on the streets and landfills who recycle waste for a living. When I started reading and talking to people, I came across a variety of names they were called such as 'scavengers', 'recyclers', 'reclaimers', 'vultures', 'waste harvesters', 'skarrelaars' (scramblers), 'garbage pickers', 'minza' (trying to survive), 'miners', 'grab-grab', and 'waste pickers'. One waste picker mentioned to Van Heerden (2015) that in the Phillippi/Gugulethu area in Cape Town they are referred to as '*mabuyze*' (people who come back with nothing). Each name tells the story of how people view them.

The waste pickers Van Heerden (2015) interviewed indicated that the waste pickers in Cape Town prefer to be referred to as 'skarrelaars' as this tells what they are doing. But, the chairperson from the waste pickers association based in Gauteng shared that they now have agreed upon the term 'waste picker' as what they should be called, as the word refers to their actions and the work they are doing – for them it is not a reflection on the person (Mbata, 2018, personal interview). This name, agreed upon by a community, through a process of reflection and discussion, is a social construction. It is a way of making sense of and telling a story about people who work on the streets and landfills, recycling waste. In this case, this name tells a story about a group having a valid, meaningful and valuable job.

4.4.3   Example 3: Trauma

Butt and Parton (2005) provide a third example illustrating the difference between positivist and social constructionist thinking in social work. Social workers often find clients who will explain that they are 'traumatised' or experienced a 'traumatic incident', or they will narrate an incident of rape, abuse, or the loss of a partner that affects them deeply. From a Western positivist perspective, during the 1980s, trauma has been officially recognised and classified as post-traumatic stress disorder (PTSD) and incorporated into the *Diagnostic and Statistical Manual for Mental Disorders* (then the DSM-III, American Psychiatric Association, 1980). So, by recognising the symptoms of PTSD, we can diagnose the person based on the symptoms, and recommend a therapeutic process (linear thinking). However, what should happen with the person who does not show the DSM symptoms, but believes that he or she is traumatised?

Butt and Parton (2005) explained from a social constructionist perspective that people often refer to 'being traumatised' to make sense of an experience. The reason why so many people now feel 'traumatised' is that the word is now known to people and they assign painful experiences to being traumatised. They have a vocabulary available that assists in helping to make sense of their painful experiences. In many communities and languages, the word trauma does not exist, but that does not mean people are not experiencing woundedness and pain. Marsella et al. (1996) explained that the concept 'trauma' is a Western term for such experiences ('trauma' comes from the Latin for 'wound'). According to Mokgatlhe (2001), there is no word for trauma in the African languages. There are perspectives on illness and healing, and the causes of the illness or pain will be searched for, be it angered ancestors, witchcraft, natural causes, disruptive social relationships, or punishment from gods/ancestors (Wade & Schenck, 2012).

Social workers, working from a social constructionist perspective, will not identify traumatic incidents or symptoms or dictate imposed stages of recovery. Instead, they will focus on the clients' processes of co-creating multiple views and meaning making of their lives. This will be further explained below.

🔮 ACTIVITY 4.3

1 You have now spent considerable time getting to understand what social constructionism is and how it manifests in daily life. Is there a word for 'social constructionism' in your home language? Probably not, since it is such a technical term. If not, construct a short phrase in your home language that captures the essence of what it means. Write this down in the margin of the book and then compare it to the following definition: 'Social constructionism is the view that realities and knowledge are created between people and in relationships.'

2 Consider the idea that *Ubuntu* (see Chapter 6) also captures what social constructionism is about. *Ubuntu* suggests that our personhood ('*umuntu ngumuntu*' or 'I am a person ...') is rooted in our relationships or interactions with other persons ('*ngabantu*' or '... through other people'). In other words, personhood is socially constructed. In similar ways, social constructionism argues that everything (e.g., family, work, religion, science, education) is socially constructed. See if you can use this as a platform from which to construct an African version of 'social constructionism'.

3 In light of this, have a look at the reflective questions in section 11.3 of Chapter 11 (person-centred approach). How does social constructionism fit with the points made there about African notions of 'the self' and in relation to Menkiti's chapter?

4.5 Social constructionism's assumptions about people

Let us unpack social constructionism. Any theory or approach has building blocks of thought processes or assumptions, explaining the world and providing values that guide our actions or practice.

4.5.1 Ideas about the self

According to Lax (1992), the self in social constructionism is not seen as an intrapsychic entity, but rather as a narrative within a context and in interaction with people. Identities are formed in interaction with other people. The responses from your family, partners, community and other people and institutions form your identity. This idea is similar to *Ubuntu* (Chapter 6), which argues that our self is rooted in our relationships with others, in the collective.

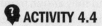 **ACTIVITY 4.4**

1 Write down some of the 'identities' you have and how they developed (e.g., loyal friend, student, party animal, troublemaker, peacemaker, member of a church, political party, and so on).
2 Which of the names are positive and which are negative?
3 What are the effects of the negative and or positive names/labels allocated to you?

Van der Watt (2016:179) provides an example of identities; the women in her groups shared that names given to them by their families were important but became labels:

> Some tried by all means to live out their names: Malethola, 'the quiet one', believed she should be quiet, while Seboeng, 'talkative' or 'chatterbox', had to talk. Seberekane was almost killed because of her name: it means 'strong woman' and 'everybody is giving me a lot of work and abuse my power.' One was called Nkwapo [like to fight] and 'I still like fighting'.

Van Heerden (2015:64) also provides an example of a waste picker called '"Troubles" because he's Islamic and drinks alcohol', to which he responds, 'it's true – I do just want to drink'.

4.5.2 People or the system is closed to information

Bateson (1979) views the person as closed to information. Bateson (1979) is of the opinion that all systems are connected and have an effect on one another, but we cannot determine how one system will respond to the other. As a lecturer, I cannot predetermine what effect my lectures will have on the students. Reading this chapter will have a different effect on each reader. Some will like it, while others may regard is as insignificant. Something in this chapter may trigger a meaningful emotion in one person, while another may be bored and stop reading halfway through the chapter.

As social workers we will not be able to influence or guide people if what we suggest does not make sense to them, or if what we share has no meaning. We often wonder why people do not 'follow' or do what they have been told. If the 'solution' or the way forward has not been crafted together and is not meaningful and owned by the client, he or she will not be able to follow it or act on it. There might be incidences where they will act on instructions in order to please you, but it will not be internalised and sustainable change. Freire (1972) confirmed this viewpoint by saying that people are not empty vessels and we cannot bank information. We must work with their realities, which is described in the next section.

4.5.3   Realities are constructed collectively

As indicated, social constructionists are of the view that there are no realities out there to be discovered; there are no wrong or right facts. Rather, they believe that there are stories or narratives about wrong or right, stories about what is true and false, or facts for people in particular contexts. There are experiences and perceptions, belief systems and cultural values constructed collectively among families, groups and communities. This does not mean that 'anything goes'! Knowledge and realities are ruled and determined by historical and cultural norms of what is right and wrong for certain communities, groups and families, which can of course change and evolve.

4.5.4   A process of meaning making through language

According to Efran and Fauber (1995:275), language and meaning making are the essence of social constructionism. When a person describes a problem, he or she uses language to give meaning to his or her perceptions or experiences. For example, when a person talks about a tree, we understand it as something with roots, a trunk, branches and leaves. For many people, a tree might be much more than a physical object. For some it may mean a place of shade, firewood to survive the winter, or firewood to bake bread for an income (a livelihood), while it may have spiritual value for others and is regarded as the source of oxygen by the environmentalists. In some communities it creates a space of gathering or serves as a classroom for children. We have earlier given the example of the importance of the tree for rainmaking in a part of Zimbabwe. A 'tree', therefore, is not 'just a tree'. It is an object that has meaning, which society constructs (hence, social constructionism) through language.

 Self-reflection   Thinking about theory

By now it should be clear why we should reflect on our thoughts, decisions and actions. As a social worker you will choose a certain theoretical framework from which to work with people. If the assumptions/ principles or propositions of the person-centred approach, strength-based perspective, resilience theory, *Ubuntu* or social constructionism make sense to you, this is what will guide your perceptions and actions. There is not one 'true' theory that makes sense to all people in the helping profession. All theories are attempts to explain human behaviour and change. So when 'choosing' a theory or an eclectic mix of theories, we must take responsibility for the choices we make. These theories or assumptions are not unrelated to you.

Hence, Bateson's (1997) comment that we are closed for information; your social work lecturer cannot determine which of the theories will become part of your epistemology. You choose to view the behaviour of the person, group or community from a certain perspective that makes sense to you and is known to you at a given time. You will then facilitate the change process accordingly. As social workers we are therefore part and parcel of the change process. This requires us to be very conscious of our decisions, thinking, action (our epistemology), and the part we play in the change process.

It might be of value to start writing down the theories or parts of the theories in this book that make sense to you. In so doing, your own theory will become clear. It may change as you continue on the social work journey. It is important to make it a conscious process.

Social workers' role in the change process

How come that I am part of the change process, when it is the client that needs to change?

What do you think will happen if student B facilitates the interview from a different theoretical approach. Will they come to the same result or change process?

Maybe, but she is more person-centred than I am. I will perhaps focus more on the strengths of the client ...

Yes, exactly! You as a social worker with your theoretical lens are part of the relationship. Let us make it simple. Let's say you are scared of dogs and I am not. I grew up with dogs as pets in my home. Maybe you are scared because you have not grown up with dogs, or you have been told they are dangerous ... the relationship between dogs and I and you and dogs will be different not because of the characteristics of dogs, but because of our different ideas of dogs.

4.5.5   Social constructionism's view of change

Anderson and Goolishian (1992:28) describe the change process as the collaborative dialogical (narrative) creation of new and multiple narratives and meanings. Change cannot be imposed from the outside or on behalf of the person, group or community. The change process is a process of co-creating new and different realities and meanings that can open up opportunities and choices for the person/group and community (Schenck, 1998:337; Van der Watt, 2016).

This section has addressed the theory of social constructionism at some length. The next section will now discuss how social constructionism can be applied in social work practice.

4.6   Applying the social constructionist approach

Fisher (1991:3) refers to social constructionism as not only a theory, but more as a way of thinking about people, events and problems. Carl Rogers (Grobler et al., 2013) and Paulo Freire (Schenck, 2012) regard their theories as 'a way of being'. It is not merely a theory or model that you use when necessary; it becomes a way of thinking about life and the world around you and a way of interacting with people.

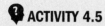 **ACTIVITY 4.5**

Think for a moment about what we mean when we say that social constructionism is 'a way of being'. What is the implication of this viewpoint?

4.6.1   Importance of the relationship in social constructionism

Social constructionism emphasises the importance of the relationship between the social worker and the person, group or community (Lax, 1992; Neimeyer, 1995; Van der Watt, 2016) as the lifeline and safe context within which new narratives and meanings can be co-constructed. The relationship is built on respect for the individual, group or community's ideas, their resourcefulness and perspectives, and knowledge and trust in their abilities. The stories, explanations and their meanings are not judged but accepted (which is different from accepting behaviour). The social worker will, therefore, create a free and safe conversational space for emerging dialogical processes in which 'newness' and differences can occur.

4.6.2   Dialogue

A social constructionist interviewer is not directive or advice oriented, but rather strives to put power into the hands of the interviewee, or rather helps them to acknowledge and experience the power they already have to construct new and different narratives. Dialogue is therefore the most important process to follow. Through dialogue, stories are constructed, co-constructed or co-authored and re-constructed and meanings are made. The relationship reflects respect for the participants' abilities. It shows a strong belief in the self-determination of the person to make his or her own choices and attach his or her own meaning. It creates a sense of responsibility and empowerment for the client, which helps the client to separate him or herself from others' definitions and to become self-reflective. This provides a greater sense of autonomy and increases the client's ability to take responsibility for his or her own thoughts and behaviour. Clients should experience that they are 'active agents' in constructing their lives (Fisher, 1991:143). Freire (1998) also emphasised dialogue as the vehicle for change as equal partners towards new constructions and meanings.

To understand social constructionism dialogue facilitation, O'Hanlon (1993) and Van der Watt (2016) describe some of its characteristics, which contrast with the characteristics of positivistic interviews (see Table 4.1 below).

Table 4.1: Positivistic interviews and social constructionism dialogue facilitation

Traditional positivistic interviews	Social constructionism relational dialogue
• *Discussions are aimed at exploring emotions (e.g., how do you feel?).* • *Discussions aim to develop insight into the problem.* • *Discussions focus on the inabilities of the person or community (e.g., they lack education).*	• *Discussions should generate, acknowledge and respect differences, new constructions, multiple and new stories, and multiple perspectives, and should open up new opportunities.* • *They should explore the political, psychological, and the social significance of differences and perceptions.* • *Good listening to all the perspectives and experiences is required. A participant was quoted by White (1995:9) as saying: 'If there are going to be any real changes, the very step has to be having our voices and our stories heard and acknowledged.'*

• *Discussions label people (e.g., they are passive, do not want to change, uneducated).* • *Discussions are prescriptive and even confrontational.*	• *Dialogues focus on competencies, strengths, opportunities, possibilities and capabilities (compare with the strength perspective).* • *Dialogues also include discussions of responsibility and accountability of thoughts, decisions and actions as the participants own the newly constructed realities.* • *Discussions focus on the participants' preferred ways of living and interacting.* • *Both facilitator and the participants are regarded as equal experts. The participants are knowledgeable about their lives and as the social worker you are an expert of the process. You may also have some experiences and different perspectives to share. According to Van der Watt (2016), this is now the time for social workers to let go of image, power, and what they want to be admired for and enter into equal relationships with people.* • *Dialogues do not focus on summaries and conclusions (deductive) but are inclusive, rich, and descriptive. It moves away from thin (positivistic) conclusions to rich, inclusive, inductive descriptions. It moves away from one dominant truth to acknowledging multiple truths.*

📍 ACTIVITY 4.6

To let go of power, image and admiration need a pause, and a reflective moment to consider what it really means to let go of an image, and that for which we want to be admired.

Reflect on this comment and discuss it in class or with colleagues. The implication of the comment needs some deep reflections and honesty.

The question you may ask now is: How do we do this and where does it take us? To facilitate the dialogical process does not mean that we only sit in the office with our client or group; in fact, the dialogical process can be facilitated through various creative ways such as theatre, writing, mapping, storytelling, and art. Any method is appropriate if it allows clients to tell their stories, explore their own lives, and create new stories in the best possible way (see Annotated websites and activities at the end of this chapter).

Social constructionism, as with the person-centred approach, does not guide the direction of the change process as this is a collective co-constructed process. It cannot be determined what the outcome of the change process will be. The outcome cannot be predetermined by the experts or outsiders. It is a respectful facilitated relational process.

 A constructionist approach to parenting

A group of mothers (farm workers) participated in a workshop on 'parenting'. They explained their power-lessness and not knowing how to discipline their children. They see themselves as 'bad parents', which is also the perception of the school their children attend. The only discipline they know is to beat their children and to scold them, telling their children how naughty and bad they are.

The social constructionist social worker explored the mothers' own childhood experiences, their own abusive relationships they were and are in, their experiences of oppression and submissiveness in the political context, and their experiences of poverty. The mothers shared stories of abuse, being scolded, labelled and being beaten up by their own parents, employers and partners. They also shared their need to be loved and accepted. They expressed a wish for their own parents or husbands to take them in their arms, listen to them, and protect them.

Without us 'teaching' these parents how to parent, they were able to find their own painful experiences and their need for revenge, which they took out on the children, and then they co-constructed new ways of parenting, which they tried out and fed back to the group. This was a new journey they embarked on. In addition, Van der Watt introduced red and green-coloured paper with which they could express their experiences. If something was painful, they will touch the red, and if they feel good or comfortable, the green will be brought forward (case study adapted from Van der Watt, 2016:210).

4.7 Relevance of social constructionism for decolonised social work

This epistemological social constructionism 'way of thinking' was carefully selected for this book, and located early in the book, as it moves away from positivistic thought, which is associated with colonialism.

Social constructionism moves away from dominant power and exclusion to embrace all the realities and constructions of the people with whom we work. It requires that we respect people's realities, cultural practices, traditions, religions, sexual orientations, values and perceptions as a point of departure, rather than imposing views and norms from outside, particularly from the Global North. For the South African context, with its rich multicultural, multireligious society, social constructionism allows social workers to embrace and respect the person, group or community with whom they are in interaction. No single reality or worldview is more important than the other.

A social constructionism epistemology listens to the voices, stories and constructions of people. It explores the socio-political and economic experiences, contexts, hardships, oppression and abuse. It embraces belief systems and co-creates new ways of doing that make sense for the people. It moves away from the reductionistic diagnosis and problem identification towards exploring the power relationships that hold people captive; it reconstructs the ideas about the self and thought processes. It facilitates critical self-reflection, which opens dialogue about power, domination, oppression and pain. It is an inclusive process.

A final note is the relevant comment from Archbishop Emeritus Desmond Tutu (2004:25):

> *A person is a person through other people. None of us comes into the world fully formed. We would not think, walk, or speak or behave as human beings unless we learned it from other human beings in order to be human.*

It is through our interactions and relationships with others that we will find new and different constructions, which may put us on new journeys of thinking and acting. Social constructionism therefore recognises our collective being.

4.8 Conclusion

This chapter introduces you to a different thought process, which we regard as assisting us to move away from dominant reductionistic Western thought processes as the main truth. With this chapter, we hope to have sparked a different and decolonial way for you to view the world, as a person and also as a social worker.

You have been introduced to a view of social work as a relational practice, where we collectively and inclusively create safe spaces for people to open up conversations focused on co-creating new meanings (not facts) through language. We view people as interconnected, and realities are created in relation to others (*Ubuntu*) through language. Applying social constructionism requires the social worker to be aware of relational processes, to be open and curious, to view people as the experts, and to spend time exploring meaning and co-creating new meanings based on people's local knowledge and experiences. It further requires the social workers to become critically reflexive practitioners who are able to be conscious of their own thinking and actions and the role they play in relation to the individual, group or community, and the new realities they co-create.

The next quotation by Bawden and Macadam (1990:139) concludes this chapter:

> *"Think about things" in a quite different way: for what we do in the world reflects what we know about it, and what we know depends on how we go about knowing! In other words, when we are thinking about change we should start by thinking about thinking.*

If this social constructionism chapter could start your *thinking about thinking* process, your social work training will be an interesting journey that never ends, since we reflect and co-construct throughout our lives!

Chapter activity

1. **Reflective question**. It may be of value if you reflect on your thoughts about social constructionism. Describe what makes sense and what is still confusing. Bring this to your class or a colleague for discussion.
2. **Personal context**. At the beginning of the chapter, I asked you to tell of or write down a painful event in your own life. Can you start to think of different ways or perspectives that can be created on this event? Can you change the narrative of your story? If so, what is the effect of having a different construction?
3. **Critical questions**. Share your thoughts on the relevance of social constructionism for the South African context and decolonised social work. Revisit the chapter on decoloniality (Chapter 2), and then provide arguments for whether or not social constructionism is facilitating the process of decolonising social work in your context.

References

Anderson, H & Goolishian, HA: 'The client is the expert: A not knowing approach to therapy'. *In*: McNamee, S & Gergen, K. 1992. *Therapy as social construction*. pp. 25–39. Newbury Park, CA: Sage.

Bateson, G. 1979. *Mind and nature: A necessary unity*. London. Wildwood House.

Bawden, R & Macadam, RD. 1990. Towards a university for people-centred development: A case history of reform. *Australian Journal of Adult and Community Education*, 30(3):138–53.

Berger, PL & Luckman, T. 1966. *The social construction of reality: A treatise in the sociology of knowledge*. Harmondsworth: Penguin.

Boal, A. 1995. *The rainbow of desire: The Boal method of theatre and therapy*. London: Routledge.

Boal, A. 2000. *Theatre of the oppressed*. 2nd ed. London: Pluto.

Butt, T & Parton, N. 2005. Constructive social work and personal construct theory: The case of psychological trauma. *British Journal of Social Work*, 35(6):793–806.

Carr, W & Kemmis, S. 1991. *Becoming critical: Education, knowledge and action research*. London: Farmer.

Chambers, R. 1983. *Rural development: Putting the last first*. Harlow: Prentice Hall.

Efran, JS & Fauber, RL: 'Radical constructivism: Question and answers'. *In*: Neimeyer, RA & Mahoney, MJ. 1995. *Constructivism in psychotherapy*. pp. 275–304. Washington, DC: American Psychological Association.

Epstein, L: 'The therapeutic idea in contemporary society'. *In*: Chambon, AS & Irving, A (eds.). 1994. *Essays on postmodernism in social work*. pp. 3–18. Toronto: Canadian Scholars.

Fisher, DDV. 1991. *An introduction to constructivism for social workers*. New York: Praeger.

Freire, P. 1972. *Pedagogy of the oppressed*. London: Penguin.

Freire, P. 1998. *Pedagogy of freedom: Ethics, democracy and civic courage*. Lanham: Rowman and Littlefield.

Gergen, KJ. 1991. The saturated family. *Family Therapy Networker*, Sept/Oct, 15:27–35.

Gergen, KJ. 1994. *Realities and relationships: Soundings in social construction*. Cambridge, MA: Harvard University.

Grobler, H, Schenck, R & Mbedzi, P. 2013. *Person-centred facilitation*. 4th ed. Cape Town: Oxford University Press Southern Africa.

Hope, A & Timmel, S. 1995. *Training for Transformation Book 1-3*. Gweru, Harare: Mambo Press.

Keeney, BP. 1983. *Aesthetics of change*. New York: Guildford.

Krog, A. 2008. My heart is on my tongue: The untranslated self in a translated world. *Journal of Analytical Psychology*, 53(2):225–239.

Lax, WD: 'Postmodern thinking in a clinical practice'. *In*: McNamee, S & Gergen, K (eds.). 1992. *Therapy as social construction*. pp. 69–85. Newbury Park, CA: Sage.

Leitch, R & Day, C. 2001. Reflective processes in action: Mapping personal and professional contexts for learning and change. *Journal of In-Service Education*, 27(2):237–260.

Marsella, AJ, Friedman, MJ & Spain, EH: 'Ethno-cultural aspects of post traumatic stress disorder: An overview of issues and research directions'. *In*: Marsella, AJ, Friedman, MJ, Gerrity, ET & Scourfield, RM (eds.). 1996. *Ethno-cultural aspects of post traumatic stress disorder: Issues, research and clinical applications*. pp. 29–62. Washington: American Psychological Association.

Matose, F & Mukamari, B: 'Trees, people and communities in Zimbabwe's communal lands'. *In*: Scoones, I & Thompson, J (eds.). 1994. *Beyond farmer first: Rural people's knowledge, agricultural research and extension practice*. pp. 69–74. London: ITP.

Mokgatlhe, PB. 2001. Psychopathology from an African perspective. *Only study Guide for PYC 302: Abnormal behaviour and mental health*. Pretoria: UNISA.

Ncube, N. 2006. The tree of life project: Using narrative ideas in work with vulnerable children in Southern Africa. *International Journal of Narrative Therapy and Community Work*, 1:3–16.

Neimeyer, RA. 1995. Limits and lessons of constructivism: Some critical reflections. *Journal of Constructivist Psychology*, 9:339–361.

O' Hanlon, HW: 'Possibility therapy: From iatrogenic injury to iatrogenic healing'. *In*: Gilligan, S & Price, R (eds.). 1993. *Therapeutic conversation*. pp. 258–271. New York: WW Norton.

Reason, P (ed.). 1994. *Participation in Human Inquiry*. London, UK: Sage.

Rogers, C. 1951. *Client-centered therapy: Its current practice, implications and theory*. London: Constable.

Saleebey, D (ed.). (1992). *The strengths perspective in social work practice*. New York City, NY: Longman.

Saleebey, D. 1994. Culture, theory and narrative: The intersection of meanings in practice. *Social Work*, 39(4):351–359.

Schenck, CJ. 1998. *Paradigma ontleding van en paradigma beskrywing vir deelnemende werkswyses [Paradigm analysis and paradigm description of participatory methods]*. Unpublished DPhil thesis in social work. University of South Africa, Pretoria.

Schenck, R. 2012. Revisiting Paulo Freire as a theoretical base for participatory practices for social workers. *Social Work/Maatskaplike Werk*, 38(1):71–81

Tutu, DM. 2004. *God has a dream: A vision of hope for our time*. London: Rider.

Van der Watt, D. 1993. *Constructions of constructivism*. Masters dissertation. University of South Africa, Pretoria.

Van der Watt, P. 2016. *Engaging with the 'soil and the soul' of a community: Rethinking development, healing and transformation in South Africa*. PhD thesis. University of the Free State, Bloemfontein.

Van Heerden, AD. 2015. *Valuing waste and wasting value: Rethinking planning with informality by learning from skarrelers in Cape Town's Southern Suburbs*. MSc in City and Regional Planning. University of Cape Town, Cape Town.

Wade, B & Schenck, R. 2012. Trauma is the 'stealing of my sense of being me': A person-centred perspective on trauma. *Social Work/Maatskaplike Werk*, 48(3):340–356.

White, M. 1995. *Re-authoring lives: Interviews and essays*. Adelaide: Dulwich Centre publishing.

Winter, R. 1989. *Learning from experience: Principles and practice in action research*. London: Falmer.

Annotated websites and activities

https://dulwichcentre.com.au/wp-content/uploads/2014/01/tree-of-life-community-context.pdf
Paulo Freire's problem-posing material – such as problem tree and river of life – is very usable in social work practice.

https://vimeo.com/15676699
Kenneth Gergen provides and introduction to social construction.

http://www.fao.org/docrep/003/x5996e/x5996e06.htm
Robert Chambers' appraisal techniques – such as mapping and transect walks – can be of great help to facilitate dialogue in groups, families and communities. It is also applicable to individuals.

https://dulwichcentre.com.au/.
Dulwich centre and the work by Michael White can be explored to see how they co-create
new narratives with individuals, families and communities.

Try to access and read at least one of the following sources on social constructionism:
> The work of Augusto Boal – *Rainbow of desire: The Boal method of theatre and therapy*
  and *Theatre of the oppressed* – are good examples of recreating stories.
> N Ncube's (2006) journal article The tree of life project: Using narrative ideas in work
  with vulnerable children in Southern Africa.
> Consult Hope & Timmel's (1995) *Training for transformation Book 1–3.*

Annotated websites and activities are also available on Learning Zone.

oxford.co.za/learningzone

Ecosystems

Paul Mbedzi

By the end of this chapter, you should be able to:

✓ *Describe the ecosystems theory*

✓ *Explain the historical background and an overview of the ecosystems theory*

✓ *Describe key concepts in ecological and general systems theories*

✓ *Describe the levels of the social ecology*

✓ *Demonstrate the practical application of the ecosystems theory in social work practice*

✓ *Critically reflect on the significance of the ecosystems theory for decolonial social work practice in South Africa.*

Maluta and his social environments

Maluta, a 14-year-old boy, was raised by his maternal grandmother in a village, after losing his parents in a car accident when he was only 6 months old. His grandmother, Tshavhungwa, is a former school principal and a devout Christian who always aspired the best for her only grandchild. When Maluta was promoted from primary to high school, his grandmother secured a space for him in one of the best schools in the city and she rented a flat for him to avoid travelling long distances to and from the school. While at school, Maluta began to use substances excessively due to peer pressure and, at times, he would not attend classes nor write tests. The situation got worse to such an extent that he was given three warning letters to sign before he was expelled from the school. Maluta did not inform his grandmother about his expulsion, as he feared that she would want him to return to the village, something he did not want.

After his expulsion from the school, Maluta got seriously involved in drugs and criminal activities, such as shoplifting and housebreaking. Because of his criminal activities, Maluta was arrested on a number of occasions and that was when his grandmother became aware of his ordeal. The grandmother immediately vacated the flat she rented for him, as she wanted him to return home as soon as possible. Since Maluta did not want to return to the village, he ran away and stayed on the streets for four months before he was placed at the Child and Youth Care Centre (CYCC) by the social worker. Through the social worker's intervention, Maluta was admitted at the local school and, while at the CYCC, he was reported to be a troublesome and uncontrollable child. He attempted to return to the streets three times. The neighbours, church members, teachers and other learners complained about Maluta's conduct.

Maluta's case exemplifies the many factors that influence how people react to what is going on in their lives. Now that you have familiarised yourself with the above case study, you can read more about the ecosystems approach in the sections below. As you work through this chapter, there will be reflective questions to answer based on this case study.

5.1   Introduction

In this chapter, we explore how ecosystems theory assists social workers to understand the social problems and issues that individuals, families, groups and communities face in today's world. We all exist within relationships with the world around us, which include our relationships with our families, employers and neighbours (see Chapter 6 on *Ubuntu*). Ecosystems theory is among the most widely adopted theoretical frameworks in social work. In ecosystems theory, persons and environments are inseparable, as they exist in continuous transactions with one another (Miley et al., 2009). This tells us that human beings and environments evolve in continuous interconnected relationships. However, it should be noted that the environments referred to here are both social and physical, including the natural environment (see Chapter 3's discussion on sustainable development and environmental justice). This reciprocal connection between humans and the environment is the process by which people continually shape their environments and are shaped by their environments. The imbalance in the continuous interaction between individuals and their environments often leads to psychological tension and creates social problems.

Social workers, more than any other profession, have directed their profession beyond people towards the broader environment (Ambrosino et al., 2012). One of the key functions of the social work profession is to enhance the social functioning of people and promote responsive environments that support human growth. This means that social work practice considers individuals within their environment, also known as person-in-environment, and helps them cope with or challenge the societal and environmental demands. Indeed, social work has a keen interest in intervening at the point where people interact with their environments, to facilitate goodness of fit between people and their environments (Teater, 2014).

According to Miley et al. (2009:38):

> *A fundamental principle of the ecosystems perspective states that a change in one part of the system creates a change in another part of the system, which, in turn, changes the functioning of the entire system.*

Thus, ecosystems-oriented social work practice centres on promoting a balance between the person and his or her environment, by changing the person or the environment or both. For example, if a girl is experiencing some challenges or problems in the family (system), this may affect her relationship with other systems, for instance, her performance at school (another system) may be affected. This tells us about the interconnectedness of the systems in that the change of relationships within one system is likely to affect the relationship with the other systems. It is for this reason that a social worker who works from the ecosystems perspective focuses on enhancing and maintaining relationships between the people and their environments.

Ecosystems theory, a blend of systems theory (which focuses primarily on the dynamics within systems) and the ecological perspective (which focuses primarily on the dynamics between one system and the systems around it).

After presenting a bit of history about ecosystems theory, this chapter will present key theoretical concepts that emerge from the ecological perspective and general systems theory, which together comprise 'ecosystems' theory. Then, the levels of the ecology, from micro to macro, will be described. This is followed by a discussion on the application of ecosystems theory in social work practice, and specifically in decolonial practice.

Reflective questions
- Think of the systems/structures in your own community/environment and describe the relationship you have with these systems.
- In your own opinion, what is the significance of such systems to you and the entire community?
- If these systems disappeared, do you think there would be changes in your community? Motivate your answer.

5.2 Historical background and overview of ecosystems theory

The term 'ecosystems' is a combination of two separate but overlapping bodies of theory: the ecological perspective and general systems theory.

The ecological perspective was originally proposed in the 1970s by an American developmental psychologist called Bronfenbrenner (1979) and its interest is in understanding individuals in context (Neal & Neal, 2013). Since its inception, the ecological perspective emphasises the interaction and interdependence of individuals and their environment. It stems from the study of the natural ecology, i.e., the study of the interdependence and interaction between the plants or animals and their natural environment (Teater, 2014). The ecological perspective argues that we cannot understand an individual (e.g., a bird or a fish) in isolation; we can only understand the individual within its natural environment or context.

General systems theory was initially developed in the 1950s by biologist Ludwig von Bertalanffy (Segal et al., 2013). Von Bertalanffy described the functioning of living systems, including the human body. Historically, the major focus in the behavioural sciences, prior to the understanding of systems theory, had been on individual functioning as reflected in such approaches as psychoanalytical theory, classical behaviourism, and neo-behaviouralism, as well as learning theory (Bowers & Bowers, 2017). General systems theory, however, provided conceptual tools to understand how whole systems function, such as a family, an organisation, or a community.

As a combination of the ecological perspective and general systems theory, 'ecosystems theory was developed to arrange, integrate and systematise knowledge about the interrelationships of people with one another and with their environments' (Maistry, 2010:170). Social workers focus on the interrelationships and connectedness of people with one another and their environment because of the challenges and problems people face when such relationships are in jeopardy. And so, ecosystems theory seeks to understand and enhance the relationship and connectedness of people with one another and the broader systems in their environment.

Ecological perspective, a view of people as existing within layers of relationships with systems in their social environment. It is concerned 'with the progressive accommodation between a growing human organism and its immediate environment, and the way in which this relation is mediated by forces emanating from more remote regions in the larger physical and social milieu' (Bronfenbrenner, 1979:13).

General systems theory, a theory that explains the 'rules' according to which a system (such as an organism, an individual, a family or an organisation) operates.

Bronfenbrenner, however, did not invent the ecological perspective. It actually dates back to the earliest thinking in social work. Mary Richmond wrote about it in 1922 (Cornell, 2006), saying (using the gender-exclusive language common in her time), '[s]ocial case work consists of those processes which develop personality through adjustments consciously effected, individual by individual, between men and their social environment' (Richmond, 1922:98–99). She went on in this same passage to stress that social workers were to focus equally on the person and on his or her environment. In 1940, Gordon Hamilton (34 & 153) wrote of 'person and situation' and 'person in his situation' in a similar way. Herbert Strean (1979:46) wrote that 'social workers by the 1950s were actively talking about the person-situation constellation and recognized that we cannot help a client unless we appreciate how and why his situations influences him and vice-versa'. And Florence Hollis discussed it in her seminal book *Casework* (1964:10), where she explained that '[c]entral to casework is the notion of "the-person-in-his-situation" as a threefold configuration consisting of the person, the situation, and the interaction between them'.

The social work concept of person-in-environment (or person-in-situation) thus has a long history, dating back to the origins of the profession. Strean (1979:46) in fact argued that 'the person-in-situation focus ... is what makes social work unique and what social workers should stress more today'; many social workers today would echo his view of 40 years ago. It is based in the premise that the social work profession provides both care and social justice and seeks to enhance the ability of individuals, families, groups and communities to solve their problems and realise their potentials, while effecting social reforms and transformation intended to remove societal obstacles to the well-being of people (Weiss-Gal, 2008).

Person-in-environment approach, (in its simplest expression) a person can only be properly understood when considered within his or her social environment. 'It views the individual and his or her environments as forming an ecosystem consisting of the individual, all the systems with which the individual has reciprocal relationships, the wider environment in which the individual acts, and all the mutual interrelationships that occur between the individual and the various subsystems. Within this ecosystem, individuals are influenced by and influence their environments through their actions' (Weis-Gal, 2008:65).

In the late 1970s and early 1980s, Alex Gitterman and Carel Germain, revived the ecological perspective for social work (Teater, 2014). The development of the ecological perspective within the social work profession was based on the criticism of the non-human language of systems theory, such as 'system', 'equilibrium' and 'homeostasis', and a lack of direction for the social worker after the assessment of systems. The ecological perspective has since become widely used in social work, because it assists social workers to understand their client systems in totality. In other words, the ecological perspective helps the social worker to understand different systems that the client system interacts with and the effect of such interaction on the client system. By addressing these relationships – interactions and interdependence between people and the environment – their social functioning is enhanced. According to Gitterman and Germain (2008:8), the focus of the ecological perspective is on:

> ... the growth, development and potentialities of human beings and with the properties of their environments that support or fail to support the expression of human potential.

When there is a good fit between person and environment, people feel that they are in harmony with their life world. They feel connected to their environment, a sense of security, and that they and their environment have the resources they need to cope with life's challenges. Conversely, a negative person-environment fit leads to the individual experiencing stress, because in the ecological perspective, stress is perceived to be an outcome of imbalance between environmental demands and the person's capacity to manage them with available internal and external resources. When people attempt to maintain a positive level of fit with their environment in their lives, they may also encounter stress during difficult life transitions such as puberty, adolescence, getting married, loss of a loved one, and lack of resources (Teater, 2014:27). The above experiences may pose a serious challenge to individuals who do not have adequate resources to deal with the challenge. Thus, the ecological perspective provides social workers with a conceptual perspective that can guide them on how people perceive the world and how they interact with various systems in their social environment.

The person-in-environment approach has become well established in the general understanding of the social work profession that social workers should use interventions at both the individual psychological level and the social level (Weiss-Gal, 2008). Thus, a social worker using ecosystems theory would evaluate and assess the level of person-environment fit and then focus her or his intervention on either the person or environment, or both, to increase the level of fit. Although Bronfenbrenner (1979) was not a social worker, it is worth noting that his ecological perspective is widely used today by many other disciplines and helping professions.

Reflective questions
Read Case study 1 again and answer the questions.
- Briefly describe your understanding of Maluta's case in terms of ecosystems theory.
- What are the systems that relate to Maluta's case?
- How would you intervene in Maluta's case using both the individual and social levels?

5.3 Key concepts in the ecological perspective

There are number of concepts that are useful for understanding the ecological perspective, as outlined by Zastrow and Kirst-Ashman (2016). These concepts are useful for social work practice. Some of the major concepts used in the ecological perspective include: social environment; transactions; energy; interface; adaptation; coping; and interdependence.

5.3.1 Social environment

The social environment includes the actual physical setting that the society or culture provides (Zastrow & Kirst-Ashman, 2016). It may also comprise the type of home a person lives in, the type of work a person does, and the type of laws and social rules that govern him or her. Moreover, social environment may include the individuals, groups, communities, organisations and other systems with which the person interacts, for instance, friends, family, colleagues and government structures that provide essential services for the person to survive, like health care, social welfare and educational systems. Thus, the *social environment* is about the actual physical setting around a person and the interactions/relationship that a person has with that setting. A negative relationship with the social environment results in challenges for a person, which may require the intervention of a social worker to help in improving that relationship.

5.3.2 Transactions

Transactions are when people interact and communicate with others in their environment (Zastrow & Kirst-Ashman, 2016). The transactions may be positive or negative. A *positive* transaction results in happiness/contentment, whereas a *negative* transaction leads to psychological tension/problems.

An example of a positive transaction is when someone is told that he or she has passed the interview for a job that he or she has been looking forward to wholeheartedly. On the other hand, an example of a negative transaction could be when a married man is told by his wife that she wants a divorce. Social workers are mainly involved when there are negative transactions between people, and their role is to improve these transactions to enhance everyone's well-being.

5.3.3 Energy

Zastrow and Kirst-Ashman (2016) describe *energy* as the natural power of energetic connection between people and their environment. The authors further state that energy can take the form of input or output. In this regard, *input* is the form of energy coming into a person's life and adding to that life, while *output* is a form of energy going out of a person's life or taking something away from it. An example of an input can be a device to enhance the mobility of a group of people living with physical disability. Conversely, an example of an output is when someone takes time off her or his busy schedule to go and fetch her or his children from school daily. In this regard, both the input and output energy may give rise to problems if they are not managed properly. For instance, if the group of people living with disabilities does not have any form of assistance to improve their mobility, they may experience problems. Equally, taking time off to fetch children daily may cause problems, because some of the work will lag. In both instances, social work intervention may be required.

5.3.4 Interface

Interface is the exact point at which the interaction between an individual and the environment takes place (Zastrow & Kirst-Ashman, 2016). During the counselling session, the social worker focuses on the interface as the primary target of the most appropriate interactions for change. It is of paramount importance that the interface be identified to deal efficiently with the challenges people face. For instance, a family attending counselling may point to the behaviour of one of the children as the main problem. Upon further exploration, it might be found that the problem is actually tensions in the marital relationship, which the child is merely indicating. The interface is the parental marriage, not the child. The social worker's role is to ensure that the interface is correctly identified to avoid wasting time and energy before getting into the real problem.

5.3.5 Adaptation

Adaptation is the capacity of people to adjust to their surrounding environmental conditions (Zastrow & Kirst-Ashman, 2016). This concept refers to change, because it is understood that people must change to adapt to new situations or circumstances to continue functioning effectively. Social workers help people adapt to new situations they are confronted with in their lives. For instance, think of a situation where electricity is cut off in a community for a long time due to heavy rains. In this instance, people cannot just sit and live in the darkness waiting for the government to fix the problem. Instead, they may devise other means for lighting and cooking, such as using candles for lighting and wood for cooking. In this way, they adapt to the current crisis. The social worker's role is to help people adapt optimally to their current conditions, because failure to adapt may result in further challenges or problems.

5.3.6 Coping

There are similarities between adaptation and coping in that *coping* implies a struggle to overcome problems. Although adaptation may involve responses to new conditions that are either positive or negative, coping refers to the constructive ways people deal with the negative experiences they encounter (Zastrow & Kirst-Ashman, 2016). For example, a divorced person may have to cope with the aftermath of divorce and being a single parent. To do this, he or she will need skills to be able to cope with such adversity. The social worker's role is to assist people to unleash and utilise their potentials and capabilities to cope with any adverse life event (see Chapter 7 on resilience and Chapter 13 on strengths-based practices). If people are not assisted to develop their coping skills, it would be difficult for them to deal with their life challenges.

5.3.7 Interdependence

Interdependence, the last ecological concept, refers to the mutual reliance of each person upon every other person (Zastrow & Kirst-Ashman, 2016). This means that people do not live in isolation; instead, they are interdependent and reliant upon other people in the social environment. This links perfectly with the most well-known African phrase, which says in Tshivenda *'muthu ndi muthu nga vhathu'* or, in English, *'a person cannot exist without other people'* (see Chapter 6 on *Ubuntu*). Thus, in life, people need other people to function optimally. For instance, in a family, children need the guidance and support of their parents, and, on the other hand, parents need their children to assist them with some activities at home. When the support from other people is not available, it often creates problems, because such support is vital for the optimal functioning of the other person.

🔍 ACTIVITY 5.1

1 Focusing on the community you live in and the types of systems you often interact with, how would you describe your social environment?
2 Briefly describe two examples each of positive and negative transaction you once experienced in your life.
3 Looking into your own life experiences, how would you describe energy, particularly focusing on input and output?
4 How would you describe interface, specifically looking at your own interaction with family members?
5 Briefly differentiate between adaptation and coping by giving practical examples.
6 What is your understanding of interdependence? Give practical examples.

5.4 Key concepts in general systems theory

In addition to the above concepts from the ecological perspective, there are other concepts from general systems theory. These concepts, which are important in helping you understand ecosystems theory and its relationship to social work practice, include: boundaries; subsystems; homeostasis; differentiation; entropy; negative entropy; and equifinality. The sections below briefly discuss Zastrow and Kirst-Ashman's (2016) descriptions of these concepts.

5.4.1 Boundaries

Boundaries refer to the borders or margins that separate one entity from the other (Zastrow & Kirst-Ashman, 2016). For example, the police officers, social workers, teachers and social auxiliary workers serve in the best interests of children. Although they all serve in the best interests of children, there are specified boundaries in their designated job responsibilities, and each group may require the services of the other during service delivery. In other words, groups know what is expected of them and will stick to that without crossing the line by doing what they are not expected to do. Tension may arise if one of the groups crosses the boundaries and takes over another group's role.

5.4.2 Subsystems

A *subsystem* is a secondary or subordinate system that is a component of a larger system (Zastrow & Kirst-Ashman, 2016). There is a connection between boundaries and subsystems, in that the subsystem is part of the larger system, although there are boundaries between them, such as different roles and responsibilities. Consider, for example, a polygamous marriage, wherein a man is married to three wives and each of these wives stays in her own little household with her children. The family as a whole is a system. But it is made up of three wife-headed subsystems, which are connected but also separate – there is a boundary between each subsystem. If one wife takes more of the husband's time than is reasonable, there will be conflict between the subsystems. Or, if one of these wives interferes in another wife's household, this crossing of the boundaries between subsystems can result in conflict.

5.4.3 Homeostasis

Homeostasis is the tendency for a system to maintain a relatively stable, constant state of balance. In fact, homeostasis means maintaining the status quo, whether positive or negative (Zastrow & Kirst-Ashman, 2016). Thus, homeostasis may be harmful, making problems even worse. The status quo is supposed to be maintained when something happens to disturb a system's balance and therefore the system will readjust itself and regain stability (it recovers, finds its feet again). Think of a situation in which one member of a singing group dies. Obviously, there will be an imbalance in the voices in the group and the relationships amongst themselves. However, the group will strive hard to maintain or regain balance and stability, perhaps by finding a replacement singer (homeostasis). A challenge may arise when the substitute does not step up to the position or does not reach the expected outcome.

5.4.4 Differentiation

Differentiation is a system's tendency to move from a more simplified to a more complex existence. This is based on the premise that relationships, situations and interactions tend to become more complex over time (Zastrow & Kirst-Ashman, 2016). When people find themselves in complex situations, they try hard to seek and devise means that will help to overcome their complex situations. For example, when a man who is a sole breadwinner in the family gets retrenched, it often leads to more complex situations in that family, because there will not be any means of income to meet the family's basic needs. As a way of bringing the situation to a better stance, the husband may find himself seeking assistance from the social welfare services. It becomes problematic if social welfare does not have policies in place on how to take care of the retrenched who are struggling to make ends meet.

5.4.5 Entropy

Entropy is the tendency of a system to progress toward disorganisation, depletion and death (Zastrow & Kirst-Ashman, 2016). This process of change usually results in problems because the system will be compelled to adapt to these changes. Entropy is inevitable as long as people live, for instance, people are born, age and die, and sometimes marriages are dissolved through divorce. These kinds of experiences normally lead to problems, especially if people are not able to cope with the changes. Therefore, social work intervention may be required.

5.4.6 Negative entropy

Negative entropy is the process of a system toward growth and development and it is the opposite of entropy (Zastrow & Kirst-Ashman, 2016). It is expected that people, families, groups and communities develop physically, intellectually and emotionally as they grow. Challenges may arise when they do not develop and grow as expected or when the development and growth is so sudden and rapid such that it was not anticipated or expected.

5.4.7 Equifinality

Equifinality refers to the idea that there are many different means to the same end (Zastrow & Kirst-Ashman, 2016). For example, there are various means of thinking; therefore, people cannot just look at one way of thinking. When people come to a social worker for help, there is not only one way of helping them, not only one solution to their problem. People might follow a path to resolve their problem that the social worker doesn't support, but if their problem is solved, then they have achieved what they wanted. This is equifinality – there are many ways to achieve a goal. In this regard, social workers encourage people to look at different methods or ways of dealing with the negative situations that confront them.

 ACTIVITY 5.2

1 How does each of the above concepts in general systems theory relate to your cultural ways of doing things?
2 How do these concepts help you to understand your family or the community you come from?
3 Do you find any relationship between the ecological perspective concepts and the general systems concepts? Please motivate your response.

 ACTIVITY 5.3

We have covered many technical terms in sections 5.3 and 5.4. Make a list of these terms in English (there are 12 of them), define each one in your own words and then try to translate them into another language (ideally, your home language, if that's not English). Maybe there is not one word in your language for each of these terms. That's okay; use a phrase, a sentence or even a metaphor. Take those translations to someone in your family and ask them to explain what they understand by each term. How similar or different are their explanations to the explanations in this chapter?

5.5 Levels of the ecological system

In his initial articulations of the ecological perspective, Bronfenbrenner (1979) identified four levels of structures or systems that are nested around a focal individual like a set of concentric circles, namely microsystem, mesosystem, exosystem and macrosystem (Neal & Neal, 2013). These levels are interconnected to make a whole and they involve numerous components that function together to make a whole. There is a similarity between these levels and the concept of social environment as discussed in section 5.3.1 above. Figure 5.1 illustrates the interconnectedness of these levels.

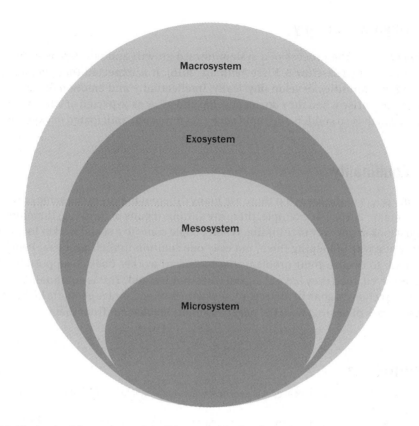

Figure 5.1: The levels of the ecology originally proposed by Bronfenbrenner (1979)

5.5.1 Microsystem

The microsystem is the lowest level of Bronfenbrenner's hierarchy. It is the setting where the focal individual plays a direct role and has direct experiences and social interactions with others (Neal & Neal, 2013). For example, a family could be regarded as a microsystem where family members interact directly with their children, siblings, and/or other immediate family members. At this level, the social worker recognises the significance of the relationship and interactions between the family and its members or amongst family members themselves. The social worker bears in mind that an imbalance in this interaction or relationship may result in tension or challenges. Moreover, the social worker recognises the dynamics of each family as a unique entity with its own unique beliefs, customs and ways of doing things.

5.5.2 Mesosystem

The mesosystem, within which microsystems are nested, includes social interactions between two or more of the focal individual's settings (Neal & Neal, 2013). In other words, the mesosystem could include a meeting between a woman and her employer. Thus, the individual person and her employer become the two microsystems that are nested and that she has direct contact and interaction with. At this level, the social worker looks at the balance in the relationship and interaction that the woman has with the two nested systems, namely the family and the employer. The assumption here is that an imbalance in the interaction or relationship between the woman and the two nested systems will create problems or challenges that will inhibit her optimal functioning.

5.5.3 Exosystem

The exosystem, within which mesosystems are nested, includes settings that influence the focal individual, but in which the focal individual does not directly participate (Neal & Neal, 2013). This could refer to social welfare policies or legislation that regulate how services should be provided to a group of people who are vulnerable, for instance, people living with disability. In this instance, people living with disabilities become the recipients of social services, but they may not be involved in the decision-making process regarding the 'what' or 'how' of these services. Therefore, this disjuncture may bring about psychological tension in people as they may feel that they do not have an influence on the policies that will benefit them.

5.5.4 Macrosystem

Finally, the macrosystem, within which exosystems are nested, includes broad cultural influences or ideologies that have long-ranging consequences for people (Neal & Neal, 2013). For instance, society holds a strong view that a young pregnant girl should be compelled to marry her boyfriend as soon as it is discovered that she is pregnant, regardless of whether she believes in it or not. Thus, the disconnect between the young pregnant girl's cultural beliefs and her personal beliefs may give rise to tensions.

It is worth bearing in mind that Bronfenbrenner was not a social worker and therefore his description of the levels of social ecology differs somewhat from the description of some of the authors who wrote about the ecosystems from a social work perspective. For instance, according to Kirst-Ashman (2013), microsystems concern work with individuals, mezzo with groups and macro with organisations and communities. So, these terms are used differently in different contexts. However, the similarity is that both Bronfenbrenner and Kirst-Ashman's descriptions focus on the interaction between people and the external systems in the environment and how these systems are interconnected.

Reflective questions

Read Case study 1 again.
- Briefly describe Maluta's situation in terms of the four levels of the ecological perspective approach by Bronfenbrenner as discussed above.
- Which of these levels are more relevant (applicable) to Maluta's situation? Motivate your response.
- In view of Kirst-Ashman's (2013) description of micro, mezzo and macro systems, how would you intervene in Maluta's situation?

5.6 Ecosystems theory in social work practice

Among the applications of various theoretical frameworks applied in social work practice, ecosystems theory may be applied from a variety of perspectives (Bowers & Bowers, 2017). With ecosystems theory, social workers are given a theoretical understanding that people are interrelated, interconnected, and interdependent with external systems in the social environment and therefore they observe the effects of such relationships in the social functioning of the people. According to Kirst-Ashman (2013), a social worker working from ecosystems theory intervenes at micro (working with individuals), mezzo (working with groups) and macro (working with organisations and communities) levels.

There are many challenges or problems people experience that may require intervention by a social worker. According to ecosystems theory, these challenges or problems relate to the imbalance in the interconnection or relationship between people and their social environment. Gitterman and Germain (2008) suggest that everyone has problems at some point, which they term '"problems in living"'. They differentiate three common types of problems in living that may require intervention by a social worker:
- Problems associated with life transitions, such as marriage/entering a long-term partnership, birth of a first child or movement of a child out of the family, or movement into middle age or retirement.
- Problems associated with tasks in using and influencing elements of the environment.
- Interpersonal problems and needs in families and groups.

The above problems can easily lead to a disconnect between people and their social environment; social work intervention may be required to enhance or strengthen such relationships. Gitterman and Germain (2008) further suggest three ways in which social workers may apply the ecosystems theory in practice to create or maintain an adaptive person-environment fit, namely:
1. Change the individual to meet the environment's perceived expectations or demands and take advantage of its opportunities.
2. Change the environment so that the social and physical environments are more responsive to the individual's needs and goals.
3. Change the person-environment transactions to achieve an improved fit.

As the first people to systematically apply ecological theory to social work practice in the early 1980s, Gitterman and Germain (2008) developed the life model of social work practice. The model is aimed at assisting in the level of fit between people and environments by helping them to find and utilise their personal and environmental strengths and resources to assist in alleviating life stressors and/or to intervene in the environment to create better resources to meet the needs of individuals (Teater, 2014). The life model of social work practice comprises the preparatory, initial, ongoing and ending phases.
- **Preparatory phase**. The preparatory phase involves gathering information and preparing to enter the life of the individual, group or community members. In this phase, the social worker gathers information about the individual, group or community, including the information about different systems that are connected to them.
  Gathering of information helps the social worker to have a holistic understanding of the individual, group and community in terms of their experiences, resources, weaknesses and strengths. For example, a social worker working with a family that has a high level of conflict may want to gather information about this family as a way of preparing her or himself to work with them. In so doing, the social worker will be able to develop a

holistic understanding of that family and the kind of relationships or connections it has with the social environment.

- **Initial phase**. The initial phase involves assessing the current level of person-environment fit, including personal biopsychosocial features and environmental properties. This stage follows the preparatory phase and requires the social worker to assess the nature and kind of relationships and connections the individual, groups and community have with the social environment or other systems. This would help the social worker to ascertain if there is a person-environment fit and, if not, to devise strategies together with the individual, group or community on how a balance/fit between them and the social environment could be created.

  For example, a dance group comprising young people from a particular village may feel that they are not given the necessary support by their parents, schoolteachers and communities. In this regard, the social worker working with the group assesses the relationship/interconnection between the group/group members and their immediate social environment comprising parents, teachers and the community. By focusing on enhancing the relationship between the group/group members and the social environment, the social worker aims to improve their social functioning and enhance their well-being. Assessment is critical, because it sets up the goals and intervention plans for the individual, group and community (Segal et al., 2013).

- **Ongoing phase**. This phase involves interventions that can be tailored to the individual, group and community members by working to increase self-esteem, self-worth, competence and autonomy or by attempting to change the physical or social environment to create a better person-environment fit. At this stage, the social worker often engages in a problem-solving process that includes engaging the individual, family, group or community, assessing the problem area and situation, developing a list of potential solutions, coming up with an action plan, and supporting the individual, family, group or community in implementing the plan (Segal et al., 2013). The social worker further encourages the people with whom he or she is working to take ownership and responsibility for the change process to improve the person-environment fit. For instance, a social worker will assist community members with the establishment of a community project that will help changing their lives. In so doing, the social worker will engage the community members in identifying their needs, developing and implementing a plan, and evaluating the project.

- **Ending phase**. In the ending phase, the social worker and the individual, group or community members address feelings around termination and develop plans for addressing any future life stressors. At this stage, the social worker and the individual, group and community complete their work together. It is important to note that people must be prepared for termination, because abrupt endings without preparation can damage the therapeutic process.

  It should be noted that the above process is not exclusive to ecological theory, as it is closely aligned with the generic planned change process (Kirst-Ashman, 2013).

Reflective questions

Answer the questions below in relation to Case study 1.
- Briefly describe how you would apply the ecological life model of social work practice when working with Maluta.
- How will working ecologically look different from working only with Maluta and ignoring his social environment? Which do you think will be more effective? Why?

5.7 Ecosystems theory for decolonial social work practice

Understanding how and why people are different is a foundation for social work practice (Segal et al., 2013). In other words, social workers need to understand the situations and conditions in which people find themselves. Since social workers work with people from various cultural backgrounds, who are members of numerous identity groups, they need to develop skills to navigate cultural differences (Segal et al., 2013). For instance, there are many different types of families in South Africa, such as single parent families, nuclear families, extended families and reconstituted families. A single parent family comprises one parent and a child or children; a nuclear family consists of two parents and a child or children; an extended family includes different members of a family, e.g., parents, children, aunts, uncles and grandparents living together; and, lastly, a reconstituted family comprises previously-married parents who live with their children, including children from their previous marriages/relationships (Grobler et al., 2013). Thus, if the social worker fails to understand families of different cultures, it would be difficult for her or him to find the basis for intervention.

When working with different types of families, a social worker should be aware that each of these families has its own unique needs and ways of doing things. Families from different ethnic or cultural backgrounds have unique practices or ways of doing things. For instance, what is regarded as a problem to one family may not be considered as such by another family. Decolonial social work practice based on the ecosystems theory creates awareness among social workers of working in situations where families comprise members from mixed ethnic or cultural backgrounds. This could be a situation whereby a person with a Christian background marries someone with a Muslim background.

Therefore, decolonial social work practice from the ecosystems perspective takes into account the uniqueness of people and the unique relationships they have with the external world. Think of a situation where somebody of Indian origin marries a Tsonga person and the couple relocates to Giyani after marriage. What kind of challenges do you think the couple will experience with their social environment? And what adjustments to you think need to happen? In this regard, the relationship or interconnectedness between the couple needs to be adjusted or the individual partner with a different ethnic background needs to make the necessary adjustment to the environment. This includes adjusting to the physical environment and forming new relationships with the members of the new family or the community.

Ecosystems theory states that failure to initiate and maintain a good relationship/connection with the environment often leads to challenges/problems. Decolonial social work practice from the ecosystems perspective focuses on enhancing such relationships without any form of prejudice or imposing one's own frame of reference. What it also means is that a social worker should understand a particular family, its ways of doing things and, where possible, use indigenous methods of practice to intervene. For example, different families may understand 'respect' differently. Thus, what is regarded as 'respect' by the social worker or another family may not be regarded as such by the other.

Earlier we spoke about the well-known phrase in African culture, which in isiZulu is *'umuntu ngumuntu ngabantu'* and in English, *'a person cannot exist without other people'*. This phrase equally relates to families since families also need support from the external environment (such as relatives, community or church) to survive and maintain themselves. Therefore, maintaining a good relationship with the external environment helps in sustaining the family and a negative relationship results in problems, which may require social work intervention. Moreover, the interactions amongst members within the family are also key, because once there are negative interactions, problems begin. Another example would be that of a university student who travelled from the rural areas to seek education in the city. This student may find him or herself sharing an apartment with other students to survive the high costs of living. Applying decolonial social work practice from the ecosystems perspective requires the social worker to consider the situations of the student and the significance of the systems around him or her.

Ecosystems theory is particularly useful for decolonial practice in turning the social worker's attention not only to the kinds of social environmental factors mentioned so far, but also to the kinds of structural factors in the social environment that facilitate or impede psychosocial well-being and flourishing. For example, the social environment may present individuals and families with experiences of racism, sexism, xenophobia, homophobia, religious intolerance and so on. These experiences are located within the social environment, though they can also infiltrate the minds of individuals (Biko, 2004). Attention to the social environment, using ecosystems conceptual tools, can support the processes of political conscientisation described in Chapter 2 (Darder, 2018).

Assessment tools, such as the genogram, which is a classic ecosystems assessment tool (Hartman, 1995), can be utilised in innovative ways to assess a far more inclusive definition of 'family', to include also 'extended' family and even non-kin family members (Watts-Jones, 1997). The genogram can also be used to trace one's ancestry (Mitchell & Shillingford, 2017), which may be particularly relevant for people of mixed-race heritage or those living in the diaspora. The genogram can be used also to identify the intergenerational transmission of racial identity, internalised racism and bias, and feelings of shame and guilt (Halevy, 1998), and in promoting critical consciousness about a range of oppressions (Kosutic et al., 2009).

By recognising the social forces interacting with individual psychosocial well-being and functioning, ecosystems theory can lay an important foundation in recognising and challenging systematic social exclusion and oppression. This serves as a healthy counterpoint to a form of social work that focuses on the individual and neglects the social environment, which inevitably leads to the privatisation of political concerns.

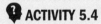 **ACTIVITY 5.4**

1   How would you describe a family from your own cultural perspective?
2   Briefly describe some of the systems that are significant in sustaining and maintaining the family.
3   What are some of the ethical and cultural aspects that you would consider when working with families?
4   Briefly discuss some of the indigenous tools that you can use in working with families.

5.8   Conclusion

This chapter has provided an overview of ecosystems theory. We started by defining the ecosystems theory followed by the description of the historical background of this theory. The connection between general systems theory and the ecological perspective was explained together with the main concepts underlying each of these theories. Subsequently, the levels of the ecosystem, as originally proposed by Bronfenbrenner, were described. This led to descriptions of the practical application of ecosystems theory in social work practice. In conclusion, the application of decolonial social work practice was outlined, using the ecosystems theory in working with African and multicultural families, and in addressing structural oppression.

Chapter activities

1. **Reflective question**. Think about your family of origin and the kind of support you sought and received as a family from the social environment. In view of ecosystems theory, how would you describe your own relationships amongst yourselves as family members and the relationship/interconnectedness you had with the social environment? Do you think that ecosystems theory provides you with a holistic understanding of your own family and its relationship with the external world?
2. **Personal context**. What is considered a 'family' in your own culture and what are the different types of families found in that community? How do these families interconnect/relate with one another and what are the other systems in the social environment they connect with?
3. **Advocacy**. How can you use the ecosystems theory to understand the social challenges/problems that your country is facing and how can you use this theory to deal with such challenges/problems?
4. **Critical question**. One of the challenges that we are facing in South Africa is xenophobic attacks, whereby African foreign nationals are attacked and accused of enjoying the privileges that are supposed to be enjoyed by South African citizens. How can ecosystems theory assist you in reducing such attacks on foreign nationals?

References

Ambrosino, R, Heffernan, J, Shuttlesworth, G & Ambrosino, R. 2012. *Social work and social welfare: An introduction*. 7th ed. Belmont, CA: Brooks/Cole.

Biko, S. 2004. *I write what I like*. Johannesburg, RSA: Picador Africa.

Bowers, NR & Bowers, A: 'General systems theory'. *In*: Turner, F (ed.). 2017. *Social interlocking work theoretical treatment approaches*. 6th ed. pp. 240–247. New York: Oxford University Press.

Bronfenbrenner, U. 1979. *The ecology of human development*. Cambridge, MA: Harvard University Press.

Cornell, KL. 2006. Person-in-situation: History, theory, and new directions for social work practice. *Praxis*, 6 (Fall 2006), 50–57.

Darder, A. 2018. *The student guide to Freire's 'Pedagogy of the oppressed'*. London, UK: Bloomsbury.

Gitterman, A & Germain, CB. 2008. *The life model of social work practice: Advances in theory and practice*. 3rd ed. New York: Columbia University Press.

Grobler, H, Schenck, R & Mbedzi, P. 2013. *Person-centred facilitation: Process, theory and practice*. 4th ed. Cape Town: Oxford University Press Southern Africa.

Halevy, J. 1998. A genogram with an attitude. *Journal of Marital and Family Therapy*, 24:233–42.

Hamilton, G. 1940. *Theory and practice of social case work*. New York: Columbia University Press.

Hartman, A. 1995. Diagrammatic assessment of family relationships. *Families in Society*, 76:111–122.

Hollis, F. 1964. *Casework: A psychosocial therapy*. New York City, NY: Random House.

Kirst-Ashman, KK. 2013. *Introduction to social work and social welfare: Critical thinking perspective*. 4th ed. Belmont, CA: Brooks/Cole.

Kosutic, I, Garcia, M, Graves, T, Barnett, F, Hall, J, Haley, E, Rock, J, Bathon, A & Kaiser, B. 2009. The critical genogram: A tool for promoting critical consciousness. *Journal of Feminist Family Therapy*, 21:151–176.

Maistry, M: 'Community development'. *In*: Nicholsa, L, Rautenbach, J & Maistry, M (eds.). 2010. *Introduction to social work*. pp. 156–177. Cape Town: Juta.

Miley, KK, O'Meila, M & Dubois, B. 2009. *Generalist social work practice: An empowering approach*. 6th ed. Harlow, UK: Pearson Education, Inc.

Mitchell, MD & Shillingford, MA. 2017. A journey to the past: Promoting identity development of African Americans through ancestral awareness. *The Family Journal*, 25:63–69.

Neal, JW & Neal, ZP. 2013. Nested or networked? Future directions for ecological systems theory. *Social Development*, 22(4):722–737.

Richmond, ME. (1922). *What is social case work? An introductory description*. New York: Russell Sage Foundation.

Segal, AE, Gerdes, KA & Steiner, S. 2013. *An introduction to the profession of social work: Becoming a change agent*. 4th ed. Belmont, CA: Brooks/Cole.

Strean, HS. 1979. The contemporary family and the responsibilities of the social worker in direct practice. *Journal of Jewish Communal Service*, 56(1):40–49.

Teater, B. 2014. *An introduction to applying social work theories and methods*. 2nd ed. Maidenhead, UK: McGraw Hill.

Watts-Jones, D. 1997. Toward an African American genogram. *Family Process*, 36:375–383.

Weiss-Gal, I. 2008. The person-in-environment approach: Professional ideology and practice of social workers in Israel. *Social Work*, 53:65–75.

Zastrow, C & Kirst-Ashman, KK. 2016. *Understanding human behavior and the social environment*. 10th ed. Belmont, CA: Brooks/Cole.

Annotated websites and activities

http://citeseerx.ist.psu.edu/viewdoc/download?doi=10.1.1.471.7361&rep=rep1&type=pdf
This link takes you to an article by Eileen Johnson on how ecosystems theory can be used in practice.

Think of your interaction with the social environment and describe how you connect with different systems at the level of microsystem, mesosystem, exosystem and macrosystem. At what level do you interact more with the other systems? Have a discussion with your classmates about this.

https://tinyurl.com/iasswethics
This link will take you to the *Global social work statement of ethical principles* (IASSW), which is designed to facilitate social workers' aspirations to achieve the highest possible standards of ethical practice.

Take time to go through these ethical principles. Write down some of the core values and ethical responsibilities for social workers and how they relate to working with individuals, groups, families and communities from the ecosystems perspective.

https://www.youtube.com/watch?v=npUqHIlMfKs
This YouTube link takes you to the presentation of ecosystems theory by Malvika Choudhary, explaining the biotic and abiotic elements of the ecosystem.

After listening to this presentation, how would you contextualise the ecosystems theory in relation to social work practice? Give practical examples.

Annotated websites and activities are also available on Learning Zone.

oxford.co.za/learningzone

Ubuntu

Johannah Sekudu

CHAPTER OUTCOMES

By the end of this chapter, you should be able to:

✓ *Describe the origin of the concept Ubuntu*

✓ *Define the concept Ubuntu*

✓ *Identify the relevance of Ubuntu in social work practice at micro and macro levels*

✓ *Argue the relevance of Ubuntu in decolonising social work practice in South Africa.*

 Case Study 1   *Ubuntu*: **Locating individual concerns in community relationships**

You are employed as a social worker in a hospital where you operate as a member of the multidisciplinary team. Your role as a social worker is not confined just to patients who are admitted to the hospital, but also includes the communities from which these patients are coming. Every day you are confronted with addressing the challenges faced by mothers of children who are admitted to hospital due to severe malnutrition. Despite the fact that the referral letters from other members of the multidisciplinary team inform you of neglect on the part of the mothers, in your interaction with the mothers you realise that the situation is compounded by poverty and a lack of resources. The stories you hear from the mothers during your interviews give you an indication that they feel helpless as they watch their children suffer from a preventable condition, because they have no resources to counteract this condition.

After realising that a number of these mothers are from one community, you visit this community to assess and map out the available resources that you could link them with. You involve all the stakeholders in your assessment process in trying to identify the resources that could be mobilised by a collective, which could be used to address the challenge of malnutrition in the community. In your community meetings you allow all members to share what they know about their community and what they think could be done to address this common challenge. Guided by the belief in the need to have a sharing community, you facilitate the discussion by encouraging community members to share what they have to the benefit of the entire community. At the end of the community meeting, it is agreed that the members are going to work together as a collective to grow vegetables in a section of the school yard that has not been utilised for any educational activity.

Reflective questions

• Using the above case study, what do you think is the role of the social worker as a member of a multidisciplinary team in a hospital?

• At the micro level of social work intervention, what do you think the social worker should do to assist the mothers of those children who are diagnosed with severe malnutrition?

• Can you identify any activity in the case study that the social worker could be involved in while trying to assist the community as a whole to deal with malnutrition?

6.1 Introduction

Social work is a profession that concerns itself with assisting human beings to improve their well-being at individual, group and community levels. This calls for social workers to be vigilant in utilising social work knowledge and skills when facilitating the change that needs to be achieved in the lives of their clients. In the process of facilitating change, the professional code of ethics forms the framework that guides social workers to address the needs of their clients in ways that are empowering and not creating dependency. Social work values and principles must always be considered when social workers interact with client systems at all levels of intervention.

Ubuntu is an African principle that could be said to date back to the origins of humanity itself. According to Tellinger (2013), *Ubuntu* has been characterising different African communities since ancient times. Community members in these communities were living in harmony with one another as a unit. They had a common understanding that they belong to the whole. As a result, each individual made efforts to contribute to the well-being of the whole through sharing. But, *Ubuntu* was dismantled and disturbed by the explorers who arrived in Africa. Due to the colonisation of these communities (see Chapter 2), division and materialism emerged. Community members became divided and lived in fear of one another, rather than being united and striving continuously towards unity. This breakdown of *Ubuntu* can still be seen across communities in Africa today, including South Africa.

Ubuntu has been adopted by the South African government as a core principle in the democratic dispensation. It is one of the principles that is highlighted in the *White Paper for Social Welfare* (RSA, 1997) that needs to be understood and utilised within the developmental welfare approach to social welfare service delivery. This chapter is aimed at unpacking the origins and concept of *Ubuntu* and illustrating its relevance in social work practice at micro and macro levels of intervention. The chapter is concluded by considering the relevance of *Ubuntu* as a principle in decolonising social work practice in South Africa.

6.2 The origin of *Ubuntu*

Broodryk (2006) suggests that *Ubuntu* as a philosophical concept is as old as the beginning of the creation of the human race. According to Broodryk (2009), until the 1990s, the philosophy of *Ubuntu* had never been recorded in written form, but dates back to before the Ten Commandments were given to Moses at Mount Sinai. There is no evidence of an exact timeframe for when *Ubuntu* came into existence, but it has been observed as a value in Africa as far back as people can remember. It is a value that was continuously transmitted from generation to generation through spoken words and behaviour, leading to a lack of written evidence. The younger generation was able to learn from the older generation how community members have to live together in harmony.

> **Ubuntu**, a philosophy that considers the success of the group above that of the individual (Lundin & Nelson, 2010). *Ubuntu* emphasises that human beings exist because of their connections to the human community.

As a result, no human being saw him or herself in isolation from or above other community members. With South Africa as a country that is characterised by a variety of cultures and subcultures, the community members have been glued together by *Ubuntu* before the colonisation of the country.

Ndlovu (2016) states that *Ubuntu*'s origins can be traced back to the village life before colonisation, where communities lived under well-defined structures characterised by common understanding. Traditional leaders provided caring authority for and protection to communities under their rule, and this spirit of caring transformed into a caring community. The spirit of *Ubuntu* became visible when people in a community encountered challenges, as they always supported one another in their attempts to address these challenges. Ndlovu (2016) further asserts that *Ubuntu* provides people with a meaning of self-identity, self-respect and accomplishment that assists individuals in dealing with their tribulations in a positive way. Before colonisation, African people used *Ubuntu* to reinforce the notion that community members have to share what they have with their neighbours who might be having less than them. This was gladly done by all who had more without any problems; as a result, a spirit of belonging was fostered. In this manner, community members lived in harmony and respect for one another, without seeing others as less important.

According to Broodryk (2006), Steve Biko found that certain Western values and traditions made him uncomfortable as they were foreign to the African way of living. These Western cultural practices were not in line with humaneness as lived by Africans. It could be that the writings of Steve Biko triggered the realisation that the spirit of *Ubuntu* was eroded and there developed a move towards revitalising it. This could be the reason that *Ubuntu* was then adopted by the government of South Africa in 1997 as one of the principles that has to govern how social welfare services are provided to all people in the country (RSA, 1997:section 24).

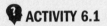**ACTIVITY 6.1**

1 Find the oldest person in your community and ask what he or she knows about *Ubuntu*.
2 Use what they have told you to map out where the principle of *Ubuntu* might have originated.

6.3 **What *Ubuntu* means**

The word *Ubuntu* is derived from the Southern African Nguni languages, mainly the Zulu and Xhosa groups, and means 'humanness' (Metz, 2014:6761). Kumalo (2017:23) states that the term *Ubuntu* is an isiZulu and isiXhosa word that means 'the positive attributes of being human, such as the sense of belonging, selflessness, hospitality, sharing, humility and respect'.

Marston (2015:424) states that 'the concept "*ubuntu*", a Nguni word, is found in many Southern African cultures and means that we are part of all humanity and we are who we are through our interconnectedness with others'. According to Nussbaum (2003:1), *Ubuntu* is 'a way of being, a code of ethics, deeply embedded in African culture'. She goes further to state that *Ubuntu* acknowledges, among other things, that 'your pain is my pain, my wealth is your wealth and your salvation is my salvation'. Nussbaum (2003:2) further states that the above definition is confirmed by the phrase '*Umuntu ngumuntu ngabantu*', meaning 'a person is a person because of others'. The word *Ubuntu* is known as *Botho* in Sesotho, Setswana and Sepedi, *Vhutu* in Tshivenda, *Bunhu* in Xitsonga and *Mensheid/Medemenslikheid* in Afrikaans

(Broodryk, 2006:23–24). This means that all the cultures in South Africa know what *Ubuntu* is, confirming its African origin.

According to Broodryk (2006), defining *Ubuntu* is not an easy task due to the different perspectives that exist on what it means, but he maintains that it originates from Africa. He describes *Ubuntu* as 'manifesting in group solidarity, mutual support, respect for human dignity, a de-emphasis on individualism, a culture of *esprit de corps* and the existence of a "we" feeling' (Broodryk, 2006:22). He further defined *Ubuntu* as a comprehensive African worldview based on the values of intense humanness, caring, sharing, respect and compassion, aimed at ensuring a happy community that lives in harmony.

From the above descriptions, we can see that the concept *Ubuntu* refers to the interconnectedness of human beings at all times, with its origins in Africa. This means that no human being can consider him or herself self-sufficient to survive in isolation. We need one another to survive, through sharing pain, joy and successes. To be a human being is to affirm one's humanity by recognising the humanity of others and establishing humane relations with them. As a result, we are forced to become human beings and continue to live our lives, making efforts to maintain humaneness in all interactions with our fellow human beings. People in a locality need to be aware of the benefits that they could get from being compassionate towards one another, such as sharing and living in harmony, and realising the need to respect and care for one another.

The individualistic manner in which community members live, surrounded by high security walls and not knowing their neighbours, is contrary to *Ubuntu*. This individualistic pattern can be traced back to the colonisation process that led to industrialisation, urbanisation and the migrant labour system. People found themselves leaving their communities where they lived as a unit and settling in foreign surroundings, surrounded by strangers. This led to a lack of trust; as a result, each person tries to protect him or herself and his or her household by erecting a security fence that would prevent an uninvited person from entering. The development of these highly secured homesteads results in neighbours not knowing one another and also not having any interest to get involved in what is going on in their neighbour's yard. This leads to people not caring for one another, to the extent that you look the other way when you see someone being attacked. We have developed the spirit of '*I do not want to get involved in other people's business*', which is entirely not what the African worldview stands for through the value of *Ubuntu*. In the African way of living, 'a child belongs to the community' and not to his or her parents, meaning that when an elderly person comes across the neighbour's child misbehaving, he or she does not have to hesitate to reprimand the child. Furthermore, when the parents learn about the incident, they will express gratitude instead of anger with the elderly person. This is how the mutual existence was lived by communities in past times, but is not the case in the present era.

In this era, each family cares about its own members only and does not care what happens in other families. The principle of 'it takes a village to raise a child' has been done away with. Elderly people in the community are no longer afforded the respect that was cherished by all community members. It is time and again reported in the media how our elderly persons are robbed of their pension money, some raped, and some murdered for the little grant money with which they are supposed to meet their basic needs. This clearly shows that the value of *Ubuntu* has been eroded. For the society to be restored to normalcy, *Ubuntu* as a value needs to be instilled from a young age, for every member to grow up knowing what it means to be human. This is in alignment with a decolonial agenda (see Chapter 2), since it requires a recovery of indigenous values and ways of life that were lost under colonial rule.

The issue of highly secured fences can also be linked to the high rate of crime in our society that forces people to try every means to protect themselves. This further disturbs the neighbourly arrangement where people would know one another in the neighbourhood and be one another's keeper. In adopting the value of *Ubuntu*, neighbours could form neighbourhood watch movements and ensure that they protect one another as a collective. The underlying value of *Ubuntu* is the development and maintenance of mutuality in relationships. *Ubuntu* embraces and requires justice, therefore it could be said to create a firm foundation for our common humanity. Nussbaum (2003:2) states that, according to Bishop Dandala:

> *... ubuntu is not a concept easily distilled into a methodological procedure. It is rather a bedrock of a specific lifestyle or culture that seeks to honor human relationships as primary in any social, communal or corporate activity.*

Ubuntu demands that human beings respect one another, as it embraces and requires justice. *Ubuntu* is said to be a worldview; a worldview is a broad thinking framework that groups of people use to make sense of the world. Adopting an *Ubuntu* worldview more than an individualist one could strengthen social justice and true community living.

Worldview, 'a coherent collection of concepts allowing us to construct a global image of the world, and in this way to understand as many elements of our experience as possible' (Vidal, 2008:3).

 **ACTIVITY 6.2**

1   In your own words, describe *Ubuntu* and apply its meaning to your everyday life.
2   Identify elements of *Ubuntu* that could make a difference in your own life and community as a whole.

6.3.1   *Ubuntu* as a foundation for practical mutual existence

I grew up in a village, where the community members knew one another, and mutual sharing was the order of the day. The community was closely knit and *Ubuntu/Botho* characterised the behaviour of community members towards one another. Most of the men in the community were migrant labourers, and the women remained at home raising the children and taking care of the households. During the men's absence from the community, women made all efforts to ensure that their children had meals by networking with one another. The households who had enough food would share with those who did not have, knowing that those who did not have would share with them once their food supply had arrived. This was possible because the men would send food supplies for their families at different times of the month according to their remuneration dates, resulting in all the community members having food throughout every month by sharing.

It was also common practice for the families to visit one another to check how everyone was doing. In cases when there were problems with one family, the whole community would come together to assist in every possible way. For example, if one family had a death case, one community member would bring maize meal, another would cook the meals and others would fetch water from the windmill reservoir. It was an easy task to eventually have the family comforted and have the departed one buried with the support of the community members. This *Ubuntu*-motivated communitarianism is in stark contrast to the trends of today, where we see a lot of competition and individualism.

These kinds of practices, which were commonplace, confirmed mutuality and perpetuated caring and sharing. It demonstrated that no-one is an island, but rather that a person is a person through other people. In many South African communities today, it is unheard of to see a neighbour visiting another neighbour with the aim of borrowing food portions or asking for assistance with any other matter. We live as individuals, behind our walls, not wanting to be bothered by uninvited guests. Perhaps this is because of the cost of living that is so high in our country. But, the high inflation and cost of living cannot justify the spirit of individualism that is observable amongst community members. Instead, community members need to rally behind one another to mitigate the effects of this situation by helping one another. We know that our country is currently plagued by high levels of unemployment and poverty, but still the sense of mutual existence and sharing does not seem to be cultivated amongst community members.

Reflective questions
- Consider patterns of interaction in your community. To what extent is *Ubuntu* practised in your community?
- Do you think *Ubuntu* as a way of life can be helpful in addressing the social challenges that we find in different communities?

6.3.2   Principles and values that guide *Ubuntu*

Let us now move to the unique principles that denote *Ubuntu* within the African worldview. According to Tshabalala (1991), in trying to demonstrate collective tendency among Africans, *Ubuntu* is said to be guided by the following values.

- *'The importance of family'*. The importance of a family in an African worldview is demonstrated by how the family as a unit tries to stick together. This can be observed when there are family issues such as the birth of a child with a disability. As seen in the study by Mathebane (2017), all the family members made it their business to assist the mother to cope. The family is brought together by such occurrences and uses its strengths as a unit to raise the child.

- *'The importance of the group'*. The principle of *Ubuntu* is guided by mutual co-existence, hence the saying amongst the African people that *motho ke motho ka batho ba bangwe* (a person is a person through other people). This emphasises the importance to a person of belonging to a group, because no person can exist and enjoy fulfilment in isolation. The humanness of a person can be understood only when in interaction with other people, not in isolation.

- *'Respect for elders'*. Respect for elders is one of the important values amongst the African people. While every person is valuable and valued under *Ubuntu*, older persons enjoy a special respect because of their age and their contribution to the life of the community over many years. Older persons are always respected because they are seen as sources of wisdom for the younger generations.

- *'Fear of God'*. People of African descent believe in a higher power, which people describe in different ways according to their beliefs. They believe that there is a higher power that governs their lives. In the study conducted by Mathebane (2017), it was clear that the African people have a strong fear of God. This was illustrated when a child with Down Syndrome was born. The whole clan felt that the child was a gift from God; therefore, the child could not be placed at a special school or be given up for adoption. They felt that God would punish them for doing that with the gift He has given to them. With this in mind, the whole clan focused all their energy on caring for the child.

- *'Deep commitment to sustaining meaningful community life through shared produce, problems and sorrows'*. Informed by *Ubuntu*, the community life of the African people is characterised by common sharing and mutual existence. Every community member has a responsibility to add value to the common benefit of the community as a whole, through participating in every activity that takes place within the community. If one family experiences a death case, all the community members come together to assist in the whole process until the loved one is buried. It is never a family affair, but always a community affair, guided by the spirit of *Ubuntu*.

In addition to these *Ubuntu* values formulated by Tshabalala, Nussbaum (2003:3) identified the following as the general principles of *Ubuntu*.

- *'Listening to and affirming others with the help of processes that create trust, fairness, shared understanding, dignity and harmony in relationships'*. When a community is governed by the spirit of *Ubuntu*, each member has time to listen to what the other member has to say. In this way, community members are able to develop trust in one another that leads to common understanding, respect and harmonious relationships. As a result, the community becomes able to lead a life of mutuality and sharing, without seeing this as a burden.

- *'The desire to build a caring, sustainable and just response to the community'*. Each member of a community that is characterised by *Ubuntu* is always concerned about the well-being of other community members. This then translates into a spirit of common caring for one another that leads to sustainable mutual coexistence. A community that lives by the spirit of *Ubuntu* is able to maintain social justice amongst its members, because of the level of caring and sharing that it maintains.

- *'Because of its emphasis on our common humanity … Ubuntu offers an alternative way to recreate a world that works for all, [characterised by] respect, compassion and dignity and justice'*, where resources are reorganised to be utilised by all. In a community that is characterised by *Ubuntu*, each member enjoys respect and harmonious relationships. Each community member is always aware of the fact that he or she has to share what he or she has for the common benefit of the community as a whole. The resources that are found in the community belong to all, without any member trying to get a bigger share at the expense of other members. The resources in our country are currently benefitting the few, and I believe if the government could strive towards reorganising this situation by adopting *Ubuntu*, we could see a better country that caters for the needs of all.

- *'Sharing wealth and making ... basic services ... accessible and visible to all'*. This value is directly linked to the macro level, where the government needs to seriously consider making services available to all the citizens of our country. Our country is rich in minerals, yet we see the majority of the citizens living in abject poverty. This could be linked to the unequal distribution of resources that began during the apartheid era, which is, to some extent, still the case in the democratic era.

Finally, Shonhiwa (2006:54–55) outlined the following as additional principles guiding *Ubuntu*.

- *'Consultation on all issues'*. It is a way of life amongst the African people to consult the elderly members in every decision that has to be taken. In cases where the elderly people within the family are unable to give answers, the higher being is consulted. This is done to demonstrate respect for the elderly, as well as recognising that one cannot exist in isolation. This assists in cases where the decision that was taken did not yield the expected results; everyone in the family assumes responsibility and the family bond becomes stronger.

- *'Desire for consensus on major problems'*. A community that is characterised by *Ubuntu* always tries to deliberate and reach consensus regarding every issue that affects its members. Members have a feeling of belonging that enables them to be part of the solutions that are geared towards improving community life. With the help of the community's elders, deliberations are conducted in a respectful manner to the satisfaction of all.

- *'Fair, honest and humane'*. Fairness is one of the values that can be observed in a community that has *Ubuntu* as one of its principles. Each member tries his or her best to interact with other members in a fair manner where mutual coexistence is always the goal. The elders also treat younger community members with fairness, without any discrimination. In such a community, social justice is the norm and enjoyed by all, not just by a segment of the community.

- *'Compassion ... politeness and dignity'*. With fairness comes compassion and dignity for all community members in a community that is guided by *Ubuntu*. All community members become mindful of one another's existence as members of a common group. As a result, they all make efforts to relate to one another with honesty, compassion, politeness and respect that foster dignity.

- *'Generosity and helpfulness'*. Generosity and helpfulness flow directly from the notion of belonging together and having the spirit of sharing and mutual existence. No community member is left to suffer alone; instead, other members make it their business to share what they have in an effort to help one another in times of need. A problem of one community member becomes a problem of the whole community when there is a spirit of *Ubuntu*.

- *'Self-respect, sincerity, goodwill and tolerance'*. With the spirit of self-respect, community members become sensitive towards one another because a self-respecting person will always behave in an acceptable manner towards his or her fellow human beings. This confirms the principle of *Ubuntu* that leads to guarding one's behaviour so that it does not affect other community members in a negative way.

These *Ubuntu* values and principles, presented by different authors, converge in regard to group cohesiveness, respect and mutual coexistence, which are all central to *Ubuntu*. The common factor in the principles and values that guide *Ubuntu*, as indicated by the above authors, is the notion of mutual existence and sharing of the resources among community members, regardless of their different backgrounds. This gives us an indication that *Ubuntu* should be the guiding principle in social work practice as it is guided by social justice and respect for all.

> **Reflective questions**
> - Identify the above principles in your community.
> - Identify the similarities and differences, if any, between the social work values and principles and the ones outlined above.
> - Do you know any person in your community who display the above principles and values? In your opinion, do these principles and values make their lives different from that of other community members?

6.4 Relevance of *Ubuntu* for decolonial social work practice

Social work practice in South Africa is based on the developmental approach, as you have seen in Chapter 3. Social work intervention is implemented at micro, mezzo and macro levels, where the social worker uses relevant skills and techniques at each level of intervention. The professional code of ethics applies to all methods of social work practice, therefore demanding from the social worker to always adhere to ethics as he or she interacts with clients, irrespective of the field of practice. As we have seen earlier in the chapter, *Ubuntu* has been eroded by the colonisation of South Africa as a country. As a result, social work training and practice has been guided by Eurocentric philosophies and theories, with no written material on *Ubuntu* in the field of social work. In an effort to decolonise the way social work has been practised all along (see Chapter 2 on decolonisation), this chapter is included with other chapters on the different social work theories.

The #FeesMustFall movement highlighted that the social work curriculum was not assisting social workers to address the needs of the indigenous people. A need was thus identified to develop social work theories that are both responsive to the needs of African people and informed by their experiences and values. The efforts to decolonise the social work curriculum began with the decoloniality workshops organised by the Association of South African Social Work Education Institutions (ASASWEI) in 2016. It was in these workshops that *Ubuntu* was identified by the participants as one of the important philosophies that could be adopted in social work to ensure that client systems are provided with social work services that meet their actual needs (ASASWEI, 2017). By adopting *Ubuntu*, social work practice could be transformed to enable social workers to effectively play their advocacy role to the benefit of their client systems, especially in the reorganisation and redistribution of resources.

Case study 1 at the beginning of this chapter talks about mothers who do not have resources to ensure that their children do not develop malnutrition and who now need assistance from the social worker. Using the principles and values that guide the practice of *Ubuntu* outlined in section 6.3.2, it is important to realise that the social worker cannot provide meaningful intervention without respecting the clients. Let us now address the intervention at individual and community levels.

6.4.1 Using *Ubuntu* in social work with individuals

As we have already established, *Ubuntu* refers to mutual coexistence and compassion towards one another. In this regard, the social worker has the responsibility to interact with the clients in the same way as he or she would like to be treated, guided by the professional code of ethics. In interacting with the individual mothers whose children have been admitted to hospital for the treatment of severe malnutrition, the *Ubuntu*-informed social worker begins by respecting them. This respect will facilitate the establishment of the helping relationship that is so important in the social work intervention process. Respect also leads to the development of trust between the social worker and the client, where the client will feel comfortable to share his or her situation without fear of being judged by the social worker. In this instance, the social worker needs to assess the family circumstances of each mother so that all the factors that led to the current situation could be unearthed. In this manner, the professional value of individualisation will be observed by the social worker.

Following assessment, the social worker needs to involve the mother in the establishment of an intervention strategy that will be responsive to the needs of her family, as it was established above that family is central in the implementation of *Ubuntu*. The social worker needs to listen carefully and make efforts to affirm the mother by communicating fairness and dignity throughout the intervention process. The social worker also needs to establish the belief system of the client and ensure that it is respected throughout. If, for example, the mother believes in a higher power, this must be fully respected, even if the social worker does not share the mother's belief, as the mother's belief will affect how she interprets her situation.

All the social work skills and techniques should be employed in the process of assisting the mother to emerge as an empowered person after the intervention process. The mother should be linked with resources that have been identified in the community, as well as those that will be developed together with the community after the need has been identified.

The social worker is expected to provide emotional counselling for the mother to support her as she deals with having a child admitted to hospital. The other family members should be assessed with regard to their emotional situation and then provided with the necessary support. Family therapy could be used to ensure that the challenges the family is faced with do not disturb its normal functioning.

The social worker can educate members of the multidisciplinary team about the realities that the mothers of children suffering from severe malnutrition are facing. This is necessary to dispel the misconception that some of the team members might have, thinking that the children developed severe malnutrition due to neglect. This is particularly needed in South Africa in this era, as we are aware of the high levels of poverty and unemployment that affect many families negatively. It might be that some of the team members, who are not exposed to people who are faced with poverty, may conclude that the child developed severe malnutrition due to neglect by the mother. Team members should be made aware of the fact that the Child Support Grant that is available to unemployed mothers is helpful but not sufficient to meet all the needs of the developing child.

Locating personal challenges in community context

The social worker in Case study 1 visited the mother in the ward after receiving the referral from the doctor.

Good morning, Lebo's mother.

Good morning, Ma'am.

Can we go to my office for us to have a relaxed conversation in privacy?

Okay, Ma'am, we can go. We are lucky Lebo is now asleep.

(Interview continues in the social worker's office.)

How are you feeling now that you are in the hospital with Lebo?

Hey, Ma'am, it is tough. My other children at home do not have anyone to take care of them. I wish I could be in two pieces, for one piece to be here with Lebo and the other at home.

I realise that it is not easy for you in this situation. Is there no one in your neighbourhood whom we could approach to assist with the children at home?

Hey! I never thought about it that way. People are just concerned with their own business.

Can you please explain what you mean by this, for me to have a better understanding?

In the above conversation, the social worker ensured that the interview takes place in a private space with the aim of maintaining the confidentiality of the patient. The social worker is aiming at assisting the client to explore her environment in order to identify the resources that might be there in her community. Guided by the principle of *Ubuntu*, the social worker is using mutual existence and caring to assist the client to carefully come up with a solution that could alleviate her current distress regarding her children who are left at home without any adult supervision. With our country plagued by the phenomenon of fatherless families, it would be beneficial if the mothers who are raising their children alone are provided with comprehensive social work services that would help them to become self-reliant. The need to inculcate the spirit of mutual sharing could assist in this regard.

6.4.2   Using *Ubuntu* in social work with communities

At community level, the social worker should use community work skills and techniques to address the challenges that are identified. In accordance with the principles and values guiding *Ubuntu*, the social worker needs to have the desire to build a caring, sustainable and just response for the benefit of all community members. The strengths of the community will be identified and utilised to minimise the weaknesses. Chapter 13 gives you a detailed discussion on community development using the ABCD approach, which is well-aligned with the principles of *Ubuntu*. The social worker also needs to mobilise the community members to realise the importance of adopting the principle of *Ubuntu*.

Regarding Case study 1, the social worker could use the assessment to identify the available resources during the appreciative inquiry meetings and then assist the community members to come up with possible solutions in order of their priority. The social worker should not dictate any solution to the community but should be guided by *Ubuntu* values like common humanity, respect, compassion and dignity, and the desire to seek consensus on major problems among community members. All these efforts are geared towards reorganising and developing resources for the benefit of all community members.

The mothers of children with severe malnutrition can be motivated to be actively involved in community projects that could assist them in alleviating the challenges that they are facing. Community members who have enough could be encouraged to contribute towards developmental projects, specifically the community vegetable garden that could be cultivated in the community. Sponsorships, through a community committee, could be attracted with the help of the social worker in writing the proposals. In this way, the social worker is fostering *Ubuntu* principles of mutuality, the group, sharing, caring and co-operation.

Taking into consideration the burden of HIV infection in the country, where many mothers have left their children in the care of grandmothers, the social worker could organise these grandmothers to empower them to belong to neighbourhood groups that work towards supporting one another. This is already observable in many communities, but, with the professional guidance of the social worker, this mutual sharing and care could be strengthened as an expression of *Ubuntu*. By going this route, the community members could be empowered and developed for the benefit of the coming generations.

While all these activities may sound like ordinary community development, drawing on literature from the Global North, they can become an expression of deeply African ways of working. As mentioned, *Ubuntu* emphasises mutual coexistence and compassion. Working explicitly within the value framework of *Ubuntu*, the social worker not only implements a good community development process, but he or she also works to revitalise a fundamental African value system in the community, contributing at a local level to an African renaissance. By facilitating the recovery of traditional African values, which were undermined and often lost under colonial rule, the social worker is conducting decolonial social work practice that decentres dominant colonial ways of engaging at community level.

ACTIVITY 6.3

Using the *Ubuntu* principles covered in section 6.3.2, do a thorough exploration of your own community, or the community where you are doing your field practice, to identify the pressing needs and then map out how you would go about engaging the community to address those needs. Be deliberate in choosing to adopt an *Ubuntu* lens for your work, both in understanding the community and in shaping your work in the community.

6.5 Conclusion

Ubuntu is a way of life of the African people that was disrupted by colonisation. Colonisation led to the abandonment of humanness and caring that characterised African communities, which was replaced by individualism and isolation. Community members find themselves in a world characterised by everyone minding his or her own business without being bothered by what is happening in the life of his or her neighbour. Social work intervention could benefit clients more if the principles and values that underpin *Ubuntu* could be adopted and applied. Communities need to be reminded of the peace and mutual coexistence that they enjoyed before the colonial system eroded the spirit of *Ubuntu*. The principles of the ABCD approach (Chapter 13), in particular, could assist social workers in this regard.

Chapter activity

1. **Reflective question**. Now that you have established what *Ubuntu* stands for, its origin, and principles and values, think about the community that you grew up in. Do you think you observe some of these principles in your everyday life? If so, how do you think they help you to cope with the demands brought upon you by your interactions with your social environment? If not, why do you think these principles are no longer part of your everyday life?
2. **Personal context**. Identify the principles and values that are commonly held by the members of your community of origin or your current community, and link them to those discussed in this chapter. Do you think your community is living in harmony? Substantiate your response by indicating the possible underlying causes of the situation in your community.
3. **Advocacy**. Identify one social challenge that is common in your community. Use the *Ubuntu* approach to suggest possible intervention strategies at individual and community levels to deal with this social challenge.
4. **Critical question**. It has been established in this chapter that colonisation interferes with the practice of *Ubuntu* amongst indigenous Africans. Think broadly about the different communities that you have observed in real life and figure out how the colonisation process might have affected their practice of *Ubuntu*.

References

ASASWEI. 2017. *Decolonising social work education in South Africa: A report emerging from a series of workshops held in September 2016.* Johannesburg, RSA: Association of South African Social Work Education Institutions.

Broodryk, J. 2006. *Ubuntu: Life coping skills from Africa.* Randburg: Knowres Publishers.

Broodryk, J. 2009. *Understanding South Africa: The uBuntu way of living.* Waterkloof: Publiself Publishers.

Kumalo, RS: 'The challenging landscape of South Africa and implications for practicing Ubuntu'. *In*: Dreyer, J, Dreyer, Y, Foley, E & Nel, M (eds.). 2017. *Practicing ubuntu: Practical theological perspectives on injustice, personhood and human dignity.* pp. 22–33. Zürich: Deutsche Nationalbibliothek.

Lundin, S & Nelson, B. 2010. *Ubuntu: An inspiring story about an African tradition of teamwork and collaboration.* New York: Random House, Inc.

Marston, JM. 2015. The spirit of "Ubuntu" in children's palliative care. *Journal of Pain and Symptom Management,* 50(3):424–427.

Mathebane, MS. 2017. *Towards indigenous social work practice guidelines for assisting African families raising children with Down Syndrome.* Unpublished PhD thesis. University of South Africa, Pretoria.

Metz, T: 'Ubuntu: The good life'. *In*: Michalos, AC (ed.). 2014. *Encyclopedia of quality of life and well being research.* pp. 6761–6765. Dordrecht, Netherlands: Springer.

Ndlovu, PM. 2016. *Discovering the spirit of Ubuntu leadership: Compassion, community and respect.* Houndmills, UK: Palgrave Macmillan.

Nussbaum, B. 2003. African culture and *Ubuntu*: Reflections of a South African in America. *Perspectives,* 17(1):1–12.

Republic of South Africa. 1997. *White Paper for Social Welfare.* Pretoria: Government Printer.

Shonhiwa, S. 2006. *The effective cross-cultural manager: A guide for business leaders in Africa.* Cape Town, RSA: Struik.

Tellinger, M. 2013. *UBUNTU Contributionism: A blueprint for human prosperity.* Waterval Boven: Zulu Planet Publishers.

Tshabalala, M. (1991). Kinship networks: An analysis on the use of kinship systems for promotion of mental health among the Nguni. *Social Work/Maatskaplike Werk,* 22(2):72–79.

Vidal, C: 'Wat is een wêreldbeeld?' [What is a worldview?]. *In*: Van Belle, H & Van der Veken, J (eds.). 2008. *De wetenschappen en het creatieve aspect van de werkelijkheid [The sciences and the creative aspect of reality].* pp. 71–85. Leuven: Acco.

Annotated websites and activities

http://www.newworldencyclopedia.org/entry/Ubuntu_(philosophy)
This website contains detailed descriptions of what the word *Ubuntu* means, Samkange's explanation of *Ubuntu*, and Western Humanism.

Read through this article to broaden your understanding of what *Ubuntu* means and how it can assist in affecting the social ills that we are confronted with in South Africa. Think about your own community of origin and try to identify areas where the application of *Ubuntu* can bring a positive change.

http://www.youtube.com/watch?v=ODQ4WiDsEBQ
This YouTube link takes you to the conversation that former President Nelson Mandela had with Tim Modise about *Ubuntu*.

Take time to watch this video for you to understand how *Ubuntu* impacted the lives of community members in the past. Observe your interactions with your close friends and begin to consciously implement the principles and values of *Ubuntu;* then observe if there are any changes, record them and share them with your classmates.

https://www.virgin.com/virgin-unite/business-innovation/how-ubuntu-philosophy-can-have-positive-impact-your-business
This link takes you to an article by Keith Bete on how the principle of *Ubuntu* could be used to instill 'Oneness' as a principle that could change how a business is run.

Think of your interaction with the service providers in your area and analyse how they run their businesses in relation to other human beings. Use your imagination to think about what would happen if all businesses were run based on the principle of *Ubuntu*. Do you think community members would benefit from such a situation? Have a discussion with your classmates on this matter.

Annotated websites and activities are also available on Learning Zone.

oxford.co.za/learningzone

Resilience

Adrian van Breda

Case Study 1 — Orphans and vulnerable children

You are a social worker employed by the Department of Social Development in a rural community. During your first weeks in this community, while negotiating entry into the community and doing your community profile, you realise that there are numerous orphans and vulnerable children (OVCs). As you listen to community members and the OVCs themselves, you realise that there is a tremendous sense of hopelessness about these many children and their vulnerability. You also start to feel helpless. You ask yourself, 'What can I do to make a difference here? Did my social work training teach me anything of use?'

Remembering learning about resilience theory, you decide to see if this might be useful. Resilience theory says we should look at people who have better-than-expected outcomes, so you decide to find those OVCs who are doing better than other OVCs. You locate teachers, pastors, community leaders, older women and some young adults who used to be OVCs. They point you to some OVCs who seem to be 'doing quite well', despite their vulnerability. You go to interview them, asking them about the difficulties they have faced as an OVC, and also about what they think helped them to 'grow up well' despite these difficulties. You start to feel hopeful about being able to do something of value for all the OVCs in this community.

Reflective questions
- What might 'doing well' look like in this community?
- What might these OVCs have told you that gives you hope?
- What might you do with what you heard from them to help other OVCs?

7.1   Introduction

Social work is concerned with problems in human life – problems in individuals, families, groups, communities, organisations and society. We are often confronted with the most tragic and stubborn of social problems – poverty, unemployment, crime, child abuse, gender-based violence and substance abuse. With such a heavy focus on the problems of society, it is easy for social workers to become obsessed with these problems and overwhelmed by their enormity. This can lead to social workers developing a cynical outlook on their work, and even to burnout.

Resilience theory offers an alternative way of viewing social problems. While recognising that the challenges of human life do indeed have negative consequences for society, resilience theory also recognises that these consequences are not inevitable.

There are times that people do not succumb to life's challenges. Even in the worst circumstances, people often get on with life and even thrive. Resilience theory is keen to understand what enables that to happen.

This chapter provides the conceptual building blocks and theoretical framework to understand how people cope with and recover from adversity. It lays a foundation for the strengths-based practices that are addressed in Chapter 13. It starts by mapping out two approaches to thinking and practice in social work: the pathogenic and salutogenic approaches. We then explore three important aspects of resilience theory: the three components of resilience theory; definitions of resilience; and the distinction between individualised and ecological approaches to resilience theory (the latter links back to Chapter 5 on ecosystems theory). Finally, we reflect critically on the relevance of resilience theory for a decolonial approach to social work in South Africa.

7.2   Two approaches to social work thinking and practice

Resilience theory invites us as social workers to turn the mirror on ourselves and question how we make sense of the world around us. This is not so much about theory, as it is about perspectives or paradigms. Our perspective on the world underlies how we think about things and thus how we act or practise (see Chapter 1 for a discussion on 'perspectives'). Perspectives are often unconscious – they are based on assumptions about how the world is. We take our perspectives for granted, and so we don't question them. Resilience theory, however, asks us to question these taken-for-granted perspectives.

Back in the 1970s, Aaron Antonovsky (1979) began to ask these questions. He was a health sociologist who worked in Israel. In his classic book *Health, stress and coping* he coined the terms 'pathogenic' and 'salutogenic' to help us think about how we make sense of the world. While this work is quite old, it is still used extensively in many disciplines today (e.g., Mittelmark & Bauer, 2017).

7.2.1   Pathogenic approach

The pathogenic approach to thinking about health and social issues is focused on the problem and its origin. The word 'pathogenesis' has two parts – 'patho' meaning illness and 'genesis' meaning the origins of (Antonovsky, 1979). Thus, the pathogenic approach is interested in the origins of illness. In social work terms, the pathogenic approach is interested in the origins of social problems.

> **Pathogenesis**, the origins of illness, or more broadly, the origins of problems. This is an approach to the social sciences that is focused extensively on people's problems – what causes them and what negative impact they have on people.

Social workers with a pathogenic perspective are very focused on social problems. Fundamentally, they believe that there should not be any problems in the world – they see problems as abnormal and wrong. So, when there are problems, this causes them great concern. They tend to divide the world into two groups – those who have social problems and those who don't. (Of course, they find that most people do have social problems.) These social workers are really interested to understand what causes these social problems, and consequently investigate the personal history and social dynamics that result in these problems. They believe that if they can get rid of these causes, the problems will go away. They are thus interested in risk factors and how to reduce risk.

Social work training inadvertently fosters a pathogenic approach, by heavily emphasising social problems. For example, your lecturers teach you about poverty, crime and violence. They teach you theories to help you make sense of these problems at a macro level: conflict; functional; and critical theories. They teach you to assess these problems: taking client histories; understanding the pathways that lead to problems; and assessing problems in their social context. They require you to develop intervention plans that are designed to eliminate people's problems. They ask you to evaluate your interventions in relation to how well you have resolved people's problems. In short, there is much in social work training that fosters a pathogenic perspective, by overemphasising social problems (Weick & Saleebey, 1995; Van Breda, 2001).

The pathogenic approach is problematic. In reality, the world is full of problems. Problems are the norm, not the exception. What is surprising is not that there are problems, but that people get on with life despite their problems! The world is not divided into two distinct groups – rather there is a continuum of having more or fewer problems. Identifying the causes of people's problems, while important in facilitating understanding of their problems, often does not lead us to a solution to their problems. Thus, a different approach is needed.

Reflective questions
Look back at Case study 1 and then answer the following questions:
- If you were using a pathogenic approach to work with the OVCs in this community, what kinds of questions would you be asking?
- The pathogenic approach might lead you to speak more to adults about the OVCs, than to the OVCs themselves. Do you agree with this statement? Why or why not?

7.2.2 Salutogenic approach

The salutogenic approach to social work thinking and practice invites us to focus on psycho-social functioning and well-being. The word 'salutogenesis' has two parts – 'saluto' meaning health and 'genesis' meaning the origins of (Antonovsky, 1979). Thus, the salutogenic approach is interested in the origins of health. In South Africa, Strümpfer (1995) coined the term 'fortigenesis', meaning the origins of strength, to make salutogenesis more relevant to psychologists. But the term 'salutogenesis' remains widely used in disciplines like psychology, nursing and social work (Mittelmark & Bauer, 2017).

> **Salutogenesis**, the origins of health, or more broadly the origins of well-being or psychosocial functioning. This is an approach to the social sciences that is focused extensively on people's well-being or health – what causes it and what enables people to flourish despite adversity.

Fundamentally, the salutogenic approach invites us to ask a different question. Whereas the pathogenic paradigm asks 'Why do people develop social problems?', the salutogenic paradigm asks 'Why, when people are exposed to the same stress which causes some to develop problems, do some maintain psychosocial well-being?' (Van Breda, 2018). We call this the salutogenic question. Hlungwani (2017), for example, was interested in the experiences of young women's transition out of residential care into young adulthood. Much of the research on this topic asks pathogenic questions about the poor outcomes of this group (e.g., unemployment, unplanned pregnancies, dropping out of education). Instead, Hlungwani asked a salutogenic question, viz. 'What are the social processes that facilitate resilience as female care leavers journey towards successful independent living?' (Hlungwani, 2017:8). She found, for example, that faith in God was important in enabling these young women to successfully transition out of care towards young adulthood.

The salutogenic approach does not require us to abandon a focus on social problems. These problems are very real and require our attention. However, it does invite us to expand our focus from only problems and their causes to psychosocial functioning and its enablers.

In summary, a salutogenic approach in social work has three main implications (Mittelmark & Bauer, 2017):

1. Instead of categorising people as having or not having social problems, we view people on a continuum from many problems to few problems. In truth, we all have at least some problems. But some have more problems than others. What we strive for in social work is to reduce the number and severity of people's problems.
2. Instead of focusing only on risk, we are also particularly interested in what enables people to function well and thrive in the face of life's difficulties, and to rise above and change their difficulties.
3. Instead of focusing on the problematic individual, we are concerned for groups of people and aim to make changes in the social environment. We also work not only with the problems that people have, but with the whole person, since people are not defined by their problems.

Reflective questions

Look back at Case study 1 and then answer the following questions:

- Formulate a salutogenic question that is relevant to the case study (much as Hlungwani did for women leaving care).
- If you were using a salutogenic approach to work with the OVCs in this community, what kinds of questions would you be asking?
- The salutogenic approach might lead you to speak less to adults about the OVCs, and more to the OVCs themselves. Do you agree with this statement? Why or why not?

Assessing the client

 My lecturer taught me that I must assess my clients' problems: what's bothering them; when it started; how it's negatively affected their lives; and why it is continuing. She said that having a thorough understanding of clients' problems is essential to developing an intervention plan for my clients.

 That's weird! My lecturer taught me that I must assess my clients' strengths: what abilities and resources they have to draw on; how they have overcome problems in the past; and what they've tried to do to solve this problem. He said that having a thorough understanding of clients' strengths is essential to developing an intervention plan for them.

 How can two lecturers teach us such different things about doing assessments? That's crazy!

 I agree. But I remember one of my other lecturers saying that we should assess the person, rather than their problem. She said that our clients are people first – people who have both problems and strengths.

 I like that! Maybe if we focused on assessing the whole person, we'd get to know them much better, including their problems and strengths, and that might help us develop an even better intervention plan specifically for them.

 Yes, I like that too. If I was your client, I'd really like you to get to know me as a person. Sure, I have some problems, but that's not the whole story of who I am. I'm more than just my problems.

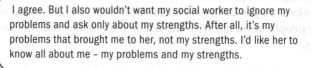 I agree. But I also wouldn't want my social worker to ignore my problems and ask only about my strengths. After all, it's my problems that brought me to her, not my strengths. I'd like her to know all about me – my problems and my strengths.

7.3 Conceptual building blocks of resilience theory

Resilience theory emerged from studies of vulnerability. These studies found that higher levels of adversity lead to negative outcomes. In other words, the more bad things you've experienced, the less well you'll be doing today. But researchers began to recognise that this was not always true – some people who experienced bad things recovered and were now doing okay. This prompted the salutogenic question: What enabled these people to do better, when others were doing worse? The answer to this question is protective factors – the factors that protect us when we go through hard times. Thus, resilience theory has three building blocks: adversity; outcomes; and protective factors.

> **Resilience**, 'the multilevel processes that systems engage in to obtain better-than-expected outcomes in the face or wake of adversity' (Van Breda, 2018a:4)

7.3.1 Adversity

Life is full of difficulties. We live in a country with high levels of unemployment, poverty and inequality. The equitable availability of quality education and health services remains a challenge. Health issues like HIV and tuberculosis continue to impact negatively on people's lives. And we face extraordinarily high levels of gender-based violence and crime. These issues impact not only on society, but also on communities, groups, families and individuals. We can call all of these challenges 'adversities'. Collectively, adversities make people 'vulnerable' to psychosocial problems like depression and anxiety, poor academic performance, substance abuse and criminal activities. Consequently, some people refer to these difficulties as 'risks', because they increase people's risk of developing other social problems.

> **Adversity**, life events that are statistically associated with maladjustment or negative outcomes (Luthar et al., 2015). Adversity can be broadly divided into single-incident traumas, such as a car accident or rape, and chronic adversity, such as poverty or long-term political conflict (Bonanno & Diminich, 2013).

For many years, researchers studying adversity have made use of the Social Readjustment Rating Scale (Holmes & Rahe, 1967). This scale measures a set of 43 life events, each of which is weighted according to how severely each event is judged to impact one's health and well-being. The most impactful event is 'death of spouse', which has a weight of 100, followed by 'divorce' (at 73). Death of a close family member is fifth with a weight of 63 and getting married is seventh with a weight of 50. The weights of all the events that happened to you over the past year add up to your level of vulnerability.

A contemporary way of measuring adversity that has become increasingly popular in recent years is called 'adverse childhood experiences' or ACEs. This term was coined in a massive study conducted in the USA from 1995 to 1997, which found that the more bad experiences adults had had as children, the greater chances they later have of falling ill or engaging in risk behaviour, for example, alcohol or drug abuse, depression, suicidal thoughts and multiple sex partners (Felitti et al., 1998). There are now several questionnaires available to measure ACEs, such as the Adverse Childhood Experiences International Questionnaire (ACE-IQ), developed by the World Health Organization, which has been revised for use in South African township communities (Quinn et al., 2018). The ACE-IQ measures a variety of experiences such as abuse, witnessing community violence, family dysfunction and peer violence.

7.3.2 Outcomes

Outcomes refer broadly to how well a person is doing at present. In vulnerability studies, outcomes are typically defined negatively, e.g., mental health problems, academic failure or dropping out, illness, criminal involvement and death. In resilience studies, outcomes are often defined as the absence of negative outcomes, e.g., no mental health problems or the absence of significant illness. But other resilience studies define outcomes positively, as the presence of something desirable, e.g., academic persistence and progress, well-being and positive relationships with others. Most commonly, outcomes relate to age-appropriate development and the absence of psychopathology (Masten, 2015).

Vulnerability studies have repeatedly demonstrated that higher levels of adversity in the past (or present) are associated with poorer outcomes. For example, a recent study of university students in Johannesburg found that higher levels of adversity during the students' first year were associated with poorer academic performance and lower satisfaction with life a year or two later (Van Breda, 2017b). A similar study with social work students in Johannesburg found also that greater adversity over their lives to date was associated with failing more modules in their social work studies (Van Breda, 2013).

Resilience studies, while recognising and agreeing with the results of vulnerability studies, point out that these results are not true for all participants. Thus, for example, Van Breda (2017a) has shown that while, in general, higher adversity is associated with poorer outcomes among university students, there are many students who do well despite their vulnerability. Qualitative research is often better at identifying these exceptions. For example, Dykes (2016) found that student social workers in Cape Town reported how their experiences of adverse childhood events contributed to personal growth and how they wove these experiences into their development as social workers.

> **Positive outcomes**, 'adjustment that is much better than what would be expected, given exposure to the risk condition under study' (Luthar et al., 2015:2).

The selection of outcomes is a controversial issue in both vulnerability and resilience research. Who, for example, decides what outcomes are important? And who decides whether an outcome is a good or a bad one? And what are the cultural considerations for the outcomes? For example, in some cultures, leaving the family and establishing your own home with no parental interference is considered a good outcome, while in other cultures, staying at home with one's parents or maintaining close connections with one's parents is considered a good outcome. Many would argue that for teenagers, having prosocial peers who are not part of a gang is a good outcome, but in violent communities, being part of a gang may be seen as a positive outcome, providing a sense of belonging, learning skills and acquiring social status (Ungar, 2004). Outcomes, it seems, are subjective, value-based judgements, and can vary from context to context.

7.3.3 Protective factors

Having recognised that adversity does not inevitably lead to negative outcomes, resilience theory prompts us to ask the salutogenic question: In the face of the same adversity, what factors enable some people to recover or do well, when others are negatively impacted? These factors are called protective factors, because they protect people from the negative effects of adversity; they are also called mediating processes, because they mediate the relationship between adversity and negative outcomes. Over the years, researchers and theorists have identified various protective factors that enable people to withstand adversity, including sense of coherence, hardiness, learned resourcefulness, self-efficacy and locus of control (Van Breda, 2001). The hope of researchers is to identify a 'magic key' that can be passed on to others so that they can become stronger in the face of adversity.

> **Protective factors**, 'modify the effects of [adversity on outcomes] in a positive direction' (Luthar et al., 2015:4).

For example, Van Breda's (2017a) study of university students referred to above found that, among highly vulnerable students, stronger community relationships and higher levels of family financial security contributed to their life satisfaction, while a positive orientation to learning contributed to their academic progress. Warm family relationships also emerged as an important protective factor for both academic progress and life satisfaction. These findings can have important implications for the provision of support services to vulnerable university students. For example, they imply that it is important to foster positive and continuous relationships between students and their home community during their studies.

Seminal resilience researcher Ann Masten (2015:148) has reviewed decades of research from many countries on the resilience of children experiencing adversity and generated a 'short list' of protective factors. These include: relationships (with family, other caring adults and romantic partners); intelligence; problem-solving skills; self-control and emotional regulation; motivation to succeed; self-efficacy; faith and hope; and effective schools and communities. She argues that, regardless of the nature of the adversity children experience, these factors appear to be the most consistently important to help children recover after adversity.

 ACTIVITY 7.1

Analyse an adversity that is relevant in your own life or in the life of the people in your family or community using the following guidelines:
- Make brief notes about the adversity – what it is, what caused it, what makes it continue, what contextual factors are associated with it.
- Make brief notes on the negative outcomes that can result or have resulted from the adversity. In other words, how has that adversity harmed you or other people?
- Identify someone who seems to be doing better than the negative outcomes you've just described. Perhaps you are that person. Or, if you can't think of someone, imagine someone who is doing better than others. Write brief notes on his or her better-than-expected outcomes.
- Now think about what protective factors or mediating processes might be present in the life of this last person that helped him or her to achieve these better-than-expected outcomes.

7.4 Definitions of resilience

So far, this chapter has laid the foundation of thinking about resilience. We've looked at two main approaches to thinking about people and their problems, and we've unpacked the main building blocks of resilience theory. This section now pulls these thoughts together into the definition of resilience.

There are no universally accepted definitions of resilience. There is among theorists and researchers, across a wide range of disciplines (e.g., psychology, social work, education, political studies, engineering), much debate still about how to define resilience. Here we will look at three definitions.

Ann Masten is a Professor of educational psychology in the USA. She is one of the pre-eminent resilience scientists whose work has been very influential in resilience theory and research, especially in psychology and also in social work. Her thinking about resilience has matured over the years, and her definition is widely used today. She defines resilience as:

> ... [t]he capacity of a dynamic system to adapt successfully to disturbances that threaten system function, viability, or development (Masten, 2015:10).

A few comments about this definition:

- Masten refers to the resilience of 'a dynamic system' because she wants her definition to be applicable not only to an individual, but also to other kinds of systems such as body organs, families, organisations, forests and computers. In other words, her definition of resilience can be scaled across a system of any size, from extremely small to very large, and is applicable not only to humans, but also to non-human systems.
- She focuses on resilience as the 'capacity ... to adapt'. There is a tension in resilience theory between resilience as outcome and resilience as process (Olsson et al., 2003). The outcome definition of resilience focuses on the outcome after going through a period of adversity. Rutter (2012:335), for example, writes, '[r]esilience is an inference based on evidence that some individuals have a better outcome than others who have experienced a comparable level of adversity'. Masten, by contrast, emphasises the process definition of resilience, which focuses on what enables people to adapt successfully.

Michael Ungar is a Professor of social work in Canada. He has become one of the leading scholars in resilience research over the past decade or two. He has a particular interest in the social ecologies of resilience (which we'll discuss in section 7.5.2). He has led large multinational research projects on resilience, including in South Africa. He defines resilience as follows:

> Where there is potential for exposure to significant adversity, resilience is both the capacity of individuals to navigate their way to the psychological, social, cultural, and physical resources that build and sustain their well-being, and their individual and collective capacity to negotiate for these resources to be provided and experienced in culturally meaningful ways (Ungar, 2012:17).

A few comments about Ungar's definition:

- In contrast to Masten, Ungar focuses on the resilience of individuals. His definition cannot be transferred to larger systems or non-human systems.
- Like Masten, he focuses on resilience as a process: 'the capacity of individuals'.
- What is most distinctive about Ungar's definition is his emphasis on the role of the social environment in the resilience of individuals. This is particularly evident in the second part of his definition, where he constructs resilience as a negotiation between people and their environment.

- Ungar also gives significant attention to cultural issues in resilience, recognising that protective factors are not universal, but rather are influenced and shaped by culture.

Adrian van Breda is a Professor of social work in South Africa. He has been researching the resilience of young people, families and organisations for over 20 years, and has worked to promote a social work construction of resilience (Van Breda, 2016). He has defined resilience as follows:

> *The multilevel processes that systems engage in to obtain better-than-expected outcomes in the face or wake of adversity* (Van Breda, 2018a:4).

A few comments about Van Breda's definition:

- Like both Masten and Ungar, he adopts a process definition of resilience, but instead of using the word 'capacity', which emphasises internal attributes of systems (what we are and what we have), he uses the phrase 'processes that systems engage in' to emphasise activities – what systems do. Thus, resilience becomes a verb (a doing word) rather than an adjective (a describing word).
- While Masten's use of 'adapt successfully' seems too normative (i.e., she makes her own judgement about what constitutes successful adaptation), Van Breda's definition uses a more relative definition of outcomes, viz. 'better-than-expected'. This allows us to consider what constitutes a positive outcome within a specific context or community, rather than imposing an external (colonial) judgement of success.
- His definition considers the challenges of living in the Global South, with its rolling inequality and violence. Thus, he speaks of resilience being not only about recovering from a time-limited adversity (such as the death of a loved one or an experience of abuse), using the phrase 'in the wake of adversity', but also about resilience being about coping with or withstanding adversity that is chronic (such as intergenerational poverty or structural racism), using the phrase 'in the face of adversity'.

For Van Breda, resilience can thus be thought of as the protective factors (or mediating processes) that enable people to obtain better-than-expected outcomes during or after adverse conditions. This is summarised in Figure 7.1.

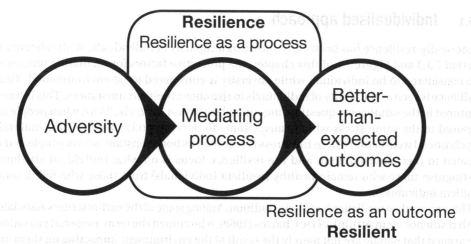

Figure 7.1: Resilience as process and outcome
Source: *Van Breda*, 2018a:4

> **⚓ ACTIVITY 7.2**
>
> 'Resilience' is quite an obscure word. It comes from the Latin word *resilire*, meaning to jump back, to recoil or rebound. In English, we might use 'the ability to bounce back' as a metaphor for resilience. (People don't literally 'bounce', do they?) It conveys the idea of being knocked down by life's challenges, and then getting back up on your feet again – 'bouncing back'.
>
> 1 Is there a word for resilience in your home language? If there is not a single word, is there a short phrase or metaphor that captures the concept of resilience? Make a note of that word/phrase in the margin of this page.
> 2 What is the difference between (a) being knocked down by hard times and getting back up again, and (b) being able to stand firm during hard times? If (a) is termed 'resilience', what word could we use for (b)?
> 3 Considering the three definitions of resilience above, try to formulate your own definition of resilience, in your home language, using terms that will be familiar to your friends and family. Write your definition in the margin of this page.

7.5 Individualised versus ecological approaches to resilience

Having considered a few definitions of resilience, it may be helpful for us to consider some of the critical developments in resilience theory in recent years. One of the key critiques has been that resilience theory has been overly individualised in its thinking, focusing almost exclusively on what individuals do in the face of environmental adversity. This has been critiqued by some social workers who advance an ecological approach to resilience theory and by those who are concerned about the impact of neoliberal policy on social welfare. While there have been significant strides to address the individualisation of resilience, this remains an ongoing point of debate in this field. It is important that we, who read, use and produce resilience literature, be aware of and sensitive to this debate.

7.5.1 Individualised approach

Historically, resilience has been constructed as a capacity of individuals. With reference to section 7.3.3 and Figure 7.1 of this chapter, the protective factors (or mediating processes) are considered to be individual, while adversity is considered to be environmental. Thus, resilience is seen as the ability of individuals to rise above their circumstances. This is nicely captured in the salutogenic question, mentioned in section 7.2.2, viz. 'Why, when people are exposed to the same stress which causes some to develop problems, do some maintain psychosocial well-being?'. Here the stress is regarded as both constant across people and as located in their environment, and the resilience focus is on what individual attributes distinguish those who remain healthy (resilient individuals) from those who fall ill (non-resilient individuals).

This approach to resilience has a long tradition. Among some of the earlier writers associated with resilience we may think of De Charms (1968), who coined the term 'personal causation'. He argued that people are not merely the result of the environment impacting on them and shaping them. Rather, there is an inherent drive in all of us to impact our environment. He writes (using gender insensitive language typical of his generation):

> *Man's primary motivational propensity is to be effective in producing changes in his environment. Man strives to be a causal agency, to be the primary locus of causation for, or the origin of, his behavior; he strives for personal causation* (De Charms, 1968:269).

Another good example of the individual approach, which also nicely illustrates the process of resilience research, is Kobasa's (1979) work on 'hardiness'. She began her research by identifying a group of businessmen who had experienced similar levels of adversity over the previous three years – thus the environmental adversity was consistent among these men. Roughly half of them became ill as a result, while the other half did not – thus, there are two very different outcomes. A vulnerability or pathogenic approach would give emphasis to the group who became ill, to determine what about the stress caused their illness; but, Kobasa's resilience approach led her to ask the salutogenic question of what enabled half of the men not to fall ill. Through her research she found that the individual, psychological construct she called 'hardiness' distinguished these two groups – thus, the protective factor or mediating process was an individual, psychological capacity. *Hardiness* means to 'have a stronger commitment to self, an attitude of vigorousness toward the environment, a sense of meaningfulness, and an internal locus of control' (Kobasa, 1979:1).

More recently, and in South Africa, Truter et al. (2014) conducted research on the perceptions of experienced designated social workers (i.e., child protection social workers) on what makes designated social workers resilient, i.e., able to maintain positive functioning despite the difficulties of working with abused children. Their research participants identified 15 protective factors: eight personal strengths; six values; and one support network. Thus, the overwhelming emphasis was on individual factors such as self-confidence, standing up for oneself, choosing to see the positive in difficult circumstances, faith in a higher being, and seeing social work as a calling. The one protective factor that was not personal was to 'have active and reciprocal personal or professional support networks' (Truter et al., 2014:314).

This individualised construction of resilience is particularly prominent in popular literature. For example, Mapela (2015), a South African social work graduate, has written a book called *Rise above your circumstances* in which she recognises the many challenges that face young South Africans today, which can suppress them. Her book is intended to motivate young people to transcend these challenges, by focusing on an individualised 'spirit of resilience' (Mapela, 2015:12). She writes:

> *Life is what you make out of it. … circumstances should not be the reason people fail to reach their full potential. … It is always easier to look at the challenge rather than focusing on the strengths of every human being. It is crucial for each individual [sic] to look deep within oneself to search [for] and find inner strength* (Mapela, 2015:13).

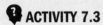 **ACTIVITY 7.3**

What do you think of the individualised approach to resilience? Does it appeal to you? If so, what about it appeals to you? If not, what don't you like about it?

7.5.2 Ecological approach

There has, in recent years, been a growing concern about the individualised approach to resilience, both outside and within the community of resilience scholars. In particular, the concern has been raised that this approach to resilience makes individuals responsible for social issues that should be the responsibility of the state. This concern is often linked to a critique of neoliberalism, which is becoming increasingly prominent in social policies across the world, including South Africa. Neoliberalism involves a reduction of the state's role in providing for the social welfare of its people, the privatisation of social welfare services and the responsibility of individuals to take care of themselves (Patel, 2015).

> **Neoliberalism**, 'a loosely demarcated set of political beliefs which most prominently and prototypically include the conviction that the only legitimate purpose of the state is to safeguard individual liberty, understood as a sort of mercantile liberty for individuals and corporations. This conviction usually issues, in turn, in a belief that the state ought to be minimal or at least drastically reduced in strength and size, and that any transgression by the state beyond its sole legitimate raison d'être is unacceptable' (Thorsen, 2010:203).

Garrett (2016), for example, has been highly critical of resilience, arguing that it has been co-opted by neoliberalism. He is critical of the overemphasis of the individual and the lack of attention to structural factors that impact human well-being. He argues that adversity is typically a macro factor that requires state intervention. Instead, resilience appears to argue that individuals are responsible to deal with the impact of these macro factors, thereby relieving the state of its responsibility. Boyden and Cooper (2007:5), similarly, write:

> Attention is diverted away from the state and other actors with the power
> and moral responsibility to intervene and bring about change, with popu-
> lations living in poverty being charged with using their own resources to
> support themselves through crisis.

There has, however, been a distinct shift among many resilience researchers over the past several years towards a social ecological approach to resilience (Van Breda, 2016, 2018b). Social workers such as Hamilton McCubbin (McCubbin & McCubbin, 1996), Mark Fraser (2004) and Roberta Greene (2006) have been prominent in advocating for an ecological approach to resilience, which layers the protective factors from individual, through family and peer networks, to social and structural levels.

For example, in a South African study on the family resilience of single-mother households in an informal settlement, Raniga and Mthembu (2017) identified three sets of protective factors. The first, 'determination to survive', is an individual-level factor that can be thought of as psychological, involving positivity, purpose and hope. The second, 'rising above harsh economic conditions', is also an individual factor, but is more action oriented than the previous factor, focusing on the practical things women do to address their economic well-being. The third factor, 'establishing networks within and outside the community', focuses on the social environment around the family, at mezzo and macro levels. Similarly, a study on youth-headed households (Soji et al., 2015) identified a range of individual, family and community-level protective factors.

Michael Ungar (2012) has taken this yet further with his 'social ecologies of resilience'. He argues that, drawing on empirical evidence to support his point, social factors are more useful than individual factors in differentiating more resilient individuals from less resilient individuals. He thus writes:

> This shift in focus to a contextually-relevant understanding of resilience de-centers the individual as the primary unit of analysis. Instead, the role played by the individual's social and physical ecology is emphasized and patterns of coping that are synonymous with resilience are identified (Ungar, 2012:18).

Social ecologies, concern the social environment (e.g., networks of relationships, educational and health services, religious institutions) and the physical environment (e.g., buildings, roads, physical safety, access to water) (Ungar, 2012).

Liebenberg (a South African social worker) and Hutt-Macleod (2017) have argued similarly for the social ecologies of resilience. They mobilise a range of evidence showing that social capital – expressed as social identity, community cultural engagement, the adoption of cultural frames of reference, community cohesion and a strong network of community-based social connections – contributes significantly to mental health outcomes and well-being among young people. Consequently, they argue that community development processes, including asset-based community development (see Chapter 13), be advocated to promote resilient outcomes.

Angie Hart and her colleagues in the UK (Hart et al., 2016) have done ground-breaking work in addressing the human rights, social justice and inequalities dimensions of resilience. They define resilience as 'overcoming adversity, while also potentially changing, even dramatically transforming, (aspects of) that adversity' (Hart et al., 2016:3). In response to the popular understanding of resilience as 'overcoming the odds', they have coined the phrase 'changing the odds' (Hart et al., 2016:7), thereby emphasising that resilience is about changing the social environment as much as it is about changing individuals, and foregrounding the advocacy role in holistic social work interventions.

Van Breda (2017c), drawing on his South African research on the resilience of young people transitioning from the child protection system into young adulthood, has adopted the person-in-environment (PIE) framework that is foundational in social work (see Chapter 5). His model (Figure 7.2) is, in some ways, a harmonisation of the individualised and ecological approaches to resilience discussed so far. In line with Patel's (2015) social development call for the harmonisation of the micro and macro perspectives, Van Breda argues for the integration of personal and environmental in the construction of resilience. According to his model, the social environment comprises both relational factors (between people and other people) and environmental factors (referring to structural factors like access to services, employment, safety, and financial and food security). He attends particularly to the 'I' in PIE, that is, to the interaction between the personal and environmental, for example, social skills, empathy, the ability to work in teams and negotiation skills. He argues that this holistic approach to resilience is most appropriate for social workers.

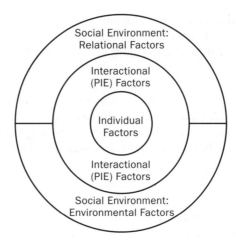

Figure 7.2: Person-in-environment framework
Source: *Van Breda,* 2017c:250

   Person-in-environment, 'views the individual and his or her multiple environments as a
dynamic, interactive system, in which each component simultaneously affects and is affected by the
other ... It views the individual and his or her environments as forming an ecosystem consisting of the
individual, all the systems with which the individual has reciprocal relationships, the wider environment
in which the individual acts, and all the mutual interrelationships that occur between the individual and
the various subsystems' (Weiss-Gal, 2008:65).

To illustrate the importance of these interactional factors, Van Breda (2018a) draws on social
work research conducted in New Zealand (Sanders & Munford, 2014; Munford & Sanders,
2015) among young people who were using two or more social welfare services. They
hypothesised that the services would contribute to improved outcomes among these young
people. In this way, they located the services in the 'Social environment: Environmental
factors' of Figure 7.2. Surprisingly, however, service use did not improve outcomes! This
suggests that environmental factors on their own are not sufficient to promote resilience.
However, they found that when young people had the opportunity to shape the kinds of
services they used and to influence how services were rendered in ways that were relevant
and meaningful to them, they perceived these services to be of good quality, and this led to
improved outcomes. In other words, the protective factor was in the interaction between the
young person and the services, not in either the young person alone or in the services
themselves.

7.6   Relevance of resilience theory for decolonial social work

Does resilience theory have relevance for a decolonial or African approach to social work?
Or, is it a concept that has relevance only in the Global North? If resilience theory is complicit
with neoliberalism, as suggested in section 7.5.2, is it appropriate in the South African context,

with its massive structural challenges of poverty and inequality, and a legacy of racism and patriarchy?

It is the view of the authors of this book that resilience theory does have relevance for decolonial social work, and for this reason we have included it in this book. The practical relevance of resilience theory will become more apparent in Chapter 13, which describes strength-based (or resilience) practices. The focus of this chapter is primarily on the theoretical foundation of these practices. Thus, these questions will be addressed here from a primarily theoretical perspective, and in Chapter 13 from a practice perspective.

For the most part, resilience theory adopts a culturally relativist stance, meaning it does not believe in universal truths that apply equally across all contexts (Ungar, 2015). Instead, resilience theory suggests that so-called truths are local constructs, relevant within particular social contexts at specific points in time. It would, therefore, be unusual (though not impossible) for resilience writers to make truth claims about the resilience of all people. As such, resilience thinking is sensitive and responsive to the local contexts in which research or practice is being done, and is therefore less likely to uncritically impose perspectives from the Global North onto the Global South. This is not to say that this cannot or does not happen, but rather that the theory itself does not lend itself to such cultural impositions.

> **Cultural relativism**, a paradigm which sees all concepts as socially constructed and as varying across cultures. Meaning is thus made within specific cultural frameworks.

Resilience theory has good potential to champion and raise up the voices and experiences of local communities, thereby promoting personal and social agency among groups who may be marginalised or oppressed. By asking a version of the salutogenic question – 'What enables you in your community to deal with the challenges you face?' – resilience theory turns people's attention to their capacities and strengths, validating what may otherwise be hidden or even denigrated.

For example, a resilience researcher could ask a group of people with a long history of colonial oppression about what enables them to retain their sense of cultural identity and pride. The answers to such a question may foreground a culture of resistance that has emerged in response to a lengthy period of oppression, the deliberate cherishing of cultural practices that have been denigrated by colonial powers, and the building of strong networks of relationships between people within their group, including those who are now living elsewhere. These answers point towards a resilience of decoloniality. By recognising and validating these protective factors, the researcher is strengthening them.

Resilience theory, however, is neither the most appropriate tool for analysing structural forces of poverty, nor the most appropriate tool for analysing colonisation. There are other theories that can do this work far better. No one theory is suitable for the whole of social work's endeavours. Thus, we should not require resilience theory, or any another theory, to serve all our purposes. Nevertheless, resilience theory does offer a useful framework for moving from asking questions about vulnerability to asking questions about survival, coping and flourishing. It is also useful for opening potential pathways for change that might otherwise be hidden under an overwhelming sense of hopelessness and despair. In this way, resilience theory is a theory for hopeful change and liberation.

> **ACTIVITY 7.4**
>
> 1 What do you think about the relevance of resilience theory for decolonial social work?
> 2 How is resilience theory relevant for your culture and community group?
> 3 How can it contribute to indigenous or African social work thinking and practice?
> 4 In what ways can it contribute to decoloniality?

7.7 Conclusion

This chapter has provided an overview of resilience theory. We started by considering two broad approaches to social work thinking and practice: the pathogenic approach, which is interested in life's challenges and people's vulnerabilities; and the salutogenic approach, which is interested in what enables people to live full and satisfying lives despite life's challenges. This led to an analysis of the main building blocks of resilience theory, viz. adversity, outcomes (particularly positive outcomes) and protective factors. This led us to consider formal definitions of resilience, three of which were presented and discussed. Two broad approaches to resilience were critically reviewed: the individualised approach, which is regarded as dated and not fully suitable for social work; and the more relevant and contemporary ecological approaches, several of which were highlighted. And finally, we considered how relevant resilience theory is to decolonial social work practice in Africa. This chapter has focused primarily on the theoretical aspects of resilience. Implications for practice will be more fully explored in Chapter 13.

Chapter activity

1. **Reflective question.** Think about some difficulty (adversity) you have faced in your life. Using the PIE resilience model (Figure 7.2), what personal, interactional, relational and environmental protective factors helped you get through that difficulty? What does that tell you about yourself that may be useful when you go through difficulties in the future?
2. **Personal context.** Give some thought to the community that you come from, or a group that you are part of. What community or group-level adversity has that group experienced? Can you distinguish between those members of your group/community who have broken down in some way as a result and those who have better-than-expected outcomes? If so, are you able to identify what protective factors may distinguish between them?
3. **Advocacy.** Think of a contemporary social issue that bothers you (e.g., youth unemployment, crime, gender-based violence). How might resilience theory inform your approach to tackling this macro issue?
4. **Critical questions.** Consider South Africa's long history of cultural, racial and gender oppression. How might social work be making these matters worse? How might resilience theory equip social workers to transform society for the better?

References

Antonovsky, A. 1979. *Health, stress, and coping.* San Francisco, CA: Jossey-Bass.

Bonanno, GA & Diminich, ED. 2013. Annual research review: Positive adjustment to adversity: Trajectories of minimal-impact resilience and emergent resilience. *Journal of Child Psychology and Psychiatry,* 54:378–401.

Boyden, J & Cooper, E. 2007. Questioning the power of resilience: Are children up to the task of disrupting the transmission of poverty? *Chronic Poverty Research Centre Working Paper No. 73.* Oxford, UK: University of Oxford.

De Charms, R. 1968. *Personal causation: The internal affective determinants of behavior.* New York City, NY: Academic Press.

Dykes, G. 2016. Coping, resilience and post-traumatic growth: Adverse childhood experiences and social work students. *The Social Work Practitioner-Researcher,* 28:18–35.

Felitti, VJ, Anda, RF, Nordenberg, D, Williamson, DF, Spitz, AM, Edwards, V, Koss, MP & Marks, JS. 1998. Relationship of childhood abuse and household dysfunction to many of the leading causes of death in adults: The Adverse Childhood Experiences (ACE) Study. *American Journal of Preventive Medicine,* 14:245–258.

Fraser, MW (ed.). 2004. *Risk and resilience in childhood: An ecological perspective.* Washington, DC: NASW.

Garrett, PM. 2016. Questioning tales of 'ordinary magic': 'Resilience' and neo-liberal reasoning. *British Journal of Social Work,* 46:1909–1925.

Greene, RR. 2006. *Social work practice: A risk and resilience perspective.* Belmont, CA: Wadsworth.

Hart, A, Gagnon, E, Eryigit-Madzwamuse, S, Cameron, J, Aranda, K, Rathbone, A & Heaver, B. 2016. Uniting resilience research and practice with an inequalities approach. *SAGE Open,* 6:1–13.

Hlungwani, J. 2017. *Young women's journey towards successful independent living after leaving residential care.* Masters dissertation. University of Johannesburg, Johannesburg.

Holmes, TH & Rahe, RH. 1967. The Social Readjustment Rating Scale. *Journal of Psychosomatic Research,* 11:213–218.

Kobasa, SC. 1979. Stressful life events, personality, and health: An inquiry into hardiness. *Journal of Personality and Social Psychology,* 37:1–11.

Liebenberg, L & Hutt-Macleod, D: 'Community development approaches in response to neo-liberalism: The example of Eskasoni Mental Health Services, Canada'. *In:* Dolan, P & Frost, N (eds.). 2017. *The Routledge handbook of global child welfare.* pp. 47–58. Milton Park, UK: Routledge.

Luthar, SS, Crossman, EJ & Small, PJ: 'Resilience and adversity'. *In:* Lerner, RM, Bornstein, MH & Leventhal, T (eds.). 2015. *Handbook of child psychology and developmental science,* Volume 3. 7th ed. pp. 247–286. New York: Wiley.

Mapela, M. 2015. *Rise above your circumstances.* Durban, RSA: Expand Your Mind.

Masten, AS. 2015. *Ordinary magic: Resilience in development.* New York: Guilford Publications.

McCubbin, MA & McCubbin, HI: 'Resiliency in families: A conceptual model of family adjustment and adaptation in response to stress and crises'. *In:* McCubbin, HI, Thompson, AI & McCubbin, MA (eds.). 1996. *Family assessment: Resiliency, coping and adaptation: Inventories for research and practice.* pp. 1–64. Madison, WI: University of Wisconsin.

Mittelmark, MB & Bauer, GF: 'The meanings of salutogenesis'. *In:* Mittelmark, MB, Sagy, S, Eriksson, M, Bauer, GF, Pelikan, JM, Lindström, B & Espnes, GA (eds.). 2017. *The handbook of salutogenesis.* pp. 7–13. Cham, Switzerland: Springer.

Munford, R & Sanders, J. 2015. Components of effective social work practice in mental health for young people who are users of multiple services. *Social Work in Mental Health*, 13:415–438.

Olsson, CA, Bond, L, Burns, JM, Vella-Brodrick, DA & Sawyer, SM. 2003. Adolescent resilience: A concept analysis. *Journal of Adolescence*, 26:1–11.

Patel, L. 2015. *Social welfare and social development*. 2nd ed. Cape Town: Oxford University Press Southern Africa.

Quinn, M, Caldara, G, Collins, K, Owens, H, Ozodiegwu, I, Loudermilk, E & Stinson, JD. 2018. Methods for understanding childhood trauma: Modifying the Adverse Childhood Experiences International Questionnaire for cultural competency. *International Journal of Public Health*, 63(1):149–151.

Raniga, T & Mthembu, M. 2017. Family resilience in low income communities: A case study of an informal settlement in KwaZulu-Natal, South Africa. *International Journal of Social Welfare*, 26(3):276–284.

Rutter, M. 2012. Resilience as a dynamic concept. *Development and psychopathology*, 24:335–344.

Sanders, J & Munford, R. 2014. Youth-centred practice: Positive youth development practices and pathways to better outcomes for vulnerable youth. *Children and Youth Services Review*, 46:160–167.

Soji, Z, Pretorius, B & Bak, M. 2015. Coping strategies and resilience in youth-headed households: The case of the Nelson Mandela Metro. *Africa Insight*, 44:124–141.

Strümpfer, DJW. 1995. The origins of health and strength: From "salutogenesis" to "fortigenesis". *South African Journal of Psychology*, 25:81–89.

Thorsen, DE. 2010. The neoliberal challenge: What is neoliberalism? *Contemporary Readings in Law and Social Justice*, 2:188–214.

Truter, E, Theron, LC & Fouché, A. 2014. Indicators of resilience in resilient South African designated social workers: Professional perspectives. *Social Work Practitioner-Researcher*, 26:305–329.

Ungar, M. 2004. *Nurturing hidden resilience in troubled youth*. Toronto, Canada: University of Toronto Press.

Ungar, M: 'Social ecologies and their contribution to resilience'. *In:* Ungar, M (ed.). 2012. *The social ecology of resilience: A handbook of theory and practice*. pp. 13–31. New York: Springer.

Ungar, M: 'Resilience and culture: The diversity of protective processes and positive adaptation'. *In:* Theron, LC, Liebenberg, L & Ungar, M (eds.). 2015. *Youth resilience and culture: Commonalities and complexities*. pp. 37–48. New York: Springer.

Van Breda, AD. 2001. *Resilience theory: A literature review*. Pretoria, South Africa: South African Military Health Service.

Van Breda, AD. 2013. Psychosocial vulnerability of social work students. *Social Work Practitioner-Researcher*, 25:19–35.

Van Breda, AD: 'Contribution du travail social à la théorie de la résilience' [Social work's contribution to resilience research]. *In:* Ionescu, S (ed.). 2016. *Résiliences: Ressemblances dans la diversité [Resiliences: Similarities in diversity]*. pp. 93–118. Paris, France: Odile Jacob.

Van Breda, AD. 2017a. Resilience of vulnerable students transitioning into a South African university. *Higher Education*, 75:1109–1124.

Van Breda, AD. 2017b. Students are humans too: Psychosocial vulnerability of first-year students at the University of Johannesburg. *South African Journal of Higher Education*, 31:246–262.

Van Breda, AD. 2017c. The Youth Ecological-Resilience Scale: A partial validation. *Research on Social Work Practice*, 27:248–257.

Van Breda, AD. 2018a. A critical review of resilience theory and its relevance for social work. *Social Work/Maatskaplike Werk*, 54:1–18.

Van Breda, AD. 2018b. Reclaiming resilience for social work: A reply to Garrett. *British Journal of Social Work*, 49:272–276.

Weick, A & Saleebey, D. 1995. Supporting family strengths: Orienting policy and practice toward the 21st century. *Families in Society*, 76:141–149.

Weiss-Gal, I. 2008. The person-in-environment approach: Professional ideology and practice of social workers in Israel. *Social Work*, 53:65–75.

Annotated websites and activities

http://www.resilienceresearch.org/
This is the website of the Resilience Research Centre in Canada, which is headed by Prof Michael Ungar, arguably the leading social work resilience theorist internationally. He hosts a regular Pathways to Resilience Conference.

https://class.coursera.org/resilienceinchildren-001
This is a free on-line course, running over six weeks and led by international expert Ann Masten. It is focused on the resilience of children exposed to trauma, disaster and war, but also provides excellent foundational material on resilience itself. It is supported with readings and videos.

http://www.boingboing.org.uk/
Boing Boing is a community organisation in the United Kingdom, led by Prof Angie Hart, working with young people with disabilities. It is an advocacy group, informed by social justice resilience theory, and shows how resilience theory can make a difference in people's lives.

https://www.youtube.com/watch?v=TXCAMThmbbA
This is a video of Prof Adrian van Breda's professional inaugural lecture, delivered in 2018 and titled '*We are who we are through other people*': *The interactional foundation of the resilience of youth leaving care in South Africa*. It presents his innovative ideas about interactional resilience.

http://www.up.ac.za/centre-of-the-study-of-resilience.
Visit the Centre for the Study of Resilience, located at the University of Pretoria.

Scan the website, particularly the section on research. Now imagine that you are the deputy director of a subdivision on resilience in social work. What kinds of focus areas would you develop for your subdivision, which both contribute to the achievement of social work aims and position social work as an important role player in the interdisciplinary field of resilience?

Annotated websites and activities are also available on Learning Zone.

Attachment

Johannah Sekudu

CHAPTER OUTCOMES

By the end of this chapter, you should be able to:

✓ Describe the important concepts of attachment theory

✓ Identify the role of attachment in the child-rearing process

✓ Explain the effects of attachment on the behaviour of a person later in life

✓ Identify the importance of understanding attachment theory by social workers in decolonising social work practice

✓ Apply the principles of attachment in a given case study.

 Case Study 1   ### The experience of disrupted attachments

Mpho is a 16-year-old girl staying in an informal settlement near Soshanguve, north of Pretoria. She grew up as an orphan after her mother passed away immediately after her birth. She spent her first month of life with her maternal grandmother, who found herself overwhelmed by the responsibility, and then relinquished it to her younger daughter who was staying in the neighbourhood with her nuclear family. Within nine months at this family, her aunt's husband decided that they could no longer take care of her and took her back to her grandmother. At that time, the grandmother was no longer emotionally prepared to take care of Mpho and then negotiated with her other daughter to take over the responsibility. However, this arrangement did not last either. When Mpho reached 10 years, she was moved again as this aunt's husband was no longer prepared to continue with the responsibility since their family had also grown bigger.

The family had a meeting to decide on who would take care of Mpho because the grandmother indicated her unwillingness to take over this responsibility. Mpho felt rejected as she grew up being shifted around by family members who could not establish long-lasting relationships with her. She indicated that every time when she felt she was getting used to the environment and developing relationships with the family, she was moved to another family. She ultimately developed behavioural problems as she was trying to adapt to the different environments that she found herself exposed to. Due to the feelings of rejection, she then attempted suicide as she felt she had nothing to live for since no one was prepared to care for her. She ended up in hospital to be treated for the biopsychosocial effects of taking rat poison, where the social worker was part of the multidisciplinary team. Mpho's life story above was uncovered by the social worker during the intervention process.

Reflective questions

• Mpho was exposed to several caregivers during her formative stage. Establish how this could have affected her challenging behaviour.

• In your opinion, what could have been done differently to ensure a healthy environment for Mpho by the family during this period? Relate your opinion to the practices you have observed in your community.

• Think of your upbringing. How was it similar to and different from Mpho's?

8.1 Introduction

Attachment theory is one of the theories used by social workers to understand the behavioural challenges[1] that clients present with. It is important to note that this theory, like all the theories in this book, evolves with time as new information is obtained by different scholars.

This theory assists in providing the social worker with the relevant information pertaining to the client's past experiences that might have a bearing on the present challenging behaviour of the client. Attachment theory was first developed by John Bowlby (1958) and provides a major perspective on human relationships in early life (Zastrow & Kirst-Ashman, 2013). An assumption behind attachment theory is that infants who become exposed to an environment that allows them to establish socio-emotional bonds with their caregivers are likely to survive later in life. This is based on the argument that their socio-emotional stability empowers them to face the challenges in life with a positive outlook and ultimately find the way forward. Without the development of socio-emotional stability in infancy, people tend to be lost later in life, when faced with life challenges. Based on social learning theory, because behaviour is learned, if a person is not exposed to a positive environment from infancy that allows him or her to learn positive problem-solving skills, it becomes difficult later in life to overcome challenges without displaying unacceptable behaviour.

> **Attachment**, 'any form of behaviour that results in a person attaining or maintaining proximity to some other clearly identified individual who is conceived as better able to cope with the world' (Bowlby, 1988:26–27). The relational patterns of attachment established in childhood tend to be replicated in adult relationships.

Socio-emotional stability in an infant's environment enables the infant to develop trust and a sense of safety, and to later develop the skills to make meaningful choices, using the strong bond they have with their immediate caregiver. The caregiver could be a parent, grandparent, older sibling, aunt or any other person. In the South African context, caregivers are often the grandparents, a phenomenon that was observable after the outbreak of the HIV pandemic.

According to Leverson (2017), attachment theory assists the social worker to see the linkage between early adversity and adult psychosocial troubles. This shows that the human experiences during the infancy period have a bearing on the behavioural challenges that a person might have later in life. Attachment theory enables social workers to unpack clients' past experiences in relation to their current behavioural challenges. Without this understanding, it will be difficult to assist the client to see the link between the past and the present, and then to learn more adaptive behaviour.

This chapter presents the stages of attachment in relation to human behaviour, styles of attachment, the patterns of attachment, and the long-term effects of attachment. The relevance of attachment theory in decolonising social work practice is also discussed.

---

1   In the context of this chapter, I choose to refer to behavioural challenges and not problems, because the concept 'problem' seems to be insurmountable and demoralising. The concept 'caregiver' is used deliberately in the context of this chapter, since many children in South Africa are raised by their grandparents or other family members, instead of the parents.

8.2 Overview of attachment theory

According to Page (2011), attachment theory was formulated by John Bowlby in the mid-twentieth century (e.g., Bowlby, 1958, 1982). He emphasises that the interactions between parents or caregivers and the infant, beginning from birth, are motivated by the infant's needs for safety and protection. These interactions are said to be central to the development of the infant. Furthermore, these interactions lead to the development of an emotional bond that will later in life enable the child to develop other healthy relationships (see also Cooper et al., 2009).

The child in this instance is regarded as an active participant in these relationships and not just a passive recipient. Even if the child depends on the caregiver for survival, he or she is actively participating in the development of the emotional bond when interacting with the caregiver. Riley (2011) argues that the development of attachment starts at birth, with the baby's intense interest in and responsiveness to the human face. This process continues developing throughout life. Attachment is the bond felt by the infant to the particular person who responds to his or her needs to be cared for.

Cassidy and Shaver (2008:5) state that the attachment behaviours are thought to be organised into 'attachment behavioural systems' that are used to describe specific behaviours that lead to certain predictable outcomes. According to Page (2011), these attachment behaviours are categorised into the fear/wariness and exploratory behavioural systems. These two behavioural systems represent the instinct to withdraw from frightening circumstances and the instinct to explore novel situations. Howe (2009:42) is of the view that the attachment behaviour is always geared towards recovering closeness to the primary caregiver, where safety and comfort is found. It could be said that the infant's attachment behaviour is triggered by the responses from the caregiver.

Attachment behaviours are viewed as inherent or instinctive, rather than the result of any learning process. Cassidy and Shaver (2008) indicate that the infant continues to be attached to the caregiver irrespective of whether this caregiver meets his or her needs. It is also important to realise that this attachment is not a bond between two people but a bond that an infant has to a caregiver. It is within this bond that the caregiver could be emotionally distant from the infant and just provide the physical needs, also leading to the infant developing a sense of insecurity, as will be discussed later.

Following are the stages of attachment according to Bowlby, as presented by Zastrow and Kirst-Ashman (2013).

8.2.1 Stages of attachment

According to Zastrow and Kirst-Ashman (2013:131), Bowlby's conceptual framework of attachment develops in four stages that move from the child's general preference for human beings to a partnership with the primary caregiver. The stages were found to be developing in the following manner:

Stage 1   Pre-attachment stage
Babies are said to be able to distinguish between people and objects during their first two months of life. After developing this ability, they then respond more to people with smiling and vocal cues and not to objects. They are able to differentiate between human beings and

objects. This illustrates the inherent need of a human being to interact with other human beings to develop relationships. The ability to develop these relationships at an early age in life can be seen to be important in laying the foundation for future relationships.

Stage 2   Attachment in the making

According to Bowlby, from two to eight months, babies learn to distinguish between primary caregivers and strangers. Babies tend to respond more positively to the primary caregiver; they become excited as they interact with the caregiver and upset when the caregiver moves away. This shows their involvement and the fact that they are not just recipients in the inter-action process. Becoming excited in the presence of the caregiver and upset when the caregiver leaves, shows the development of attachment to the caregiver. The development of emotional attachment occurs as the infant and the caregiver respond appropriately to each other.

Stage 3   True attachment

Bowlby found that from 8 to 18 months, babies make an effort to search for their primary caregivers and try by all means to get closer to them. It is during this stage that the baby is able to crawl, enabling him or her to follow the caregiver around the house. The baby also tends to pay attention to the caregiver's reaction to his or her behaviour and then responds accordingly. Paying attention to the caregiver's reactions enables the baby to develop a detailed internal picture of the caregiver, leading to the ability to predict the response of the caregiver to a particular behaviour. It is during this stage that the infant develops skills in interpreting the reaction of the caregiver and anticipating the response of the caregiver to his or her display of distress.

Stage 4   Reciprocal relationship

During this stage, infants begin to show affection to their caregivers and expect to receive love, attention and physical contact. At the beginning of this stage, 18 months, infants become sensitive to their interaction with the caregiver and show a high level of enjoyment in the presence of the caregiver. For example, during the feeding time, infants would try to prolong the time they spend with their caregivers by playing whilst maintaining eye contact instead of focusing on feeding. The baby enjoys being held by the caregiver and finds it pleasurable to prolong this period. In a situation when the caregiver finds herself (or himself, though in practice most caregivers are women) having some chores to do, the infant's behaviour may become irritating, and could trigger a negative reaction that may affect the attachment with the caregiver. The trust that was supposed to develop could also be disturbed and the infant could give up trying to prolong the time spent with the caregiver, leading to a withdrawn unhappy infant, who could also develop to be an unhappy adult.

A conducive environment is required for this process to develop, allowing the infant to develop trust in self and the environment, which enables him or her to establish meaningful relationships later in life.

8.2.2   Role of attachment

The role of attachment is illustrated in the attachment process. According to Riley (2011:13), this process unfolds through a period he termed 'set goal attachment', which is between six months and three years. During this period, the infant sees the caregiver as the only secure base, leading to always trying to keep closer and going back to the caregiver every time the exploration process does not go well. It should be remembered that it is during this stage that the infant begins to explore his or her environment, starting with crawling and then walking. When the infant experiences the distance from the caregiver as too great, the infant always gives out a danger signal, mostly in a form of crying, which Bowlby called separation protest. This cry alerts the caregiver that the infant is no longer feeling safe and her (or his) reaction to this behaviour assists the infant to develop a level of expectation. If the caregiver responds by picking up the infant, who is then comforted by this, this type of behaviour will be repeated in future to attract the caregiver's attention, with the expectation of being picked up again. This shows the active involvement of the infant in the development of attachment.

By the age of three years, as the infant develops language, reciprocal relationships characterised by negotiation, pleading, bribing and charm begin to develop. The aim of this behaviour is mainly to maintain and prolong the proximity to the caregiver. According to Knox (in Riley, 2011:13), this behaviour contains three broad dimensions, namely self-representation, the physical world representation, and the other representation. Should the infant not get an opportunity to go through this stage in a conducive environment, the development of these dimensions becomes disturbed, leading to an inability to develop meaningful relationships later in life. During this period, the nature of the attachment between the infant and the caregiver is recognisable as either secure or insecure, depending on the responses from the caregiver, and forms the basis of the future relationships that the infant will develop. A secure attachment is said to lead to the development of stable and healthy relationships in future, unlike the insecure one, as will be shown later.

The above discussion shows that the environment in which infants find themselves plays an important role in their lives, specifically in developing relationships. When taking Mpho's situation into consideration (Case study 1), it becomes evident that her early childhood was not conducive for the development of a secure attachment, leading to her developing self-doubt and feeling unloved and unwanted. Her self-worth was also dented, to an extent of deciding to take her own life. As a result of this evaluation, she doubted her self-worth and found suicide to be the only answer for her. The social work intervention in her situation is discussed later.

Reflective questions
- After studying the process of attachment above, take Mpho's case study and describe the process she went through. Scrutinise each stage and relate it to Mpho's life.
- In your opinion, was Mpho exposed to an environment that could equip her to establish meaningful relationships later in life?
- Given Mpho's situation, do you think she was able to establish a meaningful emotional attachment during her formative period?

8.2.3 Styles of attachment

The quality of attachment that people experience with their caregivers, during infancy and early childhood, influences the style of attachment that they habitually enact in their other relationships in childhood and typically well into adulthood. According to Hutchison (2015), the development of the attachment style is mostly dependent on the parenting style that the infants are exposed to. She also identified the two attachment styles according to Ainsworth, Blehar and Waters and the third one according to Madigan, Moran and Pederson (as cited in Hutchison, 2015:149). These attachment styles are discussed below.

8.2.3.1 Securely attached infants/Secure attachment

This style of attachment is named 'secure attachment' by Riley (2011), while Hutchison (2015) prefers to refer to 'securely attached infants', and Gray and Webb (2013) refer to 'secure patterns of attachment Type B'. This is the 'ideal' attachment style associated with healthy adult relationships. According to Riley (2011), the development of secure attachment depends on the caregiver responding consistently and predictably to the infant's needs. This is supported by Hutchison (2015) who stated that the infant raised by a very sensitive and accepting caregiver ends up developing a secure attachment. Howe (2009) states that care that is loving, emotionally attuned, responsive to the needs, predictable and consistent leads to secure attachments and optimal psychosocial development. In this manner, the infant is said to develop a working model of confidence in self and others, leading to the development of independence. Riley (2011) further indicates that this results in the caregiver being able to predict the infant's needs and, through empathy, to keep the infant in mind during their interaction.

This consistent parenting style by the caregiver provides the infant with a safe and secure environment to explore, allowing the infant to develop self-efficacy in dealing with the physical and social environment. Hutchison (2015) argues that a securely attached infant becomes distressed when separation with the caregiver happens and becomes overjoyed and excited when the caregiver reappears. Gray and Webb (2013) state that when distressed, securely attached infants approach their caregivers directly and positively, knowing that their distress will be recognised and responded to with comfort and understanding. They also confirm that care-giving that is responsive, reliable and consistent in the development of a secure attachment in infants, leads to the development of the self as lovable and loving. If this pattern of interaction continues into adulthood, the person develops a balanced approach towards relationships that create a sense of comfort and autonomy.

These infants tend to be more content and actively involved in exploratory activities in their environment as compared to their counterparts who are exposed to inconsistent, unavailable or rejecting caregivers. As a result, this infant will return to the caregiver should the exploratory activities not yield pleasure, unlike the infant who lacks consistency and empathy from the caregiver. The latter tends to lose curiosity about the environment and is reluctant to return to the caregiver when the exploratory activities are not fulfilling. This shows that the response of the caregiver to the infant plays an important role in facilitating the development of security in a human being, from very early in life. This sense of security has a bearing on how human beings develop relationships throughout their entire lives. A secure person is able to develop meaningful relationships that are fulfilling to him or her and to discard toxic relationships.

8.2.3.2 Anxious-ambivalent attachment/Insecure attachment

This style of attachment is named 'anxious-ambivalent attachment' by Hutchison (2015) and 'insecure attachment/avoidant-ambivalent' by Riley (2011) and Howe (2009). Howe (2009:45) refers to two insecure attachment patterns/styles, namely 'ambivalent attachments' and 'avoidant attachments', while Gray and Webb (2013) refer to avoidant patterns of attachment as 'Type A' and ambivalent patterns of attachment as 'Type C'.

Howe (2009) and Riley (2011) agree that caregivers of infants who develop ambivalent attachment are inconsistent, unpredictable and caught up with their own needs and anxieties, resulting in them being unable to be sensitive to the needs of their infants. Gray and Webb

(2013) argue that when caregivers reject expressions of need, vulnerability and dependence by the infants, they are likely to develop avoidant attachment. The parents of the infants with ambivalent attachment are said to be not overly rejecting but often unpredictable and inconsistent with their responses (Hutchison, 2015).

Infants with an ambivalent attachment are said to minimise their unmet needs for attachment in order to lessen the pain of separation when it occurs. Hutchison (2015) states that, in contrast to securely attached infants, anxious-ambivalently attached infants become distressed when the caregiver leaves and continue to be distressed when the caregiver returns. When this happens, they tend to demand and prolong the period of being held and comforted. Such infants are always afraid of being abandoned by the caregiver, resulting in them maximising their efforts to maintain close parental attachments by being too sensitive to any threat of rejection. This could be seen as being too clingy to the caregiver, resulting in irritation and behaviour that the infant could experience as rejection. Howe (2009) states that infants who develop this style of attachment see themselves as ineffective in securing love and sustaining comforting relationships. They also see themselves as not only unworthy of love, but also unlovable.

Infants who develop avoidant attachments are said to be cared for by caregivers who are indifferent, emotionally rigid or rejecting of their infants' needs (Howe, 2009). These caregivers respond reasonably well when the infant appears to be content and occupied, but they withdraw emotionally or react with irritation when the infant is distressed and in need of comfort and attention. Even if the infant tries to be clingy to the caregiver, the caregiver does not become moved by this behaviour, leading to the forced development of independence in the infant. Infants with avoidant attachment develop into adults who find it difficult to form intimate relationships, as they are afraid of being hurt by getting close to other people.

Riley (2011:14) states that insecure attachment was conceived in two types, namely avoidant or ambivalent, and disorganised attachment was conceived later for infants who displayed both forms of avoidant and ambivalent attachment. Infants with insecure attachment are distrustful of others and their own feelings and intuitions about relationships. They tend to be more defensive to protect themselves from the pain of not having their genuine attachment needs met. The infant may display distant contact with the caregiver, even when she is in close proximity, or may be excessively clingy. Riley (2011) further states that the development of insecure attachment in childhood resulting from abusive or neglectful attachment figures leads to maladaptive behaviour later in life. Children whose caregivers are 'consistently insensitive, anxious, uncertain and inconsistently responsive develop ambivalent attachment' (Gray and Webb, 2013:81). These infants are inclined to whining, clinging and complaining, just because their caregivers do not respond favourably to their needs. It is evident that an infant who is not afforded an opportunity to have a meaningful relationship with a caregiver who is responsive to his or her needs struggles to develop meaningful relationships later in life.

8.2.3.3   Disorganised attachment/disordered attachment

The disorganised or disordered type of attachment was developed later when researchers and practitioners encountered a category of infants who did not fit in the two types discussed above. Infants with a disorganised style of attachment are said to lack a consistent strategy for dealing with the stress of separation (Cassidy & Shaver, 2008). Gray and Webb (2013:81) state that infants develop a disorganised pattern of attachment when they are cared for by caregivers who are trapped in dealing with their own unresolved feelings of loss, anxiety, anger and fear, and thus do not attend consistently to their children's attachment needs. In this situation, the infant fails to find any strategy that increases feelings of security and comfort.

Such infants were observed to approach their caregivers with averted heads and rocking hands and knees following their unsuccessful attempts to get their caregivers' attention. They tend to display contradictory intentions by showing interest to be picked up by the caregivers, but when the caregivers reach out, they withdraw. Hutchinson (2015) states that infants with disorganised attachment display chaotic and conflicted behaviour, character-ised by approach and avoidance at the same time. The caregiver, in this instance, is frightening to the infant, but the infant does not have any option but to run to the caregiver when afraid and in need of reassurance. The caregiver may be hostile or fearful and unable to hide her or his apprehension from the infant. In either case, the infant's anxiety or distress is not lessened.

Cassidy and Shaver (2008) further state that an infant can be categorised as having a dis-organised attachment when the infant's behaviour fits one or more of the following descriptions:

- Continuous display of contradictory behaviour patterns, where a desire to be attached and indifferent behaviours are communicated at the same time.
- Display of behaviour that does not give direction to the caregiver regarding what the infant needs.
- Display of behaviour that is outside the normal range of behaviour expected from an infant during this period of development in the presence of the caregiver.
- Showing behaviour that suggests that the infant is not in need of the caregiver's comforting hands.
- Display of direct fear for the caregiver through facial expressions.
- Display of disorganised and disorientated behaviour such as disoriented wandering, confused or indifferent expressions, or rapid changes in affect.

The above types of behaviour show that the infants with disorganised attachment do not display behaviour patterns that give caregivers direction about what to expect from them, in contrast to infants with secure attachment.

Reflective questions
- In your view, which parental style is most appropriate in raising children who will have control of their future relationships with minimal disturbances?
- Taking Mpho's situation into consideration (Case study 1), discuss the type of parental style that she was exposed to. If you happen to identify more than one, substantiate your answer by explaining the reasons behind your choice.

8.3   Attachment theory for decolonial practice

South Africa is a multiracial country characterised by diverse cultures, which creates a unique context for social work practice. The fact that there are 11 official languages in South Africa confirms the diversity in the country. It is important to note that the diversity of languages is not the only element to be considered. Cultural diversity should also be considered as it plays an important role in how people perceive their world and experiences. Cultural and ethnic diversity in the country challenges professionals in the helping professions to go a step further to explore issues of diversity with each client and, in this way, ensure that their helping efforts are relevant and responsive to the needs of their clients. The use of professional values and principles must always be accompanied by an understanding of the unique cultural background of each client.

Kirst-Ashman (2013:70) suggests four aspects that social service professionals should bear in mind when working in a culturally diverse setting. First, social workers need to refrain from believing that people from different cultural backgrounds have become one, just because they are occupying the same geographical area – which is known as the 'melting pot' model (see also Segal et al., 2013:108). It has been believed that, with exposure to the mass media and a common educational system, people will ultimately lose their cultural uniqueness and adopt what is believed to be the dominant and acceptable culture, as some cultural practices have been labelled as barbaric.

This has been the case in South Africa during the apartheid era, where the cultural practices of black people have been seen as barbaric and unacceptable. With careful observation, this line of thinking is still observable. Incidents at schools, where learners were judged based on their hair styles, as reported by the media in 2016, bear evidence of this. The melting pot ideology is based on an unrealistic belief and has to be discarded to allow each individual to express his or her culture without any fear of judgement. The reality is that we are living together, but people are mindful of their own culture and continue to practise it, irrespective of the geographical area they find themselves in or the other cultural practices observed in the neighbourhood.

The second aspect of working in a culturally diverse context mentioned by Kirst-Ashman (2013:70) is that the professionals from the helping professions must consider how people from different cultures have different ideas and expectations of what has to happen in the intervention process. Every person who approaches the social worker for assistance has a level of expectation regarding how he or she should be assisted by the professional. The social worker who is mindful of this notion will always take it upon him or herself to explore the client's expectations within the client's own cultural background. For example, in Mpho's situation, the social worker has to involve her in exploring her expectations of the intervention process, bearing in mind her past experiences and her cultural context. The family members need to also be involved in trying to understand the cultural practices that were used in her upbringing.

Kirst-Ashman (2013:70) goes further to mention 'worldviews' of the clients as the third aspect of multicultural practice that needs the attention of the social workers. 'Worldview' means how the world is perceived by people from different cultural groups, as well as how relationships are formed and maintained in those groups. It is important to also realise the influence of ethnocentric worldviews on different people, whereby some people perceive their own ethnicity and culture as superior to that of others. Regarding attachment processes, it is important for the social worker to consider the worldview of the client by displaying a non-judgemental attitude. All aspects pertaining to cultural practices need to be explored and understood, as they may have had a role in how the attachment process unfolded.

The fourth aspect that should be taken into consideration is the importance of family as perceived by the client, within the context of the client's own cultural background (Kirst-Ashman, 2013). The worldview within black African communities is that a family does not consist of parents and their offspring only, but includes also all the relatives with whom they might find themselves sharing a common home. This notion is confirmed by Mathebane (2017), who states that the worldview of black African people is characterised by connectedness to the whole, contrary to the segmentation seen in the Eurocentric worldview. In the

Western notion of families these types of families are known as extended families. But, in black African culture there is no 'extended' family – there is just a family, which Mathebane (2017:252) refers to as a 'clan'. Within this structure, which could be seen as a large family, multiple relationships are formed and maintained; therefore, the social worker has to make an effort to understand the dynamics of these relationships, how they were formed, and how they are maintained. This understanding is crucial in assisting the social worker to intervene appropriately to address the challenge that the client presents to him or her.

For example, in Case study 1, Mpho grew up within different families that had their own members and she had to develop some relationships that would enable her to survive. Even if the different families are from a common cultural background, it could be that their practices are different, with different effects on Mpho's ability to form relationships. She did not have a primary caregiver with whom she could develop attachment that could enhance the development of trust and believe in self, and this could have impacted on her future relationships, leading to her losing trust in relationships and self-worth. Attachment theory within black African cultures needs to be applied by taking the family structure into consideration in order to ensure that the primary caregiver is identified and her or his interaction with the child is explored thoroughly, with the aim of establishing how the attachment process unfolded. This is based on the fact that the interaction of the infant with the primary caregiver forms the foundation on which future relationships will be established. If the infant has to interact with a number of people without a clear-cut boundary of who the primary caregiver is, he or she could be confused and, at times, develop a sense of rejection.

As already indicated, the type of parenting style sets the tone for the infant to either be securely or insecurely attached. As a result, the social worker has to use the assessment process to establish how the infant's life has been allowed to unfold with regard to the attachment process within a particular culture; this will enable her or him to understand the current maladaptive behaviour that is displayed by the client. It is important to always remember that attachment itself is a universal human phenomenon (Page, 2011:44). It is only the *patterns of attachment* that seem to vary, depending on the culture they unfold within. Attachment behaviour of a developing infant is mostly shaped by how the caregiver responds to the infant's expressions of the attachment needs. Within a particular culture, where infants' needs of attachment are not given a priority, perhaps because of the cultural practices that might emphasise independence from early childhood, the infants will not be afforded the opportunity to develop attachment with their caregivers and this could lead to adults who struggle with establishing relationships characterised by trust and self-worth.

8.4 Application of attachment theory in social work practice

Given the above information, it is important to explore how attachment theory can be used across diverse cultures to address the behavioural challenges that the client systems present with. Mpho's situation (Case study 1) will be applied throughout the intervention process at micro and macro levels.

8.4.1   Intervention at micro level

Johnson (2003:3) states that:

> ... therapists need a broad integrative theory of relationships, one that captures the essence of the nature of our bonds of love, if we are to understand, predict, and explain such relationships and so know how to change them for the better.

In this way, social workers as therapists need to know the context of their clients' relationships that might be having an influence on their current maladaptive behaviour. Since the need to have a secure emotional connection with those close to one is innate, social workers have to consider how this need was nurtured every time they intervene in the life of a person presenting with maladaptive behaviour. In the context of the worldview of black African people regarding family, the understanding of the involved dynamics, of having relationships with a variety of people at home, will enable the social worker to intervene appropriately.

Gray and Webb (2013) argue that attachment theory is relevant to social work practice in the fields of child protection, family support and preventative services. They go further to indicate that theory does not only help practitioners make sense of children's development and behaviour in conditions of adversity, but also provides a powerful model for understanding the mental states, behaviours and responses of the caregivers who abuse and neglect their children.

According to Page (2011), the practice guidelines of attachment theory indicate to the therapists that they should be sensitive to the primacy of safety and protection in the developmental experiences of the client. This notion emphasises the important role of early childhood relationship experiences of an individual in the behaviour that is displayed later in life. Without an understanding of these experiences, it becomes impossible for the therapist to intervene appropriately. Page (2011) further argues that interpretation and analysis of the client's relational experience, including within the therapeutic relationship, should be based on an understanding of the centrality of the expression of attachment behaviour in social experience and with regard to the creation of personal identity.

Intervention from the attachment perspective focuses on the understanding of the characteristic ways in which needs of safety and protection are expressed in current relationships, including defensive strategies and the extent to which these strategies represent attempts to cope with unresponsive attachment figures, learnt early in life. For instance, the relationship between the therapist and the client might be characterised by the client's attempt to be attached to the therapist, only because early in life the client never had an opportunity to be attached to the caregiver, i.e., seeing the therapist as the attachment figure. As a result, the therapist must be sensitive to this development and respond appropriately not to reject the client, as this might jeopardise the intervention process.

In Mpho's situation, it could be concluded that she did not get an opportunity to develop secure attachment in her infancy, leading to her inability to make sense of life and develop a sense of self-worth, and this deprivation led her to attempt taking her life. In assisting her to develop some sense of meaning in life, the social worker should assess her early childhood to understand how it happened for her to ultimately lose her sense of self-worth. Understanding her past will assist the social worker to intervene in an appropriate manner at the individual level, including her family. The principle of person-in-environment (see Chapter 5 on ecosystems theory) will also assist in helping the client to understand herself in context, not as an isolated entity.

The intervention process should be guided by what the client went through in trying to mitigate against the effects of her upbringing and then assist her to develop new adaptive behaviour patterns. Cooper et al. (2009) state that experiencing reliable care that is sensitive to developmental needs leads to secure attachment. They go further to indicate that one benefit of secure attachment is good peer relationships and socio-emotional adjustment in middle childhood. Socio-emotional stability, which leads to lower rates of mental health problems, is not something that Mpho developed during her formative years. This calls for the social worker to be sensitive to the past experiences of the client and use them to assist the client to move forward in a constructive fashion, always taking the cultural context into consideration.

• Attachment-informed micro practice starts with assessment

Assessment forms an important step in the social work intervention process, irrespective of the nature of the client's challenging situation or field of social work practice. Thorough assessment equips the social worker with the relevant information and judgements that enable him or her to establish appropriate intervention strategies that would lead to empowering the client system at all the levels, and to move from the challenging situation by developing coping strategies. Hepworth et al. (in Kirst-Ashman, 2013:121) define *assessment* as 'a process occurring between practitioner and client, in which information is gathered, analysed and synthesised to provide a concise picture of the client's needs and strengths'. It is clear that assessment is not an event but a process, meaning that the social worker has to be mindful of this process from the beginning of the intervention process until termination.

Sekudu (2015) states that, in assessing the client's situation, the social worker must take aspects of diversity, including culture, into consideration, as they have a significant impact on how the client will interact with the social worker in the helping relationship. It is also important to remember that assessment is a dynamic process requiring the social worker to modify the initial judgements as new information, insights and experience in working with the client systems increase.

• Exploring the reasons that might have led Mpho to decide on taking her life

It is important during the assessment process for the social worker, addressing a challenging situation of a young person who has attempted suicide, to understand the mental state of the client, specifically the factors that might have pushed the client to behave in that manner. The cultural context within which the behaviour was displayed has to be explored as well, emphasising the meaning that the client attaches to the cultural practices in the environment.

In Mpho's situation, the reasons around her decision might be linked to the deprivation of attachment that she experienced in early childhood. It could be concluded that she lost her self-worth because she never experienced a meaningful relationship with her caregiver since she was exposed to several caregivers during the developmental phase where she could have developed attachment. As seen in the case study, she already had three caregivers before celebrating her first birthday. For the social worker to ultimately intervene appropriately, he or she needs to assess Mpho's situation thoroughly to develop adequate understanding of her background. It is also important for the social worker to explore the meaning that Mpho attaches to this situation, as she learned about it later in life. Mpho's cultural background should be explored as well, and her interpretation of how she was raised, in relation to her current behaviour that led her to be in contact with the social worker. Her family members are needed in this process, for them to explain what happened at that age, as there might be aspects identified that could have led her to the current situation.

• Building sensitive helping relationships

Every client that approaches a social worker for assistance can be assumed to be going through a difficult situation. It is thus important for the social worker to be sensitive as he or she interacts with the client. Basic communication skills should be used with care to ensure that warmth and acceptance are communicated to the client, and to avoid judgement of the client's maladaptive behaviour. Because Mpho was never afforded an opportunity to establish any emotional bond with any person, the social worker needs to be a reliable, trustworthy and consistent caring figure. The sensitive helping relationship must be anchored in the ethical principles and values of social work to assist the client to regain believe in self and others.

• Building a partnership and collaboration with the client

The social worker has to make an effort to see the client as a partner in the intervention process. This calls for the social worker not to see him or herself as a 'know-it-all' figure during the interaction. The client understands his or her situation much better than the social worker; as a result, the social worker has to allow the client to express that understanding since it will facilitate the intervention process. The social worker needs to refrain from seeing him or herself as having authority over the client, but should rather see the client as an equal partner in the process of bringing about the desired change in his or her life.

The strengths of the client need to be used in this process to minimise the challenging behaviour that the client is presenting with (see Chapter 13 on strengths-based practices). Even if Mpho feels she has lost her self-worth, the social worker should remember that Mpho has strengths that need to be unearthed and then mobilised to empower her. A client who feels that he or she is a partner in the helping process becomes a collaborator to have the desired goals met. In this process of building a partnership with the client, the social worker relies on meaningful engagement with the client from the beginning until the goals are attained.

In the case of Mpho, the social worker must remember that Mpho's attachment deprivation might interfere with her trusting the social worker when trying to establish the helping relationship. As a result, the social worker must work to communicate unconditional positive regard for Mpho to realise that, despite what she went through, she is still a human being worthy of respect and acceptance. Mpho needs to develop a sense of safety when interacting with the social worker, as we have seen earlier how important it is for a person to feel safe for him or her to develop relationships. In this process of building a partnership with the client, the social worker has to emphasise the principle of client self-determination, for the client to feel that his or her opinions are important and respected by the social worker. This feeling instills a sense of ownership of the recovery process and assists the client to reconstruct the acceptable behaviour.

• Making efforts to understand Mpho's past, including her early development (attachment experience)

Understanding the client's past experiences assists the social worker to understand the current behaviour, enabling him or her to address it without any bias. Any negative behaviour displayed by the client should be analysed based on the past experiences and not assumed to be lack of motivation to change. After learning about the client's past, the social worker may interpret the client's negative behaviour as a protective reaction that developed over a period of time, when the client was forced to deal with traumatic experiences. Having analysed the client's past, the social worker is able to assist the client to be future oriented in a constructive manner.

In Mpho's case, the social worker might find it difficult to get all the information pertaining to her early childhood; therefore, it is important to get the involvement of the other family members, so that a better understanding of the situation could be established. Listening with compassion will assist the social worker to assess Mpho's past experiences and will also shed light on her current maladaptive behaviour.

- ### Considering Mpho's current social environment

In trying to intervene appropriately in the situation of a client who attempted suicide, it becomes very important for the social worker to fully explore the current social environment. This exploration assists in observing elements that could have enabled the client to ultimately decide on taking his or her own life. Mpho's childhood social environment was found to be cold and rejecting. She never developed a meaningful relationship with any person, making it difficult for her to trust her social environment. She had no one to share her deepest experiences with and felt that she is not worthy of living as no one has ever shown her that she is. It was established from Mpho that she associated with bad company outside her family in her attempts to develop relationships. Because she could not trust any person when her life of exploration outside the family became tough, she decided to take her life.

The lack of attachment is evident in Mpho's situation, illustrating why social workers always have to make time to understand the process of attachment in their clients who present with maladaptive behaviour. Understanding the current social environment of the client will assist the social worker together with the client to target the elements that might be negative on the client's behaviour, and use the client's strengths to eliminate them. The toxic relationships that the client might have developed in an effort to cope with the felt rejection have to be identified and attended to in collaboration with the client.

- ### Considering Mpho's current maladaptive behaviour

Considering the client's maladaptive behaviour, the social worker should work to understand the root cause of each action that is being displayed by the client in relation to the client's past experiences. The social worker should also consider that the current maladaptive behaviour displayed by the client might be the only constructive way, in the client's perspective, to deal with current challenges. The interaction between thoughts and emotions must always be considered when addressing the challenges of people who have attempted suicide. Experiencing a gap in a person's life due to the deprivation in attachment, might lead to maladaptive behaviour in an effort to get some attention from the immediate environment. This might be the reason behind Mpho's maladaptive behaviour of attempting suicide. With a clear understanding of the client's current maladaptive behaviour, the social worker together with the client will be able to design an intervention process that is responsive to the needs of the client. Using the client's strengths, after creating a safe environment for the client to feel free to interact with the social worker, can enable the client to focus on developing adaptive behaviour. The client is enabled to redefine the maladaptive behaviour and strives to develop adaptive and acceptable behaviour.

Resilience is another important aspect in this process because, prior to coming to the social worker's office, the client was able to bounce back. It could not be assumed that the reason that led to the current maladaptive behaviour (suicide attempt) is the first challenge the client had to deal with. Taking into account all the coping strategies used by the client in the past and building on the positive ones will facilitate the achievement of empowerment (see Chapter 7 on resilience).

It is important for the social worker to model respectful and professional behaviour throughout the intervention process to ensure that the client experiences acceptance and dignity as a human being. Each client's reasons for attempting suicide are unique, and, as a result, must be dealt with individually, meaning that a one-size-fits-all approach must be avoided at all costs, as emphasised by the social work principle of individualisation. Culturally relevant and gender-specific responses are also very important in this regard.

8.4.2   Intervention at macro level

Cooper et al. (2009) found that the focus on the parenting activities that promote security of attachment in infancy is compromised by adverse conditions such as poverty. Their study in Khayelitsha, in the Western Cape, provided support for the mothers during the postpartum period through trained community health-care workers. The results of this study were that mothers who focused their care activities on the developmental needs of their infants had securely attached infants. The infants were found to be more inclined to move towards their primary caregivers (mothers) whenever they experienced distress. This behaviour develops throughout the life cycle of the person, leading to healthy relationships later in life.

Sekudu et al.'s (2016) study of suicide among young people in Soshanguve found that a number of the participants were not exposed to healthy attachment during infancy. The social workers in Soshanguve could have used community work principles to improve the attachment experiences of these young people. For example, the community education model could be used to educate groups of mothers and other caregivers on the importance of focusing childcare activities on the developmental needs of their infants. These community groups could also be motivated to share their experiences with other community members in order to increase the number of caregivers who focus on their children's attachment needs. In this manner, a larger number of community members could be educated, and the attachment problems could be eliminated. This could lead to a community of adults who are able to establish meaningful relationships and who are also free from serious mental health problems.

Reflective questions
- Discuss the social work intervention in Mpho's case with your classmate/study group and then identify the important aspects that need to be taken into consideration when applying attachment theory in addressing maladaptive behaviour such as attempted suicide.
- As a social worker using the community work method in addressing the problem of lack of appropriate child-rearing practices observed in the community, which specific aspects will you focus on?
- Identify other chapters in this book that address aspects that are relevant to intervention at macro level, and use the principles contained in them when discussing your answer.

8.5   Conclusion

This chapter has argued that attachment theory is relevant to all social work practice and illustrated this with the situation of a young person who has attempted suicide. Deprivation of attachment in the early childhood development process can lead to distorted processes of developing relationships in future, leading to the loss of self-worth and trust in self and others.

Social workers need to understand attachment theory and learn to apply its principles when assessing and providing interventions to their clients. Understanding the attachment process in the life of a person assists the social worker to understand the current maladaptive behaviour displayed by the person. It is also important for the social worker to understand the clients' cultural background, particularly regarding family, parenting and relationships, so that appropriate responses for decolonial practice can be provided.

Chapter activity

1. **Reflective questions**. Having read about attachment theory above, think about your family. Ask people in your immediate environment about how you were raised and relate that to your current relationships and friendships at home, school and church. How did this upbringing affect your current relationships? Is there anything in your life you would like to change for you to have meaningful and fulfilling relationships?

2. **Personal context**. Looking back at your community of origin, think about the cultural practices that are used in child-rearing and about how they affect the development of attachment in individual lives. Is there anything you wish people in your community would do differently to improve the attachment of children in your community?

3. **Advocacy**. Identify one cultural practice that you think might be negatively affecting the development of attachment in infants and then describe how you would intervene at micro and macro levels to address its impact.

4. **Critical questions**. Think about the 'melting pot' ideology. How has this impacted social work practice in South Africa? Based on the knowledge you have acquired on social work practice in South Africa up to this point, identify what you would do to contribute to the decolonisation of social work.

References

Bowlby, J. 1958. The nature of the child's tie to his mother. *International Journal of Psycho-Analysis*, 39:350–373.

Bowlby, J. 1982. *Attachment and loss, Vol. I: Attachment*. 2nd ed. New York: Basic Books.

Bowlby, J. 1988. *A secure base: Parent-child attachment and healthy human development*. London: Routledge.

Cassidy, J & Shaver, PR. 2008. *Handbook of attachment: Theory, research and clinical application*. 2nd ed. New York: The Guilford Press.

Cooper, PJ, Tomlinson, M, Swartz, L, Landman, M, Molteno, C, Stein, A, McPherson, K & Murray, L. 2009. Improving quality of mother-infant relationship and infant attachment in socioeconomically deprived community in South Africa: Randomized controlled trial. *BMJ*, 338(7701):997.

Gray, M & Webb, SA. 2013. *Social work theories and methods*. 2nd ed. London, UK: Sage.

Howe, D. 2009. *A brief introduction to social work theory*. Hampshire: Palgrave MacMillan.

Hutchison, ED. 2015. *Dimensions of human behavior: Person and environment*. 5th ed. London, UK: Sage.

Johnson, SM: 'Introduction to attachment: A therapist's guide to primary relationships and their renewal'. *In*: Johnson, SM & Whiffen, VE (eds.). 2003. *Attachment processes in couple and family therapy*. pp. 3–17. New York: The Guilford Press.

Kirst-Ashman, KK. 2013. *Introduction to social work & social welfare: Critical thinking perspectives*. 4th ed. Belmont, CA: Brooks/Cole, Cengage Learning.

Mathebane, MS. 2017. *Towards indigenous social work practice: Guidelines for assisting families raising children with Downs Syndrome*. Unpublished thesis. University of South Africa, Pretoria.

Page, T: 'Attachment theory and social work treatment'. *In*: Turner, FJ (ed.). 2011. *Social work treatment: Interlocking theoretical approaches*. 5th ed. pp. 30–47. New York: Oxford University Press.

Riley, P. 2011. *Attachment theory and the teacher-student relationship: A practical guideline for teachers, teacher educators and school leaders*. London: Routledge.

Segal, EA, Gerdes, KE & Steiner, S. 2013. *An introduction to the profession of social work: Becoming a change agent*. 4th ed. Belmont, CA: Brooks/Cole, Cengage Learning.

Sekudu, J, Monageng, K, Botes, G, Moloko, S & Kabini, M. 2016. *Factors associated with suicide attempts amongst young people in Soshanguve, South Africa: A social work study*. Athens Institute for Education and Research Conference Paper Series SOS2016-2017.

Sekudu, J: 'The helping process in social work'. *In*: Mbedzi, P, Qalinge, L, Schultz, P, Sekudu, J & Sesoko, M (eds.). 2015. *Introduction to social work in the South African context*. pp. 81–107. Cape Town: Oxford University Press Southern Africa.

Zastrow, CH & Kirst-Ashman, KK. 2013. *Understanding human behavior and the social environment*. 9th ed (intl ed). Belmont, CA: Brooks/Cole, Cengage Learning.

Annotated websites and activities

http://www.goodenoughcaring.com/the-journal/attachment-theory-and-social-work-with-looked-after-children-and-their-families/

This website takes you to an article by John Fallowfield, who applies attachment theory to social work practice with children in the care system.

http://childprotectionresource.online/tag/attachment-theory/

You will learn about how attachment theory can be used as a child protection resource from this website. There is also additional information on this theory.

http://dspace.nwu.ac.za/handle/10394/2303

Visit this website to learn more about how social workers can use attachment theory when dealing with children in foster care. The dissertation provides details on the practical application of attachment theory when dealing with children in foster care, to avoid disruptions in the foster care placements.

https://www.communitycare.co.uk/2015/09/02/using-attachment-theory.research-help-families-just-assess

Visit this website to learn about three ideas from attachment research, presented by David Shemmings, who is Professor of child protection research at the University of Kent.

Annotated websites and activities are also available on Learning Zone.

oxford.co.za/learningzone

Feminisms

Shahana Rasool

CHAPTER OUTCOMES

By the end of this chapter, you should be able to:

✓ *Define and critique various types of feminisms*

✓ *Explain the link between social, historic or political events and the emergence of varying waves of feminisms*

✓ *Underscore the contribution of feminisms to critiquing coloniality and highlighting an African perspective on women's lives*

✓ *Identify the value of feminisms in understanding your own life and the lives of women you know*

✓ *Consider which type of feminism best aligns with your values and belief systems*

✓ *Understand how feminisms can be applied in the context of decolonial social work practice in South Africa.*

 Case Study 1

A story of domestic violence

Anele has been married to Steve for 15 years. Anele and Steve met at work and began dating. From the start, Steve didn't like Anele to go out on her own, not even to visit her mother. Anele was deeply in love with Steve. Within two years of knowing each other they got married. Once they got married, Steve insisted that Anele quit her job. He said that he wanted to take care of her. She left work three months into their marriage, when she found out she was pregnant. After she fell pregnant, Steve didn't allow Anele out of the house alone, not even to go for check-ups to the clinic. He insisted on going with her. On one occasion, after they came from the doctor, he hit her for the first time, because the doctor, who was male, touched her body as part of the medical examination. As the years went by the beatings increased. Anele tried to look after the house and do whatever Steve wanted as best she could.

Anele now has three kids and Steve frequently beats her up. She is scared to leave because she has not worked for many years and will not be able to support herself and her children if she leaves. Anele is also uncertain if she would get a job that pays her adequately to pay school expenses and for day-care facilities. She is concerned that her family would have to return the *lobola* (bride price), should she leave her husband. Anele's family lives in a rural area and they are barely able to feed themselves. She is anxious that if she goes home, she would be a burden to her parents. She did tell her mother about the beatings and showed her the bruises. Her mother responded by saying: '*Ah, beatings are a part of marriage. It is the way he shows love. Your father also did that to me.*' Her in-laws were also aware of the abuse, as they visited her in hospital after her husband broke her arm during one of the incidents of abuse. They said: '*He will come right, bekezela [be patient].*' The doctors and nurses did not ask her how she was injured, so she said nothing.

Reflective questions

• What do you think Anele should do?

• Why do you think Anele continues to stay with Steve despite the abuse?

• If you knew someone in a similar situation, what would you tell them to do about it?

• Do you think Anele should report the abusive behaviour of her husband to the police? Why?

• Imagine Anele is your client. As a social worker, how would you work with her?

9.1 Introduction

Feminisms articulate that the relationships among men and women in society are unequal, and that women are oppressed because of their gender. However, since women are not a homogenous grouping, varying strands of feminisms have arisen over time. These strands emerged in response to various historical, social and political developments that have been aligned with the various waves of feminisms. Each strand of feminism understands and theorises gender relations in a unique way, and each strand provides different solutions for tackling the oppression of women. Hence, feminisms are not just theoretical perspectives, but are also social, cultural, political and economic movements for the assertion of women's rights and interests. The use of the term feminisms (plural) instead of feminism (singular) accentuates that even within each type of feminism, there is heterogeneity.

> **Feminisms**, promote women's rights and interests by endeavouring to challenge patriarchal social, cultural, political and economic structures that discriminate against women.

Reflective question
Would you consider yourself to be a feminist? Why or why not?

This chapter provides an overview of four strands of feminisms. For each strand, I firstly provide an outline and brief critique of the strand. Secondly, I provide some insights as to how social workers could apply that strand of feminism. And thirdly, I suggest options for the application of each type of feminism to Anele's experience (Case study 1) of domestic violence at the various levels in the ecosystem (see Chapter 5). Whilst many accounts of feminisms start with liberal feminism, this chapter will start with decolonial feminisms that emerged in Africa and that are more relevant to the African context. It concludes with the commonalities among the various strands of feminisms.

We focus in this chapter on domestic violence, which is one form of violence against women. As illustrated in Case study 1, violence against women is one of the most tangible forms of women's oppression. *Domestic violence* for the purposes of this chapter, as a subset of violence against women, occurs when a male abuses his female intimate partner physically, emotionally, financially and/or sexually (Rasool, 2017a). *Violence against women*, on the other hand, is a term used:

> ... to encapsulate a variety of forms of violence experienced by women because of their gender, either within the household or outside the family. The various types of violence include rape, domestic violence, sexual harassment, female genital mutilation and femicide, among others (Rasool, 2011:31).

Research indicates that many young people have witnessed domestic violence (Rasool, 2017a). Some of you may also have similarly witnessed domestic violence in your homes. And perhaps you yourself have even been a victim of rape or sexual harassment.

Feminisms provide you as a social worker with a lens from which to consider the ways in which women are oppressed and treated differently from men. This discrimination leads to women being denied equal opportunities, resources and access. As a social worker, your role is to address discrimination and enable women's access to opportunities and resources.

9.2 Strands of feminism

There are various strands of feminism ranging from liberal feminism, which is the first strand of feminism to be explicitly articulated, to African strands that are more relevant to those of us who live and work in Africa. There are also theoretical viewpoints from women in Africa who do not align themselves politically with the concept feminism, but are concerned with women's interests and activism, such as womanism. Varying strands of feminism have emerged over time, which have been conceptualised according to the waves of how feminisms have evolved historically.

Suffragettes are synonymous with the first wave of feminisms. Their struggle for women's political power during the nineteenth and early twentieth century in the USA and UK is deemed to be central to the birth of the first wave of feminisms. To expand the feminist movement beyond political transformation, the second wave of feminisms emerged between the 1960s and 1980s. The second wave extended the fight for transformation to the social and cultural domains of women's lives and proclaimed that 'the personal is political' (Hanisch, 1970:76). However, first- and second-wave feminists were seen as representing the interests of white, middle-class, heterosexual women only.

In response to the limitations of the second wave of feminisms, which ignored issues of race, sexuality, ethnicity, location and other social divisions, a third wave of feminisms emerged. bell hooks' (2007) seminal book *Ain't I a woman* is often referred to as being iconic to the third wave of feminists, since she highlighted the exclusionary nature of earlier feminisms that omitted the lived experiences of women of 'colour'.[1] The third wave of feminisms was influenced by postcolonial and decolonial thought, and thus deconstructed the perception of universal womanhood. The third wave challenges 'artificial categories of identity, gender, and sexuality' (Rampton, 2015:para 12). This chapter will begin with a discussion of pre-, post-, anti- and de-colonial feminisms, to give them prominence.

Decolonising the her-story of feminism

The contribution of the suffragettes to bringing women's oppression into the political domain cannot be underestimated. However, historical accounts of feminism seem to start only from the suffragettes and have ignored the struggles and resistance of women in the Global South before their emergence. It seems that women's roles and contributions prior to the nineteenth century are not encompassed in the ways the waves of feminism are articulated (Rampton, 2015). Hence, the roles of women in societies, prior to the suffragettes, and the resistance to male domination and sexual discrimination in the Global South are invisible. Perhaps this is because of the perception that these women had not amassed as a political movement to represent women's interests. An additional explanation for their invisibility may be linked to the way history has been written based on imperialist and colonial viewpoints, which render the contribution of women in the South invisible. Whilst, post-colonial and de-colonial feminisms are seen as responses to Western feminists and colonial imposition, many women in the Global South have been active and resistant to forms of patriarchy long before colonisation (Ntombovuyo, 2016). Perhaps the agenda for decolonisation may change the gaze of history to more actively highlight the roles of women in various societies prior to the suffragettes. Some of these histories, or rather 'her-stories', are being rediscovered and written about in some parts of the world (Ranmuthugala, 2018). To accentuate the voices of women in Africa, this chapter will start with de-colonial feminisms.

---

1 The author bell hooks does not capitalise her name because she prefers to emphasise her work and ideas. Therefore, the authors of this book decided to honour how she writes about herself.

The fourth wave of feminisms emerged through the extension of feminist activism in the online domain (Munro, 2013). Rampton (2015:para 19) states that the internet plays an important role in 'gender-bending and levelling hierarchies'. The internet creates the space for young and historically marginalised women to play a significant role in shaping feminist thought and politics (Munro, 2013). Whilst the various waves appear as analytically separate stages in history, they are rather extensions of each other, as activism in all areas remains an ongoing domain of struggle and contestation.

There are various types of feminisms. Some feminisms emerged because of women's experiences of oppression in religion – such as Jewish, Islamic, Christian, or Wiccan feminisms – whilst other feminisms emerged on particular continents such as Latin American or Indian feminisms, which speak to the issues that women are facing in specific regions of the world. Other feminisms emerged out of socio-political and historical events or movements such as Marxist, eco or transnational feminisms.

As a result, feminisms are constantly evolving in relation to women's experiences of oppression based on their lived experiences in varied socio-historical contexts, as well as resistance to feminisms. Payne (2005:257) contends that '[t]he resistance to feminism seems to lie in the refusal of male institutions, including marriage, employment and social work agencies, to give up power'. Further, as conceptions of women's oppression deepen, feminisms evolve, and as women share their varying life experiences, more strands of feminism or womanism emerge – all of which cannot be covered here (such as Islamic, township, bantu, and Transatlantic feminisms). The descriptions below are merely a summary of the salient aspects of some of the strands of feminism, rather than a comprehensive account of the various theoretical nuances that inform these perspectives. It is important to note that even within the different strands of feminism that I discuss below, there are divergent views and some overlap.

In this chapter, in each section, I provide an overview of the theory of pre-, post-, anti- and de-colonial feminisms (focusing particularly on African feminisms, Africana womanisms and nego-feminism), liberal, Marxist/socialist, and radical feminisms. You will notice that these feminisms are not presented in chronological order. Nor does the chapter start with feminisms developed in the Global North, as is typically how theory is presented. Instead, it starts with a range of feminisms that evolved in the Global South, and particularly in Africa, since it is these feminisms that speak most closely to the experiences of African women and that align most closely with decoloniality.

Each of these strands of feminism uses a different analysis to understand:

- women's oppression in society;
- its causes and consequences; and
- the appropriate strategies to attain women's liberation (Tong, 1995).

Under each type of feminism there is a practice section that provides some pointers or questions about how a social worker, working from each perspective, would engage in practice. There is also an application section for each type of feminism through which the theory is related to the case study of Anele (Case study 1). Throughout there are questions for reflections and some activities at the end to make feminism real.

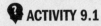

ACTIVITY 9.1

What is the word for 'feminism' in your home language? Now translate the same word back into English. How similar or different is it to the English-language explanation of feminism provided in this chapter? If you struggle to find an equivalent word for feminism in your home language, what might that tell you about the significance of feminism in your culture?

9.3   Pre-, post-, anti- and de-colonial feminisms

9.3.1   Theory

Post-, anti- and de-colonial feminists highlight the impact of the relationship between race, gender, colonialism and imperialism on women's oppression (Lewis, 2001). Post-, anti- and de-colonial thought resulted in varying forms of feminisms, including African feminisms, Latina feminisms, Indian feminisms, Caribbean feminisms and other feminisms from the Global South, all of which are diverse in their approaches, based on their locationality (Lewis, 2001). It has been argued that postcolonial thought emerged from India and decolonial thought from Latin America.

> *Pre-, post-, anti- and de-colonial feminisms*, bodies of knowledge that consider the relationship among patriarchy and the impacts of colonisation, imperialism, and other forms of racialisation.

In my discussions here, I have chosen to include also pre-colonial feminisms, since the terms post-, anti- and de-colonial imply that feminisms in Africa and in the Global South emerged only in response to colonialism. The latter two terms ignore the struggles and challenges that women engaged with during pre-colonial and colonial times in response to patriarchy and gender power hierarchies. In Africa, for example, oral traditions predominated, so women's struggles were possibly not written down. But, women from the Global South may have constructed, reconstructed and negotiated patriarchy in the way they related stories in their communities and to their children. In many African pre-colonial societies women not only could but also did occupy important leadership positions (Ntombovuyo, 2016). Hence, resistance to patriarchy occurred prior to and during colonisation in the Global South, and these her-stories may not be documented. Moreover, in many countries, women were central to the liberation struggles to end colonisation (Hassim, 1991). Women from the Global South have been engaged in writing her-stories to expand on the contributions of women in these contexts, as well as in challenging colonial impositions on their identity, subjectivities and experiences.

Pre-, post-, anti- and de-colonial feminisms and, by extension, African feminisms emerged as a critique of the way in which Western feminists mainstreamed the experiences of Western women at the expense of women from other parts of the world (Mohanty, 1991; Fennell & Arnot, 2009). Lyons (2000) contends that there have been very few attempts in mainstream Western feminisms to understand the strengths of social systems from the Global South. Due to the mainstreaming of the experiences and views of Western women, pre-, post-, anti- and de-colonial feminisms argue that the struggles of women from the Global South against oppressive systems have largely been ignored because their social status is generally viewed as subordinate in Western literature (Lyons, 2000). Western feminist movements have thereby lost opportunities to learn from the resistance methods employed by women in the Global South in fighting patriarchy and other systems of oppression (Mohanty, 1991).

Pre-, post-, anti- and de-colonial feminisms are concerned with looking at local knowledge systems and challenging imperialist, colonial, racist and patriarchal discourses about women in the Global South. Pre-, post-, anti- and de-colonial feminists call for the decentralisation of gender philosophies to include the cultures, points of reference, and experiences of black women and/or women from the Global South. Although the various feminisms that hailed from the Global South are important, due to space constraints and our location in Africa, only some types of feminisms that are relevant to African women, such as African feminisms, Africana womanisms and nego-feminism, will be discussed below.

9.3.1.1 African feminisms

African feminisms challenged the ways in which Western feminists depicted African women and are concerned with accentuating the concerns and interests of African women. However, since Africa is a huge continent, African feminist thinking and activism are as diverse as Africa itself. Nevertheless, African feminisms create the space for the lived experiences of African women to be foregrounded, and thus give life to feminist theorisation by women in Africa (Nnaemeka, 2003). This perspective reinforces the fact that Africans, and particularly African women, are not merely subjects of research, but actors in their worlds and they can, and do, define their own engagements and worldviews (Nnaemeka, 2003).

> **African feminisms**, theories that are concerned with decentring patriarchal as well as racist, colonial and imperialist discourses about African women and reinforcing self-definition and engagement that are embedded in the lived realities of African women.

African feminisms provide the space for African norms and values to be recognised, but this does not necessarily mean they are concerned with valorising the traditional, since Ake (1988:19) indicates that 'there is no fossilized existence of the African past available for us to fall back on'. Ake (1988:19) suggests we should rather be concerned with the indigenous, that is, 'whatever the people consider important to their lives, whatever they regard as an authentic expression of themselves'. African feminisms also engage with those aspects of culture that may be oppressive to women – not in a way that is denigrating but rather in ways that recognise that diverse women, especially those from different class locations, may engage and experience cultural practices differently (Coleman, 2013). Hence, African feminisms have resulted in 'strategies and approaches that are sometimes complementary and supportive, and sometimes competing and adversarial' (Nnaemeka, 1998:5).

For African women, motherhood in African society is not a subordinate position; it is imbued with power (Mekgwe, 2003). In pre-colonial Zulu society, for example, 'the importance of women's labour, as well as their reproductive responsibilities, gave women crucial rights and obligations, especially as they aged' (Mekgwe, 2003:75). Hence, African feminists argue that women in African societies play an important role in the sustenance and maintenance of the home, which they contend is a central place in African society (Ntombovuyo, 2016). African feminisms further argue that women are afforded power by being the centre of the home (Mekgwe, 2003), which differs from the arguments made by Western feminists that suggest motherhood confines women to the domestic sphere and this contributes to their oppression.

Reflective question
What makes African feminisms different from other feminisms?

Some African women are, however, not comfortable aligning themselves with the term feminist and have problematised African feminisms as being contained within a feminist framework that has marginalised African women (Hudson-Weems, 1993). Hence, some African women prefer to call themselves African womanists.

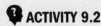

ACTIVITY 9.2

Who are the important African black women who were social work leaders in the anti-apartheid struggle? Do some internet research to find out more about people like Ellen Kuzwayo and Winnie Madikizela-Mandela.

9.3.1.2   Africana womanisms

In response to the need for African women to self-actualise, self-identify and self-name, Clenora Hudson-Weems coined the term Africana womanism in 1987 (Phillips, 2006).

Africana womanism, an ideology that aims to reflect the unique histories and needs of African women, with its roots firmly established in African culture. It differs from African feminisms in that it prioritises race over gender and advocates for a non-adversarial relationship with men (Hudson-Weems, 1993, 1989; Reed, 2001).

Hudson-Weems (1993) suggests that Africana womanisms are centrally based on the insider perspective, and hence African women themselves need to identify their priorities and find solutions to social issues affecting them. Reed (2001) confirms that women with first-hand experience are the most reliable sources of information for theorising both African experiences and possible solutions. She further argues that the solutions to the oppression of African women are present in African social systems.

Hudson-Weems (1993) also asserts that many types of feminisms are not applicable to African women, since the background and experiences of white people, as well as black people from other contexts, are vastly different from black women located in Africa. She contends that African women experience 'forms of oppression that are not necessarily a part of the overall White women's experiences' (Hudson-Weems, 1989:42), because of the complex issues that result from racial oppression. The African woman or 'Africana' woman is confronted by triple oppression: racism; classism; and sexism (Ogunyemi, 1985). Hence, the different forms of victimisation experienced by African women need to be prioritised and addressed (Hudson-Weems, 1993). However, she suggests that sexism is a result of racism and classism, and sexism is therefore a secondary problem (Coleman, 2013), which is different to what many African feminists would articulate.

Africana womanisms, like womanism, contend that, instead of alienating Africana men, 'Africanans' must work hand in glove with African men for a renegotiation of roles (Hudson-Weems, 1989, 1993). Ladner (1971) articulates that black women do not necessarily perceive black men as enemies, but suggests that social structures subjugate black men, women and children. The Southern African concept of *Ubuntu* – which translates to 'I am because we are' (Goduka, 2000) (see Chapter 6) – aligns with an Africana womanism perspective, since it is drawn from African culture and values a communalist view of humanity. This perspective gives precedence to the community over the individual (Oyewumi, 1998), which is juxtaposed with some types of Western feminisms that are argued to give precedence to the individual.

Some African writers (Makaudze, 2014; Ntiri, 2001) have shown how Africana womanisms are applied in the African context. For example, Makaudze (2014) conducted research in

Zimbabwe in which the games children played were analysed from an Africana womanist perspective. Through this research, it was argued that Shona girls are taught qualities that have strong Africana womanist foundations, such as family centeredness, respect for elders, and nurturing (Makaudze, 2014).

Reflective questions
- Why do you think some African women struggle to align with feminisms?
- Which women do you think are more likely to align with womanism?

9.3.1.3   Nego-feminism

Nnaemeka (2003), a Nigerian woman, conceptualised nego-feminism as a feminism that allows for negotiation with patriarchy. Aligned with African conceptions of shared values, compromise and balance, it disengages from egotism.

> *Nego-feminism*, incorporates negotiation, not only with respect to giving and taking, but also to 'go around' (Nnaemeka, 2003:378) patriarchy. It also advocates for mutual learning between Global West and Global South cultural systems.

Nnaemeka (2003:380) contends that 'African women working for social change build on the indigenous by defining and modulating their feminist struggle in deference to cultural and local imperatives'. So in effect, nego-feminism accounts for the contexts in which African women negotiate with or go around patriarchy to contribute to stability in the system, instead of the Western approaches to feminism that advocate for challenging and overthrowing systems of patriarchy.

Nego-feminism highlights the locatedness of feminism in relation to the real context in which women live, where negotiation with systems of power, like patriarchy, is the lived reality of African women. Nnaemeka (2003) provides the example of Burkina Faso, where women save some of their household financial allocation until they have enough to open a small shop or kiosk in or near their homes to sustain themselves and their families, whilst still maintaining their care roles. In this way, they go around patriarchy to acquire capital and negotiate the public and private spaces in non-confrontational ways to be involved in production, whilst still engaged in their reproductive roles.

Nego-feminism also asserts that in interactions between the West and the rest, learning is mutual (Nnaemeka, 2003). Nnaemeka (2003) contends that colonialists and people from the West can learn values such as connectedness, community and family from African people, as much as Africans learn individualism from the West. Hence, culture is dynamic and mutually influenced by global engagements and the transfer of knowledge and information. Therefore, nego-feminism contends that Western feminisms, the feminisms that are described in the next few sections, can learn from Southern feminisms. It also articulates how women negotiate and work around patriarchal structures, rather than actively confronting them.

Reflective questions
- Does race complicate issues of gender? Do white men have more power than black men or women?
- Should we address race, class or gender first?
- What are the implications for black women when they report their male black partners to a racist state for domestic violence?

9.3.2 Decolonial social work practice

African feminisms, Africana womanisms, township feminisms, Bantu feminisms, stiwanism, nego-feminism, etc. are particularly pertinent for South African social workers based on our location in Africa. As an African social worker, you would consider how race, colonialism, class and gender intersect to disempower African women at micro, mezzo and macro levels. You would ask African women, as individuals or in collectives, how they would prefer to solve the issue they face in ways that are cognisant of their cultural and historical contexts. At mezzo level, you could work with black women to assist them in finding ways to address their shared issues and look at ways they can go around patriarchy to achieve their objectives. At macro level, you would look at colonial and racial structures as embedded in institutions that need to be challenged and changed.

9.3.3 Application

In the case of Anele, when working with her at micro level using pre-, post-, anti- and de-colonial feminisms, you would ask her what kind of help she would like. If you suggest she should leave and go to a shelter or other safe place to escape domestic violence, you would consider with her the cultural implications of leaving the home of her husband with their shared children. You would discuss with her if there are any financial implications for her or her family with respect to *lobola* if she leaves. If you are helping her access a protection order, you would consider if the state deals with black men in harsher ways than white men, and what are the entrenched social and emotional implications for black women of using the police as a resource after domestic violence.

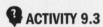 **ACTIVITY 9.3**

Interview a few young black women in townships or rural areas to ask them what their greatest concerns are and what they think can and should be done about them.

Reflective question
What are your thoughts about Africana womanisms and nego-feminism?

9.4 Liberal feminism

9.4.1 Theory

The first strand of feminism, which emerged in the eighteenth century, is liberal feminism. Liberal feminism explains women's discrimination in society as being grounded in their lack of formal equality, and frames women's rights in terms of human rights (Mill, 1984:302; Nienaber & Moraka, 2016:145). Hence, liberal feminism places strong emphasis on the state, and changing the laws in a society to increase access to equal opportunities and privileges for the attainment of gender equality (Lindsay, 2015; Bryson, 1999).

> *Liberal feminism*, concerned with challenging formal systems, particularly the state, to promote and attain gender equality. It frames women's rights as human rights.

Liberal feminism has been criticised for accepting male values. This criticism is centred on the idea that the liberal feminism goals of changing laws and creating opportunities for women are said to work within the existent male-dominated legal frameworks, and do not challenge or reconfigure these frameworks (Verloo & Lombardo, 2007). It has also been argued that liberal feminism does not provide a 'coherent analysis of women's oppression' (Waylen, 1996:424), since other aspects such as race, class and sexuality are ignored. Because of these criticisms, socialist/Marxist feminisms and radical feminisms, both offering a structuralist perspective, predominated in the early 1970s.

Reflective question
If you are a liberal feminist in an organisation that deals with domestic violence, what activities would you engage in?

9.4.2 Practice

As a social worker, from a liberal feminism paradigm, your work would focus on changing laws that discriminate against women in society and finding ways to increase women's access to opportunities in society. For instance, as a liberal feminist you would question why men dominate certain professions and you would call for the systematic introduction of policies and laws that eradicate such inequality (Nienaber & Moraka, 2016:145). You would also be engaged in lobbying for changes to all laws that are discriminatory toward women.

9.4.3 Application

To assist Anele at the micro level using liberal feminist theory, you would advise her that she could report the domestic violence to the police, if she chooses, and obtain a protection order. You would learn and understand the intricacies of the provisions of any Act in your country that addresses domestic violence to assist Anele with obtaining a protection order and reporting to the police. At the mezzo level you could work with the police and/or magistrates to educate them about domestic violence and how to implement the Act in a gender-sensitive manner. At the macro level, you could do research and lobby to improve legislation dealing with violence against women and assist with creating new legislation to enable women like Anele to deal with domestic violence (e.g., legislation that creates access to secondary housing for abused women when they leave a shelter).

9.5 Socialist and Marxist feminisms

9.5.1 Theory

Socialist and Marxist feminisms will be discussed together as they share some commonalities in terms of how they conceptualise the oppression of women, which are stronger than their differences.

Socialist and Marxist feminisms both view capitalism as a major factor in the oppression of women (Osmond & Thorne, 2009), hence they focus on issues of class. Both also focus their analysis on unequal gender relations within the areas of production and reproduction. Production refers to the labour market domain, which could include participation in the formal or informal economies that have a monetary value attached (Tattwamasi & Lakshmi, 2014:46). Reproduction refers to the areas of work in the domestic domain, such as the care of children or parents, the production of food, cleaning, and other household-related chores (Tong, 2009).

> **Socialist and Marxist feminisms**, class-based analyses of gender oppression that aim to change the balance of power in the areas of production and reproduction.

Both agree that the exploitation and oppression of women are enabled by the family as a social institution (Gimenez, 2005). They argue that women in the family are disproportionately involved in reproduction, even if they are formally employed. This is especially so in countries with high rates of female-headed households and single motherhood. On the other hand, there is *no* expectation for men to be involved in domestic duties, and they can opt out of these without consequence. For women, involvement in the sphere of reproduction is not a choice; it is an expectation (Lindsey, 2015). Subsequently, this arrangement enables women's dependence on men in the family, as work in the reproductive sphere is unpaid, unlike work in the sphere of production (Osmond & Thorne, 2009). Socialist feminists expand the Marxist analysis to argue that work in the domestic sphere such as cooking is part of production, not just consumption (Ferguson et al., 2018); hence, reproduction should have a monetary value attached and greater social value.

Socialist and Marxist feminisms are important perspectives, even in the Global South, for pre-, post-, anti- and de-colonial feminists, since sometimes elite women in the South who are engaged in feminist discussions are not inclusive of the voices of marginalised groups of women, like working class, poor, and black women (Maluf, 2011). For example, Maluf (2011:43) relates how, at a Latin-American and Caribbean Women's Meeting, 'several women from a Rio de Janeiro favela (informal settlement) arrived in a bus demanding the right to participate in the meeting without paying the registration fee'. Hence, feminists need to think of ways to include poor and marginalised women, who have limited financial resources, in decision-making bodies.

Like liberal feminisms, socialist and Marxist feminisms have been criticised for being based on masculinist ideologies. In addition, an unhappy marriage exists between feminism and Marxism since the latter argues for the primacy of class and the former for the primacy of gender (Bryson, 1999).

Reflective questions
- If you look at the earnings in your household, who brings money into the house and who decides how the money is spent? Who often takes care of children and the elderly? What are the implications of this for power dynamics?
- What are the implications, for men and women, of not giving a monetary value to care work?

9.5.2   Practice

As a social worker practising from a socialist or Marxist perspective, your activities would focus on addressing inequality that persists because of class differentiation. You would consider how issues of class, that is, where people are located in the class hierarchy, impact on their everyday functioning. For example, you may consider how working-class women have less access to care for their children than upper-class women, since they can outsource their care to nannies, who are usually women from the working class (Rasool, 2017b). In many parts of the world, like some parts of Africa and Asia, many poor women engage in domestic work in households for middle and upper-class women. You would also be concerned with issues like the wages women earn compared to both men and women from different class locations.

Reflective questions
- If you are a socialist and Marxist feminist, what issue would be more important to you: class or gender?
- What issues would you engage with at micro, mezzo and macro levels as a social worker who has adopted socialist or Marxist feminisms?

9.5.3   Application

As a socialist and Marxist feminist, your analysis of Anele's circumstances would focus on the two spheres of production and reproduction. You would consider unacknowledged costs to her personally for working in reproduction only and not production. Even though Anele and Steve live in the same household, Anele is poorer than Steve and dependent on him for survival. There would also be a class differential between Anele and Steve – if Anele leaves the abusive relationship, she would be unemployed, but Steve would still be employed. Hence, Anele's work in the sphere of reproduction has made her dependent on her husband and hampered her advancement in the sphere of production. The possibility of finding a job is encumbered as she hasn't worked for many years. At the mezzo level you could help her and other women in similar situations to enhance and update their skills in order to help them increase their chances of obtaining employment.

When working at the macro level, you would critique how in society the care work women engage in is not considered to be work, because it is not remunerated monetarily. You would look at the benefit to society and her husband (in terms of the time he has available to spend on productive labour and on himself socially) by her being a homemaker. This would involve accounting for the time she spends on the needs of her husband in her role as wife, and how much times she spends on caring for her children in her role as mother. You would therefore work with structural systems and policies to find ways to increase the value of care work in the family and community and allocate a costing to care work (Rasool, 2017b).

Even in cases where women work in either the formal or informal economy, they are expected as a 'duty' to be active in the reproductive sphere after work (cook, clean and take care of their children), with no similar expectation of men. Mchunu (as cited in Hassim, 1991:1), from the South African Inkatha Women's Brigade, has argued that:

> Women have the added burden of home-management and child-care irre-
> spective of whether they are full-time housewives or employees. These two
> roles cannot be shirked by women no matter how much we cry for equality.

As a socialist and Marxist feminist, you would attempt to reorganise social norms that permit women to work more than 15 hours a day on care work, such as household duties and child-rearing that is unpaid.

One of the ways to do this, at all levels in the ecosystem, is to encourage men to be more active in child-rearing and other domestic duties. Men tend to spend approximately 8–10 hours on productive work in the labour market, then go home to rest, assuming the women had done 'nothing' at home all day. Hence, you would engage both men and women in group work or individual counselling about their involvement in or lack thereof in both production and reproduction.

9.6 Radical feminisms

9.6.1 Theory

Radical feminisms articulate gender divisions as the primary division in society and argue that the roots of female oppression stem from men's control over women's sexuality. Radical feminisms argue that men benefit from women's oppression, through their dominant social status. They use the concept of 'patriarchy' to describe systems of male domination (Bryson, 1999; Waylen, 1996). Hence, radical feminisms suggest that society considers women to be inferior to men (Gunew, 2013) and valorises male values and attributes (Gardiner, 2005).

Radical feminisms, consider gender to be the most important consideration in understanding society, since radical feminists argue that men have more power than women in society and benefit from women's subordination.

Patriarchy, a system in which male values, priorities, privileges, and access, dominate social thought and institutions which results in alienating and excluding the needs, views and concerns of women (Rasool, forthcoming).

An important focus of radical feminisms has been to challenge patriarchal constructions of masculinity such as competitiveness, aggression, emotionally unavailability and control (Gardiner, 2005). Radical feminisms argue that these aggressive masculinities contribute to the widespread acceptance of rape and domestic violence, as well as the proliferation and glorification of wars and other types of violent activities (Whisnant, 2017). Radical feminists indicate that violence against women is rampant in societies that valorise violent behaviour. Hence, radical feminists suggest that if men incorporated more female traits such as warmth, nurturing and caring, they would be less prone to violence (Beynon, 2002). They further suggest that the oppression of women is commercialised through pornography, prostitution and the depiction of women as sex objects in the media (Jóhannsdóttir, 2009) (see Annotated websites and activities).

By assuming that men are violent and socially dominant, and presuming that women are largely nurturing and socially subservient, radical feminists have generalised the attributes and experiences of both men and women, thereby limiting their possibilities of having varying traits and characteristics that do not conform to stereotypical notions.

Reflective questions
- Do you think feminism excludes men?
- Can a man be a feminist? If so, which type of feminist?
- Do you think there is a need to advocate for women's rights?

9.6.2 Practice

The solution to women's oppression, according to radical feminists, is to challenge patriarchal constructions of masculinity and eventually overthrow patriarchy (Gardiner, 2005). A central feature of radical feminist activism has been to create institutions that respond to the needs of women; to create safe spaces to protect vulnerable women; and to produce knowledge that is sensitive to and reflective of women's lived experiences (Gunew, 2013). For radical feminists, this means the creation of 'women only' spaces that are devoid of the patriarchal gender hierarchy (Gunew, 2013). Over the years, radical feminisms have successfully campaigned for laws that criminalise coercive practices such as date and marital rape (West, 2008). Radical feminisms have been in the forefront of building safe houses for abused women and support centres for woman survivors of sexual assault and rape (Spain, 2016).

Reflective questions
- What is the core focus of a radical feminist social worker?
- If you were working with a victim of domestic violence (Anele) from this perspective, how would you assist her?

9.6.3 Application

As a radical feminist social worker, at micro level, in the case of Anele, you would refer her to a shelter for abused women, which is a safe women-only space. At macro level, social workers could challenge the structures and institutions that are patriarchal and discriminatory towards women. For example, social workers can research the struggles women face in accessing justice when reporting rape and domestic violence. Advocating and lobbying the criminal justice system to make changes in rape procedures would be powerful in increasing women's access to justice. At mezzo level, social workers can train judges, magistrates and prosecutors to improve their knowledge on sexual and domestic violence, and to consider responding more appropriately in cases of violence against women with regard to what evidence can be led in court. For instance, educating legal professionals on the implications and pitfalls of leading evidence on the sexual history of rape survivors, which should be inadmissible, would prevent the re-victimisation of women in rape trials.

First- and second-wave feminists – including liberal, Marxist, socialist and radical feminists – have been criticised by post-, anti- and de-colonial feminists for assuming a unitary and ahistorical notion of 'women', assuming they have shared interests.

Reflective questions
- What were the concerns of African women about first- and second-wave feminisms?
- Do you agree with African women about feminism? Why?

9.7 Commonalities among feminist strands

Whilst feminism is not a hegemonic concept, since women 'have different subject positions as a product of different structural conditions' (Waylen, 1996:9), there are some common threads that apply across the strands of feminism. Some of the commonalities that exist among the varying strands of feminism, according to Stanley and Wise (1983), are that: women are oppressed; the personal is political; and women's or feminist consciousness is distinctive. Each of these is discussed below.

- **Women are oppressed**. The ways in which women are oppressed has been articulated by the various types of feminisms above. Liberal feminists have argued that women are oppressed through their exclusion from state and discriminatory laws. Socialist and Marxist feminists focus on how women are excluded from the productive sphere and abused through their unpaid work in the reproductive sphere. Radical feminists articulate how patriarchy that is embedded in institutions oppresses women. Pre-, post-, anti- and de-colonial feminists highlight intersectionality and the ways in which colonialism, imperialism, racism, classism, homophobia and other forms of oppression intersect with gender. African feminisms provide the space for African women to articulate their needs and interests, as well as find ways to address them. Africana womanism was developed by women who do not align with the feminist concept, since they found it to be too challenging and exclusionary of men. However, they are still concerned with raising the voices of African women on the ground. Nego-feminism emerged to reflect the lived experiences of women in which they need to negotiate with patriarchy in order to survive. These African feminist/womanist perspectives are more inclusive of men and specific cultural requirements in an attempt to indigenise and decolonise women's experiences of oppression. They also highlight that African women are engaging with the issues that confront them and have generated culturally appropriate solutions to deal with their challenges.

- **The personal is political**. One of the core elements of feminist work has been to politicise the personal by debunking the privatisation of women's issues, since sexist power structures are replicated in the private domain (Stanley & Wise, 1983; Scott, 2004). As Hassim (1991:72) states:

  > It was feminists who first made the link between people's "inner worlds", their personal relationships and ways of living, and the organisation of society more broadly.

She further adds that this conception:

> ... [challenges] dominant (western) political theories, which have rested 'on a conception of the "political" that excludes the private domain of the home in which women mainly operate, as well as all that which is represented by femininity and women's bodies' (Hassim, 1991:72).

Violence against women, in particular, highlights the importance of making that which happens in the personal domain political. Some feminists argue that Anele's situation of domestic violence is not just a personal issue, since many women in the community are also experiencing domestic violence, sexual harassment and rape. Hence, it should not be kept silent and managed privately between the two people concerned; instead, it must be criminalised in law and dealt with by formal systems (criminal justice systems or tribal councils). Some feminists would contend that domestic violence reflects unequal power dynamics in society that gets replicated in the home context, which makes it difficult for women to escape domestic violence since it is reinforced by the social context (Rasool, 2015). Hence, some feminists argue that there is a need for action by the criminal justice system and other local powerful institutions, otherwise women will have no recourse to help.

This was evident in Anele's situation, when her mother sent her back to the abusive situation and the medical personnel did not ask about how she got the injuries. These professionals did not want to intervene because they think of domestic violence as a personal issue. In addition, because it happened in the private domain, it is hidden by the families who in many cases are aware of abuse, like Anele's in-laws, thereby making the violence women experience in the home invisible (Rasool, 2015). Some feminists, particularly liberal feminists, argue that domestic violence needs to be brought into the political arena, especially by enacting legislation. Others suggest different remedies, as was discussed throughout the chapter. Hence, Lister (1997) contends that women's position in the three spheres of the public space (namely the state, paid economy and polity) is limited by their status in the private sphere. Some feminists argue that for women to challenge their own oppression, they need to attain feminist consciousness.

• **Feminist consciousness**. Some theorists (e.g., Kabeer, 2001) argue that it is only through feminist consciousness that women can attain deeper levels of empowerment. Feminist consciousness is not something that 'oppressed groups can claim automatically' but rather something that must be achieved through struggle utilising both science and politics (Harding, 2004:8). To fight the oppression of women in its various forms at micro, mezzo and macro levels, women need to attain feminist consciousness and be involved in fighting gender inequality.

Because of our professional status as social workers, we have power to actively challenge gender discrimination. We can either maintain or challenge the status quo that contributes to women's oppression. As practitioners, we could practise in ways that reinforce gender, class and racial oppression or challenge it.

To challenge gender hierarchies and other power hierarchies, when doing research or when practising from a feminist social work approach, you need to ask the women concerned how they see the world and what is important to them, in order to work with them from within their worldview. These women's worldviews may be substantially different to your own worldview (see 'Decolonising the her-story of feminism' in section 9.2). So being aware of power relations – in society and also in our individual interactions with women in practice and research – becomes critical for us as social workers.

9.8   Conclusion

Feminism is not a homogenous concept; it has developed over time in different contexts. It is a controversial theory that is contested both within feminist circles and by those womanists who feel it alienates men. However, it provides a useful lens from which to unpack the ways in which women and girls are oppressed in society, and it provides areas to consider for challenging systems of discrimination at various levels in the ecosystem.

While most strands of feminism engage with these three concepts (women are oppressed, the personal is political, and feminist consciousness), the way in which they relate in practice and their areas of focus differ (Stanley & Wise, 1983), as was highlighted in the discussion on the various feminisms throughout. Pre-, post-, anti- and de-colonial feminists highlight the oppression of women in the Global South, which they argue was obscured and ignored by first- and second-wave feminists. African feminists particularly reflect on the differential experiences of African women, because of their location in Africa and the multiple oppressions they experience. Hence, as social workers located in Africa, we need to consider the specific and unique socio-cultural and spiritual issues that African women encounter, which may be different for women in other contexts.

Chapter activity

1. **Reflective questions**.
    1.1 In what ways were your views on feminism, prior to reading this chapter, confirmed or challenged? Explain your answer.
    1.2 Do any of these theories align with your thoughts or beliefs? Explain the alignment or lack thereof.
    1.3 What would you add or change to the theory of your choice to make it more relevant to your life?
    1.4 Would you consider yourself to be a feminist (or pro-feminist, the term we tend to use for men)? Has this changed after reading this chapter?
2. **Personal context**.
    2.1 Think about your mother or another significant woman in your life. Can any of these feminist or womanist theories help you understand their lives and roles in society?
    2.2 Would you use these theories to challenge gender oppression in your community?
3. **Advocacy**.
    3.1 Do women have enough power to negotiate patriarchy with men?
    3.2 Will men give up the power and privilege they obtain merely by being men?
    3.3 If you had to work at a macro level in your community, how would you work with men around addressing violence against women and sharing the care work in families?
4. **Critical questions**.
    4.1 Has your country done enough to address gender inequality and women's issues? Explain your views.
    4.2 How would gender equality benefit society (men, women and children)?

References

Ake, C: 'Building on the indigenous'. *In*: Frühling, P (ed.). 1988. *Recovery in Africa: A challenge for development cooperation in the 1990s*. pp. 19–22. Stockholm: Swedish Ministry of Foreign Affairs.

Beynon, J. 2002. *Masculinities and culture*. Philadelphia: Open University Press.

Bryson, V. 1999. *Feminist debates: Issues of theory and political practice*. New York: NYU Press.

Coleman, MA: 'Ain't I a womanist too?'. *In*: Coleman, MA (ed.). 2013. *Ain't I a womanist too? Third wave womanist religious thought*. pp. 1–31. Minneapolis, MN: Fortress Press.

Fennell, S & Arnot, M. 2009. Decentring hegemonic gender theory: The implications for educational research. *Research Consortium on Educational Outcomes and Poverty* (Working Paper no. 21). Development Studies and Faculty of Education, University of Cambridge.

Ferguson, A, Hennessy, R & Nagel, M: 'Feminist perspectives on class and work'. *In*: Zalta, EN (ed.). 2018. *The Stanford Encyclopedia of Philosophy* (Spring 2018 Edition). [Online]. Available: https://plato.stanford.edu/archives/spr2018/entries/feminism-class/ [Accessed 17 March 2018].

Gardiner, J: 'Men, masculinities, and feminist theory'. *In*: Kimmel, MS, Hearn, J & Connell, RW (eds.). 2005. *Handbook of studies on men & masculinities*. pp. 35–50. Thousand Oaks, CA: Sage.

Gimenez, ME. 2005. Capitalism and the oppression of women: Marx revisited. *Science & Society*, 69(1):11–32.

Goduka, IN: 'African or indigenous philosophies; legitimizing spiritually centered wisdoms within the academy'. *In*: Higgs, P, Vakalisa, NCG, Mda, TV & Assie-Lumumba, NT (eds.). 2000. *African voices in education*. pp. 63–83. Cape Town: Juta.

Gunew, S. 2013. *Feminist knowledge (RLE feminist theory): Critique and construct*. London: Routledge.

Harding, SG (ed.). 2004. *The feminist standpoint theory reader: Intellectual and political controversies*. New York: Routledge.

Hanisch, C: 'The personal is political'. *In*: Firestone, S & Koedt, A (eds.). 1970. *Notes from the second year: Women's liberation: Major writings of the radical feminists*. pp. 76–78. New York: Radical Feminism.

Hassim, S. 1991. Gender, social location and feminist politics in South Africa. *Transformation*, 15:65–82.

hooks, b. 2007. *Ain't I a woman: Black women and feminism*. Boston, MA: South End Press.

Hudson-Weems, C. 1989. Cultural and agenda conflicts in academia: Critical issues for Africana women's studies. *Western Journal of Black Studies,* 13(4):185–189.

Hudson-Weems, C. 1993. *Africana womanism: Reclaiming ourselves*. Troy, MI: Bedford.

Jóhannsdóttir, NK. 2009. *Patriarchy and the subordination of women from a radical feminist point of view*. PhD thesis. University of Iceland. [Online]. Available: https://skemman.is/bitstream/1946/3017/1/Nina_Katrin_Johannasdottir_fixed.pdf [Accessed 18 March 2018].

Kabeer, N. 2001. Conflicts over credit: Reevaluating the empowerment potential of loans to women in rural Bangladesh. *World Development*, 29(1):63–8.

Ladner, JA: 'Racism and tradition: Black womanhood in historical perspective'. *In*: Steady, FC (ed.). 1971. *The black woman cross-culturally*. pp. 269–288. Cambridge, MA: Schenkman Books.

Lewis, D. 2001. Introduction: African feminisms. *Agenda: Empowering Women for Gender Equity*, 50:4–10.

Lindsey, LL. 2015. *Gender roles: A sociological perspective*. New York: Routledge.

Lister, R. 1991. Citizenship engendered. *Critical Social Policy*, 11(32):65–71.

Lyons, LT. 2000. Disrupting the center: Interrogating an 'Asian feminist' identity. *Communal/ Plural: Journal of Transnational and Cross-Cultural Studies*, 8(1):65–79.

Makaudze, G. 2014. Africana womanism and Shona children's games. *The Journal of Pan African Studies*, 1.6(10):128–143.

Maluf, SW. 2011. Brazilian feminisms: Central and peripheral issues. Feminist Review Conference Proceedings 2011. *Feminist Review*, pp. 36–51.

Mekgwe, P. 2008. Theorizing African feminism(s): The 'colonial' question. *Quest: An African Journal of Philosophy/Revue Africaine de Philosophie*, 20:11–22.

Mill, JS: 'The subjection of women'. *In*: Robson, JM (ed.). 1984. *The collected works of John Stuart Mill, Vol. 21: Essays on equality, law and education*. pp. 290–305. Toronto: University of Toronto Press.

Mohanty, C: 'Under Western eyes: Feminist scholarship and colonial discourses'. *In*: Mohanty, C, Russo, A & Torres, L (eds.). 1991. *Third world women and the politics of feminism*. pp. 51–80. Bloomington: Indiana University Press.

Munro, E (2013). *Feminism: A fourth wave?* Political Studies Association. [Online]. Available: https://www.psa.ac.uk/insight-plus/feminism-fourth-wave [Accessed 01 March 2018].

Nnaemeka, O: 'Introduction: Reading the rainbow'. *In*: Nnaemeka, O (ed.). 1998. *Sisterhood, feminisms, and power: From Africa to the Diaspora*. 1–35. Trenton, N.J.: Africa World Press.

Nnaemeka, O. 2003. Nego-feminism: Theorizing, practicing, and pruning Africa's way. *Signs: Journal of Women in Culture & Society*, 29(2):357–385.

Nienaber, H & Moraka, NV. 2016. Feminism in management research: A route to justly optimise talent. *Acta Commercii*, 16(2):139–163.

Ntiri, DW. 2001. Reassessing Africana womanism: Continuity and change. *The Western Journal of Black Studies*, 25(3):163–167.

Ntombovuyo, L. 2016. *Gender equality and women empowerment for Africa's renewal: Existing influences and future considerations*. [Online]. Available: https://www.mbeki.org/2018/06/01/gender-equality-and-women-empowerment-for-africas-renewal-existing-influences-and-future-considerations/ [Accessed 4 June 2018].

Ogunyemi, CO. 1985. Womanism: The dynamics of the contemporary black female novel in English. *Signs: Journal of Women in Culture and Society*, 11(1):63–80.

Osmond, MW & Thorne, B: 'Feminist theories'. *In*: Boss, P, Doherty, WJ, La Rossa, R, Schumm, WR & Steinmetz, SK (eds.). 2009. *Sourcebook of family theories and methods*. pp. 591–625. Boston, MA: Springer.

Oyewumi, O. 1998. Deconfounding gender: Feminist theorizing and Western culture. *Signs: Journal of Women in Culture and Society*, 23(4):1049–1062.

Payne, M. 2005. *Modern social work theory*. 3rd ed. New York: Palgrave MacMillan.

Phillips, R. 2006. Undoing an activist response: Feminism and the Australian government's domestic violence policy. *Critical Social Policy*, 26(1):192–219.

Rampton, M. 2015. *Four waves of feminism*. [Online]. Available: https://www.pacificu.edu/about/media/four-waves-feminism [Accessed 03 March 2018].

Ranmuthugala, MEP. 2018. *Widows and concubines: Tradition and deviance in the women of Kanthapura*. Paper presented at the 4th World Conference on Women's Studies, 3–5 May 2018, Colombo, Sri Lanka.

Rasool, S. 2011. *Help-seeking by abused women in South Africa*. Dissertation submitted to the University of Oxford, Oxford, UK.

Rasool, S. 2015. The influence of social constructions of family on abused women's help-seeking after domestic violence. *South African Review of Sociology*, 46(4):24–38.

Rasool, S. 2017a. Adolescent reports of experiencing gender based violence: Findings from a cross-sectional survey from schools in a South African city. *Gender and Behaviour*, 15(2):9109–9122.

Rasool, S: 'Gender and development'. *In*: Midgley, J & Pawar, M (eds.). 2017b. *Future directions for social development*. pp. 119–139. New York: Palgrave Macmillan.

Rasool, S (forthcoming). The implications of a patriarchal culture on women's access to 'formal' human rights in South Africa: A case study of domestic violence survivors.

Scott, SJS. 2004. The personal is still political: Heterosexuality, feminism and monogamy. *Feminism & Psychology*, 14(1):151–157.

Spain, D. 2016. *Constructive feminism women's spaces and women's rights in the American city*. Ithaca: Cornell University Press.

Stanley, L & Wise, S. 1983. *Breaking out feminist consciousness and feminist research*. New York: Routledge & Kegan Paul.

Tattwamasi, P & Lakshmi, L. 2014. 'Production' and 'reproduction' in feminism: Ideas, perspectives and concepts. *Indian Institute of Management Kozhikode Society & Management Review*, 3(1):45–53.

Tong, R: 'Feminist perspectives and gestational motherhood: The search for a unified legal focus'. *In*: Callahan, JC (ed.). 1995. *Reproduction, ethics, and the law: Feminist perspectives*. pp. 55–79. Bloomington, Indiana: Indiana University Press.

Tong, R. 2009. *Feminist thought: A more comprehensive introduction*. 3rd ed. Philadelphia, PA: Westview Press.

Verloo, M & Lombardo, E: 'Contested gender equality and policy variety in Europe: Introducing a critical frame analysis approach'. *In*: Verloo, M (ed.). 2007. *Multiple meanings of gender equality: A critical frame analysis of gender policies in Europe*. pp. 21–49. Budapest, Hungary: Central European University.

Waylen, G. 1996. *Gender in Third World politics*. Buckingham: Open University Press.

West, R. 2008. *Sex, law and consent* [archive paper]. Georgetown Law Faculty Working Papers. Working Paper 71. Georgetown University. [Online]. Available: https://scholarship.law.georgetown.edu/fwps_papers/71 [Accessed 29 March 2018].

Whisnant, R: 'Feminist perspectives on rape'. *In*: Zalta, EN. 2017. *The Stanford Encyclopedia of Philosophy* (Fall 2017 Edition). [Online]. Available: https://plato.stanford.edu/archives/fall2017/entries/feminism-rape/ [Accessed 16 March 2018].

Reed, PYA. 2001. African womanism and African feminism: A philosophical, literacy, and cosmological dialect on family?.*Western Journal of Black Studies*, 25:168–76.

Annotated websites

https://ocw.mit.edu/courses/womens-and-gender-studies/
This is a link for some courses on women and gender studies offered at the Massachusetts Institute of Technology. These are all completed courses – you cannot do them, but you can view their learning guides, assignments, etc.

http://www.agenda.org.za/
The link to this journal would provide interesting articles on a range of issues faced by many African women.

www.forharriet.com/2015/04/18-phenomenal-african-feminists-to-know.html?
This link provides some information about famous African feminists.

https://www.awid.org/whrd-tribute
This website provides a profile of over 400 women who have championed women's human rights around the globe.

https://www.youtube.com/watch?v=u_4dPB9MVS8
View this video on how women are treated as sex objects as part of the way in which patriarchy is entrenched in society. It also highlights, in a fun way, the implications of gender inequality for society. Answer the critical questions above after watching this video.

https://www.youtube.com/watch?v=mGiANjf94xc
Do you think women overreact to compliments and then call it sexual harassment? Watch this video. After watching it, ask women you know what they do on a daily basis to keep themselves safe from sexual harassment and rape.

https://www.youtube.com/watch?v=MOqIotJrFVM
This inspirational video is of Malala Yousafzai, a 17-year-old girl who is speaking at the Nobel Peace Prize awards ceremony. She is a campaigner for the education of girls and was shot in the head, for her activism. In this video she discusses the plight of girls in many parts of the world, including Africa, Asia and the Middle East.

(The author of this chapter acknowledges her funders the Oppenheimer Memorial Trust and the South African National Research Foundation for their support, and her research assistant, Innocent Mwatsiya, for his assistance.)

Sustainable livelihoods

Antoinette Lombard

A community working to sustain its own livelihoods

You work for an NGO that implements developmental social work with families and children in an urban township community. The NGO embraces both micro and macro practice and focuses on the intersection of the two in particular. Psychosocial services are complemented with income from social enterprises which contribute to sustainable development goals. People participation is central in the work of the NGO, and the childcare model that the NGO adopted includes childcare workers, team leaders and auxiliary social workers from the community.

In your engagement with the community, you observe the high level of poverty in the community. Household incomes are unstable; one or more members rely on piece jobs and many households depend on pensions and other social grants for survival. Most of the families and children with whom you work are either infected or affected by HIV and Aids.

However, despite these adversities, you observe how much hope and resilience the people have. You experience how people voluntary engage in programmes and activities, including the beading income-generating project, parenting programmes, school homework classes, home vegetable gardens, life skills and entrepreneurial skills training programmes. In addition, clients are employed in the NGO's compost and vegetable hydroponic social enterprises. You recognise the roles of many stakeholders working in partnership with you for social change, including the clients, the business sector, Department of Social Development, the school, clinics, community organisations, and university students in social work and other disciplines such as engineering. You experience the impact of using strength-based and empowerment approaches in your interventions. You learn how to create opportunities within the organisation for developing both staff and clients' capabilities to increase their choices for sustainable livelihoods. You realise that human development is more than income; it is also about well-being, social inclusion and protection of the environment.

Reflective questions
- What inspires you to work in this community?
- What strengths do people have in this community?
- What options do you see in this community for sustainable livelihoods?

10.1 Introduction

Poverty, unemployment and persisting inequalities have been the key drivers in the continuous search for development approaches and models to ensure people's survival and well-being. In the 1970s and 1980s, priorities and directions for development changed rapidly (Chambers & Conway, 1992). This debate had much to do with the pressing need to find sustainable solutions to eradicate poverty. As these authors further indicate, it was the values, concepts and methods that were narrowly applied by single academic and professional disciplines, called 'disciplinary reductionism', which have been increasingly challenged in this era. Now, we recognise the interrelatedness between ecology, economics and other social sciences.

This thinking started in the 1980s and 1990s and is known as an era where the focus of approaches to development shifted to human well-being and sustainability rather than just economic growth (Solesbury, 2003). There was a need for an approach to poverty eradication that goes beyond traditional definitions and approaches that narrowly focus 'on certain aspects or manifestations of poverty, such as low income, [while ignoring] other vital aspects of poverty such as vulnerability and social exclusion' (Krantz, 2001:1). In this chapter, you will see that sustainable livelihoods emerged from the development debate during this era. Development workers now widely agree on the importance of focusing on various factors and processes 'which either constrain or enhance poor people's ability to make a living in an economically, ecologically, and socially sustainable manner' (Krantz, 2001:1). This recognition gave birth to the sustainable livelihoods concept, which is 'a more coherent and integrated approach to poverty' (Krantz, 2001:1). It presents 'a way of thinking about the objectives, scope and priorities for development' and provides a framework that facilitates logical and structured discussion of different perspectives on sustainable livelihoods (Department for International Development (DFID), 1999: Section 1.1).

The sustainable livelihoods approach (SLA) is derived from both theory and practice and thus strengthens the connection between researchers and practitioners beyond the conventional way of a one-way linear relationship where research informs policy and policy is being implemented through practice. The SLA shows a pattern of relationships where the interaction between research, policy and practice can be presented in a triangle in which all three have two-way interactions with one another (Solesbury, 2003). The SLA is thus a broad and inclusive approach to addressing 'the priorities of poor people, both directly and at a policy level' (DIFD, 1999: Section 1.2). This explains the relevance of the approach in different contexts – locally, nationally and internationally – which resonates with the social worker's role in both local and global contexts within the sustainable development agenda (see Chapter 3).

The SLA draws from participatory approaches (DFID, 1999). In relation to this book, the SLA fits with developmental social work. The SLA also has close links with resilience theory (see Chapter 7) in that it prepares people to respond to shocks and trends that influence sustainable livelihoods. Furthermore, the SLA also strongly resonates with the strengths-based perspective in its focus on people's assets and inherent strengths, capabilities and people-centred processes. Chapter 13, section 13.3.3, of this book explains the links between asset-based community development (ABCD) and sustainable livelihoods, and section 13.3.4 explains ABCD's contribution to decolonial social work practice. It will deepen your understanding of this chapter if you read these sections of Chapter 13.

We start our discussion in this chapter by giving an overview of sustainable livelihoods in the context of poverty and development. The concept 'sustainable development' is then discussed as it evolved within the agenda of sustainable development. Next, the components of the sustainable livelihoods analytical framework will be discussed, followed by a critical reflection on the relevance of developmental social work for decolonial social work practice. Finally, the conclusion summarises some of the important aspects of this chapter.

10.2 Sustainable livelihoods, poverty and development

In Chapter 3, we discussed the relevance of social investment strategies in developmental social work. The SLA fits well with developmental social work in its emphasis on: poverty reduction; equity; people participation; human rights; capabilities and strengths-based perspectives; the micro and micro practice link; partnerships (across practice, policy and research); and sustainable development. The emphasis of the SLA on economic, social, environmental and institutional sustainability makes it an appropriate analytical and intervention tool for social work to contribute to the 17 goals of the 2030 Agenda for Sustainable Development (UN, 2015).

The SLA is underpinned by three insights into poverty (Krantz, 2001:10). The first is to understand that there is no 'automatic relationship' between economic growth and poverty reduction, 'since it all depends on the capabilities of the poor to take advantage of expanding economic opportunities'. Therefore, we should ask poor people what their challenges are to improve their situation in order to plan and develop appropriate support activities for them (Krantz, 2001).

Second, a view that has been conceived by poor people themselves is the realisation that poverty 'is not just a question of low income, but also includes other dimensions such as bad health, illiteracy, lack of social services', and in general, 'a state of vulnerability and feelings of powerlessness' (Krantz, 2001:10). It helps us to see 'the important links between different dimensions of poverty', and how improvement in one area may positively influence other areas. For example, a higher educational level 'may have positive effects on their health standards, which in turn may improve their production capacity' (Krantz, 2001:11). This happens because it will reduce their vulnerability to risks, which makes them more willing to engage in other, and more productive, economic activities (Krantz, 2001).

Third, it is now recognised that poor people know what is best for them and therefore must be involved in the planning and designing of policies and projects that can improve their situation (Krantz, 2001). Having a say in matters concerning them, usually results in people's greater commitment to implementation and hence improves project performance (Krantz, 2001:11).

The core principles of the SLA, as outlined by DFID (1999: Section 1.3), are as follows:

- **People-centred** – this means 'that the approach starts with an analysis of people's livelihoods and how these have changed over time from their perspective' (DFID, 1999: Section 1.3). It also includes supporting people to reach their improvement goals that they set for themselves.
- **Holistic** – the SLA wants to achieve multiple livelihood outcomes that people themselves determine and negotiate. The point of departure is how people themselves define their challenges and opportunities, and how they acknowledge that they need to adopt multiple livelihood strategies to secure their livelihoods.
- **Dynamic** – the SLA understands and learns from change in order to support positive patterns of change and help mitigate the impact of negative ones. The SLA 'explicitly recognises the effects of external shocks' and trends on livelihoods and the scope it

presents for livelihood analysis and strategies (DFID, 1999: Section 1.3). Shocks and trends can be linked.

Shocks, 'are usually sudden events that have a significant impact – usually negative – on livelihoods. They are irregular and vary in intensity'. Shocks can be classified as: natural (disasters such as floods); human (e.g., illness); economic (e.g., losing a job, price increases); conflict (e.g., war), and 'crop/livestock health shocks' (DFID, 1999: Glossary).

Trends, 'can have either a positive or a negative effect on livelihoods and involve changes that take place over a period of time'. They include: population trends; economic trends (reduced prices, new market development); 'resource trends (e.g., soil erosion, deforestation); trends in governance/politics (e.g., increasing accountability) [and] technological trends (e.g., the development of more efficient production techniques' (DFID, 1999: Glossary).

- **Building on strengths** – 'starts with an analysis of strengths, rather than needs' (DFID, 1999: Section 1.3). It recognises people's inherent potential and removes the constraints to reach potential; it builds resilience to allow people to better achieve their own objectives.
- **Bridging the macro-micro gap** – emphasises 'the importance of macro level policy and institutions to the livelihood options of communities and individuals' (DFID, 1999: Glossary). In addition, the development and planning of macro level policy must be informed by the insights of people at the local or micro level.
- **Sustainability** – is important to ensure that progress in poverty reduction is lasting. Livelihoods will be sustainable if they can 'continue into the future, coping with and recovering from stresses and shocks, while not undermining the resources on which it draws for existence' (DFID, 1999: Glossary). External support (outside of the household) is important for sustainable poverty reduction and should supplement people's livelihood strategies, their social environments, and their ability to adapt (DFID, 1999). Sustainability is influenced on both local and global levels.

Environmental sustainability, 'is achieved when the productivity of life-supporting natural resources is conserved or enhanced for use by future generations' (DFID, 1999: Section 1.4). Productivity means the 'ability to produce a wide range of environmental services, such as the supply of food and water, flood protection [and] waste management' (DFID, 1999: Glossary).

Economic sustainability, in the context of the poor is when 'a baseline level of economic welfare can be achieved and sustained' over time (DFID, 1999: Section 1.4). The 'ability to maintain a given level of income and expenditure over time' relates to expenditure on various levels including 'individuals, households, projects, programmes, [and] government departments' (DFID, 1999: Glossary).

Social sustainability, 'is achieved when social exclusion is minimised and social equity maximised' (DFID, 1999: Section 1.4). It implies the 'ability to maintain and improve livelihoods while maintaining or enhancing the local and global assets and capabilities on which livelihoods depends' (Chambers & Conway, 1992:5).

In addition to the social, economic and environmental dimensions of sustainability, Sachs (2012:2208) adds a fourth condition, that is, 'good governance at all levels: local, national, regional, and global'. In the sustainable livelihoods analysis framework (see section 10.4), it refers to institutional sustainability.

> **Institutional sustainability**, 'is achieved when institutions, structures and processes have the capacity to continue to perform their functions over the long term' (DFID, 1999: Section 1.4). For this purpose, 'it is important to have in place: well-defined laws, participatory policy-making processes, and effective public and private governance organisations', to ensure the ongoing improvements of the livelihoods of the poor (DFID, 1999).

Partnerships for development are relevant at all levels. Defining what partnerships entail in practice is an ongoing debate. However, the vision of DFID (1999) is for deeper and more meaningful development partnerships, including with other donors. Effective partnerships require that partners share common objectives and approaches to development (DFID, 1999). This means countries that want to collaborate with DFID for sustainable livelihoods should have national strategies for sustainable development in place. These strategies should incorporate a long-term approach and wide participation of all stakeholders (DFID, 1999).

> **ACTIVITY 10.1**
>
> Refer to the features of developmental social work in Chapter 3. Reflect on how they interrelate with the core principles of the SLA.
>
> **Reflective questions**
> Look back at Case study 1 and then answer the following questions:
> - Which core principles of the SLA do you recognise in the case study?
> - What scope do you see for applying the SLA in this community?
> - What challenges do you foresee in this regard?

10.3 Defining sustainable livelihoods

The thinking about livelihoods started with the work of Robert Chambers in the mid-1980s, which was then further developed by him and Conway and others in the early 1990s (DFID, 1999). The 1992 publication of *Sustainable rural livelihoods* by Chambers and Conway is widely recognised as seminal in coining the term 'sustainable livelihoods' (Krantz, 2003).

In the following discussion, we will focus on the mainstream development of the concept 'sustainable livelihoods' as it is widely recognised in literature.

Sustainable livelihoods emerged as a new paradigm in the early 1990s, which was triggered in 1987 when the World Commission on Environment and Development published its report *Our Common Future*, also known as the Brundtland Report (Solesbury, 2003). It introduced a policy debate and thinking about development beyond economic terms (Solesbury, 2003), and proposed 'sustainable livelihood security as an integrated concept' (Chambers & Conway, 1992:5).

The Brundtland Commission defined livelihood as:

... adequate stocks and flows of food and cash to meet basic needs. Security refers to ownership of, or access to, resources and income-earning activities, including reserves and assets to offset risk, case shocks and meet contingencies. Sustainable refers to the maintenance or enhancement of resource productivity on a long-term basis. A household may be enabled to gain sustainable livelihood security in many ways –through ownership of land, livestock or trees, rights to grazing, fishing, hunting or gathering; through stable employment with adequate remuneration; or through varied repertoires of activities (Chambers & Conway, 1992:5).

Chambers and Conway (1992:5) expanded the Brundtland definition's focus of sustainable livelihoods 'as a means of serving the objectives of both equity and sustainability'. They indicated that sustainable livelihoods (SL) also present the resources and conditions for the development and implementation of capabilities:

A livelihood comprises the capabilities, assets (stores, resources, claims and access) and activities required for a means of living: a livelihood is sustainable which can cope with and recover from stress and shocks, maintain or enhance its capabilities and assets, and provide sustainable livelihoods opportunities for the next generation; and which contributes net benefits to other livelihoods at the local and global levels and in the short and long term (Chamber & Conway, 1992:6).

For Chambers and Conway (1992:5), 'a livelihood in its simplest sense is a means of gaining a living'. They argue that 'gaps and cross-linkages between ecology, economics and other social sciences offer scope and need for practical concepts'. They searched for concepts that are useful, both analytically, in order 'to generate insight and hypotheses for research, and practically, as a focus and tool for decision-making' (Chambers & Conway, 1992:3). They took as basis three concepts that they found evolving in the social and biological sciences with increased consensus, namely capability, equity and sustainability. These concepts are interrelated and each concept is 'both an end and means' – thus, has purpose in itself, but is also a means to support the others (Chambers & Conway,1992:3). When 'linked together, capability, equity and sustainability present a framework or paradigm for development thinking which is both normative and practical'. With this dual emphasis, the authors assure that nothing can and should be final (Chambers & Conway, 1992), allowing people to remain central in their sustainable livelihoods debate.

Krantz (2001) comments that Chambers and Conway's approach was rather general, leading to efforts to refine the sustainable livelihoods concept further, both analytically and operationally. However, this is most likely why their definition is widely recognised as it presented the foundation for other disciplines to expand on.

Significant contributions were subsequently made by researchers connected to the Sustainable Livelihoods Research Programme of the Institute for Development Studies (IDS) at the University of Sussex, Brighton, UK (Krantz, 2001:7). Scoones tabled an influential report in 1998, and in 1999 the British Department for International Development (DFID) started their now widely recognised work on the SLA (Krantz, 2001). Schoones (1998:5) defined sustainable livelihoods in the following manner:

> *A livelihood comprises the capabilities, assets (including both material and social resources) and activities required for a means of living. A livelihood is sustainable when it can cope with and recover from stresses and shocks, maintain or enhance its capabilities and assets, while not undermining the natural resource base.*

In this definition, Scoones (1998:5) recognised five key elements, captured in the two dimensions of the concept:

1. Livelihoods: links 'concerns over work and employment with poverty reduction with broader issues of adequacy, security, well-being and capability'.
2. Sustainability: looks at the 'resilience of livelihoods and the natural resource base on which, in part, they depend'.

He argues that people become vulnerable to not achieving sustainable livelihoods when they are unable to cope with the changes that they face or are unable to adapt by shifting livelihood strategies (Scoones, 1998). Therefore, Scoones (1998:6) argues 'that assessing resilience and the ability to positively adapt requires an analysis of a range of factors, including an evaluation of historical experiences of responses to various shocks and stresses'.

According to Krantz (2001:8), the main difference between the IDS (Scoones) definition and the earlier one by Chambers and Conway is 'that it does not include the requirement that for livelihoods to be considered as sustainable, they should also "... contribute net benefits to other livelihoods"'. In this sense, he regards the IDS version as 'less demanding' and 'more realistic'.

The next influential definition of sustainable livelihoods, which is widely recognised and used today, came from the British Department for International Development (DFID) in 1999. DFID is the British government department responsible for promoting development and the reduction of poverty. It receives its mandate from the *White Paper on International Development* that was published in November 1997 (DFID, 1999). The White Paper commits DFID to promoting human rights through policy and practice, and stresses the importance of part-nerships at all levels. DFID slightly adapted the definition of Chambers and Conway (1992):

> *A livelihood comprises the capabilities, assets (including both material and social resources) and activities required for a means of living. A livelihood is sustainable when it can cope with and recover from stresses and shocks and maintain or enhance its capabilities and assets both now and in the future, while not undermining the natural resource base* (1999: Section 1.1).

DFID (1999: Section 1.2) uses the SLA to facilitate more sustainable livelihoods for the poor through the following core objectives:

- *improved access to high-quality education, information, technologies and training and better nutrition and health;*
- *a more supportive and cohesive social environment;*
- *more secure access to, and better management of, natural resources;*
- *better access to basic and facilitating infrastructure;*
- *more secure access to financial resources; and*

- *a policy and institutional environment that supports multiple livelihood strategies and promotes equitable access to competitive markets for all.*

The SLA can be applied to various levels, including the community, household and individual levels, of which the household level is the most commonly used, as indicated by Chambers and Conway's (1992) definition. For them, the main components and relationships in a household livelihood have four categories or parts: people (their livelihoods); activities (what they do); assets (tangible, including resources and stores, and intangible, referring to claims and access, which provide material and social income); and gains or outputs (a living, and how they benefit from what they do).

We can summarise by saying that 'the concept of sustainable livelihoods is a composite of many ideas and interests, the coming together of a number of different strands in the development debate' (Scoones, 1998:7). The different definitions and intention of the SLA – to be a way of thinking and an analytical tool – explain why there is no single approach to apply sustainable livelihoods. Determined by the developing agency, the SLA can be used 'primarily as an analytical framework (or tool) for programme planning and assessment or as a programme in itself' (Krantz, 2001:2). As opposed to having only one approach, there are rather specific features common to most variations of sustainable livelihoods approaches that agencies combine in different formats to apply and implement the SLA. This is why reference in literature is made to sustainable livelihoods approaches (SLAs). Krantz (2001:2) highlights three common features of SL approaches. First, they focus on the livelihoods of the poor. Second, they 'reject the standard procedure of conventional approaches of taking as an entry point a specific sector such as agriculture, water, or health'. This is because their focus is holistic and people adopt different livelihood strategies and objectives at different times (DFID, 1999). Third, the SLA encourages people involvement in identifying and implementing activities (Krantz, 2001). Scoones (1998:7) adds that 'the important thing to recognise about the term is that it is always subject to negotiation'. This is the case because people have different views on the importance of indicators, and, when conflicts occur, they have to make choices between different elements of the definition.

Talking about people who are poor

This year, my field placement is an eye-opener to understand what poverty is really about through the eyes and voices of those that we so easily referred to as 'the poor'.

Yes, in the class it is so easy to talk about 'them' as the poor, the unemployed, and socially excluded. I came to understand that beyond the pain of struggling to put food on the table, poverty has a much bigger face than a lack of income. I was surprised to learn that poverty is also about not having access to health, education, clean water, energy and proper roads and transport, among others.

Me too, and moreover, to learn that poverty has a gender dimension. Women seems to be differently affected by poverty. Culture also plays a role in how people think and respond to poverty. What strike me most are the psychological aspects of poverty – people feel powerless, voiceless, and often humiliated.

What strikes me most is how poor people are so often just left to fend for themselves. It sometimes frightens me to wonder whether social workers are not in fact perpetuating their marginalisation. It is one thing to have sector programmes such as health clinics and free education, but quite another to get access to these. These government programmes often fail poor people. NGOs do what they can, but are in their own struggle for resources to render effective services.

Yes, I agree. You remember that class discussion that we had about policies and human rights. It is great to have a Bill of Rights and policies in place, but the challenge is to use them to bring about social change. Also, the existing policies are sometimes simply inadequate.

Yes, although we are supposed to help people to have better lives and advocate for transformation of structures and processes, I often feel so powerless myself. I do not always know where to start and whether I can really make a difference.

What surprises me most is how poor people remain hopeful and resilient despite all the adversities that they face daily. They help me to better understand the concept 'livelihoods' as they have to find many ways to survive.

I find our current study theme on sustainable livelihoods very exciting, especially the fact that the SLA puts people, and their participation, first. I find that to be the most valuable skill that I have learnt thus far as a social work student – to start where the people are. Poor people know best about their poverty, their struggles, and what they need.

That is so important, because starting where people are, show them that we treat them with dignity and respect, and see their agency and strengths to look at options which they can choose from.

I look forward to our next class on the SLA where we are going to hear more about the sustainable livelihoods framework.

10.4 **Sustainable livelihoods frameworks**

With the DFID framework being the most widely used framework in both practice and research, it is appropriate for purposes of this chapter that we discuss this framework.

Other organisations such as Oxfam, CARE International and the UNDP have developed similar sustainable livelihoods frameworks, which complement DFID's (cf. Solesbury, 2003; Krantz, 2001; DFID, 1999).

> **DFID's sustainable livelihoods framework**, 'is a tool to improve understanding of livelihoods, particularly the livelihoods of the poor'. Since it can be continuously adapted, the framework 'becomes a living tool' to eliminate poverty. It is relevant for planning of new development initiatives and also to assess how existing activities contribute to livelihood sustainability. It is people-centred and draws stakeholders with different views together to have constructive debates on factors that influence livelihoods. The framework identifies five key factors or components that are interrelated: the vulnerability context; livelihood assets; transforming structures and processes; livelihood strategies; and livelihood outcomes (DFID, 1999: Section 2.1).

The DFID framework is people-centred and prioritises partnerships among governments, private sector, civil society and researchers in its commitment to help reduce poverty. Livelihoods are influenced by different forces and key factors that keep on changing, and emphasise the importance of a context-specific analysis of livelihoods and the involvement of local people (Krantz, 2001). Figure 10.1 below illustrates DFID's sustainable livelihoods framework, indicating the key factors that affect people's livelihoods, and the typical relationships between these factors.

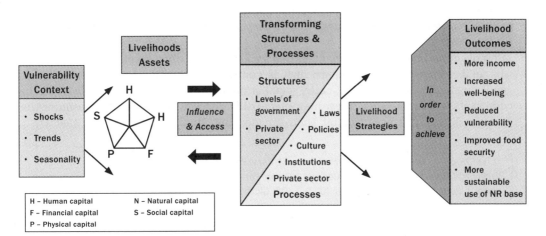

Figure 10.1: Sustainable livelihoods framework
Source: *DFID* (1999: Section 2.1)

Be mindful that the direction of the arrows between the factors does not imply a particular causality between them, but rather a certain level of influence. Furthermore, the framework allows for different entry points for a livelihoods analysis and does not necessarily start with the *vulnerability context*. You can focus on any part of the framework, provided you keep the wider picture of the framework in mind. This means conducting the analysis in a participatory manner, being committed to eliminating poverty, being committed to meaningful dialogue in order to challenge the underlying political and socioeconomic injustices that maintain poverty, and showing the ability to recognise deprivation in the field (DFID, 1999). However, in view of the people-centred focus of the framework, it is appropriate to start the analysis by concurrently exploring people's assets and their livelihood outcomes (DFID, 1999). We will start our discussion with the *livelihood assets* component.

10.4.1 Livelihood assets

The SL framework regards people first and hence wants to understand their strengths – referred to as 'assets or capital endowments' – and how they attempt to transform these strengths into 'positive livelihood outcomes' (DFID, 1999: Section 2.3). The framework identifies five core types of capital upon which people can build their livelihoods: human capital; social capital; physical capital; natural capital; and financial capital. The five capitals can be best thought about as 'livelihood building blocks'. The SLA is embedded in the belief that no single category of assets is sufficient in itself and that an innovative combination of these assets is required to ensure survival. Access implies taking ownership thereof or claiming its use as a right (DFID, 1999).

Assets are framed in the asset pentagon (see Figure 10.1), which 'lies at the core of the livelihoods framework, "within" the vulnerability context' (DFID, 1999: Section 2.3). The pentagon shows the interrelationships between the various assets. The lines meet at the centre point, which 'represents zero access to assets while the outer perimeter represents maximum access'. Pentagons are differently shaped and 'can be drawn for different communities or social groups within communities'. Because asset endowments constantly change, pentagons likewise continuously shift over time. A first step in the process of analysing livelihoods and activities to reduce poverty is to understand the complex relationships inherent to the framework (DFID, 1999).

It is of course important to remember that socioeconomic differences have an impact on what makes up peoples' livelihoods, such as 'contrasts of asset ownership, income levels, gender, age, religious affiliation, caste, social or political status' (Scoones, 1998:11). In the context of the SL framework, 'these may refer to differences in basic livelihood resources (or access to different forms of "capital") or to broader contextual factors' (Scoones, 1998:11).

> **Livelihood assets**, 'a key component in the SL framework, they are the assets on which livelihoods are built, and can be divided into five core categories (or types of capital)'. These are: human; social; natural; physical; and financial (DIFD, 1999: Glossary).

Human capital
Human capital includes the 'skills, knowledge, capacity to work, and good health that together enable people to pursue different livelihood strategies and achieve their livelihood objectives' (DIFD, 1999: Glossary). Human capital is fundamental to using the other forms of capital (DFID, 1999).

Human capital can be accumulated in direct or indirect ways. Attending school or a training session is a direct way, while accessing preventative medical services is more indirectly (DFID, 1999). Whichever way people obtain human capital, they have to be willing to develop their own human capital (DFID, 1999). This reminds us that human rights go hand in glove with responsibilities. For example, the right to education implies the willingness to use the opportunity to learn. However, if people are restricted to do so because of opposing 'structures and processes (e.g. formal policies or social norms that prevent girls from attending school) then indirect support to human capital development will be particularly important' (DFID, 1999: Section 2.3.1). However, in many instances, a combination of both types of support will be necessary (DFID, 1999).

Social capital

Social capital 'relates to the formal and informal social relationships (or social resources) from which various opportunities and benefits can be drawn by people in their pursuit of livelihoods' (DIFD, 1999: Glossary). *Benefits* include 'access to information, to influence or power, and to claims or obligation for support from others' (DIFD, 1999: Glossary).

Social resources, include interactions with others, and groups of which people are members, and building relations of trust that enable people to work together and be assisted in the development of safety nets (DFID, 1999: Glossary).

All the assets are interrelated and involvement in one asset can extend to the other. However, social capital is the most closely connected asset to *transforming structures and processes* (DFID, 1999). Social capital has its own intrinsic value, but is also an important resource for poor and vulnerable people, as it can provide a buffer against shocks, 'act as an informal safety net to ensure survival, [and] compensate for a lack of other types of capital' (DFID, 1999: Section 2.3.2). It can, however, be used in a positive or negative way (DFID, 1999).

Natural capital

Natural capital refers to 'natural resource stocks (e.g. trees, land, clean air, coastal resources) upon which people rely', and it has direct and indirect benefits (DIFD, 1999: Glossary).

There is a close relationship between natural capital and the *vulnerability context* as many shocks are natural processes (e.g., floods, fires) that destroy natural capital and thus the livelihoods of people (DFID, 1999). Seasonal changes play a key role in the *vulnerability context*, influencing assets, production activities and prices, work opportunities, and health (DFID, 1999). People are more vulnerable if all their livelihoods come from farming, and when they are hungry or become sick (DFID, 1999). We know that our health and well-being are intertwined with various ecosystems (see Chapter 5). How different natural assets are combined also play a role in SL. For example, the nutritional value of food will be higher if it is grown in high quality fertile land. However, the value of soil and nutrients will both be reduced in the case of drought or where access to water is restricted because of lack of physical capital or infrastructure to use available water (DFID, 1999).

Physical capital

Physical capital 'comprises the basic infrastructure and physical goods that support livelihoods. Infrastructure consists of changes to the physical environment that help people to meet their basic needs and to be more productive' (DFID, 1999: Glossary). *Infrastructure* comprises 'affordable transport systems, water supply and sanitation (of adequate quantity and quality, energy (that is both clean and affordable), good communications and access to information', while 'shelter of adequate quality and durability is considered by some as infrastructure' (DIFD, 1999: Glossary). The lack of appropriate infrastructure contributes to poverty. Access to water and energy is important for good health. Using human capital to collect water and wood for basic needs takes time and impinges on time to produce goods and access markets (DFID, 1999). For SL, 'development of physical capital must be led by demand from the intended users' (DFID, 1999: Section 2.3.4). The SLA should support poor people to access affordable infrastructure to obtain their livelihood objectives, such as taking produce to the market (DFID, 1999).

Financial capital

Financial capital means 'the financial resources that people use to achieve their livelihood objectives' (DFID, 1999: Section 2.3.5). There are two categories of resources. The first category includes available stocks, of which savings are prominent, 'because they do not have liabilities attached and usually do not entail reliance on others [such as] cash, bank deposits or liquid assets such as livestock and jewellery' or credit institutions (DIFD, 1999: Glossary). The second category of financial resources is regular and reliable inflows of money, which include a salary, pensions or other state grants (DIFD, 1999: Glossary).

Financial capital is an important livelihood building block, and likely 'the most versatile of the five categories of assets [because it] enables people to adopt different livelihood strategies' (DFID, 1999: Section 2.3.5). Financial capital 'can be converted ... depending upon Transforming Structures and Processes – into other types of capital' (DFID, 1999: Section 2.3.5). It can be used for 'direct achievement of livelihood outcomes' such as buying food to achieve food security, and 'it can also be transformed into political influence and can free people up for more active participation in organisations that formulate policy and legislation and govern access to resources' (DFID, 1999: Section 2.3.5).

But, because financial capital is less available to the poor, the other forms of capital are more important to them (DFID, 1999). Financial capital can be built for the poor through indirect means. On an organisational level, the benefits of existing savings can be increased while access to financial services can be increased on an institutional level, including challenging the structural barriers to get access to credit (DFID, 1999). Safety nets for the poor can be improved by lobbying government for legislation that will change the financial services' environment (DFID, 1999).

However, financial capital alone is not the answer to all the problems related to poverty. People may lack knowledge of how best to use legislation or may be constrained by inappropriate legislation and policies and hence 'inappropriate *Transforming Structures and Processes*' for micro-enterprise development (DFID, 1999: Section 2.3.5). On the other hand, it is 'important to be aware of the way in which existing social structures and relations (forms of social capital) can help facilitate group-based lending approaches' (DFID, 1999: Section 2.3.5) such as 'stokvels' and other saving clubs.

To conclude the discussion on assets, you will see in the *vulnerability context* component that assets can be destroyed but also created because of the trends, shocks, and seasonality which cause such vulnerabilities (DFID, 1999). Furthermore, you will note the role of the *transforming structures and processes* component of the framework in mobilising institutions and policies to influence access to assets (DFID, 1999). However, *livelihood strategies* that will enable people to escape from poverty depend on them having access to assets (DFID, 1999).

Reflective questions

Look back at Case study 1 and then answer the following questions:

- What assets do you identify in the community?
- What potential do you see in expanding the asset base of households/communities?
- How do you see the role of the social worker in relation to asset development in the community?

10.4.2 **Vulnerability context**

Understanding the *vulnerability context* as a key component in the SL framework and analysis is important since it 'frames the external environment in which people exist' (DFID, 1999: Section 2.2). People's livelihoods and assets are 'affected by critical trends as well as by shocks and seasonality – over which they have limited or no control' (DFID, 1999: Section 2.2). For poor people, 'seasonal shifts in prices, employment opportunities and food availability are one of the greatest and most enduring sources of hardship' (DFID, 1999: Section 2.2). Therefore, the trends, shocks and aspects of seasonality on livelihoods must be identified as well as how its negative impacts can be minimised (DFID, 1999). Understanding the local context is important in relation to the nature of local livelihoods, what livelihood strategies people implement, and the hindering factors in obtaining their livelihood objectives (DFID, 1999).

The *vulnerability context* component lies the furthest outside people's control of all the parts of the framework. This can be managed through policy changes at the level of *transforming structures and processes* (DFID, 1999). One approach is to 'help ensure that critical institutions and organisations are responsive to the needs of the poor' (DFID, 1999: Section 2.2). Another approach to managing the *vulnerability context* is by supporting poor people 'to become more resilient and better able to capitalise on its positive aspects' (DFID, 1999: Section 2.2).

10.4.3 **Transforming structures and processes**

The *transforming structures and processes* component of the framework includes 'the institutions, organisations, policies and legislation that shape livelihoods [and operate] at all levels, from the household to the international arena, and in all spheres, from the most private to the most public' (DFID, 1999: Section 2.4). The structures include the public and private sectors and civil society, while the processes include policy, legislation, institutions and culture (DFID, 1999). The structures and processes determine access 'to various types of capital, to livelihood strategies and to decision-making bodies and sources of influence; the terms of exchange between different types of capital; and returns (economic and otherwise) to any given livelihood strategy' (DFID, 1999: Section 2.4). They also influence people's experiences of inclusion and well-being, and, within the context of culture, explain how different societies do things differently (DFID, 1999). The activities related to the *transforming structures and processes* component are directed to the sixth livelihood objective of DFID – securing 'a policy and institutional environment that supports multiple livelihood strategies and promotes equitable access to competitive markets for all' (DFID, 1999: Section 2.4).

10.4.4 **Livelihood strategies**

The SLA 'seeks to promote choice, opportunity and diversity', which is most visible in its livelihood strategies (DFID, 1999: Section 2.5). Determinants such as birth, gender, the social, economic and ecological environment, education, and migration play a role in choosing *livelihood strategies* (Chambers & Conway, 1992).

> *Livelihood strategies*, indicate 'the range and combination of activities and choices that people make/undertake in order to achieve their livelihood goals' (DFID, 1999:Section 2.5).

Having a wider choice in *livelihood strategies* enhances people's ability to resist or adapt when confronted with shocks and stresses of the *vulnerability context* component (DFID, 1999). Access to *assets* influences people's choices of sustainable livelihoods, while *transforming structures and processes* can strengthen positive choices (DFID, 1999:Section 2.5).

The SLA puts poor people first and promotes their social sustainability, inclusion and equity (DFID, 1999). However, the poor compete among themselves for markets and prices for their *livelihood strategies*. It is thus important to present them with options and opportunities and, at the same, time build their assets so that they take advantage of opportunities (DFID, 1999). At the same time, it is important to advocate for safety nets for people when they cannot meet their livelihood objectives in a competitive environment (DFID, 1999).

10.4.5 Livelihood outcomes

Livelihood outcomes 'are the achievements or outputs of *Livelihood Strategies*' (DFID, 1999: Section 2.6). These achievements are determined by people and should focus on what is of importance to them, and not to us as professionals. We are the outsiders whose role it is to 'investigate, observe and listen, rather than jumping to quick conclusions or making hasty judgements about the exact nature of the outcomes that people pursue' (DFID, 1999:Section 2.6). On the other hand, 'we should also not assume that people are entirely dedicated to maximising their income' but rather 'recognise and seek to understand the richness of potential livelihood goals' (DFID, 1999:Section 2.6). In this way, we can rather appreciate what people prioritise, their reasons for doing things the way they do, and determine where they experience constraints (DFID, 1999).

There are two reasons why the framework uses 'outcomes' rather than objectives. First, in relation to its focus on sustainability, the framework presents 'a way of thinking about livelihoods and tries to promote responsiveness' (DFID, 1999:Section 2.6). Second, outcomes have a normative dimension where DFID's objective is 'to promote sustainable livelihoods', which is not necessarily shared by all partners, including the poor. The conclusion is that the *livelihood outcomes* component of the framework 'is something of a hybrid, combining the aims of both DFID and its clients' (DFID, 1999:Section 2.6). 'Outcomes' is a more neutral concept, more inclusive of all partners, and focuses on the process of analyses and planning rather than objectives, in which case one could ask 'whose objectives' are referred to (DFID, 1999:Section 2.6). Furthermore, 'outcomes focus on achievements, the development of indicators and progress in poverty elimination' (DFID, 1999:Section 2.6).

The SL framework includes the *livelihood outcomes* below. However, the local context of the particular *livelihood strategies* will determine which *livelihood outcome(s)* is applicable and should be achieved (DFID, 1999:Section 2.6). These *livelihood outcomes* are:
- More income: relates to the 'overall increases in the amount of money coming into the household (or their own pocket)' and therefore the economic sustainability of livelihoods.
- Increased well-being: focuses on non-material goods that influence people's well-being. Factors that will increase people's well-being through *livelihood strategies* include their

'self-esteem; sense of control and inclusion, physical security of household members, their health status, access to services, political enfranchisement, [and] maintenance of their cultural heritage', among others.

- Reduced vulnerability: poor people are already vulnerable and because their livelihoods are likely to be unstable, they need to be protected against 'the adverse effects of the *Vulnerable Context*'. People's vulnerability can be reduced by increasing the social sustainability of their livelihoods.

- Improved food security: hunger and dietary insufficiency is an indicator of poverty. This outcome intends 'to locate the activities of those governments and donors that focus on food security'.

- More sustainable use of the natural resource base: this outcome is listed separately from the other dimensions of sustainability because it is important, and not sufficiently covered in the other livelihood outcome categories.

Livelihood outcomes could conflict with one another. The structure of the SL framework should be used to carefully consider how *livelihood outcomes* influence the other components of livelihoods (DFID, 1999).

In conclusion of this section, adopting an SLA has operational implications, including 'methodologies for field investigation, intervention options and planning approaches' (Scoones, 1998:13). DIFD (2000) presents *guidance sheets* for investigating livelihoods for project and policy purposes, and a collection of methods for utilising the components of the sustainable livelihoods framework. Rapid and participatory methods are interrelated categories of tools proposed to conduct livelihoods analysis (DFID, 1999). However, it is important to remember that the SL framework development is ongoing and only 'summarises the main components of and influences on livelihoods' (DFID, 1999:Section 2.1). Because it is a 'flexible tool', it can be adapted as relevant to the local context (DFID, 1999:Section 2.1).

 ACTIVITY 10.2

Apply the SL analytical framework to Case study 1 by answering the following questions:
1 Explain the level(s) of your focus – individuals, households, community?
2 Reflect on the asset or capital categories that you observe.
3 Evaluate the *vulnerability context*.
4 What transformation of structures and processes are required?
5 What are the livelihood strategy options?
6 What livelihood outcomes are targeted?
7 Assess people's involvement.
8 Discuss the relevance of the SLA for poverty reduction.

10.5 Relevance of the SLA for decolonial social work practice

The SLA puts people first, which means that their voices count and their participation is central in the SL framework. It is important in decolonial social work to not impose our views on people, and to collaborate with them in a space of respect, utilising their strengths and capabilities, and allowing them to explore options and make choices on livelihood strategies that best suit their situation. The mix of assets of the SLA creates a broader scope to tackle poverty with a variety of sustainable livelihoods. The UNDP report aptly states that:

> *If the potential of all people is harnessed through appropriate strategies and proper policies, human progress would be accelerated and human development deficits would be reduced* (UNDP, 2015:iii).

Sustainable livelihoods and rights-based approaches 'are complementary perspectives that seek to achieve many of the same goals (for example, empowerment of the most vulnerable and a strengthened capacity of the poor to achieve secure livelihoods)' (DFID, 1999:Section 1.2). From a rights-based perspective, the SLA recognises the importance of the links 'between public institutions and civil society and, particularly, on how to increase the accountability of public institutions to all citizens' (DFID, 1999:Section 1.2). However, the starting point in this, which the SLA accommodates, is 'to understand the livelihoods of poor people in [their] context' and to identify the specific constraints that will prevent them from realising their rights and consequently improving 'their livelihoods on a sustainable basis' (DFID, 1999).

In Chapter 3, I argued that developmental social work is in principle decolonial because of its embeddedness in human rights; this is true also of the SLA. The SLA focuses on different forms of capital, including those that overlap with the dimensions of sustainable development: social; financial (economic); and natural (environment). In this context, sustainable development is a useful approach for developmental social work to promote ecological justice (see Chapter 3). It is particularly in their advocacy role that social workers can contribute to institutional sustainability, by challenging structural injustices that constrain people in obtaining sustainable livelihoods outcomes. Through the SLA, social workers can promote social and economic inclusion, poverty reduction, and equality.

 ACTIVITY 10.3

Throughout this chapter, we have been using this rather complex term, 'sustainable livelihoods'. It is not a word that we use in our everyday conversations.

1 How would you translate SL into your home language? If you cannot find an equivalent word or two, how would you translate it using a phrase or sentence?
2 Also, consider if there is an idiom in your language or culture that captures the essence of SL. Make notes of this in the margins of this chapter and share them with your classmates.

10.6 Conclusion

The overall aim of the SLA is to eradicate poverty. We have seen in this chapter that poverty is not just about a lack of income; there are other interrelated assets that should be harnessed to reduce poverty. As Sachs (2012:2209) states, 'traditional measures of economic performance, namely, gross domestic product and household income, capture only a small part of what determines human wellbeing'. In his words:

> *Human happiness, life satisfaction, and the freedom from suffering depend on many things in addition to meeting of material needs, including social*

trust, honest government, empowerment in the work place, mental health services, and a high level of civic participation (Sachs, 2012:2209).

These aspects are all embedded in the SLA.

The participatory focus of the SLA gives people dignity, which strengthens their agency to use and expand their capabilities in exploring various sustainable livelihoods options from which to choose livelihood strategies. The SL framework is an appropriate tool to target transformation of structures and institutions in response to people's vulnerabilities as expressed by themselves. The framework creates a platform for social workers to advocate for social justice and upholding human rights. Krantz (2001:9) adds that the 'livelihoods framework can strengthen the political voice and influence of the poor and enable them to secure social and economic rights'.

Note also that the sustainable livelihoods approach is appropriate for developmental social work because it emphasises that:

> *... the true aim of development is not only to boost incomes, but also to maximise human choices – by enhancing human rights, freedoms, capabilities and opportunities and by enabling people to lead long, healthy and creative lives* (UNDP, 2015:1).

The SL framework presents an appropriate analytical and intervention tool for social work to contribute to the 2030 Agenda for Sustainable Development and hence to a transformed society.

The SLA is attractive to governments, intergovernmental organisations and NGOs, and operates on local, national and global levels, and therefore creates a facilitating platform for development partnerships. Furthermore, it can also build on existing approaches, and it integrates participatory methods that strengthen the policy, research and practice interrelatedness of the SLA and its framework.

Chapter activity

1. **Reflective question**. Think about where you come from, your education, opportunities, hardships, oppression/privileges and vision of the future. How do you see your *vulnerabilities context*? Think about your strengths. Map your *livelihood assets* as they are, indicating the stronger and weaker interrelated links. Reflect on how you could possibly develop your assets. Which of your vulnerabilities require *transformation of structures and processes*? How can this transformation be achieved? What *livelihood strategies* do you identify with and why? Indicate how the *livelihood outcomes* apply to you.
2. **Personal context**. Think about the community where you come from. What shapes the peoples' lives there? How do they respond to life's challenges? How do you see your community through the lens of the SLA and SL framework? What link do you see between the challenges that your community faces and the way the SLA brings about change?
3. **Advocacy**. Identify any poverty related issue(s) that challenges you to respond. How could you use the SLA and SL framework in responding to this challenge?
4. **Critical questions**. Think about the high levels of poverty and inequalities in South Africa. In your view, how committed and engaged are social workers in reducing poverty and inequalities in the country? What should change and how can the SLA contribute in this

regard? Reflect on the value of the SLA for practice, research and policy. Reflect on the possibilities of the SLA for developmental social work, and social work's contribution to sustainable development. In what way could the SLA support social workers in practising decolonial social work?

References

Chambers, R & Conway, G. 1992. *Sustainable rural livelihoods: Practical concepts for the 21st century.* IDS Discussion Paper 296. UK, Brighton: IDS.

Krantz, L. 2001. *The sustainable livelihood approach to poverty reduction: An introduction.* Swedish International Development Cooperation Agency (Sida). [Online]. Available: https://www.sida.se/contentassets/bd474c210163447c9a7963d77c64148a/the-sustain-able-livelihood-approach-to-poverty-reduction_2656.pdf [Accessed 1 May 2018].

Sachs, J. 2012. From Millennium Development Goals to Sustainable Development Goals. *Lancet,* 379:2206–2211.

Scoones, I. 1998. *Sustainable rural livelihoods. A framework for analysis.* IDS Working Paper 72. UK, Brighton: IDS.

Solesbury, W. 2003. *Sustainable livelihoods: A case study of the evolution of DFID policy.* London: Overseas Development Institute.

United Kingdom. Department for International Development (DFID). 1999. *Sustainable livelihoods guidance sheets.* [Online]. Available: http://www.livelihoodscentre.org/documents/20720/100145/Sustainable+livelihoods+guidance+sheets/8f35b59f-8207-43fc-8b99-df75d3000e86 [Accessed 1 May 2018].

United Nations. 2015. *Transforming our world: The 2030 agenda for sustainable development.* Advanced unedited version. Finalised text for adoption (1 August). [Online]. Available: https://sustainabledevelopment.un.org/content/documents/21252030%20Agenda%20for%20Sustainable%20Development%20web.pdf [Accessed1 May 2018].

United Nations Development Programme. 2015. *Human development report 2015: Work for human development.* [Online]. Available: http://hdr.undp.org/sites/default/files/2015_human_development_report.pdf [Accessed 1 May 2018].

Annotated websites and activities

https://www.youtube.com/watch?v=B5NiTN0chj0
https://www.youtube.com/watch?v=7V8oFI4GYMY
These are two short animated videos on sustainable development that will help you to understand that SL consider social, economic and environmental dimensions.

Visit the following websites that show initiatives and projects on SL in South Africa and Southern Africa:
- Sustainable Livelihoods Foundation
http://livelihoods.org.za
http://livelihoods.org.za/current-projects
- South African SDI Alliance
http://sasdialliance.org.za
- African Initiatives
http://www.african-initiatives.org.uk

- Sustainable livelihoods in Southern Africa – ODI
  https://www.odi.org/projects/1225-sustainable-livelihoods-southern-africa
- ENACTUS South Africa
  https://www.youtube.com/channel/UCYyd5cvwVOMSdGbEJ3qDmVA

Learn from these examples by answering the following questions:
- What make SL projects sustainable?
- How do they manage vulnerability contexts and use of assets?
- How do SL options reflect local context?
- What livelihoods outcomes are achieved?
- What are the transformation challenges, and how are they addressed?
- What role does the local community play?
- What impact does SL have on poverty reduction?

Annotated websites and activities are also available on Learning Zone.

oxford.co.za/learningzone

Person-centred

Paul Mbedzi

 Case Study 1 Using a person-centred approach to deal with clients

Mulanga is a 36-year-old man who has been married to his wife Mishumo for the past 10 years. The couple has three children, namely Tshavhungwa (9-year-old girl), Ronewa (6-year-old girl) and Mpho (3-year-old boy). Apparently, Mulanga found out that his wife has been cheating on him with a colleague and this has been happening for the past four years. After realising that the romantic relationship between his wife and her colleague happened prior to the birth of their last-born child, Mulanga decided to go for a paternity test and the results confirmed that Mpho is not his biological son. As a result, Mulanga suffered from depression and his health significantly deteriorated. Regardless of his health condition, he did not tell anyone about his problems in fear of being judged and ridiculed. He did not know what to do as he loves his wife and the children.

One day, Mulanga decided to share his problems with his supervisor at work who informed him that the Department of Social Development provides social work services to distraught people. Early the next morning, Mulanga went to the department's social work offices for assistance. During the facilitation process, the social worker afforded Mulanga an opportunity to share his experiences in a non-threatening environment and he felt respected and not judged. Although he accused his wife of cheating on him during the facilitation process, he also blamed himself for not giving enough time and love to his wife and children. Eventually, Mulanga decided to stay in the marriage with his wife and to seek more professional assistance for himself and his wife. Both Mulanga and his wife committed to love one another and to live together in harmony.

In this case, the social worker social worker used a person-centred approach, which is one of the approaches that social workers use when they deal with clients.

Now that you have familiarised yourself with the above case study, you can read more about the person-centred approach in the sections that follow. As you work through this chapter, there will be reflective questions for you to answer based on the above case study.

11.1 Introduction

The person-centred approach was originally developed by an American psychologist named Carl Rogers. This approach is based on the precept that people have the ability to live to their optimal potential when they feel safe to do so or when a conducive environment has been created for them to do so. When a person-centred approach is used, the facilitation process allows the facilitator (social worker) to walk with people (clients) and accompany them on their journey of self-discovery. Through this process, people are able to explore who they are, their experiences, and the things that prevent them from being who they are or living to their full potential.

Rogers' basic assumptions are that people are essentially trustworthy, that they have a vast potential for understanding themselves and resolving their own problems without direct intervention on the facilitator's part, and that they are capable of self-directed growth if they are involved in a specific kind of counselling relationship (Corey, 2017). In general, the person-centred approach seeks to enable people to discover for themselves what they are struggling with and then find their own unique way forward (Grobler et al., 2013). To achieve this, the social worker must build trustworthy relationships with people and enter into collaborative partnerships with them on their journey of self-discovery.

> **Person-centred approach**, a non-directive and empathic approach to social work practice that cultivates a therapeutic environment that is conducive to personal growth.

This chapter explores the person-centred approach with specific focus on: its historical background; the 19 propositions; the core conditions for facilitation inherent in the person-centred approach; the person-centred facilitation process; professional values and communication skills embedded in the person-centred approach; and decolonial social work practice using the person-centred approach.

11.2 Historical background of the person-centred approach

The person-centred approach is intensely immersed in Rogers' own experiences as a therapist and researcher of therapeutic processes in the 1930s and 1940s. In the early 1940s, Rogers developed *non-directive counselling*, 'a powerful and revolutionary alternative to the directive and interpretative approaches to therapy practiced then' (Corey, 2016:257).

> **Non-directive counselling**, an approach to counselling where the client takes the lead and the counsellor refrains from influencing the discussion.

Through *non-directive counselling*, Rogers challenged the basic assumptions that the counsellor was the expert and the client had a reactive role. In so doing, he questioned the validity of the then widely used therapeutic procedures of diagnosis, interpretation, giving advice, suggestions, and teaching. In *non-directive counselling*, 'the therapist's realness and empathy were emphasised, and the therapeutic relationship rather than the therapist's techniques were viewed as the central factors in facilitating change' (Corey, 2016:257). The non-directive approach to counselling focused on reflecting and clarifying the feelings of individual clients, as Rogers believed that through an accepting relationship, clients were able to symbolise the unsymbolised experiences (i.e., make the unconscious conscious) and take constructive action based on their self-understanding.

In the 1950s, Rogers moved from using non-directive counselling to the *client-centred approach* (Joseph & Murphy, 2013). It is important to note that Rogers emphasised the facilitator's attitudes and personal characteristics together with the quality of client-facilitator relationship as the central determinants of change during the therapeutic process. With the *client-centred approach*, the focus was on the client as a person rather than on the non-directive methods, and there was a general assumption that the best way to understand people's behaviour is from their internal frame of reference. Rogers continued to test the underlying hypothesis of the client-centred approach during the 1960s by conducting extensive research on both the process and the outcomes of psychotherapy (Corey, 2017). This approach was broadened to include applications to the teaching/learning situation, affective/cognitive learning in workshops, and organisational development and leadership. This also marked the move from only focusing on the individual to include groups and communities.

In the 1980s, the term 'person-centred approach' became popular. According to Joseph and Murphy (2013:27):

> ... the term client-centered was later replaced with the term person-centered in an attempt to recognize that Rogers's metatheory of human functioning had implications that could reach far beyond one-to-one therapeutic work.

This change from *client-centred* to *person-centred* reflected the broadening application of the approach. It became used, not only in individual therapeutic work, but also in family work, organisational development, administration and education (Corey, 2017). Since Rogers' death in 1987, the person-centred approach has continued to develop and remained a central training topic in the helping professions. Thus, the person-centred approach has since become an important theoretical approach within social work. Many of Rogers' principles and skills form the bedrock of all social work practice, even when practitioners are not applying his full model.

In South Africa, during the 1980s, many organisations were formed in different sectors and communities to bring about transformation. Educational NGOs advocated a learner-centred approach to education. Professionals such as teachers and social workers began to see their roles in the community as change agents. The term 'people-centred' became popular and organisations, including social work organisations, advocated for the adoption of a people-centred approach when delivering services to empower communities. Person-centred encounter groups were run with racially-diverse groups of South Africans to show how person-centred principles, like empathy and congruence, could enable reconciliation and authentic relationships. Through this, the person-centred approach was recognised as an effective way to engage in cross-cultural counselling (Spangenberg, 2011).

11.3 Rogers' 19 propositions

Rogers developed 19 propositions (or statements) that provide a framework in which clients, groups and communities can be understood better. In other words, these propositions inform social workers on how they should view and think about people. Equally, Grobler et al. (2013) assert that the propositions provide tentative guidelines for social workers in their efforts to understand, think about and make sense of what they can observe of others, such as what they think, say, do and feel when they encounter others. This signifies that the propositions provide guidelines to social workers on what needs to be explored or understood when they interact with clients, groups and communities. It is important to keep in mind that the propositions are equally applicable in all these different contexts.

The extract below indicates the 19 propositions embedded in the person-centred approach as it appears in the original writing by Rogers (1987:483–522) (Note that Rogers wrote in a past time when the gender-exclusionary use of 'he' to refer to people was acceptable.):

1. *Every individual exists in a continually changing world of experience of which he is the center.*
2. *The organism reacts to the field as it is experienced and perceived. This perceptual field is, for the individual, 'reality'.*
3. *The organism reacts as an organized whole to this phenomenal field.*
4. *The organism has one basic tendency and striving – to actualize, maintain, and enhance the experiencing organism.*
5. *Behavior is basically the goal-directed attempt of the organism to satisfy its needs as experienced in the field as perceived.*
6. *Emotion accompanies, and in general facilitates, such goal-directed behavior, the kind of emotion being related to the seeking versus the consummatory aspects of the behavior, and the intensity of the emotion being related to the perceived significance of the behavior for the maintenance and enhancement of the organism.*
7. *The best vantage point for understanding behavior is from the internal frame of reference of the individual himself.*
8. *A portion of the total perceptual field gradually becomes differentiated as the self.*
9. *As a result of interaction with the environment, and particularly as a result of evaluational interaction with others, the structure of the self is formed – an organized, fluid, but consistent conceptual pattern of perceptions of characteristics and relationships of the 'I' or the 'me', together with values attached to concepts.*
10. *Values attached to experiences, and the values that are a part of the self-structure, in some instances are values experienced directly by the organism, and in some instances are values introjected or taken over from others, but perceived in distorted fashion, as if they had been experienced directly.*
11. *As experiences occur in the life of the individual, they are either (a) symbolized, perceived and organized into some relationship to the self, (b) ignored because there is no perceived relationship to the self-structure, (c) denied symbolization or given a distorted symbolization because the experience is inconsistent with the structure of the self.*

12. *Most of the ways of behaving which are adopted by the organism are those that are consistent with the concept of self.*

13. *Behavior may, in some instances, be brought about by organic experiences and needs which have not been symbolized. Such behavior may be inconsistent with the structure of the self, but in such instances the behavior is not 'owned' by the individual.*

14. *Psychological maladjustment exists when the organism denies to awareness significant sensory and visceral experiences, which consequently are not symbolized and organized into gestalt of the self-structure. When this situation exists, there is a basic or potential psychological tension.*

15. *Psychological adjustment exists when the concept of the self is such that all the sensory and visceral experiences of the organism are, or may be, assimilated on a symbolic level into a consistent relationship with the concept of self.*

16. *Any experience which is inconsistent with the organism or structure of self will be perceived as a threat, and the more of these perceptions there are, the more rigidly the self-structure is organized to maintain itself.*

17. *Under certain conditions, involving primarily complete absence of any threat to the self-structure, experiences which are inconsistent with it may be perceived and examined, and the structure of self revised to assimilate and include such experiences.*

18. *When the individual perceives and accepts into one consistent and integrated system all his sensory and visceral experiences, then he is necessarily more understanding of others and is more accepting of others as separate individuals.*

19. *As the individual perceives and accepts into his self-structure more of his organic experiences, he finds that he is replacing his present value system – based so largely upon introjections which have been distortedly symbolized – with a continuing organismic valuing process.*

Reflective questions

The phrase 'the self' appears 12 times in Rogers' 19 propositions. Find and read them again. Answer the following questions:

- What is your understanding of how Rogers' defines 'the self'?
- Taking into consideration African culture, how do we in Africa define 'the self'? How similar or different is it from Rogers' definition?
- In light of Menkiti's (1984) chapter on the self in African thought (find a link to the full text in the reference list), to what extent have Western notions of self (or personhood) dominated and even overridden African notions of self (or personhood)?
- How might we reinterpret Rogers' propositions if we replaced a personal definition of self with a social or relational definition?
- What might this imply for group and community practice?

> **Symbolised**, experiences that a person is aware or conscious of.
>
> **Unsymbolised**, experiences that a person is unaware or unconscious of. Experiences may be unsymbolised because they do not fit into the person's sense of who they are, or because they threaten the self, evoking feelings of anxiety.

Rogers' 19 propositions relate to individuals, group members and community members, and to their conscious and unconscious experiences. Conscious experiences are regarded as the experiences that are known to a person, which do not threaten the person's self. Conversely, unconscious experiences are the experiences that are hidden to the self and they threaten the self. This tells us that, when working with the individuals, families, groups or communities, the focus should be on dealing with both the conscious and unconscious worlds of experiences. Figure 11.1 illustrates the connection of the two experiential worlds, namely the conscious (symbolised) and unconscious(unsymbolised) world to the self, as outlined by Grobler et al. (2013:175), and further specifies where each of the 19 propositions belongs.

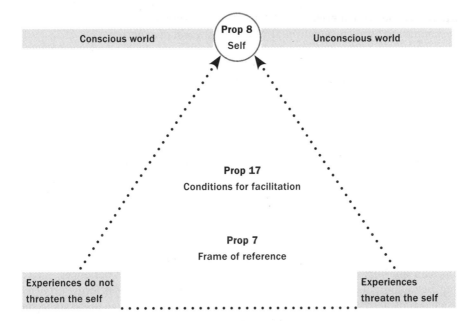

Figure 11.1: An illustration of the propositions and how they fit within the two worlds of experiences

Figure 11.1 illustrates the connection of the two experiential worlds (namely the conscious and unconscious worlds) of the person to the self. Each of the 19 propositions is attached to a particular experiential world but there are those that are found in both worlds of experiences. The propositions that focus on conscious experiences include Propositions 1, 2, 3, 4, 5, 6, 9, 10, 11 (a and b) and 12. Those that focus on unconscious experiences are Propositions 11 (c and d), 13, 14, 15, 16, 17, 18 and 19. Those that cover both worlds of experiences are Propositions 7, 8 and 17.

This chapter describes only two propositions found in the conscious world (Propositions 1 and 5), two propositions in the unconscious world (Propositions 14 and 15), and two propositions that cut across the two worlds of experiences (Propositions 8 and 17). The focus on these propositions is only to expand your understanding of the propositions and this does not mean that the propositions that are not included in the description are less important. You are encouraged to read up on the other 13 propositions to get a complete understanding of the person-centred approach. A more detailed explanation of the propositions may be found in the book *Person-centred facilitation: Process, theory and practice* (Grobler et al., 2013).

Proposition 1

'*Every individual exists in a continually changing world of experience of which he is the center*'(Rogers, 1987:483).

There are three principal elements involved in this proposition, namely that: the experiential world of every person is central, unique and personal; the personal world of every individual is continually changing; and, lastly, the individual's experiences constitute both conscious and unconscious levels. This implies that the experiences of every person, group and community are central, unique and known to that person, group and community. Therefore, an outsider will never know what is happening in somebody's life or the challenges faced by the individual, group and community, unless they decide to share with the outsider. More importantly, we should take note that the experiences are not static, which means that they continually change because people are living in a continually changing world of experiences.

Proposition 5

'*Behavior is basically the goal-directed attempt of the organism to satisfy its needs as experienced in the field as perceived*' (Rogers, 1987:491).

Any form of behaviour displayed by an individual is an attempt to satisfy his or her needs. This implies that behaviour is associated with needs and people's needs motivate behaviour. Therefore, whenever the social worker encounters people whose behaviour seems strange, the social worker may ask her or himself questions such as 'What need is this person trying to meet in this way?'.

Proposition 8

'*A portion of the total perceptual field gradually becomes differentiated as the self*' (Rogers, 1987:497).

The 'self' refers to a person's conception (perceptions and experiences) of who she or he is as a person, a unique human being. These perceptions relate to all our experiences, such as our thinking, behaviour, needs, emotions and values. All these experiences form part of who we are, which is indicated by the term 'total'. Thus, for the social worker to understand the self, the social worker has to understand it in terms of who that person believes he or she is in the here and now. This belief of who the person is (or how the person perceives her or himself) is linked to all her or his experiences. Proposition 8 of the person-centred approach rests on the premise that if people know who they are, they will also know how to behave and what they believe in, and eventually find their own way forward. Through their experiences, the social worker is able to get a clear understanding of how and/or what people think of themselves.

Link between experiences and perception

A mother shares with the social worker that every morning when she wakes up, she prepares her kids for school, takes them to school, and after school she fetches them and assists them with homework. Although she did not mention it directly, her experiences tell us that she perceives herself as a *'caring'* mother.

 ACTIVITY 11.1

Consider again Case study 1 and answer the following questions:
1 How does Mulanga, the husband, see himself?
2 Why did Mulanga believe that people will judge and ridicule him for his wife's infidelity?
3 Could this possibly be linked to patriarchy and how men and women are viewed by society?
4 If he was the unfaithful one, would he still believe that people will judge and ridicule him, or is society more accepting of men's infidelity?
5 How might these societal perceptions about gender and infidelity influence Mulanga's self-concept? And his wife Mishumo's self-concept?

Proposition 14

'Psychological maladjustment exists when the organism denies to awareness significant sensory and visceral experiences, which consequently are not symbolized and organized into the gestalt of the self-structure. When this situation exists, there is a basic or potential psychological tension' (Rogers, 1987:510).

When there are many experiences that cannot be allowed into conscious awareness, it creates psychological stress for the person. Psychological tension happens when people block out awareness of experiences they perceive as a threat to them. In other words, when people distance themselves from the experiences that are inconsistent with their self-structure, psychological tension results, which is an unsymbolised inner conflict. For example, a divorced man cannot admit that his infidelity contributed towards the divorce. In this instance, he may want to blame the church and family members for not doing enough to save his marriage and deny the fact that he might have contributed towards the divorce. Therefore, denying into awareness the fact that he cheated and thinking life would be the same after divorce, may create psychological tension for him.

Proposition 15

'Psychological adjustment exists when the concept of the self is such that all the sensory and visceral experiences of the organism are, or may be, assimilated on a symbolic level into a consistent relationship with the concept of self' (Rogers, 1987:513).

When people begin to accept into their self-structure, experiences that were denied symbolisation in the past (Proposition 11c) because they threaten the self and as a result created psychological tension (Proposition 14), psychological adjustment or reconstruction of self begins to take place. Psychological adjustment or reconstruction of self begins when people begin to accept or acknowledge their previous experiences or mistakes. In this instance, this is not the final stage of the reconstruction process, as they may want to seek further assistance.

Proposition 17

'Under certain conditions, involving primarily complete absence of any threat to the self-structure, experiences which are inconsistent with it may be perceived and examined, and the structure of self revised to assimilate and include such experiences' (Rogers, 1987:497).

A conducive environment should be created in which individuals, group members or community members feel free to share their experiences fully and explore themselves in depth. When people do not feel free during the facilitation process, the facilitation process is adversely affected. To create a conducive environment, the social worker should: respect, accept and understand people, together with their experiences; treat them as individuals; maintain their confidentiality; and allow their self-determination. In other words, the social worker must apply professional values if he or she wants to create a conducive environment. Apart from professional values, the social worker should also practise the use of appropriate skills, for instance, the social worker must be able to apply basic communication skills, such as listening, attending and empathy. Therefore, professional values and basic communication skills are key in creating a conducive environment.

Reflective questions
- Refer to Case study 1 above and indicate by means of examples how Rogers' 19 propositions can be applicable in working with Mulanga's family.
- Which of the 19 propositions can the social worker apply with Mulanga at the beginning of the facilitation process? Motivate your answer.
- At what point in the case study did the reconstruction begin for Mulanga? Motivate your answer.
- Critically evaluate whether any aspects of Rogers' propositions are directly in conflict with the African philosophy of *Ubuntu*?

11.4 Core conditions for facilitation

The attitude of the social worker towards the person in the facilitation relationship is the prime determinant of the outcome of the facilitation process. Beckett and Horner (2016:147) make the following observation:

> *Rogers believed that the relationship between the facilitator and clients is the crucial factor in a therapeutic relationship and this is based on much research, which confirms that the quality of this relationship may be a more significant predictor of success.*

In this regard, Rogers emphasised the core conditions of genuineness, unconditional positive regard and empathy as the basis of change and growth. Note that these core conditions are not only unique to the person-centred approach, but also are inherent to this approach and focus on the attitude of social workers towards their clients. This implies that person-centred social workers have to suspend their personal attributes and adopt these core conditions when dealing with clients. In the sections below these core conditions are discussed in more detail.

11.4.1 Genuineness/congruency

According to Corey (2016:262), 'genuineness [which is the same as congruency] is the state of authenticity that results from a deep exploration of self and a willingness to accept the truths of this exploration'. Rogers understood that an effective facilitator needs to be perceived as somebody who is trustworthy, dependable and consistent (Beckett & Horner, 2016).

> **Genuineness**, when facilitators are freely and honestly themselves and their experiences are consistent with the way they portray themselves. Genuineness and congruency mean the same thing.

With the condition of genuineness, social workers execute their professional duties without hiding behind their professional roles. This implies that what the social worker is thinking and feeling on the inside is what is being displayed on the outside. High levels of self-awareness, self-acceptance and self-trust are required for the social worker to maintain genuineness. In other words, the social worker must achieve a high level of personal growth to be able to support the personal growth of others. When the individual, group or community realise that the social worker is congruent and honest, they begin to trust in her or him and the counselling relationship. In addition, the social worker should express genuineness with an attitude of respect and unconditional positive regard.

11.4.2 Unconditional positive regard

As mentioned above, unconditional positive regard is also one of the core conditions for facilitation emphasised by Rogers.

> **Unconditional positive regard**, the display of a positive, non-judgemental and accepting attitude towards another person.

Person-centred social workers must consistently demonstrate the total acceptance of people and refrain from adopting judgemental attitudes towards them. Acceptance is a principle of action whereby the social worker perceives and deals with clients as they really are, including their strengths and weaknesses, their congenial and uncongenial qualities, their positive and negative feelings, and their constructive and destructive attitudes and behaviour (Arora, 2013). Similarly, a non-judgemental attitude is the recognition that the social worker's role is to understand and assist the client and not to judge or condemn her or him. According to Kondrat (2014:114), 'individuals who experience unconditional positive regard do not develop conditions of worth [i.e., the sense that their basic worth is conditional] and tend to be more psychologically well adjusted'. However, total acceptance of a client as a person should not be confused with the approval of a client's behaviour. In other words, the social worker accepts the client as a human being and does not put conditions in doing so, but it does not imply that the social worker condones the client's behaviour.

11.4.3 Empathy

Empathy, 'being able to see what the client's world is like to him/her and how the client sees himself/herself' (Grobler et al., 2013:54).

Finally, Rogers identified empathy as a core condition. In the facilitation process, empathy means that social workers must enter the person's world without losing sight of their own world (Kondrat, 2014). Social workers must temporarily set aside their frame of reference and attempt to hear and understand the client and convey this understanding without prejudice or preconceived ideas. By conveying their understanding to the client, social workers intend to confirm if they understand the client the way the client understands her or himself. Although the facilitation process involves the relationship between the social worker and the client, it should be borne in mind that the client is the focal point. The condition of empathy is often regarded as the primary relationship-building condition, because people often trust social workers more when they realise that they are being understood. When social workers demonstrate empathic understanding, people feel cared for and fully understood.

Reflective questions
Read Case study 1 again and answer these questions:
- Do you think the core condition of unconditional positive regard is applicable when working with Mulanga's wife? Motivate your answer.
- How would you demonstrate the core condition of empathy when working with Mulanga's children? Motivate your answer.

Further reflections on the core conditions
- If you were working with a client who was racist or sexist towards you, how could you apply the core condition of genuineness in a way that is professional and helpful?
- How should social workers working with prisoners apply the core condition of unconditional positive regard in a prison setting in South Africa?
- Where do you draw the line between empathy and becoming emotionally over-involved with a client?

11.5 Values inherent in the person-centred approach

Grobler et al. (2013) outlined four main values embedded in the person-centred approach, namely respect, individualisation, self-determination and confidentiality. You have already learnt about other values in social work, and therefore you need to note that all these values form part of the social work code of ethics. You should also note the similarities between the person-centred approach values and the above core conditions for facilitation, as both refer to certain attitudes that social workers should adopt to treat people with respect. Without these values, the facilitation process is more likely to be compromised. The four main values of the person-centred approach are discussed below.

11.5.1 Respect

Respecting a person implies that every aspect of the person must be accepted, including their strengths and weaknesses, attitudes, behaviours and qualities. De Jong and Berg (2013:257) point out that '[t]he commitment to respecting human dignity also demands that facilitators remain non-judgemental'. Therefore, respect for people through acceptance and a non-judgemental attitude is the basis for the development of trust in the person-facilitator relationship. The professional value of respect resonates with the core condition of unconditional positive regard on the basis that they both emphasise unconditional acceptance of people and a non-judgmental attitude. When people feel respected and accepted by the social worker, they are more likely to share their experiences freely, without fear.

11.5.2 Individualisation

We should bear in mind that all the helping professions emphasise that each person is unique, possessing her or his own distinctive beliefs, attitudes, wishes, strengths, needs and challenges. In other words, social workers must not generalise or be biased when dealing with people but should treat each person as an individual. Arora (2013:44) describes *individualisation* in the following manner:

> *Individualisation is the recognition and understanding of each client's unique qualities and the differential use of principles and methods in assisting each towards a better adjustment.*

People might have similar experiences or belong to the same ethnic group, but that does not mean that they perceive things in a similar way or would behave in the same manner. For instance, there are diverse cultural and/or religious groups with which people in South Africa associate themselves, and a social worker working with these groups or individuals should be cognisant of the fact that every individual/group has different ways of doing things. Disregarding the uniqueness of the person means that the unique potential, experiences and direction of the person you are dealing with are also being lost (Grobler et al., 2013). Individualisation resonates with all the core conditions as explained above.

Note, however, Rogers' Western bias here. He makes the unitary individual the centre of the helping process, while in an African context we give far greater attention to the collective (e.g., the family, clan or community). The rights and needs of the individual are held in tension with the rights and needs of the community. While not overriding the individual, African social work incorporates serious consideration of the individual within their environment (see Chapter 5 on ecosystems).

11.5.3 Self-determination

Self-determination is one of the key values in the person-centred facilitation process as it makes facilitators aware that every person has the innate ability to make her or his own choices and decisions. Arora (2013:52) refers to *self-determination* as 'the recognition of the right and need of every person to have freedom in making his/her own choice and decision in the facilitation process'. This implies that under no circumstances should the person-centred facilitator make decisions for clients during the facilitation process. In the person-centred approach, the inherent belief is that people are able to make their own choices and decisions regarding their lives, and the social worker's role is to create an environment wherein people feel free to make such choices and decisions (see Chapter 13). When social workers make decisions for people, it would be impossible for people to take responsibility for such decisions.

In practice, the value of self-determination means that the client will be directing the process of facilitation in terms of whether she or he wishes to discuss something, what the client wishes to discuss, and how she or he wishes to discuss it. Such decisions and actions are often made in line with the cultural values and customs of individuals, groups and communities.

Rogers' notion of self-determination can be translated up to the level of the community or even society. Under colonial and apartheid rule, African people as a collective could not exercise self-determination. The state and other people determined life for African people. A large part of the Black Consciousness movement was to reclaim self-determination. Biko (2004:92), for example, writes:

> *The philosophy of Black Consciousness therefore expresses group pride and the determination of the black to rise and attain the envisaged self. Freedom is the ability to define oneself with one's possibilities held back not by the power of other people over one but only by one's relationship to God and to natural surroundings. On his own, therefore, the black man wishes to explore his surroundings and test his possibilities – in other words to make his freedom real by whatever means he deems fit.*

Thus, while Rogers' writes of self-determination as an expression of the individual having power over her or his life, in decolonial social work it is also an expression of the collective having power over their community and society.

11.5.4 Confidentiality

Confidentiality is defined as 'the preservation of secret information concerning the client which is disclosed in the professional relationship' (Arora, 2013:53). The value of confidentiality requires the social worker to keep the information conveyed by the client during the facilitation process confidential. It is the responsibility of a social worker to see to it that the client's information is not shared with anyone else and the client should be assured of this right at the beginning of the facilitation process.

One of the challenges associated with the value of confidentiality is a situation where the social worker finds her or himself caught between maintaining confidentiality and protecting life, which is referred to as an *ethical dilemma*. It could be a situation in which the life of a client or another person is threatened and where keeping confidentiality could lead to the loss of life, for instance, when the client threatens to kill someone or her or himself. In situations like this, the social worker may be forced to inform the client's family and/or line manager (depending on the context) about the client's intentions, because protecting life precedes maintaining confidentiality.

In a collectivist society like Africa, individual confidentiality can be made complicated by a requirement of families or communities for shared confidentiality, in which multiple people are tied into an agreement of confidentiality about an individual. The global social work community has attempted to address this contextual reality by incorporating the following into its ethical statement of respect for confidentiality and privacy:

> *In some cultural contexts, characterized by we-centered, communitarian living, social workers respect and abide by the people's right and choice to shared confidentiality, in so far as this does not infringe on the rights of individuals'* (IASSW, 2018:Section 6.5).

🛈 ACTIVITY 11.2

1 How do you think you would apply the value of respect and individualisation when working with a family who are practising certain rituals that contradict your own religious beliefs?
2 Suppose you are working with the family comprising members who hold opposing views about certain cultural practices. What are the advantages of allowing self-determination to all the family members?
3 What is the importance of maintaining confidentiality when working with a group?

11.6 The person-centred facilitation process

The person-centred facilitation process involves the social worker dealing with the two worlds of experiences of the client, namely the conscious (symbolised) experiences and the unconscious (unsymbolised) experiences. These worlds of experiences centre around the self of the client. Therefore, it is important for the social worker to keep in mind that, in the person-centred approach, the focus is on the self of the client. According to Grobler et al. (2013:1–2), the person-centred facilitation process can be divided into four broad phases as discussed below.

11.6.1 Phase 1: Creating a safe space for facilitation

The process of facilitation begins with the social worker creating a conducive environment for people to feel at ease while they share their experiences (Proposition 17). During this phase, the social worker focuses on the self of the client (Proposition 8) as it is the core of the person-centred facilitation process. In so doing, the social worker focuses on how the client perceives her or himself in the here and now. (In group or community work, the social worker will similarly focus on how the group or community perceives itself as a group – as a collective – not merely as multiple individuals.) Additionally, the social worker must keep in mind that the client lives in a continually changing world of experiences (Proposition 1), thus, the self continues to change. In this phase, there are experiences that may be symbolised by the person, because such experiences are perceived to be relevant or appropriate to the self-structure (Proposition 11a), and some of the experiences may be ignored, because there is no perceived relationship to the self-structure (Proposition 11b).

As part of creating a conducive environment, the social worker should bear in mind that people may react to the environment as they experience or perceive it (Proposition 2). The social worker should also understand that a person's behaviour is motivated by a need (Proposition 5), which implies that a person's behaviour should be understood as an attempt to satisfy his or her need. Conversely, it should be understood that people's behaviour is always accompanied by emotion and the intensity of such emotion signifies the importance attached to such behaviour or need (Proposition 6). People's experiences are very important during the facilitation process and therefore the social worker must keep in mind that people react as whole beings (Proposition 3). This means that the social worker must consider all the experiences of the client and not focus on only one experience and ignore the rest.

Moreover, the social worker should consider that a person's self develops in interaction with significant others (Proposition 9). Such interaction may result in the person developing values that he or she would perceive in a distorted manner, as if he or she experienced them directly (Proposition 10). In most instances, people behave in a manner that fits with the self-concept (Proposition 12), and the best way to understand people's behaviour is from their internal frame (Proposition 7).

Lastly, under this phase, the social worker should bear in mind that every person possesses the capability of becoming the person they want to become (Proposition 4). This implies that if people are determined, they are able to reach their goals. The role of the social worker in this phase is to apply professional values and basic communication skills in order to deal with the person's symbolised (i.e., conscious) experiences.

11.6.2 Phase 2: Exploring unsymbolised experiences

The second phase of the facilitation process focuses on dealing with the unsymbolised (i.e., unconscious) experiences and involves the social worker using advanced communication skills (see section 11.8 below). During this phase, the social worker must keep in mind that experiences that are perceived as a threat to the structure of the self may be denied symbolisation (Proposition 11c) or given a distorted symbolisation (Proposition 11d). When people deny symbolisation to such experiences, they are more likely to suffer from psychological tension (Proposition 14). Psychological tension happens when people deny awareness of experiences that are inconsistent with the self-structure. In some instances, a person might demonstrate behaviour that is brought about by experiences and needs that have not been symbolised or experiences and needs that have been symbolised in a distorted manner (Proposition 13). Such behaviour is often not intentional and therefore the person does not own it. During this phase, people are likely to defend the self-structure if they perceive that there are many experiences that conflict with their self-perception or that are threatening to the self (Proposition 16). These experiences are often perceived as an attack on the self-structure. In such instances, it is crucial that the social worker creates a conducive environment to allow these unsymbolised experiences to come to the fore where they can be worked on.

11.6.3 Phase 3: Reconstruction of the self

The third phase of the facilitation process involves the reconstruction of the self. The process of reconstruction begins when the client begins to assimilate all his or her experiences into a consistent relationship with the self-concept (Proposition 15). In other words, the process of reconstruction begins when people acknowledge or accept their experiences, including their mistakes and faults. When people accept all their experiences (good or bad), the chances are that they are ready for change. In this phase, the social worker should use advanced communication skills to assist people to further explore the unsymbolised experiences and threats to the self.

11.6.4 Phase 4: Ending the process

The ending phase involves the person coming to accept other people as unique individuals (Proposition 18). This phase follows immediately after the reconstruction phase in which the person has accepted her or himself and her or his experiences (Proposition 15). Thus, the person is more likely to accept others because she or he has already accepted her or himself and her or his experiences. At this stage, the person no longer worries about what other people think about her or him because the person has developed her or his own new value system (Proposition 19). This implies that the person has developed her or his new way forward and is therefore no longer concerned about other people's views about her or him. In fact, she or he has accepted that people have different opinions in life and they are entitled to such opinions. The role of the social worker in this phase is to continue maintaining a conducive environment and applying professional values and basic communication skills for people to feel free as they share their experiences. Finally, the social worker has to use advanced skills to explore the self of the client in relation to the new values developed.

> **Reflective questions**
> Refer to Case study 1 and answer the questions below.
> • Briefly describe how you would apply the person-centred facilitation process when working with Mulanga?
> • If you were to conduct three separate sessions with Mulanga, his wife and the children, do you think the facilitation process would unfold in the same manner? Motivate your answer.

11.7 Basic communication skills

Basic communication skills are important tools used by the person-centred social worker in dealing with symbolised (conscious) experiences. You should bear in mind that there are many basic communication skills that can be used during the facilitation process, but there are three main basic communication skills used in the person-centred approach, namely attending, listening, and basic empathy (Grobler et al., 2013:205–212). Because you have already learnt about the basic communication skills in your studies, the focus in this chapter will be on the advanced communication skills.

 **ACTIVITY 11.3**

1 What do you think would be the purpose of using basic communication skills in Mulanga's case?
2 What is the purpose of applying listening and attending skills during the facilitation process?
3 Provide an example of how you would apply the skill of empathy with Mulanga's family.

11.8 Advanced communication skills

Advanced communication skills are used to deal with the unsymbolised (unconscious) experiences that threaten the person's self during the facilitation process. It is important to keep in mind that the basic communication skills are always used initially and continuously throughout the facilitation process. According to Grobler et al. (2013:82–101, 213–226), the advanced skills are divided into three categories, namely advanced empathy, exploring distortions, and immediacy.

11.8.1 Advanced empathy

Advanced empathy involves the ability of the social worker to enter people's unconscious world and see clearly what they only half see or hint at (Grobler et al., 2013). When dealing with unsymbolised experiences, advanced empathy implies that the social worker must identify the client's self and how the self-structure is threatened by the client's experiences. Advanced empathy involves deeper understanding and requires the social worker to communicate this understanding to the client. There are three types of advanced empathy, namely identifying the implied messages, connecting islands, and identification of themes.

1. **Identifying the implied messages**. The skill of identifying the implied messages is used to deal with the unsymbolised experiences of the client to assist her or him to express these experiences directly, as they are unconscious experiences. The social worker has to read between the lines to understand how these experiences threaten the person's self. When using the skill of advanced empathy, the social worker does not listen only to what the client is saying out loud, but also to the implied messages about the person's self and how the self is threatened. In other words, the social worker's response should always include the person's self and how the self is threatened, and this self is based on the person's frame of reference in terms of how she or he presents or perceives her or himself.

 Identifying how the self is threatened

A man who lost his job through retrenchment says: 'Life is not easy for me. I am no longer able to provide for my family. My kids used to attend one of the best schools in town, but now the circumstances forced them to go to a public school.' This man perceives himself as 'a caring father' who used to take care of his children/family. However, the self of 'a caring father' is threatened by the fact that he does not have a job and therefore he is asking himself if he would ever be able to take care of his children/family. The possible response would be: 'I am gathering that you seem to perceive yourself as a "caring father" to your children, who is willing to do anything necessary to ensure that your children get the best. However, the fact that you have lost your job makes you wonder if you will be able to take care of them in future.' The social worker in this instance did not only listen to what the client is saying directly, but also identified the self of the client and how the self is threatened before communicating her understanding to the client.

2. **Connecting islands**. People often share their experiences as if they are not connected to other people. In Proposition 3 (wholeness), we mentioned that people's experiences are linked to one another. For that reason, the social worker cannot focus on only one aspect, for example, the behavioural, without considering emotional aspects, such as needs and values, which could have influenced the person's behaviour. The skill of connecting islands allows the social worker to see the person's experiences in totality and to give her or him feedback.

Connecting experiences to the self

A 48-year-old single mother, whose son allegedly abuses substances, says: '*I only want good things for my son. I raised him in a Christian environment hoping that he would become somebody I could be proud of. I sacrificed everything for him. I worked hard to ensure that he would always get what he wanted. He has everything a child desires – nice clothes, toys, everything. I even send him to the most expensive Christian school.*' If all the experiences (behaviour, feelings and needs) are linked together, it appears that the woman tries hard to be the 'best mother' to her son. However, this self is threatened by the fact that her son abuses substances despite all her efforts. Therefore, a possible response could be: '*You are doing everything in your power to provide love and care to your son, ensuring that he receives the quality education he deserves, being the best mother you can be, but you seem worried that your efforts are in vain.*' In this example, all the experiences shared by the mother are connected to the self.

3. **Identification of themes**. Identification of themes relates to connecting islands in the sense that clients often share their inner world of experiences as if they are separate from one another. The reality is that these experiences are somehow connected to one another in a way that they make up a theme. Using the skill of identification of themes requires the social worker to ask her or himself what the shared experiences have in common and how they relate to the person's self. The social worker should be aware of the fact that people may give the same message in different ways and that makes it crucial for the social worker to listen attentively.

Listening for themes in a person's narrative

A 33-year-old widower says: '*I am unable to cope with my wife's death. I miss the warmth that we used to have in this house. She left with her income, care and protection. It feels like a part of my life has gone with her.*' If we listen to the man's experiences, it seems as if 'loss' is the main theme. Therefore, a possible response could be: '*I am hearing that the death of your wife makes you think that you are a loser, since you have lost all the precious things she used to provide and you wonder if your life can be the same without her.*' After identifying the themes, the social worker must communicate them to the man to allow him to explore these themes.

11.8.2 Exploring distortions or discrepancies

People sometimes unconsciously present contradictory messages during a conversation or over several sessions. However, the social worker cannot judge or accuse people of dishonesty, as it could be their way of protecting the self. The social worker should bear in mind that exploring distortions or discrepancies should be done with respect and not in a confrontational manner. However, exploring discrepancies does not refer to conflicts or disagreements between individuals, groups or communities on a conscious level only. It rather refers to nonverbal discrepancies between a person's words, nonverbal communication and the self (Grobler et al., 2013). These aspects are discussed in more detail below.

Verbal distortions. This kind of discrepancy happens when people verbally convey two contradictory verbal messages, which implies that people say something contrary to what they said earlier in the session or in a previous session. Verbal distortions are a common type of discrepancy and most social workers accurately identify it in practice. The role of the social worker is to help people explore the discrepancy.

 Case Study 6 ## Exploring verbal distortions

A boy says: *'I love my mother. She is my pillar of strength.'* Later in the session the same boy says: *'My mother is the most ruthless person I have ever seen. I do not want to see that woman.'* In this instance, the boy verbally communicated the message of both 'love' and 'hate' towards his mother and these messages contradict each other. Therefore, the social worker must assist him to explore these experiences without being judgemental. A possible response could be: *'If I heard you correctly, earlier you mentioned that your mother is the pillar of your strength and now I hear you saying that she is the most ruthless person.'* This will help the boy to explore and clarify what he meant by the two statements.

Nonverbal distortions, it is another form of discrepancy that is very common in practice. People often convey verbal messages that are contrary to their nonverbal messages (i.e., their actions). In other words, what they say contradicts what they do.

 Case Study 7 ## Exploring nonverbal distortions

For example, group members may verbally say that everything is well with the group, but their facial expressions shows the opposite. In this instance, the social worker may respond by saying: *'Correct me if I am wrong, I hear you saying that all is well with the group, but looking at your facial expressions, I am getting the opposite message.'* The role of the social worker in this instance is to help the group explore that contradiction.

Self distortions, involve a discrepancy between the self and the self, which happens when people present themselves in two or more different contradictory ways. This means that they are presenting more than one self at a time.

This type of discrepancy is not easy to identify, as it is not obvious. The best way to understand this discrepancy is through Proposition 9 (self and significant others), which indicates that the self is formed in interaction with significant others. Different forms of the self can be formed, therefore, in interaction with various significant others. From a person's experiences, the social worker is able to identify whether the person is portraying two contradictory selves. This is evidenced, for example, when a client portrays him or herself sometimes as a 'loving person' and at other times as an 'abusive person'. In this instance, the role of the social worker is to assist the client to explore the two contradictory selves that the client presents.

11.8.3 Immediacy

Immediacy is the advanced skill used by facilitators to address stumbling blocks in the professional relationship and it is applied in the 'here and now' (Grobler et al., 2013). There are three general rules that apply when responding with immediacy, namely:

1. self-based statements (the 'I' rule);
2. dealing with stumbling blocks in the professional relationship; and
3. the hypothetical (or tentative) nature of immediacy.

The skill of immediacy always involves the facilitator in the statement (the first rule). In other words, she or he applies the 'I' rule. There may be various stumbling blocks that occur during the facilitation process, however, immediacy deals specifically with the stumbling blocks in the professional relationship (the second rule). The social worker may use the skill of immediacy when the client involves her or him. For instance, when a client asks the social worker *'Are you married?'*, the client is directly involving the social worker by asking a direct personal question. Therefore, the social worker must first identify the implied message about the relationship and the threats it poses to the facilitator relationship. Instead of responding directly to the client's statement, for instance, by saying *'I am married'*, the social worker should identify the implied message and use it as an immediacy response (the second rule). In this example, the implied message could be that the client is doubtful that the social worker will be able to understand him or her unless the social worker is married. In responding to the client, the social worker must ensure that he or she applies the 'I' rule in his or her response. A possible immediacy response could be: *'I am gathering that you seem doubtful that I can understand you unless I am married.'* Such a response would be hypothetical or tentative (the third rule), meaning that the response is not valid unless the person confirms it.

Reflective questions

Refer to Case study 1. Answer the following questions:

- What is the importance of using the advanced skills in Mulanga's case?
- Briefly describe your understanding of advanced empathy and provide an example of how you would use it during the facilitation process.
- What are the advantages of using the skill of exploring distortions? Kindly provide an example from the case study.
- Why is it necessary to use the skill of immediacy during the facilitation process?

🔍 ACTIVITY 11.4

1 Briefly describe the value of listening in the context of your culture.
2 Think of idioms in your culture that best describe the advanced skills of connecting islands and identification of themes.
3 Suppose you are facilitating a group of elderly men who are cynical about being facilitated by a young social worker, how would you use the advanced skill of immediacy?
4 Do you think that the basic and advanced skills discussed above are applicable within a multicultural context such as South Africa? Please motivate your answer.

11.9 Decolonial person-centred practice

The person-centred approach has received more attention and generated more interest in multicultural settings outside of North America in the past decade (Rowe, 2017). This happened after Rogers recognised the importance of working with individuals, groups and communities in a cross-cultural setting. Decolonial social work practice using the person-centred approach recognises the uniqueness of multicultural settings. In other words, it recognises the importance of different cultural groups and its indigenous practices and beliefs.

Earlier sections of this chapter deal with the person-centred approach in relation to working with individuals. In this section, the focus shifts toward using a person-centred approach to work with multicultural groups. Rogers viewed the intensive group experience as an important vehicle for therapeutic growth and attitudinal change (Rowe, 2017). This tells us that understanding multicultural groups from their own point of view is of paramount importance.

In the South African context, applying the person-centred approach within a multicultural setting proves to be invaluable to the social worker. South Africa comprises people from many different ethnic groups with different cultural practices and beliefs. This diverse ethnicity requires social workers to be observant, considerate and respectful towards other people's cultural practices and beliefs.

> *Ethnicity*, a social group that shares a common culture, tradition or language.

Ethnic groups in South Africa include, among other, amaNdebele, amaSwati, amaXhosa, amaZulu, Bapedi, Basotho, 'coloured' Afrikaans, Hindu Indians, Muslim Indians, Vatsonga, Vhavenda and white Afrikaans social groups. Working from the person-centred approach in the South African context requires the social worker to give reasonable and appropriate consideration to the beliefs and multicultural practices of these diverse groups.

An important philosophical concept, *Ubuntu*, has been identified in the *White Paper for Social Welfare* (RSA, 1997) as one of the key principles for transforming social welfare in South Africa. This philosophy has been practised since before the colonisation of South Africa and is premised on the belief that people exist because of their connections to others. It emphasises the success of the group above that of the individual. *Ubuntu* also reinforces certain positive values, for example, children are taught to love, respect and accept everyone regardless of their age (Grobler et al., 2013). Chapter 6 of this book discusses the *Ubuntu* philosophy in more detail.

Regarding Rogers' propositions, it is important for the facilitator to realise that multicultural groups may have different perceptions about something (Proposition 2), which should be understood from within a particular group's own frame of reference (Proposition 7). This may include values inherent in that group that may be passed from one generation to another (Proposition 10) through some form of interaction amongst one another (Proposition 9). This means that a social worker who works with multicultural groups needs to work within the sense of 'self' (i.e., the group identity, the sense of 'groupness') of a particular group as presented to him or her (Proposition 8), and should respect the group's perceptions (Proposition 2) and frames of reference (Proposition 7) by creating a conducive environment (Proposition 17).

The core conditions are useful in all group facilitation, but particularly so when working with a diverse group, and even more so when running a group to address decolonial issues, for example, a group of people from different race groups to talk about racial conflicts. The person-centred approach encourages each person to express him or herself in an authentic and genuine way, by being honest and sometimes taking a risk in sharing something that might be contentious. All group members are encouraged to exercise unconditional positive regard, by listening to one another in an open-hearted way and refraining from judging or jumping to conclusions. And throughout, empathy is exercised to enable participants to step into the life world of one another, so as to see the world from one another's point of view. In this way, person-centred social work can begin to break down the walls between groups of people that have resulted from generations of colonialism and apartheid.

Using the person-centred approach from a decolonial perspective may also require the social worker to use various indigenous tools or activities that are relevant to a particular cultural group. For example, by now you have learnt that facilitating a group requires the use of various group activities to enhance group communication, among others. In this instance, it is very important that the social worker use the tools or activities that resonate with that group. This may also apply to working with individuals, families and communities.

Reflective question
Think of the unique cultural background of your community. What are some of the indigenous tools or activities that you think may be used when facilitating a group of older women caring for orphans using the person-centred approach.

 ACTIVITY 11.5

Suppose you are working with a group of elderly men who are concerned about their grandchildren who are refusing to go to the initiation school, which is one of the practices in their culture. The grandchildren are of the view that initiation school is old fashioned and is no longer relevant for them. They further point out that this kind of practice is against their religious beliefs and practices.

1 How would you create a conducive environment for mutually respectful dialogue? Motivate your answer.
2 How might you use Propositions 2, 8 and 17 to help you in this situation?

11.10 Conclusion

This chapter has provided an overview of the person-centred approach. We started by describing the historical background of the person-centred approach and how it evolved over the years. In so doing, we unpacked how the person-centred approach moved from being known as the non-directive approach in the 1940s to the client-centred approach in the 1960s and, finally, to the person-centred approach in the 1980s. This led us to the discussion of the 19 propositions and the core conditions inherent in the person-centred approach. Subsequently, the person-centred approach facilitation process was expounded, followed by descriptions of the practical application of the person-centred approach using the values and communication skills embedded in this approach. The chapter concludes by outlining the application of decolonial social work practice using the person-centred approach within multicultural contexts.

Chapter activity

1. **Reflective question**. Think about one of the challenges you encountered as a child or youth and how you dealt with it. In terms of the person-centred facilitation process, how would you describe the process that you could have followed, specifically linking it to Rogers' 19 propositions? Should you experience the same challenge in the future, do you think you would deal with it in the same way you dealt with it in the past?

2. **Personal context**. Think about different ethnic groups that are found in your community. Do you see any similarities or differences in terms of how these ethnic groups (including your own) deal with social or family problems? If so, what are those similarities or challenges?

3. **Advocacy**. How can you use the person-centred approach to deal with the pertinent social issues that you are faced with in the country you live in, especially at a macro level?

4. **Critical question**. The divorce rate in South Africa is very high (StatsSA, 2015). How do you think the social work profession is contributing towards this, and how can the person-centred approach help in strengthening marital relations to reduce the number of divorces?

References

Arora, N. 2013. *Case work: Concepts and principles*. Delhi: Book Enclave.

Beckett, C & Horner, N. 2016. *Essential theory for social work practice*. 2nd ed. London, UK: Sage.

Biko, S. 2004. *I write what I like*. Johannesburg: Picador Africa.

Corey, G. 2016. *Theory and practice of group counselling*. 9th ed. Belmont, CA: Cengage Learning.

Corey, G. 2017. *Theory and practice of counselling and psychotherapy*. 10th ed. Belmont, CA: Cengage Learning.

De Jong, P & Berg, IK. 2013. *Interviewing for solutions*. 4th ed. Belmont, CA: Brooks/Cole.

Egan, G. 2014. *The skilled helper. A problem-management and opportunity development approach to helping*. 10th ed. Belmont, CA: Brooks/Cole, Cengage Learning.

Grobler, H, Schenck, R & Mbedzi, P. 2013. *Person-centred facilitation: Process, theory and practice*. 4th ed. Cape Town: Oxford University Press Southern Africa.

IASSW. 2018. *Global social work statement of ethical principles*. International Association of Schools of Social Work. [Online]. Available: https://tinyurl.com/iasswethics [Accessed 7 May 2019].

Joseph, S & Murphy, D. 2013. Person-centred approach, positive psychology, and relational helping: Building bridges. *Journal of Humanistic Psychology*, 53(1):26–51.

Kondrat, DC: 'Person centred approach'. *In*: Teater, B (ed.). 2014. *An introduction to applying social work theories and methods*. 2nd ed. pp. 108–124. Maidenhead, UK: McGraw Hill.

Menkiti, IA: 'Person and community in African traditional thought'. *In*: Wright, RA (ed.). 1984. *African philosophy: An introduction*. Lanham: MD. [Online]. Available: http://courseweb.stthomas.edu/sjlaumakis/Reading%203-AFRICAN%20VIEW.pdf [Accessed 7 March 2019].

Republic of South Africa. 1997. *White Paper for Social Welfare*. Pretoria: Government Printer.

Republic of South Africa. Statistics South Africa. 2015. *Marriages and divorces 2013*. [Online]. Available: http://www.statssa.gov.za/publications/P0307/P03072013.pdf [Accessed 16 May 2018].

Rogers, CR. 1987. *Client-centered therapy: Its current practice, implications and theory*. London: Constable.

Rowe, WS: 'Client-centered theory and the person-centered approach: Values-based, evidence-supported'. *In*: Turner, FJ. 2017. *Social work treatment: Interlocking theoretical approaches*. 6th ed. pp. 34–53. New York: Oxford University Press.

Spangenberg, JJ. 2003. The cross-cultural relevance of person-centered counseling in post-apartheid South Africa. *Journal of Counseling & Development*, 81:48–54.

Annotated websites and activities

https://www.youtube.com/watch?v=iMi7uY83z-U
This YouTube link takes you to Carl Rogers' presentation on empathy and its usefulness.

Take time to watch this video to understand the importance of empathy as one of the core conditions inherent in the person-centred approach. Practise the core condition of empathy when communicating with family members and/or friends. As you do so, take notes of your shortcomings and/or areas you need to improve.

https://www.youtube.com/watch?v=sO5vPyWMgXQ
With this YouTube link, you shall be taken to the presentation by Rory Lees-Oakes on Carl Rogers' 19 propositions. It provides an overview of the person-centred approach in relation to practice.

After watching this presentation, briefly describe how the person-centred approach helped in shaping your perception and understanding about people and their experiences.

https://www.youtube.com/watch?v=r_yGBnZXFFA
This link takes you to Carl Rogers' interview with a client named Steve.

Take time to watch and observe how Rogers creates a conducive environment through the application of professional values and communication skills. Identify some of the values and skills that Rogers used in this interview and how these values and skills can help you to create a conducive environment when working with people.

Annotated websites and activities are also available on Learning Zone.

Learningzone
oxford.co.za/learningzone

Spirituality

Glynnis Dykes and Shernaaz Carelse

CHAPTER OUTCOMES

By the end of this chapter, you should be able to:

✓ *Critically assess the role and place of spirituality in social work*

✓ *Define and differentiate spirituality and religion*

✓ *Argue the merits of a biopsychosocial-spiritual approach*

✓ *Explain the place of spirituality in social work practice*

✓ *Reflect critically on the place of spirituality in your own professional identity*

✓ *Understand the inclusion of an African-centred worldview that human beings are spiritual.*

 Case Study 1   The influence of religious beliefs

Anna is referred to the local social development office after her husband Barry was arrested for physically abusing her. She has been married to Barry for 15 years and has had five children with him, ages 2 to 14. Barry runs his own business and supports the family well. Anna did not complete high school and has never worked. The family belongs to a traditional religious community. On one occasion after Barry physically assaulted her, Anna was on the floor crying when the police arrived. She had a large bruise on her face. Barry was arrested, but released the next day. Anna insisted she wanted to withdraw the charges. As a social worker you wonder what role the family's religious beliefs have played in Anna's insistence to stay and whether you should ask her about it, or if Anna's economic vulnerability, making her unable to leave him and care for her children alone, is the dominant story (based on a case study scenario in Senreich, 2013).

Reflective questions

• Why might you be hesitant to ask the client about her religious beliefs?

• Do you think it would be unwise to ask the client about her religious beliefs? Why do you think so?

• What, if any, are your own spiritual or religious beliefs about Anna's situation?

• Do you think that spirituality and religious beliefs are an area that social workers should include in their work with clients? Motivate your answer.

12.1 Introduction

Social workers are confronted with a variety of biopsychosocial challenges experienced by their clients. Often when asked how they have managed to cope with these challenges, clients cite prayer, meditation, rituals, visualisation or mindfulness as some of the internal resources and coping measures they draw on. These practices are often integrated in clients' spirituality, which is often engrained in their culture. Likewise, social workers' views of spirituality in their own lives play an important role in their engagement with clients. The experiences and expressions of their own spirituality influence their approach to practice.

Spiritual needs are universal and therefore a significant factor in considering clients' needs during the helping process. Understanding clients' spiritual needs is an important aspect in holistic service provision in social work and should therefore not be seen as separate from attending to clients' biopsychosocial needs. Knowledge about clients' spirituality is important to understand and contextualise their social and personal challenges (Canda, 2008; Stanley et al., 2011; Oxhandler & Pargament, 2014).

Western societies tend to favour secularism, arguing that it is neutral. However, because of its materialism, secularism does not recognise the spiritual world, by implication rejecting people's spiritual needs. Ignoring the spiritual needs of clients could be regarded as being judgemental towards people who do believe in the divine, a higher power and/or God. Spirituality discourse offers opportunities to realise values, such as the clients' right to self-determination and social justice. It also offers useful and alternative constructions of clients' needs and the role of social workers (Bhagwan, 2007; Canda, 2005, 2008; Canda & Furman, 2010; Carroll, 2001; Healy, 2005), but should be approached critically and cautiously.

In this chapter, we will discuss spirituality as an alternative discourse for social work education and practice. We start with defining the terms spirituality and religion, which are two distinct but often closely interrelated terms, and which we often refer to in combination as spirituality and religion (S&R). We present the merits for a biopsychosocial-spiritual approach to social work practice that provides for a holistic assessment and intervention with individual, families, groups and communities. We identify the value and merits of decolonising African spirituality as a more contextually relevant approach to meeting clients' needs. The chapter provides case studies and reflective questions so that you can critically engage and do introspection regarding your own professional identity.

12.2 Defining spirituality and religion

There are no universally accepted definitions for S&R, because there are various schools of thought about these terms, some of which are culturally derived. The diverse definitions of S&R reflect the complexity of its application in social work. According to Philips (2014), S&R is about the emotional state of mind, beliefs, experiences and conduct associated with the search for the sacred. Similarly, Hutchison (1998) as well as Kissman and Mauer (2002) describe S&R as a non-materialistic worldview that places emphasis on the divine, mysterious or higher power or being whose proponents promote spiritual and human well-being, as well as care and compassion for others.

While some authors use the terms spirituality and religion interchangeably, most literature distinguishes between the two, proposing that *spirituality* is associated with a broad sense of interconnectedness and self-fulfilment, while *religion* is concerned with adherence to organised belief systems (Philips, 2014). We thought it useful to deconstruct S&R to demonstrate the difference between the two concepts.

12.2.1 What is spirituality?

Spirituality, according to Koenig, McCullough and Larson (2001:18), is characterised as:

> ...[a] personal quest for understanding answers to ultimate questions about life, about meaning, and about relationship to the sacred or transcendent, which may (or may not) lead to or arise from the development of religious rituals and formation of community.

Spirituality is therefore considered a more holistic and inclusive approach because it is influenced by multiculturalism and thus takes on board different cultures and beliefs of diverse people. Cowley and Derezotes (1994:33) assert that spirituality is 'not contained by theological walls of any specific ideological system' nor is it 'equivalent with religion, religiosity or theology'. Spirituality is the search for meaning, purpose and morality, fulfilling relations with self, others, the encompassing universe and ultimately with reality however a person understands it (Furman et al., 2004:772). Spirituality has always been part of indigenous and culturally sensitive social work practice. It is therefore important to locate spirituality within culture, place and history.

Religiosity, 'strong religious feeling or belief'
(https://en.oxforddictionaries.com/definition/religiosity).

Theology, 'the study of the nature of God and religious belief'
(https://en.oxforddictionaries.com/definition/theology).

In African culture, spirituality is associated with communicating with spiritual beings, the Divine and with one's ancestors. The ancestors, who are deceased persons in one's lineage, are regarded as a source of support and strength in times of despair and stress, providing comfort and solutions to life's problems, and even healing of illness and disease. It is believed that solutions and comfort are revealed through dreams and visions (Thomas, 1999; Wheeler et al., 2002). There is therefore much reliance on the Divine (heavenly) and ancestors in African society.

These practices are not universal to all African cultures and are practised differently by different cultures within African society. In a multicultural society such as South Africa, social workers must consider the client's spirituality for the purpose of assessment and intervention. It is important also not to make assumptions about an African person's spirituality, as even within one cultural group spiritual views may be diverse.

Global North literature indicates a growing recognition and appreciation of indigenous spirituality in social work practice (Baskin, 2002; Beatch & Stewart, 2002; Ruwhiu, 2001; Stirling, 2008). Ruwhiu (2001:63) asserts that 'the spiritual realm is always present, integrated into everything, the source of both pain and suffering and healing and wellbeing'. Similarly, Jenkins (1998:493) asserts that spirituality 'penetrates and permeates through the whole of life, supporting, nurturing and guiding the natural order'. It is thus a lived phenomenon imposing a set of social obligations for engagement with other dimensions of the universe (Ruwhiu, 2001:63–65).

In her edited book, *Spirituality and social work*, Crisp (2017) considers spirituality in the context of lived experiences of clients. Crisp contends that spirituality allows exploration of the challenges experienced by clients during different life stages, whether or not the client identifies with religion and/or practises some form of spirituality. Most social work literature on S&R relates to the elderly, death and dying or sick or bereaved clients. But as Crisp (2010) points out, spirituality is a significant aspect for people of all ages and at various life stages and therefore not only during illness or loss.

Similarly, Dreyer (2015) asserts that a caring relationship with God and/or other being promotes spiritual and physical well-being and contributes towards people's resilience during times of adversity. Spirituality is an important human element in the social work helping process and is strongly linked to principles of strengths-based approaches (see Chapter 13). Dreyer further affirms that an individual, family, group or community's view of the meaning of life and their place in the world is not static and can change. This change is associated with culture, place and history, and given the fact that spirituality is embedded herein, it can change or evolve.

A definition of spirituality in social work has to take into consideration every client's perception of the unknown as equally valid. A definition of spirituality for social work education and practice should therefore meet the following criteria (Holloway & Moss, 2010):

- It should be a comprehensive definition that respects the diverse beliefs of each individual client.
- It should reflect the values that social work students are encouraged to develop.
- It should assume that there are diverse points of view about life.
- It should be clear and specific, for social work students and practitioners to understand precisely what it means to assess and intervene with a client's spirituality.

We propose the following definition of spirituality for social work.

> **Spirituality**, refers to a person's personal and communal pursuit for meaning in life, and the influence of that knowledge about the self, others and morality on the person's worldview, culture, beliefs and behaviour.

Spirituality in social work assessment and intervention (in the helping process), therefore, encompasses the personal beliefs, customs, culture, religion and history of both the social worker and the client system for the purpose of finding solutions.

12.2.2 What is religion?

Religion, according to Furman et al. (2004:772), is an organised set of beliefs and practices shared by a community that relates to the Divine. Similarly, Koenig (2008:11) defines *religion* as a 'system of beliefs and practices observed by a community, supported by rituals that acknowledge, worship, communicate with, or approach the sacred, the divine, God or ultimate truth, reality, or nirvana [spiritual enlightenment]'. Hence, religion, unlike spirituality, is considered to be institutionalised and associated with observance of and adherence to rules and rituals.

> **Religion**, 'the belief in and worship of a superhuman controlling power, especially a personal God or gods ... a particular system of faith and worship' (https://en.oxforddictionaries.com/definition/religion).

Griffith (2010:13) asserts that:

> *Religion, defined by its themes of personal spirituality, often becomes a bulwark [defence], protecting emotional and physical survival for those who suffer. Religion can contribute to the security of a group, strengthening individual's sense of worth and value and reducing personal suffering; religion is equally powerful in its ability to harm.*

Here Griffith (2010) reflects the nurturing and positive aspects of practising a religion, reflecting comforting images and actions, such as defence and protection against harm, and fostering group and individual benefits. Therefore, Ratliff (1996:171) further clarifies the significant role that religion plays in the various aspects of life:

> *Religious beliefs may dictate food choices, clothing styles, customs of birthing and dying, etiquette in the sick room, use of modern conveniences, invasive procedures, organ donation, reception, use of blood products, certain diagnostic tests, gynaecological procedures, spiritual influences on or control of sickness and healing, and the need for prayers and rituals performed by various religious specialists.*

Ratliff (1996) has clearly illustrated how one's religious beliefs influence the social and health choices and decisions that a follower of a specific religion is able to make. From the above, it can be seen that one's choices are often not one's own and very much dictated to by religious doctrines (rules and standards).

Griffith (2010) and Walsh (2009) refer to religious groups as 'faith communities', consisting of people brought together – based on their religious (and spiritual) beliefs – to form a community of mutual care, which offers spiritual care to its members throughout the life span (Dreyer, 2015; Griffith, 2010; Walsh, 2009). The community of care is characterised by internal (inherent) personal strength based on personal beliefs and by external resources of care and support provided by the faith community (Walsh, 2009). Thus, religious beliefs are associated with an individual, family, group or community's history, culture and customs.

Although religion has thus far been portrayed as having a positive influence on an individual, Griffith (2010:13) also reminds us of the other side of religion, when he writes that 'religion is equally powerful in its ability to harm'. Religion has been used to exert harm and has a long history of exclusion, violence and atrocity. Examples include the Dutch Reformed Church in South Africa under apartheid, the holocaust in Germany during Adolf Hitler's reign, and the Ku Klux Klan in America. Other forms of harm associated with religion are racism, homophobia and sexism, which are institutionalised prejudices associated with certain religions.

The harm associated with such prejudice is referred to by Saul (2014:3) as 'collective trauma'. Collective trauma is the impact of adversity on relationships in families, communities and societies and is worsened when those responsible deny accountability or refuse to make amends for the harm caused. The result of this is a betrayal of social trust, and people feeling devalued, dehumanised and humiliated. Collective trauma damages the fabric of society and destroys people's sense of community, collectivism and social order.

Restoring social trust in the wake of collective trauma requires an acknowledgement of and taking responsibility for the harm caused, so that injustice is diminished (Saul, 2014). A case in point is the Truth and Reconciliation Commission in South Africa as a means for confession, accountability and forgiveness.

So far, we have established that there is a clear distinction between spirituality and religion. Edwards (2009) argues that religion is narrow, compared to spirituality, because of religion's concern with rules, adherence and observance of such rules and rituals and therefore considered the 'bureaucratic' face of spirituality. This distinction is evident in the different approaches to worship. For example, some Christian churches follow a highly structured and ordered process of readings, prayers and sacraments, in accordance with Biblical principles and liturgical or church texts. In other churches, a very different process unfolds – while also based on Biblical principles, services are more flexible and dynamic and follow a more spiritual (charismatic) process.

Some scholars question the need for distinction between S&R, however, because social workers work with both spirituality and religion, which do not always have definable boundaries (Philips, 2014).

Reflective questions
- What are your own religious beliefs? What is your own spirituality? How are these two (S&R) related to each other, or disconnected from each other, in your own life?
- What do you think forms the basis of your own spirituality and religion and the role these play in your own life in terms of decision-making and choices?
- What, if any, are the value conflicts you have in terms of Anna's refusal to lay criminal charges against Barry (Case study 1)?

12.3   History of spirituality and religion in social work

Social work is regarded as a secular profession because it is influenced by human and biomedical sciences, which are the dominant discourses in social work education and practice. Although social scientists now concur that social work knowledge can be broadened, even transformed, by including knowledge and wisdoms from different cultures (Furman et al., 2005), this wasn't always the case. Lezotte (2010) argues that social work's relationship with S&R went through three main stages, which are discussed below.

12.3.1   Stage 1: Sectarian origins

Sectarianism means the strong support for one religion to the exclusion of or resulting from discrimination against other religions. This was common during the colonial period. A common understanding about human behaviour often emerged from conflicting explanations of behaviour, for example, between moral censure and merit (such as the deserving and undeserving poor) versus social justice and transformation (Lezotte, 2010). In South Africa, sectarianism also played itself out in colonialism, where westernised culture and knowledge became the dominant belief system, forced upon many people practising different cultures and beliefs (Dumbrill & Green, 2008; Le Grange, 2014). The brutality and discrimination of colonialism meant that traditional African spirituality and beliefs were ridiculed and Christian beliefs became dominant. Another example was people's sexual orientation and sexual identity, where these were shaped by the Judeo-Christian values, which set the dominance of the heterosexual orientation as norm (Lezotte, 2010).

In the early development of social work as a profession, its theory and practice were founded on S&R, which reflected the religious origins of social work based on Judeo-Christian beliefs (Furman et al., 2005; Lezotte, 2010; Sheffield & Openshaw, 2009; Sheridan & Amato-von Hemert, 1999). Many of the initial social work values were based on Christian values, for example, respect for persons' worth and dignity, caring for others, and the plight of the poor (Hare, 2010; Neagoe, 2013) as evidenced in the charitable work around 'the least, the last and the lost' (Hare, 2010:2). However, other fundamental values in Christianity conflict with safe sex education, abortion services, services to and acceptance of the LGBTIQ+ (Lesbians, Gay, Bisexual, Transgendered, Intersex, Queer, and other, including gender non-conforming) community (heterosexuality and homophobia), patriarchy and the subjugation of girls and women (sexism). The overemphasis on Christianity in relation to those who were deemed worthy of being assisted gave rise to the notion of sectarianism (Holloway & Moss, 2010).

> **Reflective question**
> Think of our social work values and principles. How do these values and principles link with Christian values or teachings?

12.3.2 Stage 2: Secularisation and professionalisation

Freudian and Marxist analyses of religion started to signal the shift away from S&R in social work (Holloway & Moss, 2010). Freud argued that people should look deep within themselves for meaning, rather than to religious supreme beings for fulfilment. Marx (1970:127) criticised religion as 'the opium of the people', drugging them into accepting subservience and their lot in life (Holloway & Moss, 2010). Consequently, social work academics and practitioners began to critique sectarianism and agitate for the processes of secularisation and professionalisation to be the dominant forces, rather than S&R.

This change meant that social work moved towards scientific, rational explanations. These processes changed the fundamentals of social work education and practice. This could be seen in the changes brought about in social work's ethical principles and values, which in the past were grounded in S&R, but now became based on *empiricism* (knowledge based on experience and observation), *secular humanism* (a non-religious view of the world and how it should function), *medical science* (the study of health from a science and disease perspective), and *libertarian morality* (individual liberty as a primary moral principle) (Furman et al., 2005; Lezotte, 2010; Sheffield & Openshaw, 2009; Sheridan & Amato-von Hemert, 1999).

> *Secularisation*, 'religion loses its authority in all aspects of social life and governance' (Togarasei, 2015:58).

The impact of secularisation was felt not only in the profession of social work, but also in decreasing church membership, in the declining institutional power of organised religion, and in waning religious beliefs (Furman et al., 2005). Fulcher and Scott (1999) identified two components of secularisation worth noting (Table 12.1):

Table 12.1: Components of secularisation

Disengagement	Disenchantment
The socio-political developments by which S&R and its consequential far-reaching power become dissociated from other forms of modern society and structures thereby reducing its dominance and significance in society.	The diminished belief in the power of S&R as ways to find meaning and fulfilment in an increasingly challenging world.

Disengagement and disenchantment together reduced the strong and dominant role that S&R had played in people's lives and in society as a whole. Social work services increasingly became disconnected from the role of S&R in clients' lives (Canda, 2005; Crisp, 2017). The additional disregard for indigenous beliefs and practices, historically seen in Africa, Australia, New Zealand and Canada, also caused a further disconnect with S&R. In terms of disengagement and disenchantment, S&R were no longer part of the therapeutic relationship and helping process, fieldwork learning, professional practice and research.

Reflective questions
- Do you agree that social work should only be practised within the context of secularisation? Why do you think so?
- Is S&R incompatible with the principles of social work? In what ways?

The secularisation of social work went hand in glove with the professionalisation of social work. Since the 1860s, social work has developed into a global profession practised in over 144 countries. Its growth and expansion were associated with its strive for professionalisation (Weiss-Gal & Welbourne, 2008). The professionalisation of social work is related to the trend of helping professions to shift away from religious foundations towards a scientific medical approach to practice. Social work thus enacted the move from its S&R roots, as it did not sufficiently reflect a scientific foundation (Oxhandler & Pargament, 2014). Professions can be described as occupations that fulfil specific characteristics for their functioning and contribution to society and in terms of its power and dominance in areas of practice which together reflect its professional status (Weiss-Gal & Welbourne, 2008). Whether or not social work has achieved its professional status is still a matter of debate, as it differs in each country in terms of political will and resource provision.

Reflective question
What do you think are factors that are enabling and constraining to the professional status of social work in SA?

12.3.3 Stage 3: Resurgence of interest in S&R in social work

You might well ask why S&R should be relevant for social work now. What caused the resurgence of interest in S&R in social work? The turnaround in the value and relevance of S&R for social work was contingent on the following factors (Bullis, 1996; Carroll, 2002; Furman et al., 2005; Lezotte, 2010; Sheffield & Openshaw, 2009; Sheridan & Amato-von Hemert, 1999):

- Social work scholars have begun to realise the significance of S&R and its impact on the historical foundation of social work.
- A burgeoning interest in S&R in modern social work education and practice (with the proviso that *proselytism,* converting others to one's own religion, be avoided).
- A shift from the pathological approach (focus on deficits and problems) to a strengths and resilience perspective.
- The increasing number of social workers having religious beliefs with increasing disconnect to the dominant value base of the profession.

Charlotte Towle (1896–1966), a social work academic who pioneered a client-centred case work curriculum, already realised the importance of S&R in practice in 1945 (Bullis, 1996). Social work's realisation was initially founded on the psychological impact of S&R on the lives of their clients, as S&R often strongly influence how people feel about themselves and how they perceive the world and their place/role in it. Knitter (2010) says the connection to S&R and its psychological impact is premised on the close relationship between behaviour and beliefs, which is a process we are exposed to when still young:

- We are all taught to behave or make decisions to act in certain ways through the teachings of our primary caregivers, which are essentially based on socio-cultural and religious belief systems.
- We learn and develop these values and beliefs through these teachings during our formative years and are reinforced through these beliefs and in many ways we add to them.

Since we all have values and beliefs in whatever form they take, we know that our communities are no longer homogenous but multicultural. Multiculturalism is broadened as people move in and out of a community, or they become influenced by the beliefs of others, for example, through multi-ethnic marriages and relationships or just by meaningful interaction with others. If we look at South Africa and the many cultures and ethnic identities according to which people enact their lives, then we know that we practise S&R in different ways through, for example, formal (or charismatic) church, mosque (*masjid*), synagogue (*beit knesset*) membership and/ or worshipping of ancestors (*Ukuqula izinyanya* where *qula* means worshipping and *zinyanya* means ancestors) for sources of meaning in life. Abdullah (2015) argues that assimilating a multicultural focus in social work will ensure that all clients receive needed services no matter their beliefs. Maintaining clients' cultural and religious beliefs and perspectives also ensures that clients are viewed as key to positive interventions (Abdullah, 2015).

12.4 Decoloniality and spirituality

Knowledge production in HEIs should be based on localised realities and contexts focused on that community's experience (then and now) in order to challenge Western claims to knowledge dominance and generalisability (Hadebe, 2017). Hadebe (2017:7) therefore argues that 'critical appropriation' is needed to address idealised and unchanging perceptions of culture not in sync with reality. *Critical appropriation* means the relevant use of culture to become open and progressive, rather than prolong repressive structures. This might be a long and uncomfortable process, depending on how invested people are in their viewpoints. Yoruba (2014) asserts that religious colonialism is not as well known, but that its psychological impact has been enduring. Through religious colonialism, most indigenous peoples have derived negative opinions about their own spiritual beliefs and customs, believing these to be backward and primitive (Graham, 1999; Ugiagbe, 2012; Yoruba, 2014).

An *Afrocentric worldview* purports that human beings are spiritual in that they are connected to others and a higher being, and they are understood within a collective, where the mind, body and spirit are one (Payne, 2014). Molefi Kete Asante, a prominent proponent of Afrocentrism, had argued that 'when we center each ethnic group in their own historical and cultural experiences, we expand our knowledge of, and appreciation of, the human experience' (cited in Graham, 1999:256). The Afrocentric viewpoint thus argues for African knowledge and traditions to be at the forefront and not on the periphery of decisions and processes that have direct impact on and involve black people (Graham, 1999; Ugiagbe, 2012). This viewpoint is founded on the *philosophy of holism* that focuses on the completeness of being and involves culture, beliefs, and the way that Africans have traditionally lived their lives (Graham, 1999; Ugiagbe, 2012). Afrocentrism represents a transforming paradigm focused on an epistemology that intends to restore and develop African worth and self-respect (Ugiagbe, 2012). The Afrocentric worldview should compel social workers to broaden their traditional knowledge base and world perspective and to liberate themselves from a Eurocentric past (Graham, 1999). These are principles that are relevant to working in African (including South African) contexts and should be centralised within social work practice.

12.5 Spiritual assessment and intervention

Historically, social work had neglected the place of S&R in social work practice (Zastrow, 2010). Essentially this was mistakenly founded on the perception that S&R was focused only on 'heavenly concerns' and social work only on 'earthly concerns' (Zastrow, 2010:392). In recent years, there has been a realisation of the role of S&R in clients' decision-making and therefore spirituality should be a part of the assessment of clients' lives.

Spiritual assessment and intervention involve a systematic process of exploring clients' ability, capacity and available resources to overcome adverse experiences, building hope, self-esteem and resilience (Bhagwan, 2007; Crisp, 2017; Healy, 2005; Payne, 2014). Services based on spirituality and religion are holistic, focusing on the biological, psychological, social and spiritual needs of clients. These spiritual and religious needs are considered as part of the diverse needs of the client. Insufficient knowledge about the client's S&R beliefs can result in a deficient assessment of the important parts of the client's life (Greeff & Loubser, 2008). These authors therefore stress that spirituality should not be neglected because it is a significant part of human existence. In the next section, we consider how to start including S&R in the helping process.

12.5.1 Starting the helping process

When you as a social worker have clients with a different S&R, you will need to do more than just 'respect' their S&R. The following four techniques suggest how to incorporate clients' religious beliefs and values into the helping relationship (Knitter, 2010):

- Explore and engage with clients' beliefs, values, and convictions.
- Understand clients' beliefs as personal commitments.
- Value the worth and coherence of S&R in clients' life.
- Distinguish between positive or negative aspects of S&R and address sensitively through helping process.

If you as a social worker are engaging your clients in this purposeful way about their religious beliefs and the role these beliefs play in their lives, then Knitter (2010:260) calls this 'a religious dialogue', and describes this dialogue as:

> *An interaction between two or more parties in which each one recognises their own beliefs and values, describes these values to one another, try to learn from one another, and are ready to change their minds in view of what they have learnt, to the mutual benefit of all.*

This description ensures a conducive environment for a respectful discussion on what can become quite a sensitive (and often conflictual) engagement. Prerequisites (or principles) for a dialogue are, according to Knitter (2010):

- Humility: the belief that all will have something to learn in the interaction.
- Commitment: the confidence in your beliefs and to own up to these.
- Trust in our common humanity: the belief in the commonality of our humanity.
- Empathy: the ability to see into and understand the world of the other person.
- Openness to change: to be open to the effects of the engagement on yourself.

The above principles do set the premise upon which mutually respectful and engaging dialogues can be created with our clients regarding these sensitive topics. Although knowing does not always equate to knowing how, it is important to also provide possible ways in which these principles can be enacted.

The response to clients' needs also include the collective responsibility of the faith community, which may be managed by a social worker who is often part of a team that may include priests, traditional leaders, spiritual leaders, and laypersons in the religious community (Healy, 2005).

Consider Anna's case for example. A social worker in this case will likely explore Anna's exposure to domestic violence over the past 15 years. Questions could include 'How have you managed to stay in a relationship that is characterised by continued physical violence against you?', 'What motivates you to stay in the relationship?' and 'What are your coping resources?'. Then you could consider what Anna might expose about the role of religion in her life, in her decision-making, and the options that have been available to her.

Several authors confirm the significant positive outcomes when clients' holistic needs are met by focusing on their spiritual and religious needs (Bhagwan, 2007; Crisp, 2017; Koenig et al., 2012). Studies also found that clients want social workers to address S&R (Crisp, 2017; Leitz & Hodge, 2013; Stanley et al., 2011). According to Payne (2014:290–291), social workers can enhance clients' holistic well-being through:

- Transcendence: providing clients with hope, purpose and affirmations.
- Transformation: enabling clients to deal with, prevent, and enhance adverse situations and experiences.
- Wholeness: focusing on all aspects of a client's life to enhance their sense of self.
- Hope: helping clients to identify resources to help them increase their quality of life and develop interest in future possibilities.

- Resilience: helping clients to develop coping resources and see problems as opportunities for growth and development even in the face of adversity.

Because social work is predominantly seen as a secular profession, a social worker assessing and responding to a client's spiritual and religious needs should be cognisant to be objective, non-judgemental and unbiased, offering a safe space in which clients' challenges can be shared and addressed. Showing real interest in all aspects of a client's life (including S&R) will further illustrate genuineness, regard and empathy. These are key ingredients in establishing a helping relationship (Kirst-Ashman & Hull, 2012; Payne, 2014).

One way in which we can assess client's (like Anna) strengths and challenges is through an assessment tool such as the biopsychosocial and spiritual framework.

12.5.2 A biopsychosocial-spiritual approach as assessment tool

By 1933, Swiss psychiatrist Carl Jung (1875–1961) had already proposed in his theory of personality that there are physical, mental and spiritual selves which all work together for balance and wholeness within ourselves (Lezotte, 2010). Jung argued that the development of consciousness and striving to obtain a spiritual perspective were the driving forces in life as an individual aged. In the late 1950s, Abraham Maslow (1908–1970), founder of humanistic psychology, added a sixth level to the traditional five in his hierarchy of needs called self-transcendence, where he argued that an individual sought meaningful experiences beyond the boundaries of the self (Koltko-Rivera, 2006; Lezotte, 2010). In social work, Holloway and Moss (2010:2) also argued eloquently that the search for S&R brings one to the 'heart and spirit' of social work, and that social work is not a 'morally-neutral' profession.

Reflective question
What do you think you need to do to respectfully assimilate the client system's S&R into the social work helping process?

A powerful argument for the inclusion of S&R in social work is its importance in multi-ethnic communities and the overall human experience (Lezotte, 2010; Oxhandler & Pargament, 2014). Furthermore, religion may be the primary means through which people of diverse cultures express their spirituality (Holloway & Moss, 2010). Senreich (2013), therefore, advocates for the inclusion of a spiritual component in the conventional biopsychosocial (BPS) assessment framework. In South Africa, social work students are expected to understand and engage with clients using a BPS approach; see the Council on Higher Education, CHE, standards 3.1, 3.2, and 3.4 below (CHE, 2015).

> 3.1 *Recognising humans as bio-psycho-social (BPS) [sic] beings, as the biological, psychological and social (including the spiritual) dimensions of life are inter-connected and mutually reinforcing;*
>
> 3.2 *Undertaking holistic BPS assessments to facilitate holistic intervention directly and/or through referrals to appropriate professionals and resources; [and]*
>
> 3.4 *Understanding of how historical and contemporary BPS approaches impact on human functioning and capabilities development[.]*

These three sub-standards cohere under the main standard of assessment and social work students are required to show competency in this standard. The BPS model was originally developed by American psychiatrist George Engel (1913–1999) in 1977 at Rochester University Medical Centre, New York (Borrell-Carrió et al., 2004; Miles, 2013) based on general systems theory (Melchert, 2011). The model advocated for three components to be considered when diagnosing patients, i.e., biological, psychological and social factors and their complex connections and interplay in appreciating the health of patients (Miles, 2013). In this way, Borrell-Carrió et al. (2004) contended that the BPS must be viewed not only as a diagnostic (assessment) tool but also as a philosophy of care, because it represented a paradigm shift from a biomedical view of disease and health to a multiple causative perspective. Engel believed that the model allowed for a more humanistic and empowering engagement towards a holistic diagnosis because of its multidisciplinary perspective (Borrell-Carrió et al., 2004).

Eugene Gendlin (1926–2017), an American philosopher and psychotherapist, however, maintained that people interacted and responded to life, not only physically but with all that they are, and that there was a place for spiritual enlightenment (Watson, 2013). Therefore, Watson says that it is unwise to think about the body as separate from the spiritual. Health professionals have long realised the health benefits of S&R on patients' positive outcomes and that holistic health care must include all the facets of a person's being (Saad et al., 2017). This realisation led to the inclusion of the spiritual dimension into the existing BPS model, which also called for the inclusion of the patient's subjective experiences (i.e., a patient's health from his or her own viewpoint) and thereby broadening the assessment framework (Saad et al., 2017).

Figure 12.1 below represents the original model (Sulmasy, 2002) plus the added dimension of S&R, which can be used as an assessment tool in social work with individuals, families, and groups.

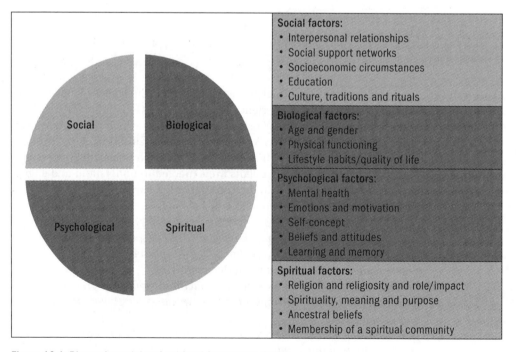

Figure 12.1: Biopsychosocial and spiritual framework (BPSS)

The biopsychosocial-spiritual (BPSS) model emphasises the initial motives of George Engel to create a holistic and humanistic view of the patient's (client) health. Senreich (2013) argues that the beliefs and opinions of clients about S&R should become part of the process of assessment. Each quadrant therefore focuses on a dimension of a person's life, which together form a holistic whole. This would be relevant for both micro and mezzo applications. The underlying principle is that each person's view on how he or she perceive his or her strengths and challenges is equally important in the helping process whether as an individual client or in a group. This principle would be valuable, for example, in family counselling and group work in promoting equity and individual value within a collective context. Consequently, social workers and students need to comprehend the inter-linkages between clients' S&R and their biopsychosocial challenges (Senreich, 2013). S&R represents the valuable resources in the lives of clients (Greeff & Loubser, 2008; Knitter, 2010), for example, as sources of self-worth, of strength to overcome hopelessness, and of a sense of empowerment and advocacy. It is therefore imperative that social workers and students include in their intervention plan how to engage the client's S&R, if it has been assessed; this has a vital impact on their difficulties and a role in achieving positive outcomes (Senreich, 2013).

The intervention plan for an individual client or with a family is therefore based on the strengths and limitations that have been assessed in accordance with the BPSS model.

12.5.3 Macro assessment and intervention

Assessment and intervention on the macro level take into consideration the role that S&R may play in the community or the dominant values and beliefs in that community. Spirituality has a key role in maintaining the healthy life cycle of African families (Greeff & Loubser, 2008). Traditional African children are taught from young to respect the role of spirituality and ancestor worship in their daily routines and in communal worship ceremonies (Greeff & Loubser, 2008). Traditional Africans turn to ancestor worship for reassurance, support and answers. S&R plays a key role in fostering overall well-being and belonging, which are essential ingredients in quality of life (Pillay, Ramlall & Burns, 2016). The relationship between spirituality and quality of life can be viewed through feelings of well-being and authentic relationships (Pillay et al., 2016) with others and spiritual others.

> **Quality of life**, a general understanding of what constitutes the health and welfare (well-being) of a person or community reflecting their perception of their social roles, relationships, strengths and surroundings (Pillay et al., 2016).

The linkages between spirituality and community development (macro work) underscore the relationship between the well-being of the individual and the well-being of the community (Chile & Simpson, 2004; Mthembu et al., 2017). The main principles of this relationship are equity, social justice, and access to resources. Ife (2002) identified six dimensions of community development, namely economic, social, political, spiritual, cultural, and environmental (see also Chile & Simpson, 2004; Murray, 2013). These dimensions are founded on the spiritual values consisting of holism, enduring (sustainable), multicultural, balance, and social justice (Chile & Simpson, 2004). These dimensions are not always clear-cut and often overlap in intricate ways highlighting the reciprocal relationship that exists amongst the dimensions (Murray, 2013).

Murray (2013) contends that an important resource in community development is the spiritual possibilities that people hold. A spiritual focus could assist communities to tap into their personal resources (strengths) and wisdoms. However, spirituality is not yet fully recognised as a key component in community development (Mthembu et al., 2017; Murray, 2013). Murray (2013:26) explains the purpose of community development as follows:

> ... to facilitate or guide people towards growth, equity, and well-being by acknowledging and encompassing the richness and complexities of human life and of the experiences of the community.

Reflective questions
- How can spirituality be used as a resource to address the needs of a community battling gang violence/substance abuse?
- What are potential implications for the integration of spirituality in macro social work, particularly in the South African context?

12.6 Self-awareness and professional identity in spirituality and religion

We all need to assess any aspects of counter-transference responses towards clients who have unequivocal opinions regarding their religious viewpoints that you may or may not agree with (Senreich, 2013). We all may have strong views and convictions that may be difficult to reconcile with the principles and values inherent in S&R (Sheffield & Openshaw, 2009). It is thus imperative that as students you should start to differentiate your own S&R from those of clients and have ground rules for separating your personal and professional lives so as to set clear boundaries in your professional relationships. We develop our beliefs throughout our formative years (Lezotte, 2010) and these may be fully ingrained by the time you enter the social work academic programme. Sheffield and Openshaw (2009) advocate developing your self-awareness regarding who you are and how your beliefs may impact on the helping process.

Self-awareness is defined as 'involving an ability to accurately perceive one's emotions, beliefs and motivations' (Reupert, 2007:108). This would mean the recognition and bringing to the fore of your own definition of S&R and how this will relate to the S&R beliefs of your clients. Religious beliefs also bring taboo topics into our consciousness, for example, the relationship between what we believe the religious teachings are about homosexuality and LGBTIQ+ persons. This may be a source of deep anxiety and stress for you as a student especially as you may grapple with this contradiction between your religious convictions and the humanistic principles espoused by social work's code of ethics about non-judgementalism and acceptance.

Your lecturers may be using self-awareness tools that may include genograms, autobiographies, journaling, and mindfulness (Aten & Leach, 2009). These four tools are used in the classroom to teach you self-awareness. Mindfulness, in particular, is a cognitive (mental) activity to raise your awareness of your internal and external lenses that would enable you to pay unencumbered attention to your own viewpoints, beliefs and emotions being evoked from a topic under discussion (Coholic, 2011; Napoli & Bonifas, 2011). The outcomes of mindfulness include self-acceptance, trust, non-judgementalism, and self-awareness (Birnbaum, 2008), which are vital principles and ingredients in the helping relationship.

Reflective question
What are the possible ways in which your own S&R would have impacted on your assessment and intervention with Anna and her family?

Reflecting on S&R beliefs

When our lecturer told us in class that we as social workers are often called on to draw on our own S&R beliefs when engaging with diverse client issues, what does this mean for you since you are an atheist?

What do you mean? Being an atheist is believing in something!

Yes, but you don't believe in God, you don't believe in heaven, you don't believe in Christianity, and you don't believe in the Church. It's a lot of 'don't believes'!

But it's a belief in people's ability to live their own lives and to make their own choices, and that is how I will frame my engagements with clients because I do believe in people having the right to choose.

The above conversation reflects that spirituality is an open and inclusive construct that underscores the definition of spirituality by Furman et al. (2004:772). Their definition highlights the 'search for meaning, purpose and morality however a person understands it', which is what the conversations by the person identified as an atheist is also purporting to do. Spirituality is thus an inclusive construct as opposed to religion where the connections to a religion are the belief in God and the adherence to rules and creeds.

12.7 Conclusion

Theories on S&R challenge the dominant discourses in social work. As social work students you must interrogate your own spirituality commensurate with the organisations that will employ you, the type of services offered, and the client population.

The S&R discourse, as we pointed out in this chapter, is not without critique, especially in terms of its limits on clients' opportunities to achieve their goals and social workers' commitment for achieving humanistic values. We encourage you to incorporate S&R into your fieldwork services currently and your future professional practice. By now you are able to recognise the potential conflicts between your own beliefs and those of your clients. We hope that by studying this chapter you were able to see the range of S&R practices available as sources of strength and opportunity for your clients.

Chapter activity

1. **Reflective question**. Now that you have gone through the chapter of S&R, what are the ways in which you are now able to help Anna? What would be the main factors in S&R that you would bear in mind? And how would you use the BPSS model with Anna?
2. **Personal context**. Consider your own S&R principles. What are the possible ways in which these would have impacted on your helping relationship with your client?
3. **Advocacy**. Consider a social issue that you have become aware of in your community or in SA generally (think of human rights issues, e.g., abortion rights or access to water and sanitation). Using an S&R and macro lens, how would you go about advocating for the social issue you have identified to the benefit of the affected people or community? How would you see this from a decoloniality viewpoint?
4. **Critical question**. Think about the discrimination against people who align themselves with the LGBTIQ+ community. How do you think your knowledge of decoloniality and S&R might be useful for knowledge building, empowerment and transformation?

References

Abdullah, S. 2015. An Islamic perspective for strengths-based social work with Muslim clients. *Journal of Social Work Practice*, 29(2):163–172.

Aten, J & Leach, M. 2009. *Spirituality and the therapeutic process: A comprehensive resource from intake to termination*. Washington, USA: American Psychological Association.

Baskin, C. 2002. Circles of resistance: Spirituality in social work practice, education and transformative change. *Currents: New scholarship in the human services*, 1(1):1–9.

Beatch, R & Stewart, B: 'Integrating Western and Aboriginal healing practices'. *In*: Nash, M & Stewart, B (eds.). 2002. *Spirituality and social care: Contributing to personal and community well-being*. pp. 151–170. London: Jessica Kingsley.

Bhagwan, R. 2007. Tools and techniques to facilitate spiritually sensitive clinical assessment and intervention. *The Social Work Practitioner-Researcher*, 19(3):25–40.

Birnbaum, L. 2008. The use of mindfulness training to create an 'accompanying place' for social work students. *Social Work Students*, 27:837–852.

Borrell-Carrió, F, Suchman, A & Epstein, R. 2004. The biopsychosocial model 25 years later: Principles, practice, and scientific inquiry. *Annals of Family Medicine*, 2(6):576–582.

Bullis, R. 1996. *Spirituality in social work practice*. Washington, USA: Taylor & Francis.

Canda, ER. 2005. Integrating religion and social work in dual degree programs. *Journal of Religion and Spirituality in Social Work*, 24(1/2):79–91.

Canda, ER. 2008. Spiritual connections in social work: Boundary violations and transcendence. *Journal of Religion and Spirituality in Social Work: Social Thought*, 27(1–2):25–33.

Canda, ER & Furman, LD. 2010. *Spiritual diversity in social work practice: The heart of helping*. 2nd ed. New York: Oxford University Press.

Carroll, MM: 'Conceptual models of spirituality'. *In*: Canda, ER & Smith, ED (eds.). 2001. *Transpersonal perspectives on spirituality in social work*. pp. 5–22. New York: The Haworth Press Inc.

Carroll, MM: 'Social work's conceptualization of spiritualization'. *In*: Canda, ER (ed.). 2002. *Spirituality in social work: New directions*. pp. 1–14. New York: Routledge.

Chile, LM & Simpson, G. 2004. Spirituality and community development: Exploring the link between the individual and the collective. *Community Development Journal*, 39(4):318–331.

Coholic, D. 2011. Exploring the feasibility and benefits of arts-based mindfulness-based practices with young people in need: Aiming to improve aspects of self-awareness and resilience. *Child Youth Care Forum*, 40:303–317.

Cowley, AS & Derezotes, D. 1994. Transpersonal psychology and social work education. *Journal of Social Work Education*, 30(1):32–41.

Crisp, BR. 2010. Belonging, connectedness and social exclusion. *Journal of Social Inclusion*, 1(2):123–132.

Crisp, BR (ed.). 2017. *The Routledge handbook of religion, spirituality and social work*. New York: Taylor & Francis.

Dreyer, Y. 2015. Community resilience and spirituality: Keys to hope for a post-apartheid South Africa. *Pastoral Psychology*, 64(5): 651–662.

Dumbrill, G & Green, J. 2008. Indigenous knowledge in the social work academy. *Social Work Education: The International Journal*, 27:489–503.

Edwards, S. 2009. *Titirowhakamurikiamarama ai tewaonei: Whakapapa epistemologies and Maniapoto Māori cultural identities*. DPhil thesis. Massey University, New Zealand.

English Oxford *Living* Dictionaries. 2019. [Online]. Available: https://en.oxforddictionaries.com [Accessed 4 June 2019].

Fulcher, J. & Scott, J. 1999. *Sociology*. New York: Oxford University Press.

Furman, L, Benson, P, Canda, E & Grimwood, C. 2005. A comparative international analysis of religion and spirituality in social work: A survey of UK and US social workers. *Social Work Education*, 24:813–839.

Furman, L, Benson, P, Grimwood, C & Canda, E. 2004. Religion and spirituality in social work education and practice at the millennium: A survey of UK social workers. *British Journal of Social Work*, 34:767–792.

Graham, M. 1999. The African-centred worldview: Developing a paradigm for social work. *British Journal for Social Work*, 29:251–267.

Greeff, AP & Loubser, K. 2008. Spirituality as a resiliency quality in Xhosa-speaking families in South Africa. *Journal of Religion and Health*, 47(3):288–301.

Griffith, JL. 2010. *Religion that heals, religion that harms: A guide for clinical practice*. New York: Guilford Press.

Hadebe, NM. 2017. Commodification, decolonisation and theological education in Africa: Renewed challenges for African theologians. *HTS Theological Studies*, 73(3):1–10.

Hare, J. 2010. *Christian social workers and their sense of effectiveness in social work practice*. MA thesis. School of Health and Social Services, Massey University, Albany campus, New Zealand.

Healy, K. 2005. *Social work theories in context: Creating frameworks for practice*. Basingstoke, UK: Palgrave Macmillan.

Holloway, M & Moss, B. 2010. *Spirituality in social work*. Basingstoke, UK: Palgrave MacMillan.

Hutchison, W: 'The role of religious auspiced agencies in the post-modern era'. *In*: Meinert, R, Pardeck, J & Murphy, J (eds.). 1998. *Postmodernism, religion and the future of social work*. pp. 55–69. New York: The Haworth Press.

Ife, J. 2002. *Community development: Community-based alternatives in an age of globalisation*. 2nd ed. New South Wales, Australia: Pearson Education Australia.

Jenkins, K. 1998. *Te hono ki te wairua*. The spiritual link: A Māori perspective on the spiritual dimension of social wellbeing. *Royal Commission on Social Policy*, 3(1):491–496.

Kirst-Ashman, K & Hull, G. 2012. *Understanding generalist practice*. 6th ed. Belmont, CA: Brooks/Cole, Cengage Learning.

Kissman, K & Mauer, L. 2002. East meets west: Therapeutic aspects of spirituality in health, mental health and addiction recovery. *International Social Work*, 45(1):35–43.

Knitter, P. 2010. Social work religious diversity: Problems and possibilities. *Journal of Religion and Spirituality in Social Work: Social Thought*, 29:256–270.

Koenig, HG. 2008. *Medicine, religion, and health: Where science and spirituality meet*. Philadelphia: Templeton Foundation Press.

Koenig, HG, King, DE & Carson, VB. 2012. *Handbook of religion and health*. 2nd ed. New York: Oxford University Press.

Koenig, HG, McCullough, ME & Larson, DB. 2001. *Handbook of religion and health*. New York: Oxford University Press.

Koltko-Rivera, M. 2006. Rediscovering the later version of Maslow's hierarchy of needs: Self-transcendence and opportunities for theory, research and unification. *Review of General Psychology*, 10(4):302–317.

Le Grange, L. 2014. Currere's active force and the Africanisation of the university curriculum. *South African Journal of Higher Education*, 28:1283–1294.

Leitz, CA & Hodge, DR. 2013. Incorporating spirituality into substance abuse counseling: Examining the perspectives of service recipients and providers. *Journal of Social Service Research*, 39:498–510.

Lezotte, E. 2010. *Spirituality and social work*. [Online]. Available: https://cdn.ymaws.com/ www.naswma.org/resource/resmgr/imported/FCE_SpiritualityandSocialWork.pdf [Accessed 16 February 2019].

Marx, K. 1970. *Critique of Hegel's "Philosophy of right"*. Cambridge, UK: Cambridge University Press.

Melchert, T. 2011. *Foundations of professional Psychology: The end of theoretical orientations and the emergence of the biopsychosocial approach*. London: Elsevier.

Miles, E: 'Biopsychosocial model'. *In*: Gellman, M & Turner, J (eds.). 2013. *Encyclopedia of Behavioral Medicine*. pp. 227–228. New York: Springer.

Mthembu, TG, Wegner, L, & Roman, NV. 2017. Spirituality in the occupational therapy community fieldwork process: A qualitative study in the South African context. *South African Journal of Occupational Therapy*, 47(1):16–23.

Murray, I. 2013. *Spirituality as dimension of integrated community development*. PhD thesis. Faculty of Theology, Stellenbosch University, South Africa.

Napoli, M & Bonifas, R. 2011. From theory towards empathic self-care: creating a mindful classroom for social work students. *Social Work Education*, 30:635–649.

Neagoe, A. 2013. Ethical dilemmas of the social work professional in a (post-) secular society, with special reference to the Christian social worker. *International Social Work*, 56(3):310–325.

Oxhandler, HK & Pargament, KI. 2014. Social work practitioners' integration of clients' religion and spirituality in practice: A literature review. *Social Work*, 59:271–279.

Payne, M. 2014. *Modern social work theory*. 4th ed. New York: Palgrave MacMillan.

Philips, C. 2014. Spirituality and social work: Introducing a spiritual dimension into social work education and practice. *Social Work Research*, 26(4):65–77.

Pillay, N, Ramlall, S & Burns, J. 2016. Spirituality, depression and quality of life in medical students of KwaZulu-Natal. *South African Journal of Psychiatry*, 22(1):1–6.

Ratliff, SS: 'The multicultural challenge to health care'. *In*: Julia, MC (ed.). 1996. *Multicultural awareness in the health care professions*. pp. 164–181. Needham Heights, MA: Allyn & Bacon.

Republic of South Africa. Council on Higher Education (CHE). 2015. Higher Education qualifications sub-framework. Qualifications standard for Bachelor of Social Work, South Africa.

Reupert, A. 2007. Social worker's use of self. *Clinical Social Work Journal*, 35:107–116.

Ruwhiu, LA: 'Bicultural issues in Aotearoa/New Zealand social work'. *In*: Connolly, M (ed.). 2001. *New Zealand social work: Contexts and practice*. pp. 54–71. Auckland, New Zealand: Oxford University Press.

Saad, M, De Medeiros, R & Mosini, A. 2017. Opinion. Are we ready for a true biopsychosocial-spiritual model? The many meanings of 'spiritual'. *Medicines*, 4:1–6.

Saul, J. 2014. *Collective trauma, collective healing: Promoting community resilience in the aftermath of disaster*. New York, US: Routledge/Taylor & Francis Group.

Senreich, E. 2013. An inclusive definition of spirituality for social work education and practice. *Journal of Social Work Education*, 49:548–563.

Sheffield, S & Openshaw, L. 2009. *Integrating principles of spirituality into the social work classroom*. Conference presentation at NACSW Conference, October 2009, Indianapolis, Indiana, USA.

Sheridan, M & Amato-Von Hemert, K. 1999. The role of religion and spirituality in social work education and practice: A survey of student views and experiences. *Journal of Social Work Education*, 35:125–141.

Stanley, MA, Bush, AL, Camp, ME, Jameson, JP, Philips, LL & Barber, CR. 2011. Older adults' preferences for religion/spirituality in treatment for anxiety and depression. *Aging and Mental Health*, 15:334–343.

Stirling, B. 2008. *Moving beyond acknowledgement: An investigation of the role of spirituality and religion within the professional practice of social work in Aotearoa/New Zealand*. DPhil thesis. University of Otago, Dunedin, New Zealand.

Sulmasy, D. 2002. A bio-psychosocial-spiritual model for the care of patients at the end of life. *The Gerontologist*, 42:24–33.

Thomas, LE. 1999. *Under the canopy: Ritual process and spiritual resilience in South Africa*. Columbia, SC: University of South Carolina Press.

Togarasei, L. 2015. Modern/charismatic pentecostalism as a form of 'religious' secularisation in Africa. *Studia Historiae Ecclesiasticae*, 41(1):56–66.

Ugiagbe, E. 2012. African-centred approach to social work practice: The relevance of Afrocentrism in social work practice in Nigeria. *EBSU Journal of Social Sciences Review*, 4(1):12–20.

Walsh, F: 'Religion, spirituality and the family: Multifaith perspectives'. *In*: Walsh, F (ed.). 2009. *Resources in family therapy*. 2nd ed. pp. 3–30. New York: Guilford Press.

Watson, J. 2013. Editorial. Spirituality and physicality: Crossing thresholds. *International Journal of Children's Spirituality*, 18(1):1–3.

Weiss-Gal, I & Welbourne, P. 2008. The professionalization of social work: A cross-national exploration. *International Journal of Social Welfare*, 17:281–290.

Wheeler, EA, Ampadu, LM & Wangari, E. 2002. Life span development revisited: African-centred spirituality through the life cycle. *Journal of Adult development*, 9(1):71–77.

Yoruba, C. 2014. Decolonising the mind: The misunderstanding of traditional African beliefs. *Opinion*, 6 May 2014.

Zastrow, C. 2010. *The practice of social work: A comprehensive text.* 9th ed (intl ed). Belmont, CA: Brooks/Cole, Cengage Learning.

Annotated websites and activities

https://youtu.be/0XWOW0LP3F0?t=22 [3 mins]
This video clip on religion vs spirituality is hosted by Sean Meshorer who has an avid interest in both the philosophy and understanding of the West and East. He is an ordained non-denominational minister, has authored the book *The bliss experiment,* and has also written for CBS News, *The Huffington Post*, AskMen, among others. He teaches and travels throughout the world sharing his philosophies and life lessons.

https://youtu.be/yfR5XeGt-5E?t=154 [10 mins]
This video on religion vs spirituality (the differences and which we need more) is hosted by Koi Fresco, YouTube vlogger and spiritual teacher whose KoisCorner channel has over 500,000 subscribers and 33 million views. His published books are *A (not so) enlightened youth* and *The meditation manual.*

https://youtu.be/90kRJjh-F80?t=149 [1hr 29mins]
This video called *Spiritual diversity in social work: the heart of helping* is hosted by Edward Canda (PhD) who is Professor and Coordinator of the Spiritual Diversity Initiative in the School of Social Welfare at the University of Kansas. His research focuses on the linkages between cultural diversity, spirituality, and resilience in relation to health, mental health, and disabilities. For the past 40 years he has also delved into Eastern philosophy for social welfare. One widely cited book is *Spiritual diversity in social work practice.*

https://youtu.be/ZQSvSQDRB7o?t=143 [7 mins]
Spirituality and social work is hosted by Jasmine Ama, a practising social worker, who is sharing her experiences and knowledge about various topics in her development as a professional social worker, including the role of spirituality in social work.

Annotated websites and activities are also available on Learning Zone.

oxford.co.za/learningzone

Strengths-based

Adrian van Breda

CHAPTER OUTCOMES

By the end of this chapter, you should be able to:

✓ *Outline the principles of a strengths approach to social work practice*

✓ *Explain the main theoretical concepts underlying Asset-Based Community Development (ABCD)*

✓ *Apply ABCD to decolonial social work practice*

✓ *Explain the main theoretical concepts underlying narrative therapy*

✓ *Apply narrative therapy to decolonial social work practice.*

 Case Study 1   ## Working from a deficit perspective

Ntando is a social worker in a rural village, not too far from a small town. She is employed to provide generalist social work services to the community. She conducts a community needs assessment, speaking to many members of the community and studying what data she can find at the local municipality. She finds that there are many, many problems – poverty, child-headed households, child neglect, ill health, lack of transport, and so on.

Recognising that poverty is a major problem in this community, she decides to contribute to improving their living conditions. She writes a funding proposal to a company that has a shop in the nearby town, to pay for a community centre. She explains in her proposal that the centre will provide a meeting place for the community, which will enable them to talk about their problems. She is very pleased that the company agrees to her proposal – they send in builders and quickly build the community centre.

Ntando calls a community meeting in the new building, but is disappointed that only nine people came. Nevertheless, she tells them about all the problems she has identified while she has been working in the village and asks them what they think should be done about these problems. (She is trying to get them to participate in her work.) But they don't have anything to contribute to the discussion. Ntando makes some suggestions for starting a knitting group and vegetable garden. The community members nod and smile, but don't seem very enthusiastic about her ideas. A month later, nothing has been done about these ideas, and the community centre remains an empty building.

Reflective questions
- Despite her enthusiasm, Ntando's efforts do not seem to be fruitful. What is happening that has led to these disappointing results?
- What do you think Ntando could do differently to achieve better results?

13.1 Introduction

Chapter 4 discussed social constructionism, showing it to be an epistemology (a way of making sense of the world) that says there is no objective reality 'out there', but that we collectively construct reality by the way we talk about it. Thus, we co-construct the world through our interactions with others. Chapter 7 later discussed resilience theory, showing it to be a framework for making sense of the ways people navigate through adversity towards better-than-expected outcomes. These chapters were both rather theoretical, offering conceptual ways of making sense of the world and doing research, more than guiding social work practice.

In this chapter, I draw on both social constructionism and resilience theory to present a set of strengths-based practices. These practices – which include the strengths perspective, asset-based community development (ABCD), appreciative inquiry (AI), narrative therapy, and solution-focused therapy – explicitly or implicitly draw on or are based in social constructionism and resilience theories. Some of these practices (viz. narrative and solution-focused therapies) are particularly useful at micro and mezzo levels (with individuals, families and perhaps also small groups), while others (viz. ABCD and AI) are particularly useful at mezzo and macro levels (with action groups and communities). Thus, I have selected practice theories that address the full range of generalist practice.

I also aim to show in this chapter how these theories can be particularly useful for decolonial social work practice, by championing and celebrating indigenous solutions to life's challenges or by working to subvert unjust patterns of colonial oppression.

There are whole books written on each of these practice theories, so I cannot present them in detail. I encourage you to do further reading on those that grab your interest, using the references I provide as a starting point.

13.2 Strengths perspective

While the earliest social work thinking was interested in the strengths and capabilities of people, it rapidly adopted a pathogenic perspective (Chapter 7), in its attempt to profession-alise (Van Breda, 2001). From the 1950s, however, social work gradually began to work towards a greater focus on the strengths of clients, as seen in the work of Hamilton and Hollis, and later Perlman. Van Breda (2001:200) thus writes:

> Social work theories and models which have evolved over the past few decades tend to provide a greater opportunity for the incorporation of a strengths or resilience perspective: Germain and Gitterman's life model, Shulman's interactional model, Middleman and Goldberg's structural model and Pincus and Minahan's systems model.

It was in 1989, with a publication entitled *A strengths perspective for social work practice* (Weick et al., 1989), that the strengths perspective really gained recognition. The authors state, 'A strengths perspective rests on an appreciation of the positive attributes and capabilities that people express and on the ways in which individual and social resources can be developed and sustained' (Weick et al., 1989:352).

> **Strengths perspective,** an approach in social work that centres on the social worker's perception of people as possessing or having access to the strengths and capabilities to deal with their life challenges.

The strengths movement gained significant momentum in 1992 with the publication of *The strengths perspective in social work practice* by Dennis Saleebey. This book, now in its sixth edition (Saleebey, 2013b), has become the definitive text on the strengths perspective in social work. Saleebey (2013a:17–21) presents a set of six principles that underlie the strengths perspective:

1 *Every individual, group, family, and community has strengths...*
2 *Trauma and abuse, illness and struggle may be injurious, but they may also be sources of challenge and opportunity...*
3 *Assume that you do not know the upper limits of the capacity to grow and change and take individual, group and community aspirations seriously...*
4 *We best serve clients by collaborating with them ...*
5 *Every environment is full of resources ...*
6 *Caring, caretaking, and context.*

In essence, the strengths perspective argues that focusing on people's problems traps people in these problems, resulting in social work being oppressive and disabling. Instead, the strengths perspective believes that all people, even in the most deprived and adverse circumstances, have strengths, and that by mobilising these strengths, people find ways to resolve their problems and flourish.

An important contribution of the strengths perspective in social work is its capacity to recognise and celebrate indigenous knowledge and practice. Instead of coming in with external definitions (typically from America and the rest of the Global North) of people's problems and what they need to do to overcome their problems, the strengths perspective asks people, at the local level, 'What works for you?'. It draws on solutions from the ground up. In so doing, it is far more likely to elicit indigenous ways of making sense of the world and indigenous ways of behaving (Shield, 2009; Brownlee et al., 2010).

Reflective questions
Look back at Case study 1 and then answer the following questions:
• What would Ntando have done in this village had she adopted a strengths perspective?
• What could she do to implement each of Saleebey's six principles?
• What kinds of results do you think Ntando may have obtained had she applied these principles?

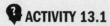 **ACTIVITY 13.1**

How would you translate English words like 'strengths', 'resources' and 'assets' into your home language? In doing these translations, do the meanings of the words change? And if so (as is likely), do these changes bring useful new meanings to the English words? Are there other words in your home language that speak to the concept of 'strengths'? More importantly and usefully, are there idioms or expressions in your culture or language that convey the idea of strength, in relation to the strength of individuals, families, groups and communities? Make notes of these in the margins of your text book. Give thought to how you could make better use of these words and expressions in your social work practice. Compare notes about what you are learning with a classmate from another language or culture group.

13.3 Asset-based community development

Asset-based community development (ABCD) was developed by Kretzmann and McKnight (1993) in response to what they saw as the problems with traditional deficit-oriented or needs-based community development approaches. They aimed to construct an approach to community development that recognised and mobilised the existing assets or strengths in communities. Their work has been taken up by the Coady International Institute in Canada (Mathie & Cunningham, 2003) and achieved a small but significant following. ABCD has been widely adopted in developing countries like Ethiopia (e.g., Butterfield et al., 2016), and also in South Africa, where it is most associated with the work of Hanna Nel (2018).

> **Community development**, a model of macro practice that involves the majority of community members in shaping and driving their own development.

I decided to focus on ABCD in this chapter because it offers a macro strategy for community change that is strongly rooted in the tradition of the strengths perspective. Moreover, ABCD lends itself to identifying and celebrating indigenous community processes, and in this way, can make a meaningful contribution to decolonial social work practice. The following section sets out the basic methodology for ABCD, though interested readers will need to read further to get the details required to apply this approach. The links between ABCD and appreciative inquiry (AI) and sustainable livelihoods (SL) are then explained. Finally, the contribution that ABCD can make to decolonial social work practice is critically discussed.

13.3.1 ABCD methods

Kretzmann and McKnight (1993) argue that traditional approaches to community development, which focus on addressing the needs and resolving the deficits of communities, inadvertently compound the problems (Pretorius & Nel, 2012). When community workers and development agencies enter communities to help them with their problems, communities learn that:

> *... their well-being depends upon being a client. They begin to see themselves as people with special needs that can only be met by outsiders. They become*

consumers of services, with no incentive to be producers (Kretzmann & McKnight, 1993:2).

They argue further that keeping communities in this dependent or client state is in the interests of universities, researchers and social service organisations, whose livelihood depends on having vulnerable communities that need their services. (This deficit-oriented approach is illustrated in Case study 1.)

Instead of these needs-based approaches, Kretzmann and McKnight (1993:4) call for an approach 'based on the capacities, skills and assets of lower income people and their neighbourhood'. This is for three main reasons. First, a shift to assets avoids the problems associated with needs-based approaches mentioned above. Second, they say that evidence shows communities' engagement in their own development is essential for successful and sustainable community development. And, third, the availability of external help and funding is limited and likely to decrease over time. Kretzmann and McKnight (1993:4) remark that '[t]he hard truth is that development must start from within the community and, in most of our [American] urban neighborhoods, there is no other choice'.

They thus argue for an approach that identifies and mobilises the assets and strengths that are already present in a community. In line with the principles of the strengths perspective set out above, Kretzmann and McKnight (1993) argue that this abundance of assets is the engine that drives community development. They locate these assets in individuals, in citizen associations (such as churches and block clubs), and in local institutions (such as schools and businesses). ABCD argues that as people realise their capabilities, they grow in confidence and thus progress with their own development (Nel, 2015).

> **Assets**, internal and environmental knowledge, skills, culture, resources and processes.

Mathie and Cunningham (2003:477), who have continued to build on the ABCD approach, summarise the ABCD methodology as follows:

1 *collecting stories about community successes and analysing the reasons for success;*
2 *mapping community assets;*
3 *forming a core steering group;*
4 *building relationships among local assets for mutually beneficial problem-solving within the community;*
5 *convening a representative planning group; [and]*
6 *leveraging activities, resources and investments from outside the community.*

In addition to these steps, Mathie and Cunningham (2003) also link ABCD to a number of other influential concepts in macro practice:

• *Social capital.* Central to ABCD is social capital, that is, the networks of relationships between people. There are two kinds of social capital that are important in ABCD – bonding and bridging social capital. Bonding social capital is the existing relationships between members of a community. Because these relationships already exist, either in reality or in potential, the ABCD worker here is primarily concerned to facilitate and mobilise these relationships. Bridging social capital, on the other hand, is relationships that link the community to other networks within or even beyond the community. Thus, the ABCD worker will help the community identify and engage with social capital on the edge of or outside their own network, in ways that cultivate goodwill and elicit supportive responses.

- *Community economic development.* Economic development is a key focus of ABCD, and community economic development theory offers various approaches to achieving this goal. While much economic development takes place at the level of the individual, for example, through microloan systems (classically illustrated by the Grameen Bank in Bangladesh), ABCD tends to emphasise 'developing the economic capacities of groups to undertake community economic development' (Mathie & Cunningham, 2003:480). Thus, groups are mobilised to develop co-operative economic ventures designed to generate a sustainable income for the group and their families.
- *Participatory approaches.* ABCD, in contrast to approaches used by some international development agencies, aims to locate power and control over development in the hands of the community itself, and not in a developmental agency or community worker. Thus, participation is central to the working approach of ABCD. While probably all developmental work strives for participation, ABCD is distinctive in placing significantly more control and power in the hands of the community, rather than reducing 'participation' to 'consultation'. ABCD workers take pains to step back from community decisions. Funding agencies similarly have to agree to be led by the community regarding their priorities, rather than the funder dictating priorities to the community.

It may be helpful to note the similarities between ABCD and the person-centred approach (see Chapter 11). When mobilising communities, the ABCD process requires the social worker to: (1) enable the community to decide on the issues they want to address; and (2) facilitate the community to decide how to take action to address these issues. In this way, the community, not the social worker, will own the process. In a very similar way, the person-centred process (Chapter 11) requires clients, including communities, to identify the issues that concern them and to determine their own process, facilitated by the social worker, to address these.

13.3.2 Appreciative inquiry

As could be seen in the last paragraphs of the previous section, ABCD has connected with various other approaches to address social development and poverty. Two important links in South African research and practice are with appreciative inquiry and sustainable livelihoods (Mathie & Cunningham, 2003; Nel, 2011, 2015).

Appreciative inquiry (AI) emerged in the 1980s and is most closely associated with David Cooperrider (Lewis et al., 2008). It was developed as a way of facilitating organisational change and development, and was influenced by various emerging ideas, including social constructionism (see Chapter 4) and an interest in strengths and capabilities (see section 13.2 on the strengths perspective). Essentially, AI is an approach to organisational change that focuses on the stories that people in the organisation tell about themselves and the organisation about what works, and that seeks to increase people doing what works. It emphasises its two constituent words: to appreciate what is good and workable; and to inquire or ask questions about what works (Zandee & Cooperrider, 2008). Although AI was developed for and is written primarily around organisations, it is now also being used in community work.

Appreciative inquiry, a process of organisational and community development centred on fostering and pursuing a vision of what people most appreciate about their organisation or community.

The AI model uses a 4D methodology: discovery; dream; design; and destiny (Lewis et al., 2008; Ludema & Fry, 2008):

1. *Discovery.* The first phase is about discovering the best of what works in an organisation. While there may be many problems in an organisation, the AI worker is interested rather in hearing what is working. Discovery is not so much about listing success criteria as it is about listening to the stories people tell about what most excites them about their organisation and about experiences of accomplishment. It is in these stories that the most important learning takes place. Discovery is thus about appreciating the best of what is.

2. *Dream.* Dreaming is about building on the best of what is. This stage invites people to imagine what the organisation would be like if everyone continued to embody this best and to become even better and more fulfilled. The AI worker is interested to hear of people's hopes and aspirations, and what they strive towards. Dreaming is thus about innovating and envisaging what could be.

3. *Design.* Once people have articulated and been captivated by the dream, they begin to dialogue about how to create an organisation that is able to accomplish the dream. This includes the 'norms, values, structures, strategies, systems, patterns of relationship, [and] ways of doing things' (Ludema & Fry, 2008:283) – that is, everything that makes an organisation an organisation. In summary, this envisaged organisation needs to be the one that people really want to work and invest in. Designing is thus about co-constructing their ideal organisation.

4. *Destiny.* Finally, destiny, which is sometimes called delivery (Nel, 2011), is about helping people move in the direction of this new organisation they have designed. People now need to behave and relate in ways that embody the new organisation. It is in the doing of the dream that the organisation transforms. Thus, destiny is about sustaining change through figuring out how to 'learn, empower, execute and improvise' (Ludema & Fry, 2008:283).

The entire AI process unfolds through a process of conversation (Lewis et al., 2008), in which people exchange ideas, feelings and experiences in ways that transform all participants. Conversation is not merely the exchange of information, but a true meeting or encounter between people that draws on various levels of their being. Stories are the most powerful way to facilitate conversation and so form the basis of AI practice.

Nel (2011) concludes that AI and ABCD are highly compatible approaches, drawing on a similar foundation of principles, even if they originally developed in quite different fields (wealthy businesses and poor communities), as illustrated in Case studies 2 and 3 below. This integration has been so successful, that the University of Johannesburg's Bachelor of Community Development and Leadership now bases its approach to community development on an integration of AI and ABCD.

Using AI with community organisations

In South Africa, Nel and Pretorius (2012) used the AI method with the management committee of the Kliptown Youth Programme in Soweto. Using participatory action research (PAR) techniques, they implemented AI, monitored the committee's experience of undergoing the AI process and evaluated the outcomes of the process. Fifteen three- to four-hour sessions were held to implement the first three phases of the AI process. Members were positive about the process; reporting on the Discovery phase, for example, they commented that '[t]he strengths and assets we have identified take us forward and not backwards' and '[i]t was nice to realise that we are the ones who did this; we are proud that we are the owners of the organisation' (Nel & Pretorius, 2012:49).

 Using AI with community groups

Nel (2011) has gone further by applying AI not only to organisations (as in Case study 2), but also to community groups. In this study, she used a combination of AI and ABCD 'to facilitate a community of refugees [in the inner city of Johannesburg] in identifying their strengths and applying them towards building a better future' (Nel, 2011:344). An action committee of refugees was established to drive the process, in partnership with community development workers. The committee was trained in AI methodology, and then co-facilitated a three-day AI workshop with the entire community of refugees (42 individuals).

For the Discovery phase, for example, the community formulated the following question to facilitate storytelling and conversation: 'Please would you tell a story that illustrates the kind of help that you gave on a personal basis to people and what kind of help you received on a personal basis from people since you have lived in South Africa?' (Nel, 2011:351). Other creative methods were also used in the Discovery phase, such as photos and maps. This process, which lasted the whole of the first day, generated positive working relationships in the community and unearthed numerous assets. For example, many community members were professionals back home (e.g., lawyers and engineers), while others had artisan skills (such as shoemaking or hairdressing). They also identified organisations that some individuals were drawing resources from (e.g., banks and clinics). Some members were part of civic associations (e.g., a 'stokvel'). They also identified community resources that were underutilised (e.g., a library).

Through the Discovery and remaining AI stages, over a period of several months, which are recounted in Nel's (2011) article, this community established a network of small businesses that provided 275 meals a day (with cuisine from seven different countries), a dressmaking shop, a hair salon and a shoe repair shop. Together, these businesses provided a sustainable livelihood to 40 families.

13.3.3   Sustainable livelihoods

The sustainable livelihoods approach (SLA) (discussed in detail in Chapter 10) was developed by the UK Department for International Development (DFID, 1999:Section 1.1), which defines sustainable livelihoods as follows:

> *A livelihood comprises the capabilities, assets and activities required for a means of living. A livelihood is sustainable when it can cope with and recover from stresses and shocks and maintain or enhance its capabilities and assets both now and in the future, while not undermining the natural resource base.*

The sustainable livelihoods approach to community development places people at the centre of the development process and is focused on promoting the livelihoods of people who are poor (DFID, 1999). These people are located in a context of vulnerability, but also have access to various assets or capital that they can use to reduce their poverty, viz. human, social, natural, physical and financial assets. The social environment influences the meaning and value of these assets and also the ways in which they are used in achieving positive livelihood outcomes.

Nel (2015) has linked ABCD and the SLA to community development. She argues that the SLA has much in common with the strengths perspective broadly and with ABCD in particular. For example, the SLA includes principles of being people-centred and strengths-oriented (DFID, 1999), which are central principles of ABCD. In addition, having multiple categories of assets enables SL workers to identify not only areas of poverty, but also strengths; strengths in one area frequently offset vulnerabilities in another (Cooper, 2009).

Nel (2015) does, however, note that there are some differences in the two approaches. For example, ABCD has been critiqued for overemphasising the responsibility of community members and underestimating the role of the state, while the SLA gives greater weight to the role of the state in supporting community initiatives. Furthermore, the SLA is criticised for giving more attention to assets than to people, while ABCD has a very strong focus on the development of people. In these ways, Nel argues, the SLA and ABCD could be meaningfully integrated into a holistic community development approach.

Nel (2015:514) has developed an integrated SL/ABCD practice model, which includes the following principles: people-centredness; participation; inside-out approach; self-reliance and ownership; relationship-driven; focus on assets; local leadership; and holism. She also proposes an integrated SL/ABCD process of community development, viz. 'analysing of assets, activities and capabilities; exploration of the vulnerable context within which the community members live; determining of livelihoods strategies; and sustainable outcomes' (Nel, 2015:514). In this study, she utilised her integrated model in assessing Bapong, a rural community in North West Province, South Africa.

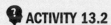 **ACTIVITY 13.2**

Using SL's five categories of capital or assets, do a quick assessment of your own community. See how many assets you can identify in each category (ATHA, 2014:section 2):

1. *Human capital (i.e., the amount and quality of knowledge and labor available in a household)*
2. *Natural capital (i.e., the quality and quantity of natural resources, ranging from fisheries to air quality)*
3. *Financial capital (i.e., savings and regular inflows of money)*
4. *Physical capital (i.e., the infrastructure, tools, and equipment used for increasing productivity)*
5. *Social capital (i.e., social resources, including networks for cooperation, mutual trust, and support)*

13.3.4 ABCD's contribution to decolonial social work practice

ABCD intuitively has much value to add in advancing indigenous social work practice, though little has been published on this topic. Hipwell (2009), however, reports on ABCD work in Taiwan with indigenous groups who had experienced centuries of colonisation by the Chinese, Dutch and Japanese. He provides three case examples of ABCD work with these groups. One example relates to an area of natural beauty, called Tanayiku, which had been severely compromised by tourism. This area had spiritual significance for the indigenous people, seen as the home of the guardian spirit of nature. ABCD mobilised indigenous cultural resources, such as 'the notion of *"ayutyutsyu"* (responsibility to the natural world) ... and the practice of religious customs such as *do beo bitt*, or thanks to the spirit of an animal taken by hunting' (Hipwell, 2009:297).

Culture can be seen as a major asset of communities, and thus an important resource to leverage for community development (Kihl, 2015). As a result, an ABCD approach that recognises cultural and indigenous assets will serve to strengthen a community's awareness of their cultural heritage and generate experiences of living out this heritage. This fosters cultural identity and pride, which are important facets of decolonial social work practice, particularly regarding the decolonisation of the mind (Ngũgĩ wa Thiong'o, 1981; Fanon, 2008).

ABCD's optimism is not shared by all, however. MacLeod and Emejulu (2014:431), for example, argue that 'ABCD is a response and a capitulation to the rise of neoliberalism and its values of individualization, marketization, and privatization of public life'. They construct a persuasive narrative of ABCD's emergence in the Reagan era in the USA, during which there was major dismantling of Lyndon Johnson's welfare programmes. In this era, there was a shrinkage of the role of the state in taking care of its citizens, and a return to individualistic approaches to welfare. In this context, ABCD emerged, with the rhetoric that individuals and communities are responsible for their own development, and deliberately minimised the state's responsibility for addressing macro developmental issues, such as poverty and inequality. ABCD also rose up to replace social action models of community mobilisation, which would increase conflict between communities and the state.

MacLeod and Emejulu (2014:437) state:

> Supporters of ABCD do not seem to recognize that systems can both harm and protect liberty and rights, and it is a role of community development not to simply disavow the state but to pursue an agenda that makes the local and national state work better for the most marginalized. We suggest that transferring various state responsibilities to individuals and communities is not the best, or even the most effective, means for reforming the state.

This point is illustrated in a curious way by two versions of a manuscript published by Mathie and Cunningham (2002, 2003). In the 2002 version, published as an occasional paper, Mathie and Cunningham (2002:10) address the subject of 'civic engagement', which they say is important for 'advocating for, and holding governments accountable for, the redistribution of more concrete assets through redistribution of land, employment opportunities, public facilities and services to which the "one billion absolute poor" are entitled'. This facet of ABCD – holding the state accountable for delivering on its social mandate – is not aligned with a neoliberal agenda; indeed, it suggests activism. However, in the 2003 version of the same manuscript, published in the journal *Development in Practice*, the entire topic of civic engagement was dropped. In deciding how to shorten the original manuscript to fit the journal requirements, the authors apparently saw civic engagement as least central to ABCD.

Given ABCD's apparent complicity with neoliberalism, and its tendency to foster inward-looking community development, and not challenge social structures and processes that oppress and marginalise, does ABCD have relevance for the decolonisation of society? I have been unable to locate any literature that addresses this question, but, in a conversation with Mathie and Cunningham (26 February 2018), some possibilities were raised. ABCD is effective in mobilising communities towards collective action, and while this action is typically focused inwardly on taking care of the community, it could also be turned towards advocacy, lobbying and social action. A goal of ABCD is to help communities become agents rather than subjects. Agency has the potential to position communities to challenge, critique, and hold Power to account. But, while communities challenge the state, they can also get on with the business of cultivating community and fostering growth and identity (Westoby, 2014). Thus, it appears that ABCD could be a useful method for facilitating decolonisation.

 ACTIVITY 13.3

Scan the material in section 13.3 again. What are your thoughts about the potential contribution of ABCD to decolonial social work practice?

13.4 **Narrative therapy**

Narrative therapy is one of social work's own practice theories (Kelley, 2011). It was developed by Michael White, an Australian social worker, in the 1970s, together with David Epston, a Canadian-New Zealand social worker. Many of White's foundational writings and case studies are published in *Selected papers* (White, 1989c) and 'narrative therapy' was born in their joint book *Narrative means to therapeutic ends* (White & Epston, 1990). White's last book was *Maps of narrative practice* (2007).

Narrative therapy has a rich theoretical foundation, which aligns with much of the thinking in the strengths perspective, but which also addresses important issues of power, culture and oppression. This makes it a practice theory that is particularly useful for decolonial social work practice. It has been extensively used with individuals and families, usually with a keen awareness of the community or social network around the family, and thus is a model well suited for micro and mezzo practice.

Narrative therapy, a model of family therapy that works to deconstruct oppressive and disabling accounts of life and construct new narratives that foreground agency and power.

13.4.1 **Narrative practice**

Martin Payne (2006:10–17) provides a useful process model of narrative therapy, which is briefly summarised here as a series of steps:

Step 1: Narrative therapy starts by inviting clients to tell their story in detail. This is termed the 'problem-saturated description', because clients typically come with a strong sense of being overwhelmed (or saturated) by their problems, leading them to feel disempowered and helpless. For this reason, this description is also termed the 'dominant story'.

Step 2: During this initial conversation, the social worker personifies the problem by giving it a name, drawing on the kind of language used by the client, rather than from the social worker's own clever ideas. For example, in a classic case of working with a child with encopresis (defecating (pooing) in his pants), White (1984) named the problem 'sneaky poo', because the child had spoken about how poo snuck out when it was least wanted. 'Sneaky' was a playful way of talking about a messy problem.

Step 3: The social worker continues to use 'externalising language' during the rest of the work with the client. This is a way of speaking about the client's problems that places the problem outside the client. Thus, 'the person isn't the problem: the problem is the problem' (Epston, as cited in Payne, 2006:44). Naming the problem, as in Step 2, is one way of doing this. Further externalising can be done by talking about how the problem dominates the client, e.g., 'The [problem] has invaded your life/caused you grief/created chaos'. This way of talking helps to create some distance between the client and his or her problem.

Step 4: The client's problem is located within broader socio-political issues. Narrative therapy is not an individualised therapy; it is always located within the power dynamics at play in society. Thus, personal problems are considered in relation to macro themes, like gender, age, culture and race. Clients are helped not to make macro issues their own problems, by being critical of the world around them.

Step 5: A series of 'relative influence questions' are asked, concerning the influence of the problem over the client and the influence of the client over the problem. Examples of the latter include (White, 1989b:41): 'Can you recall an occasion when you could have given into the problem but didn't?'; and 'Can you recall an occasion when John was nearly overtaken by the problem, but instead managed to intervene and undermine it?'. Instances where the client was not dominated by the problem are called 'unique outcomes'. They are unique in that one would not expect to find these instances in the person's life, given the extent to which the person is dominated by the problem.

Step 6: Drawing on these unique outcomes, the social worker begins to construct an alternative narrative with the client. This 'reauthoring conversation' involves linking three or more unique outcomes together with interpretations of each outcome. These interpretations speak to the meaning that the outcomes have for the client, for example: 'What does this tell you about yourself that it is important for you to know?'; and 'What does this new direction tell you about your relationship that is pleasing for you to know?' (White, 1989b:43). This weaving together of unique outcomes, which are events in time (past, present and future), with interpretations of these events, leads to the formation of a new narrative about the client's life in which he or she has power over the problem. The new narrative is not fantasy; it is based on actual experiences that the client has had, but had overlooked or forgotten.

Step 7: The client is then invited to take a position on the problem, namely to consider whether they want to continue being under the oppression of the problem as they have been up to now, or whether they want to embrace this new narrative in which they are powerful and in control. This further reinforces the undermining of the problem-saturated story and the emboldening of the new narrative.

Step 8: Narrative therapy makes extensive use of a range of therapeutic documents. These include writing process notes (or rather, 'session letters') and mailing them to the client between sessions and creating certificates of accomplishment (White & Epston, 1990). Classic examples are the Monster Taming Certificate and the Fear Busting Diploma (White, 1989a).

Step 9: Narrative therapy often starts out with an individual client, but frequently winds up with a group of people. Friends and family of the client, and even a panel of social workers or previous clients of the social worker, can be invited to witness the client's telling of his or her new narrative. In this way, narrative therapists decentre themselves, recognising that they are not the primary therapeutic agents, but rather that the people with whom the client interacts daily exert far greater influence over the client's life.

Step 10: In addition to connecting the client to other people in the living community, narrative therapy also encourages the use of 're-membering' conversations. Here the client identifies people who have moved on or died and explores the nature of their history and relationship. The social worker asks what that person would say about them and their journey if they were present today.

🔖 ACTIVITY 13.4

1   Consider the important people who have been in your own life in the past, but who are no longer present. Perhaps they have moved away and you've lost touch, or perhaps they have died. Drawing on the idea of re-membering conversations, what would you like them to know about your life today? What would they be proud of about you? What would they say about these things that you have accomplished? What advice would they give you?

2   What was it like to make these people members of your life again? Would you like them to continue to be part of your life? Even if you don't see them, they can still be a member of your life. You can just think about them.

13.4.2   Solution-focused brief therapy

Narrative therapy has many similarities to solution-focused brief therapy, developed by Steve de Shazer and Insoo Kim Berg, both social workers (De Shazer & Berg, 1988; De Shazer & Dolan, 2007). The two practice theories appear to have developed independently of each other, though around the same time. While narrative therapy is particularly influenced by a range of theories, solution-focused therapy was developed as a result of empirical research by De Shazer and Berg into the actions of therapists that appeared to produce positive results (Lee, 2011). Their method avoids 'problem talk' and instead focuses on identifying and exploring solutions. They use the term 'exceptions' to refer to what in narrative therapy is called 'unique outcomes'.

Solution-focused therapy makes use of a range of questions that are useful in leading clients to focus on solutions to their problems and reducing the amount of problem talk. These include (Lee, 2011; Macdonald, 2011):

- *The miracle question.* The clients are asked to imagine what they would see if they woke up to find that their problems had miraculously disappeared.
- *Coping questions.* Here the social worker asks what the client is doing that enables him or her sometimes to not have the problem.
- *Scaling questions.* Clients are asked to rank themselves on a scale of one (where the problem is the worst it can be) to ten.
- *Relationship questions.* Clients are invited to reflect on what other people in their lives would say about their improvements or motivation to solve a problem.

Many social workers use a combination of both narrative and solution-focused therapies, because the various techniques and processes are highly compatible.

13.4.3 Narrative therapy for decolonial social work practice

Narrative therapy, and the work of the Dulwich Centre, which was co-founded by Michael White (https://dulwichcentre.com.au), lends itself to decolonial social work practice. This is because of its deep roots in critical theory and philosophy (White & Epston, 1990; Payne, 2006).

Narrative therapy draws, for example, on Michel Foucault's work on power and knowledge. Foucault argued that those who have power in society exercise that power through selectively setting forth what is 'true'. This 'truth' in turn shapes society and thus the lived experiences of people. This construction of truth is a 'technique of subordination' (Payne, 2006:35). Thus, Foucault (1980:93) writes:

> There can be no possible exercise of power without a certain economy of discourses of truth which operates through and on the basis of this associa-tion. We are subjected to the production of truth through power and we cannot exercise power except through the production of truth.

The exercise of power, of course, is central in colonial rule, and is exercised, at least in part, through selective truth. (In South Africa, for example, we remember the use of the term 'terrorist' by the apartheid government to describe people whom most others called 'freedom fighters'.) It is for this reason that, long after the withdrawal of the colonisers, these truths, which are taken up by those who are colonised, continue to exert power over the behaviour, thoughts, feelings and experiences of a postcolonial population (see Chapter 2). This exercise of power over knowledge does not permit indigenous or local knowledges space to be expressed and performed. Indigenous or local knowledges can exist only on the margins of society, in hidden and dark spaces. As a result, such knowledges are, in effect, lost.

Narrative therapy is concerned with challenging these dominant and hegemonic truths, which are often taken for granted, by questioning and subverting them. This plays out, for example, in questioning dominant approaches to grieving as requiring us to let go of the deceased person and get on with our lives (White, 1988/9), as well as in challenging patriar-chal patterns of masculinity that all-too-frequently lead men to become perpetrators of domestic violence (Jenkins, 1990). In addition, narrative therapy is concerned with recovering hidden or lost knowledges – truths about one's strength and capabilities that are otherwise overlooked.

White (1992:121) also draws on Jacques Derrida's work on deconstruction:

According to my rather loose definition, deconstruction has to do with procedures that subvert taken-for-granted realities and practices: those so-called 'truths' that are split off from the conditions and the context of their production; those disembodied ways of speaking that hide their biases and prejudices; and those familiar practices of self and of relationship that are subjugating of persons' lives. Many of the methods of deconstruction render strange these familiar and everyday taken-for-granted realities and practices by objectifying them.

The narrative method is essentially a therapeutic process of deconstruction. It seeks to decentre the dominant place of people's problems by:
- externalising and personifying their problems;
- exploring the relative influence of the problem on the person, but particularly of the person on the problem;
- identifying and highlighting unique outcomes, which reduce the power of the problem;
- constructing a new sense of identity in which the person is neither defined nor dominated by the problem; and
- charting out a way of living (that is, a narrative) in which their hidden and previous lost truths come out into the open and people reclaim their personal agency to shape their own lives.

In these ways, narrative therapy can be regarded as a process of decolonisation, particularly in the way it links personal problems to broader socio-political issues. Narrative therapy thus has the potential to be useful in dealing not only with problems at a micro level, but also with larger mezzo and macro social issues. Narrative therapy can help a people group to tell their own story about themselves, rather than having their story told to them by another (colonising) group, as illustrated in Case study 4.

 Using narrative therapy to reclaim cultural identity

Butler (2017), writing as an aboriginal person, narrates such an approach. He explains how the stories of Aborigines in Australia are typically damage-centred and told by people who are not aboriginal. These stories, albeit second-hand stories, become the dominant stories, dictating the lives of aboriginal people. But, he argues, when the story of aboriginal poverty and social problems is told by aboriginal peoples themselves and placed in its broader social context (a context of colonisation, genocide and dispossession), these problems are separated from themselves, enabling new ways of looking at, making sense of and doing something about them.

Aboriginal people (as well as Māori people of Aotearoa/New Zealand) thus introduce themselves by locating themselves in their family clans (on both maternal and paternal sides) and their ancestral land. (The video by Drahm-Butler in the annotated websites at the end of this chapter illustrates this.) Butler (2017:23) writes:

When we begin our conversations here we resist colonisation by resisting disconnection from family, kin, culture, language, lore or country. Instead, we start our story with an act of survivance, one that counters disconnection and looks to reconnect through situating ourselves in culture, identity and belonging. This is a strong story, which assists in decolonising our mind from the beginning.

Butler (2017:24) also invites communities to engage in re-membering conversations with their ancestors, by asking questions like:

> What do you think it means for your ancestors that you carry on the connection to your tribe?
>
> If they could say something to you about this, what would it be?
>
> In the face of invasion and all that we've been through, you are still able to identify with your mob [clan]. What do you think this would mean to your ancestors?
>
> What would it mean for them to hear you acknowledge their contribution to your aboriginality today?
>
> How might your responses to these questions help to shape the direction of your future from here? What does thinking about your ancestors and their thoughts and feelings make possible for you into the future?

 ACTIVITY 13.5

Scan the material in section 13.4 again. What are your thoughts about the potential contribution of narrative therapy to decolonial social work practice? How might it be applied in macro practice (community work)?

13.5 Conclusion

This chapter has introduced you to several models of practice that are based on the strengths that are present in individuals, families and communities. These models cover the full spectrum of generalist social work practice, from micro to macro. The models show significant ability to promote indigenous knowledge and the decolonisation of the mind. They also show potential to contribute to challenging oppressive and colonial social and structural patterns in society. As such, it appears that strengths-based practice approaches should be widely taken up by social workers in South Africa and, indeed, throughout the Global South.

Chapter activity

1. **Reflective question.** Identify some challenge that you are facing in your life (or that someone you care about is facing). Working playfully with that challenge, try to apply narrative techniques to that challenge, which include formulating a name for the challenge to help externalise it and identifying some unique outcomes. How does this begin to open up new energy to engage in a different way with the challenge?
2. **Personal context.** Give some thought to the community that you come from, or a group that you are part of. Are there narratives about your community or group that others have produced that disempower or marginalise your community or group in some way? What are those dominant narratives? Try to construct a new narrative of your own.
3. **Service delivery.** In your role as a social worker, what three or four lessons do you take away from this chapter that you will try to implement in your work? In what ways will

implementing these lessons help you contribute towards a decolonised, African approach to social work practice?

4. **Critical questions**. This chapter has highlighted a tension between community agency (people and communities taking responsibility to care for and develop themselves) and the role of the state (emphasising the responsibility of the state in providing for its citizens and in addressing macro issues like poverty and inequality). What are your thoughts about this tension? Where do you position yourself on this issue politically and in your role as a social worker?

References

ATHA. 2014. *Sustainable livelihoods framework*. [Online]. Available: http://atha.se/content/sustainable-livelihoods-framework [Accessed 4 April 2018].

Brownlee, K, Rawana, E, Macarthur, J & Probizanski, M. 2010. The culture of strengths makes them valued and competent: Aboriginal children, child welfare, and a school strengths intervention. *First Peoples Child & Family Review*, 5:106–113.

Butler, J. 2017. Who's your mob? Aboriginal mapping: Beginning with the strong story. *International Journal of Narrative Therapy and Community Work*, 3:22–26.

Butterfield, AKJ, Yeneabat, M & Moxley, DP. 2016. "Now I know my ABCDs": Asset-based community development with school children in Ethiopia. *Children & Schools*, 38:199–207.

Cooper, N. 2009. Promoting sustainable livelihoods: Making welfare reform truly personal. *Benefits: The Journal of Poverty & Social Justice*, 17:171–182.

De Shazer, S & Berg, IK. 1988. Constructing solutions. *Family Therapy Networker*, September/October, 42–43.

De Shazer, S & Dolan, Y. 2007. *More than miracles: The state of the art of solution-focused brief therapy*. Binghamton, NY: Haworth.

Fanon, F. 2008. *Black skin, white masks*. London, UK: Pluto Press.

Foucault, M. 1980. *Power/knowledge: Selected interviews and other writings, 1972–1977*. New York: Pantheon.

Hipwell, WT. 2009. An asset-based approach to indigenous development in Taiwan. *Asia Pacific Viewpoint*, 50:289–306.

Jenkins, A. 1990. *Invitations to responsibility: The therapeutic engagement of men who are violent and abusive*. Adelaide, Australia: Dulwich Centre.

Kelley, P: 'Narrative theory and social work treatment'. *In*: Turner, FJ (ed.). 2011. *Social work treatment: Interlocking theoretical approaches*. pp. 315–326. 5th ed. New York: Oxford University Press.

Kihl, T: 'The effects of globalisation on community development practice in remote indigenous communities in Australia'. *In*: Wilson, SA (ed.). 2015. *Identity, culture and the politics of community development*. pp. 10–16. Newcastle upon Tyne, UK: Cambridge Scholars Publishing.

Kretzmann, J & Mcknight, J. 1993. *Building communities from the inside out: A path toward finding and mobilizing a community's assets*. Evanston, IL: Northwestern University.

Lee, MY: 'Solution-focused theory'. *In*: Turner, FJ (ed.). 2011. *Social work treatment: Interlocking theoretical approaches*. 5th ed. pp. 460–476. New York: Oxford University Press.

Lewis, S, Passmore, J & Cantore, S. 2008. *Appreciative Inquiry for change management: Using AI to facilitate organizational development*. London, UK: Kogan Page.

Ludema, JD & Fry, RE: 'The practice of appreciative inquiry'. *In*: Reason, P & Bradbury, H (eds.). 2008. *The Sage handbook of action research: Participative inquiry and practice*. 2nd ed. pp. 280–296. London, UK: Sage.

Macdonald, A: 'Solution-focused therapy'. *In*: Nelson-Jones, R (ed.). 2011. *Theory and practice of counselling and therapy*. 5th ed. pp. 371–391. Los Angeles, CA: Sage.

Macleod, MA & Emejulu, A. 2014. Neoliberalism with a community face? A critical analysis of asset-based community development in Scotland. *Journal of Community Practice*, 22:430–450.

Mathie, A & Cunningham, G. 2002. From clients to citizens: Asset-based community development as a strategy for community-driven development. *Coady International Institute Occasional Paper Series, No. 4*.

Mathie, A & Cunningham, G. 2003. From clients to citizens: Asset-based community development as a strategy for community-driven development. *Development in Practice*, 13:474–486.

Nel, H & Pretorius, E. 2012. Applying Appreciative Inquiry in building capacity in a non-governmental organisation for youth: An example from Soweto, Gauteng, South Africa. *Social Development Issues*, 34:37–55.

Nel, H. 2011. An application of Appreciative Inquiry in community development in South Africa. *Social Work Practitioner-Researcher*, 23:345–364.

Nel, H. 2015. An integration of the livelihoods and asset-based community development approaches: A South African case study. *Development Southern Africa*, 32:511–525.

Nel, H. 2018. A comparison between the asset-oriented and needs-based community development approaches in terms of systems changes. *Practice*, 30:33–52.

Ngũgĩ wa Thiong'o. 1981. *Decolonising the mind: The politics of language in African literature*. Harare, Zimbabwe: Zimbabwe Publishing House.

Payne, M. 2006. *Narrative therapy: An introduction for counsellors*. London, UK: Sage.

Pretorius, E & Nel, H. 2012. Reflections on the problem-based approach and the asset-based approach to community development. *The Social Work Practitioner-Researcher*, 24:266–87.

Saleebey, D. (ed.). 1992. *The strengths perspective in social work practice*. New York City, NY: Longman.

Saleebey, D: 'Introduction: Power in the people'. *In*: Saleebey, D. (ed.). 2013a. *The strengths perspective in social work practice*. 6th ed. Boston, MA: Allyn & Bacon.

Saleebey, D. (ed.). 2013b. *The strengths perspective in social work practice*. 6th ed. pp. 1–24. Boston, MA: Allyn & Bacon.

Shield, RW. 2009. Identifying and understanding indigenous cultural and spiritual strengths in the higher education experiences of indigenous women. *Wicazo Sa Review*, 24:47–63.

United Kingdom. DFID. 1999. *Sustainable livelihoods guidance sheets*. London: Department for International Development.

Van Breda, AD. 2001. *Resilience theory: A literature review*. Pretoria, South Africa: South African Military Health Service.

Weick, A, Rapp, C, Sullivan, WP & Kisthardt, W. 1989. A strengths perspective for social work practice. *Social Work*, 34:350–54.

Westoby, P. 2014. *Theorising the practice of community development: A South African perspective*. Surry, UK: Routledge.

White, M. 1984. Pseudo-encopresis: From avalanche to victory, from vicious to virtuous cycles. *Family Systems Medicine*, 2:150–160.

White, M: 'Saying hullo again: The incorporation of the lost relationship in the resolution of grief'. *In*: White, M (ed.). 1988/9. *Selected Papers*. pp. 29–36. Adelaide, Australia: Dulwich Centre.

White, M: 'Fear busting and monster taming: An approach to the fears of young children'. *In*: White, M (ed.). 1989a. *Selected papers*. pp. 29–34. Adelaide, Australia: Dulwich Centre.

White, M: 'The process of questioning: A therapy of literary merit?'. *In*: White, M (ed.). 1989b. *Selected papers*. pp. 37–46. Adelaide, Australia: Dulwich Centre.

White, M. 1989c. *Selected papers*. Adelaide, Australia: Dulwich Centre.

White, M: 'Deconstruction and therapy'. *In*: Epston, D & White, M (eds.). 1992. *Experience, contradiction, narrative and imagination*. pp. 109–151. Adelaide, Australia: Dulwich Centre.

White, M. 2007. *Maps of narrative practice*. London: W.W. Norton.

White, M & Epston, D. 1990. *Narrative means to therapeutic ends*. New York: W.W. Norton.

Zandee, DP & Cooperrider, DL: 'Appreciable worlds, inspired inquiry'. *In*: Reason, P & Bradbury, H. (eds.). 2008. *The SAGE handbook of action research: Participative inquiry and practice*. 2nd ed. pp. 190–198. London, UK: Sage.

Annotated websites and activities

https://dulwichcentre.com.au/decolonising-identity-stories-by-tileah-drahm-butler/
This is a presentation by Aboriginal Australian social worker Tileah Drahm-Butler, where she links narrative therapy to social justice work with aboriginal people. Listen for the useful ways that narrative therapy principles inform her decolonial social work with a people group with a long history of colonial oppression.

https://www.youtube.com/playlist?list=PL035FFC4493D1687E
This is a set of six videos that I created with a former student, based on an actual person I counselled some years ago. If you can't find them at this link, search for 'Kirst-Ashman's Planned Change Process' on YouTube. They illustrate the planned change process, using elements of the strengths perspective and unique outcomes from narrative therapy. You'll notice in the fourth video that I (nearly) fall off my chair as a way of emphasising to Fikile the significance of the outcome.

https://www.youtube.com/watch?v=_muFMCLebZ4
This short animated South African video illustrates the deficit and asset-based approaches to community development.

http://coady.stfx.ca/themes/abcd/
Visit the Coady International Institute and have a look at their material on ABCD. You will notice that they have both stories and case studies on ABCD in different parts of the world. Pick any of these and read them, so that you get a better sense of what ABCD is about and how it can be used. Notice that Coady also offers a course in ABCD; maybe you can find funds to do this course!

https://dulwichcentre.com.au/courses/what-is-narrative-practice-a-free-course/
Visit the Dulwich Centre in Australia where you can sign up to do a free online introductory course on narrative therapy. As an appetiser, jump straight to the second session (The Narrative Metaphor) and watch the second video called *Dot exercise*. It's only 90 seconds long, but gives a good idea of what narrative therapy is about. If it appeals, go back and do the whole course. If you go to the home page of the Dulwich Centre, you'll also find a 30-minute video with several clips of Michael White's lectures.

Annotated websites and activities are also available on Learning Zone.

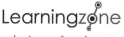

oxford.co.za/learningzone

Circle of Courage

Glynnis Dykes

 Case Study 1 ## Sipho

Sipho (14 years old) was referred to the social worker for his ongoing uncontrolled anger outbursts and aggression in the home with family and in school with his teachers and classmates. After an initial assessment, the social worker gave Sipho the Circle of Courage for his own completion and goal setting. By the third session, he had already completed the four quadrants on his own, identifying his strengths and gaps and thinking about the strategies that would help him to overcome these gaps. Sipho chose to share his Circle of Courage with each of his parents and his teacher of his own volition. He kept it in his school bag and took it out over weekends to keep by his bedside. He said it was a constant reminder to him of what his strengths and capabilities are; the positives in his life, and the coping strategies he has learnt. He also uses it to determine how far he still has to go. To him it is a hopeful and motivating tool. (based on Yamagishi & Houtekamer, 2005).

Reflective questions
• Why do you think the social worker asked Sipho to complete the Circle of Courage tool on his own?
• Do you think the social worker should have completed the Circle of Courage with Sipho and his parents together? If so, why do you think so? If not, why not?
• Who do you think should keep the Circle of Courage between sessions with the social worker?

14.1 Introduction

A century ago, youth workers had an optimistic and constructive perspective of children and youth in which the driving force was the belief in the endless possibilities in store for youth to achieve and for adults to ensure their success (Brendtro et al., 2005). However, the need for professionalisation of professions (such as social work) became entrenched with approaches that focused on shortcomings and deficiencies rather than strengths (see Chapters 7 & 13) (Brendtro et al., 2005). Traditionalists believed in the adage 'spare the rod and spoil the child' that is premised on a strong message of punishment as a means to change behaviour (Brown, 2005). This belief translated into the view that children and youth were not on the same social footing as adults, and that children were out of control and had to be corrected (Jackson, 2014). Recently, there has been a huge upswing in professions and practitioners looking towards using a more optimistic lens through which to engage children and youth (Jackson, 2014). Positive youth development has become a key research area (Lee & Perales, 2007) based on the premise that to prevent difficult and challenging behaviours from occurring, the focus should be on more positive factors such as bonding, nurturing, capability, and self-worth.

This chapter focuses on the Circle of Courage (CoC).

> **Circle of Courage**, a tool that has been widely adopted as a positive means through which the strengths and growth areas of the youth are assessed by both the youth and the youth worker in a positive and nurturing manner (Brown, 2005).

In South Africa, all social workers and child and youth care workers who work with children (e.g., in children's homes and in the court system) use the CoC to assess the child and plan services. For this reason, the authors and editors agreed that this was a vital theory to include in this book.

14.2 Origins and foundations of the Circle of Courage

Brendtro et al. (2005, 2013) argue that all children, no matter in what part of the world they may find themselves or to what culture or tribe they belong, need gateways to be unlocked to be able to enjoy what they call the common developmental needs of belonging, mastery, independence, and generosity (also see Brendtro, Mitchell & Jackson, 2014). Some communities are better able than others to provide for these needs of children and youth. Generally in traditional and tribal communities, for example, the extended family (kinship) made it possible for children to be reared and cared for by the whole clan, thereby facilitating the fulfilment of these universal needs (Brendtro et al., 2005) (see Chapter 6 on *Ubuntu*). However, colonisation and apartheid have destroyed the basic tenets of many South African communities, who are now struggling to survive themselves, let alone care for and share with others.

In 1988, on the request of the Child Welfare League of America, Doctors Larry Brendtro, Steve van Bockern, and Martin Brokenleg did a presentation at an international conference in Washington. The topic was focused on Native American child development principles. Their combined efforts became known as the Circle of Courage (CoC) and evolved into the foundation of the work of the Reclaiming Youth Network, a not-for-profit organisation networking with those helping children who are in conflict with family, school, and community

(Brown, 2005). Coughlan and Welsh-Breetzke (2002) confirm that the CoC is based on Brendtro et al.'s analysis of the ways in which tribal cultures nurture positive development through the four values of belonging, mastery, independence, and generosity. Larry Brendtro initiated the inclusion of courage as a pivotal construct and explained it as behaving with honesty and bravery, even in challenging circumstances, thus developing resilience (Oosthuizen, 2017) (see Chapters 7 & 13).

14.2.1 The philosophical base for the Circle of Courage

The CoC is in keeping with the kind of medicine wheel used by the tribal peoples of North America, which embodies the need for equilibrium and coherence of all things (Jackson, 2014; Lee & Perales, 2007; Yamagishi & Houtekamer, 2005). Medicine wheels were places where indigenous people socialised in large gatherings for celebrations, teaching, healing, and decision-making. The initial medicine wheels were fixed structures, and when the Europeans first arrived in North America, there were an estimated 20,000 medicine wheels in existence (Gilgun, 2002). The original medicine wheels were divided into quadrants that symbolised North (cultural balance and respect), South (ecological interrelatedness), East (spiritual wholeness), and West (sense of belonging) and were made of stones of different sizes (Poonwassie & Charter, 2001). Each stone symbolised an element of creation, the meanings of which differed from tribe to tribe.

The medicine wheel represents the spiritual foundations of the indigenous (first nations) peoples of particularly North America and the centrality of these beliefs in the everyday and routine lives of the people then. The concepts in the medicine wheel are symbolic understandings of the cycle of life and belonging, which then establish a base for people to develop meaning and connection to a central system (Poonwassie & Charter, 2001).

The CoC illustrates the connections with the medicine wheel and its strong spiritual base; but, whereas the medicine wheel was a physical structure and space, the CoC symbolises an imagined space (Gilgun, 2002). Just like the medicine wheel, the components (quadrants) of the CoC are interrelated and cyclical (Gilgun, 2002). The circle consists of four quadrants representing four colours to reflect the four main races (black, white, red and yellow) and their equality in the circle; at the same time, these four quadrants also represent the vital universal needs of children and youth: belonging; mastery; independence; and generosity (Brendtro et al., 2005; Brown, 2005; Frankowski & Duncan, 2013; Lee & Perales, 2007). The CoC is applicable to all children of any age and culture, who are faced with any behavioural or environmental challenges (Yamagishi & Houtekamer, 2005). In the case of Sipho (Case study 1), it was seen that the CoC helped to build trust and helped Sipho to think about all his experiences in a purposive way.

In addition to the Native American child development principles, the CoC also uses strengths-based principles to develop traditions of respect (Jackson, 2014) (see Chapter 13 on strengths-based practices). The key outcome for the nurturance and care of children is their overall development and independence. Jackson (2014) argues that if the developmental needs of children are not met, then children and youth run the risk of displaying socio-emotional behavioural challenges.

Reflective questions
- Take a page and draw the four quadrants of belonging, mastery, independence, and generosity on it, resembling the CoC. Complete the circle by inserting your strengths, achievements, capabilities, characteristics, and limitations in each quadrant.
- How easy or difficult was it for you to complete the four quadrants?

You may have found that it wasn't as easy as you thought, because the exercise made you think deeply about your childhood and the parenting practices that you experienced growing up.

14.2.2 Embedded theoretical frameworks

The CoC has strong links with other social science theories that we have become familiar with in professions like social work. This framework assimilates positive psychology and neuroscience, together with child development principles and indigenous values (Brendtro, Mitchell & Jackson, 2014). From these theories, practice principles and wisdoms have been distilled (Brendtro, Brokenleg & Van Bockern, 2014). Some of the practices and theories that underscore the CoC principles are illustrated in Table 14.1 below.

Table 14.1: Common principles

Circle of Courage	Self-worth	Maslow's Hierarchy	Positive peer cultures
Belonging	*Significance*	*Belongingness*	*Attachment*
Mastery	*Competence*	*Esteem*	*Achievement*
Independence	*Power*	*Self-actualisation*	*Autonomy*
Generosity	*Virtue*	*Self-transcendence*	*Altruism*

Source: *Brendtro, Brokenleg & Van Bockern* (2014)

Table 14.1 shows the strong similarities between positive child and youth development principles and a number of social science theories. These key principles have become the mainstay of child and youth development and practice philosophies. The theories underscoring the CoC and its practice are discussed below.

- **The CoC and Erikson's psychosocial theory**. Coughlan and Welsh-Breetzke (2002) assert that Erik Erikson's (1902–1994) psychosocial theory of child development was the first Western theory that incorporated the effects of relationships on human development. Erikson (1998) was also the first to present a lifespan model from birth to death, consisting of eight stages, where the natural conflict in one stage propelled a person into the next stage (Sokol, 2009). Erikson emphasised the impact of culture on development or the progress through each stage (Sokol, 2009). According to Erikson, ego strength (personal functioning) also emerges through the trusting relationships that an individual has with significant others. Gilgun (2002) contends that competence (mastery) is essential to Erikson's theory, where the child learns positive attachment and the ability for self-regulation.

- **The CoC and resilience theory**. Adversities in the environment of a child or youth are likely to have a negative impact on him or her, which will be evident in the four quadrants of the CoC (Gilgun, 2002). Undoing the harm of trauma or challenging circumstances and facilitating resilience are vital tasks (see Chapter 7 on resilience) and the CoC's components will indicate helpful strategies for resilience. Thus, Jackson (2014) contends that the CoC is strongly aligned with the notion of resilience. Resilience theory provides a framework for the use of strengths approaches to assess children and youth and for developing interventions (Oosthuizen, 2017) (see also Chapter 13 on the strengths-based approach). Importantly, it assists practitioners to think about why some children are at risk and become prone to inappropriate behaviours, while others advance and progress, even when they were exposed to similar social circumstances. The underlying assumption, therefore, is that the discernment of these differences will help to build knowledge of the kinds of interventions that will promote resilience (Oosthuizen, 2017).

- **The CoC and systems theory.** As human beings we live out our routines, lifestyles and cultures within various social environments, such as families, schools, friends, and communities. Within these various social systems, we interact and become influenced by these systems but in turn we also influence these systems. Even though, in many of these environments, adults are the primary caregivers and authority figures (Gilgun, 2002), children and youth also influence these systems. For example, the needs and requirements of children can be seen in the particular structure of the system (micro system) and the particular relationships amongst the role players in the system (mezzo system) aligned to the needs of the child (see also Chapter 5 on ecosystems theory). The CoC is strongly aligned to the systems perspective because of how the child's socialisation unfolds in the various systems that influence the outcomes in the CoC. The child may not be directly engaged with all the systems but will be impacted, for example, through macro-structural forces such as poverty, levels of violence, and educational and job opportunities (Jackson, 2014). This theory safeguards against the tendency towards victim-blaming because of the influences of the various social systems, which counteracts viewing clients as the source of the problem (Gilgun, 2002).

14.3 Four quadrants of the Circle of Courage

The CoC features four essential components (quadrants) for positive child and youth growth and development, namely belonging, mastery, independence, and generosity (Brendtro et al., 2005; Lee & Perales, 2007). The following discussion shows the use of each of these by child and youth practitioners, development workers, and parents/caregivers.

14.3.1 Belonging

The first component of the CoC is belonging.

Belonging, being able to meaningfully relate to and connect with others is the most vital need after the fulfilment of physical needs (Brendtro, Mitchell & Jackson, 2014; Gilgun, 2002).

In order to facilitate belonging, the child or youth needs ongoing bonding and attachment opportunities with loving carers that contribute to feeling treasured and valued (Brendtro, Brokenleg & Van Bockern, 2014). Belonging is central to the needs of a person and there is an extensive body of research that has attested to the significance of attachment in the formative years of a child (Brendtro, Brokenleg & Van Bockern, 2014) (see also Chapter 8 on attachment). The indigenous values applicable here are kinship and family (based on an expansive definition of family and, therefore, not only family through birth or marriage) (Gilgun, 2002). The consequences of not having these emotional connections can be dire for children and can lead to: attention seeking; risky sexual behaviour; gang membership; or social isolation. The positive consequences, however, are sustained confidence and trust in oneself, in others and in one's ability to be a success (Brendtro, Mitchell & Jackson, 2014).

Belonging in the South African context can be discerned in the African value of *Ubuntu* (a Nguni word that roughly translates to 'I am because we are'), which is the belief that all are responsible for the care and welfare of the children in the village (tribe or clan) that one belongs to (Coughlan & Welsh-Breetzke, 2002; Martin & Mbambo, 2011) (see Chapter 6 on *Ubuntu*). This is an Afrocentric philosophy that emphasises group or collective unity and identity (Coughlan & Welsh-Breetzke, 2002). An example of *Ubuntu* is kinship care, which is the basis for traditional adoptions and foster care provisions (Martin & Mbambo, 2011).

14.3.2 Mastery

The second component of the CoC has been termed mastery.

> *Mastery*, involves situations where a child can acquire, learn, and discover skills, talents and knowledge, especially while engaging with others (Brendtro, Brokenleg & Van Bockern, 2014). Gilgun (2002) also asserts that mastery is about doing a task well and feeling a sense of achievement and satisfaction upon completion.

The source of this component is located in the indigenous belief that children should be exposed to situations to learn in four domains, namely: cognitive; emotional; physical; and spiritual (Gilgun, 2002). Children are also exposed to opportunities to learn self-control and restraint when with elders; in this way, they learn the social rules that bring order and structure to their existence and the whole tribe (Gilgun, 2002). Through this, children mature and grow into functioning youth and adults and learn wisdom as they grow up. Key tasks involve listening to and observing their parents and elders in the tribe. Teaching and learning in a tribe take the form of storytelling, traditional games, ceremonies, artwork, household tasks, and caring for others (Gilgun, 2002). This social learning is not unlike what happens in traditional households, tribes and clans in South Africa (De Ridder, 2002). Through the various social learning opportunities, the child learns emotional control and resilience, which in turn lead to self-worth (i.e., the perception that 'I matter').

If a child or youth has not been exposed to positive opportunities for growth and competency, then that child would have ongoing fear and anxiety of failing or overachieving, or a constant feeling of being a 'loser', or a tendency to cheat or give up easily (i.e., poor resilience) (Brendtro, Mitchell & Jackson, 2014). Gilgun (2002) argues that competence and mastery are also context-dependent, as the external environment will have an impact on what the child can be exposed to and learn. In this way, resource restrictions in families, schools and communities will play a significant role in how mastery is enabled and facilitated, and the levels of mastery that can be achieved (Gilgun, 2002).

14.3.3 Independence

The third CoC quadrant is independence.

> **Independence**, 'the freedom to make choices, to have control over your own life, and to influence others, while also taking into consideration the effects on others of your own behaviours and words and modifying your behaviours in response' (Gilgun, 2002:73).

Gilgun (2002) explains that independence incorporates the dual tasks of making one's own choices, but not at the expense of others. Her description has been illustrated in the following way to show the dualistic nature (or action-reaction) of decision-making:

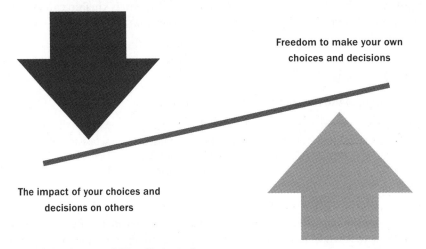

Freedom to make your own
choices and decisions

The impact of your choices and
decisions on others

Figure 14.1: Dual responsibility of independence

Coughlan and Welsh-Breetzke (2002:222) refer to independence as 'guidance without inter-ference', which shifts attention to the self-discipline and self-regulation of the individual (see also Brendtro, Brokenleg & Van Bockern, 2014; Gilgun, 2002). This would mean that appro-priate opportunities should be made available for children and youth to learn to make choices and decisions and learn to do tasks, which in the process enable them to become confident about their abilities. This confidence is created through constant positive feedback from others and through managing life's challenges (Gilgun, 2002).

Those who achieve levels of self-sufficiency are those who can make good decisions and act upon them to completion; such people can be described as independent (Brendtro, Mitchell & Jackson, 2014). However, if these traits have not been developed, these children and youth will have challenges in impulse control (impulsivity) and may exhibit reckless behaviour by taking unnecessary risks, or become bullies or rebellious, or develop shame, guilt and pessimism. However, Brendtro, Mitchell and Jackson (2014) argue that with increasing maturity, the brain is able to build new routes that enable the person to exercise better self-control. We can see this in how Sipho enjoyed the sense of fulfilment in completing the CoC in Case study 1, and the independence he showed by continuing the completion of the tool without supervision and without being prompted.

14.3.4 Generosity

The final component of the CoC is generosity, which consists of contributing to others.

Generosity, 'comes in many forms … in simple human behaviors such as giving compliments and showing respect. To be patient, to listen, to share a joke, or even a tear are powerful gifts' of generosity (Brokenleg, 1999:67).

The key ingredient in our survival as a species is helping others and forming a sense of community with others (Brendtro, Brokenleg & Van Bockern, 2014; Brendtro, Mitchell & Jackson, 2014). This activity has evolved into a natural ability to pay attention to the welfare of others.

Generosity can take different forms, for example, in relation to one's possessions, time, energy, or cognitive/supportive help (Gilgun, 2002). This benevolence or altruism involves offsetting your own interests against those of others, and often involves sacrifice. Indigenous values regard generosity as the highest of the virtues. Wealth is not created for showing off, but as a basis to help others (Gilgun, 2002). Generosity increases self-worth and thus balances stress and anxiety.

Children exposed to a nurturing environment are able to show care to others in return, forming the basis of empathy and compassion (two of the main characteristics of the social work helping relationship). Here, children and youth can contribute to *Ubuntu* where previously they might have been passive recipients of *Ubuntu* in terms of care and compassion. However, children who are not shown care and concern may develop egocentric and selfish behaviours.

The four components of the CoC discussed above are interlinked; one cannot be achieved without the other. Generosity, for example, suggests mastery (e.g., doing something for someone else) and a sense of belonging (e.g., 'I matter to others' as a precursor for doing something good to others) and independence (of thought and action).

> **Reflective question**
> In terms of what you have read so far about social work practice in South Africa and your exposure to your organisations in your fieldwork practice, how do you think these fundamental elements in child and youth development relate to children and youth in South Africa, and how have social workers generally responded?

14.4 Circle of Courage in the South African context

Brendtro, Brokenleg & Van Bockern (2014) contend that the need to belong is an essential need for human beings, and if obstructed, then physical health and mental health are affected. This is particularly relevant to the racial and cultural segregation violently forced upon those classified as black, so-called coloured and Indian people in South Africa during the colonial and apartheid historical periods. The violence of social exclusion is still experienced by many South Africans, even today. The next section will focus on the CoC in the context of decolonial practice.

14.4.1 The CoC in decolonial practice

The system of coloniality has been a brutal conduit for social exclusion and oppression. Colonialism subjugated African knowledge systems to the dregs of history and civilisation (Abdi, 2006) (see also Chapter 2 on decoloniality). This destruction of indigenous ways of life caused the annihilation of many cultures, values, traditions and knowledge systems, leaving many indigenous peoples without a sense of belonging. While the colonisation of Africa was economic and political, colonialism was essentially psychosocial, cultural, and educational. In other words, it involved colonisation of the mind (Ngũgĩ wa Thiong'o, 1986).

Frantz Fanon, a French-Martinican psychiatrist (1925–1961), wrote extensively on the violent consequences of colonisation on the mind and soul (psyche) of indigenous people and their concomitant suffering from a deeply ingrained sense of low self-worth and inadequacy (Lovesey, 2000). Ngũgĩ wa Thiong'o referred, for example, to the use of the English language in Africa as a 'cultural bomb', because it destroyed people's belief in themselves and left them without cultural connections and social rootedness (Lovesey, 2000:125).

Based on Brendtro, Brokenleg & Van Bockern's (2014) offering, social exclusion can have the following consequences in relation to the four components of the COC:
- **Belonging**: feelings of not belonging anywhere in terms of land or cultural value.
- **Mastery**: impacts on intellectual thought and severe lack of self-worth and confidence, which can be reflected in poor school attendance and premature dropping out.
- **Independence**: deficient or underdeveloped self-management and increased impulsivity, decreased personal power, and increased gang membership.
- **Generosity**: in some instances, decreased sense of community, but yet in others, a heightened community spirit and togetherness.

The CoC presents a unique opportunity to reclaim identities, unlearn internalised oppression, and throw off dominance. We can see how filling the four components of belonging, mastery, independence and generosity with positive reinforcement can begin to heal the deep wounds left by coloniality. Such positive reinforcement could happen in the following ways:
- in belonging, by rekindling the value and pride in being connected to a tribe or clan that is beyond the person itself;
- in mastery, through the opportunities that have become available for young people, especially to expand their world and try new things that had been prohibited and limited under colonial rule;
- in independence, by being enabled to exercise one's freedom and power to make one's own choices unhampered by laws and policies limiting these; and
- in generosity, through a nurturing environment that will enable one to develop feelings and behaviour of care and caring about others.

14.4.2 The South African child: Status and care

In South Africa, in isiXhosa, a child is called *umntwana*, which means 'little person'. In its original application, this word conferred status and value to the child, so much so that the birth of a child was announced with excitement as a significant happening for the whole village (De Ridder, 2002). The birth of a child was also met with many spiritual rituals for the protection of the infant from evil spirits and malevolent intent (De Ridder, 2002). In traditional households, the child grew up in a social group context with his or her peers. In most of the main tribes in South Africa, children were exposed to traditional learning from a young age. They were viewed by the tribal elders from a group perspective (not individually), where the group had joint responsibilities and tasks in gender-specific duties (De Ridder, 2002).

Many African customary laws are still practised by communities today. These laws were initially protective of children (Martin & Mbambo, 2011). However, they have been negatively transformed through the years due to the impact of outside socioeconomic and political demands on traditional communities. Many positive laws and traditions have been eroded, but patriarchal and unequal gendered roles still prevail, contributing to, for example, adverse relationships between children and their fathers and to the phenomenon of absent fathers (Martin & Mbambo, 2011). Some harmful traditional practices are still prevalent, many of which relate only to girls, such as female genital mutilation, virginity testing and child marriages (Maimela, 2009; Makundi, 2009) (see also Chapter 9 on feminisms). These practices are kept in place because of large-scale poverty (especially child poverty) and the low status of the child. They often take place within the home or clan (outside of the law), in isolated rural areas that go unrecorded (thus outside of monitoring mechanisms) (Maimela, 2009). As a consequence, children are often the victims of extreme violence and neglect (Martin & Mbambo, 2011).

This might well be the social context that confronts social workers and youth development workers in terms of the four CoC components. The positives and negatives with regard to the traditions of children and youth might be a source of contention for practitioners and bring value conflicts into play. The influence of these examples of harmful practices on the components of the CoC can be seen in the following ways:

- in belonging, where children and youth might have a skewed sense of belonging and not want to expose or challenge these kinds of abuses;
- in mastery, where their sense of self and self-worth might be compromised by being absorbed and immersed only in terms of their connection to the tribe or clan;
- in independence, where opportunities to learn self-regulatory skills and decision-making are severely limited in terms of the hierarchical and patriarchal social order; and
- in generosity, where self-care and being cared about might compromise the care for, and caring about, others.

🗨 ACTIVITY 14.1

1 The CoC emerged from a study of indigenous wisdom regarding parenting, particularly among Native American people in the USA. While it is now widely used in South Africa, its links to indigenous wisdom in South Africa have not been explored. Give some thought to constructing an African version of the CoC that draws on indigenous knowledge from your own culture group.

2 Formulate terms for the quadrants in your home language, rather than English, to make it more relevant to social work in your community. Discuss your initial ideas with friends or elders from your language or culture group to get their inputs.

3 Based on this, draft your own indigenised version of the CoC. Maybe you can present a paper on this at a conference or write a journal article.

14.5 Social work use of the Circle of Courage

In the first years following the transition to democracy in SA, the late former President Nelson Mandela established the Inter-Ministerial Committee on Young People at Risk as a means to transform the kinds of services rendered to children and youth (Coetzee, 2005; Jackson, 2014). A training programme was also established for service providers in several state departments, such as Social Development (DSD), Education, Justice and Health.

Subsequently, DSD developed a policy providing for Individual Development Plans (IDPs) that must be completed for each child who becomes caught up in the childcare system (Khoza, 2011). The IDP is structured according to the four quadrants of the CoC. Each child coming into the care system is comprehensively assessed according to the CoC. After the assessment information has been analysed for meaning, a care plan is then developed for the child or youth. The emergent care plan establishes the therapeutic strategies (with timelines) that will be implemented for the child. A six-month review is instituted to assess the progress of the child and the implementation and appropriateness of the programme (Khoza, 2011). Thus, the CoC is central to the provision of social services to children in South Africa.

Key service providers in child and youth work are social workers and child and youth care (CYC) workers. A unique programme, established through a partnership among DSD, Childline and the National Association of Child Care Workers (NACCW), is the *Isibindi* (isiZulu for 'courage') Circle of Courage Child and Youth Care Model (NACCW, 2015). This model was implemented as a community-based intervention programme for vulnerable children living in remote rural areas. The programme is implemented by CYC workers and community workers from local communities who have been appropriately trained (NACCW, 2015). Next, the use of the CoC is discussed in relation to the levels of assessment and intervention in social work.

14.5.1 Micro and mezzo practice

The CoC can be used with efficacy on both micro and mezzo levels, as the techniques and skills can be easily applied to both levels. If we look at Sipho (see Case study 1), the use of the CoC helped Sipho to uncover his strengths. Many young people are not aware of their own strengths until they are pointed out to them. An individual client or each group member within a group can be asked to complete the CoC, leading to them recognising their strengths.

For example, the social worker can use the CoC in the following way with Sipho (Frankowski & Duncan, 2013):

- Reflect his positives to conscientise him of all that is good and positive about him.
- Engage in a discussion about the different ways to increase his strengths.
- Use the strengths discussion as a gateway to discuss other challenging or difficult behaviours and ways of addressing these.

The social worker could just as easily have done this in a group with other young people like Sipho. In a group setting, each child could complete her or his own CoC. Each one could be asked if they would feel comfortable in sharing their CoCs with another group member or buddy. This could be an opportunity for others to affirm each group member's strengths. Group members may also recognise strengths that individuals have that the individuals do not recognise in themselves. Furthermore, through the group interactions over time, new strengths can be developed and recognised, where the information in the CoC can be used as building blocks for growth over the duration of the group sessions.

Yamagishi and Houtekamer (2005) caution that the CoC is not a quick fix to be completed in one sitting, but rather that it is a tool that should be added to over a significant period in the person's life. In the same way, when one is completing the tool, it would also be advisable to go around the circle in a purposeful way. It would therefore be useful to first find a child-centred setting when doing an assessment. For children, it can be very useful when they are assisted to name their feelings, to articulate them in a constructive manner, and to identify what strengths they have from which to draw resources that will help them to endure a difficult situation. For adults, the CoC is viewed from the perspective of the child that they remember being and then recalling significant incidences that they might have forgotten but that have a vital bearing on their present (Yamagishi & Houtekamer, 2005).

Figure 14.2 below is an example of a CoC assessment tool (Lee & Perales, 2007).

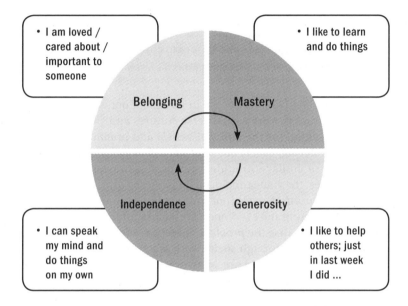

Figure 14.2: Assessment essentials
Sources: *Jackson* (2014); *Lee & Perales* (2007)

Figure 14.2 shows the kinds of statements that children can make to reflect their character-istics, traits or behaviour in each of the four quadrants. A child's positive socialisation during the formative years can be attributed to the assimilation of the values and principles in the CoC (Jackson, 2014). The social worker doing the assessment could add many more statements or questions that can reflect the essence of each quadrant. When there are gaps in the circle, the CoC can facilitate unique insight into and understanding of the child or youth's needs (Coetzee, 2005). This would set the stage for the creation of the child's own developmental plan. In mezzo level assessment, each group member can complete his or her own CoC and would be able to set goals for the group work sessions.

Positive outcomes of a child's social interactions are affected by the kinds (and quality) of relations and connections with other individuals and within her or his social environment. This is in keeping with the ecological theory of Urie Bronfenbrenner, because all the facets of a child's environment have an impact on how she or he will mature (Jackson, 2014). In the same way, colonialism has deeply eroded the once close-knit (*Ubuntu*) functioning of many communities, so much so that the kinds and quality of social relations mentioned above are few and far between.

Case Study 2 — **Mogamat**

Mogamat is a 16-year-old Muslim high school learner who is brought to the school social worker as he was found in possession of dagga (cannabis). He lives at home with his mother and younger siblings. His father has been in prison for the past six months. Mogamat has been trying to fulfil the fatherly role to his brothers. He is usually a good student, but he has failed all his subjects for the first semester and has become angry and aggressive with everyone at home and school, which was out of character as he now was often in trouble. (based on Frankowski & Duncan, 2013)

Reflective questions
- How could you use the CoC to assist Mogamat?
- Identify at least one of Mogamat's strengths in each quadrant. How would these be able to help Mogamat?
- How might it be useful to remember that Mogamat follows the Muslim faith?

Through their work with First Nations people in Canada, Poonwassie and Charter (2001) argue that if counsellors want to work with diverse cultures and groups, they must acquire knowledge and positive regard for the cultural beliefs and practices of others. This is an imperative for service rendering, as it is not necessary then for 'ethnic matching' of clients and social workers, because similar ethnic identities do not always eliminate potential value conflicts. For some cultures, the values and principles may be different to those practised by social workers, such as *non-interference* (not intervening without invitation or necessity), *non-competitiveness* (everything and everyone have equal standing), and *problem distancing* (using storytelling to contextualise the *problem,* thereby creating an emotional *distance*).

But how can one ensure that, through social work practice for example, attention is paid to the four quadrants of the CoC? Here are some examples of what practitioners can do in micro and mezzo work (Brendtro, 2009; Laursen, 2010):

1. **Belonging** – nurturing attachment
   > Create a therapeutic environment for positive encouragement for all to participate and share.
   > Foster social connectedness. Create a distinctive identity for the group (mezzo).
   > Recognise individuality. Each one is a person apart from the family or group. Learn to notice discerning features, characteristics and talents.
   > Focus on the deed and not the doer.

2. **Mastery** – developing achievement
   > Connect psychosocial growth and learning to the specific personal needs of each one (family or group).
   > Ensure that each client gets a turn to do something in a group or at the home.
   > Help the client to set realistic goals and ways to go about achieving these.
   > Help the client to solve and find appropriate solutions.
   > Celebrate achievements through awards, certificates or badges or other treats.

3. **Independence** – fostering autonomy
   > Help with decision-making processes, setting out possible consequences and risks.
   > Give choices for activities/social learning, so that each one can decide on his or her preferences.
   > Help with strategies for internal control and discipline.
   > Teach alternative behaviours in role-play activities.

> Help with personal responsibility/accountability.
> Allow the child/youth to face consequences (home/residential context).

4. **Generosity** – fostering altruism
   > Nurture co-operative interpersonal relationships (partnerships).
   > Cultivate good listening and communicating.
   > Encourage helping nature – options of helping and what can be done.

The above ideas represent a starting point of what practitioners can do or use to develop the four components of the CoC. The following strategies can also be considered in conjunction with the above for helping and healing (Poonwassie & Charter, 2001):

1. **Storytelling**. This is an effective and imaginative way of infusing cultural values and beliefs through narratives. It is one way of using the principle of non-interference, by using a narrative for others to gain insight into their difficulties without explicitly naming or discussing them. The opinions of all are elicited and encouraged, which reflect the principle of non-competitiveness. The storyteller uses imagery to ignite consciousness about each one's inner resources and power to be able to accept responsibility or find solutions.

2. **Teaching and sharing circles**. These groups could relate to mezzo intervention where they could provide a valuable setting for transformation and change. The groups also offer a sense of connectedness to one's culture and roots. In this particular group context, group members are not compelled to disclose personal challenges unless it emerges as a natural consequence of the group process. Additionally, the labels of expert are removed in keeping with the principle of non-interference and non-competitiveness as all have a place and knowledge and therefore all learn from one another. If, for example, the social worker is asked for an opinion, she or he may share her or his experiences but not give guidance and advice.

3. **Role modelling**. Role models fulfil important roles individually or in group context to show others different kinds of behaviour and responses in different circumstances so that the person onlooker can learn and benefit. Feedback is a vital part of role modelling for discussion and clarification to strengthen positive behaviour.

To fulfil professional obligations and the needs of indigenous people, it would be helpful for social workers to examine the crucial parts in the helping process and counselling relationship to enable decoloniality and empowering tasks (Poonwassie & Charter, 2001).

14.5.2 Macro practice

People's perspectives and opinions develop from their life experiences and endurance, which shape their political, social, spiritual and cultural viewpoints (Poonwassie & Charter, 2001). When oppressed people are not given opportunities for their voices and input to be heard, or when there is ignorance about the contexts of people that propagates racism and discrimination, then a situation arises of blaming the victim; Freire calls this a culture of silence (Sinclair, 2004). Raising awareness isn't enough if it is not accompanied by purposeful action, because socio-political will and legitimacy are not always embedded in awareness-raising (Sinclair, 2004). It is therefore imperative that social work and other helping professions take the necessary time to learn about the people with whom they will be engaging.

In macro interventions, social workers must become aware of the key role players in the tribe or clan, because it is through these role players that the social worker can gain access to the rest of the community. Social workers will also have to surrender their expert role and be prepared to suspend their own beliefs and accept the beliefs of others as being of equal value. For the sustainability of macro projects, it is vital that projects be created and implemented by community members themselves (Poonwassie & Charter, 2001).

How does the CoC relate to macro intervention? Samjee (2000) provides some useful ideas for youth engagement and participation in macro work by establishing peer counselling, coaching and mentoring programmes. Through her CYC work in Kimberley, she has become convinced that youth represent unused resources in helping other youth by tutoring, facilitating, coaching, modelling and supporting. In terms of the CoC, involving youth in appropriate training on interpersonal communication skills and helping and caring approaches will develop their own sense of belonging, mastery, independence and generosity (Samjee, 2000).

Petersen and Taylor (2009) offer two suggestions for whole-school interventions that social workers and youth workers will find useful, namely:

1. **Building a caring community**. This is still an appropriate means of fostering all four components in the CoC. They argue that participating and being involved in a project beyond themselves cultivate unique qualities in keeping with the CoC, for example, courage, persistence, skills, and altruism. Caring is a component of *Ubuntu* also and this value can be reignited and nurtured in young people. The *Isibindi* CoC project (referred to earlier) is also a worthy community-based programme to mention here.

2. **Empower citizens for democracy**. Helping young people to find their niche and their voice in situations that matter to them is a significant goal in itself. Leadership, communication, responsibility, and generosity are valuable qualities that can emerge from their participation and involvement in projects that develop equality and equity (social justice) for their communities.

Being given responsibilities that others find meaningful and valuable can have a significant positive impact on youth (Petersen & Taylor, 2009). In macro work, the generosity component is emphasised, as it is giving something you have or value to others. When we are willing to become involved and show our caring towards others in real and practical ways, this becomes a powerful endorsement of ourselves as worthy human beings and therein lies the true value in developing a generous nature (Petersen & Taylor, 2009).

> **Reflective questions**
> Think about your fieldwork placements that you have been assigned to as a social work student:
> • How do you think you would be able to use the CoC in your fieldwork placements in micro, mezzo, or macro work?
> • How do you think your fieldwork organisations could incorporate the CoC in their general work with children, families, and communities?

14.6 Conclusion

Culture and traditions may always challenge us to think outside of the box. By this is meant that culture and traditions make it imperative for professions and professionals to become flexible about the customs and beliefs of those whom we engage with and support in the carrying out of our professional duties. The Circle of Courage (CoC) has shown that there are ways of knowing and doing that fall outside of the boundaries of formal knowledge. The question then arises of how long we are going to ignore the role that culture and traditions play in the lives of people. The CoC is a philosophical and practice tool that is deeply rooted in tribal lore and spirituality, and to be able to use this tool, we must familiarise ourselves with the underlying philosophies and principles that go with it. If we do, then we will be connecting with people from different cultures and beliefs on a much deeper level. The CoC is a significant and positive tool in the assessment and intervention of children and youth, especially in the context of the decoloniality process in South Africa.

Chapter activity

1. **Reflective question**. Now that you have gone through this chapter on the CoC, what are the ways in which you are now able to help Sipho or Mogamat? How would you incorporate the principles of non-interference, non-competitiveness and problem distance?
2. **Personal context**. Consider your own cultural beliefs and values. What are the possible ways in which these would have impacted on your helping relationship and engagement with either Sipho or Mogamat?
3. **Advocacy**. Consider a social issue that you have become aware of in your community or in South Africa more broadly (e.g., gangsterism, community violence, fear). Using the CoC and a macro lens, how would you go about initiating advocacy with the participation of the people or community affected by your identified social issue?
4. **Critical question**. Think about the discrimination against and oppression of people who are different to you and whose lifestyles and beliefs are different. How do you think your knowledge of the CoC might be useful for knowledge building, empowerment and transformation?

References

Abdi, A. 2006. Eurocentric discourses and African philosophies and epistemologies of education: Counter-hegemonic analyses and response. *International Education*, 36(1):15–31.

Brendtro, L. 2009. *The Circle of Courage and RAP training: The evidence base*. Sioux Falls, South Dakota, US: Circle of Courage Institute at Starr Commonwealth.

Brendtro, L, Brokenleg, M & Van Bockern, S. 2005. The Circle of Courage and positive psychology. Editorial. *Reclaiming Children and Youth*, 14(3):130–136.

Brendtro, L, Brokenleg, M & Van Bockern, S. 2013. The Circle of Courage: Developing resilience and capacity in youth. *International Journal for Talent Development and Creativity*, 1(1):67–74.

Brendtro, L, Brokenleg, M & Van Bockern, S. 2014. Environments where children thrive: The Circle of Courage model. *Reclaiming Children and Youth*, 23(3):10–15.

Brendtro, M, Mitchell, M & Jackson, W. 2014. The Circle of Courage: Critical indicators for successful life outcomes. *Reclaiming Children and Youth*, 23(1):9–13.

Brokenleg, M. 1999. Native American perspectives on generosity. *Reclaiming Children and Youth*, 8(2):66–68.

Brown, K. 2005. *Understanding the Circle of Courage*. [Online]. Available: http://dib.sa.edu. au/mentmoodle/file.php/20/Understanding_the_Circle_of_Courage.pdf [Accessed 1 March 2018].

Coetzee, C. 2005. The Circle of Courage: Restorative approaches in SA schools. *Reclaiming Children and Youth*, 14(3):184–187.

Coughlan, F, & Welsh-Breetzke, A. 2002. The Circle of Courage and Erikson's psychosocial stages. *Reclaiming Children and Youth*, 10(4):222–226.

De Ridder, J. 2002. *The personality of the urban African in South Africa: A Thematic Apperception Test study*. London: Routledge.

Erikson, EH & Erikson JM. 1998. *The life cycle completed (extended version)*. New York: WW Norton & Company.

Frankowski, B & Duncan, P. 2013. Always searching for strengths: Interviewing and counselling with the Circle of Courage. *Reclaiming Children and Youth*, 21(4):32–36.

Gilgun, J. 2002. Completing the circle: American Indian medicine wheels and the promotion of resilience of children and youth in care. *Journal of Human Behavior in the Social Environment*, 6(2):65–84.

Jackson, W. 2014. *The Circle of Courage: Childhood socialization in the 21st century*. DPhil thesis. Wayne State University, Detroit, Michigan USA.

Khoza, S. 2011. *Application of a developmental assessment tool by social workers practicing foster care in the Far East Rand, Ekurhuleni*. MA mini-dissertation. University of Witswatersrand, South Africa.

Laursen, EK. 2010. *Focusing energy in schools and youth organizations: Attending to universal developmental needs*. Sandy, UT: Aardvark Global Publishing.

Lee, B & Perales, K. 2007. Circle of Courage: Reaching youth in residential care. *Residential Treatment for Children and Youth*, 22(4):1–16.

Lovesey, O. 2000. *Ngũgĩ wa Thiong'o*. New York: Twayne Publishers.

Maimela, M. 2009. *Combatting traditional practices harmful to girls: A consideration of legal and community-based practices*. LL.M. mini-dissertation. University of Pretoria, South Africa.

Makundi, l. 2009. *Harmful cultural practices as violations of girls' human rights: Female genital mutilation in Tanzania and South Africa*. LL.M. mini-dissertation in Comparative Child Law. North-West University, Potchefstroom, South Africa.

Martin, P & Mbambo, B. 2011. *An exploratory study on the interplay between African customary law and practices and children's protection rights in South Africa*. A study commissioned by Save the Children Sweden Southern Africa Regional Office. Pretoria, South Africa.

National Association of Child Care Workers (NACCW). 2015. Development of a service delivery model for community based professional child and youth care services. *Hands-On* issue 9 (NACCW) Learning Brief 53.

Oosthuizen, J. 2017. *Restoring the Circle of Courage in the lives of youth at risk through mentoring*. DPhil thesis. Faculty of Theology, Stellenbosch University, South Africa.

Petersen, J & Taylor, D. 2009. *Whole schooling and the Circle of Courage*. [Online]. Available: http://www.wholeschooling.net/WS/WSPress/WS%20&%20C%20of%20C.pdf [Accessed 21 February 2019].

Poonwassie, A & Charter, A. 2001. An Aboriginal worldview of helping: Empowering approaches. *Canadian Journal of Counselling*, 35(1):63–73.

Samjee, S. 2000. The Circle of Courage. *CYC-Online*, 15. [Online]. Available: https://www. cyc-net.org/cyc-online/cycol-0400-circle.html [Accessed 21 February 2019].

Sinclair, R. 2004. Aboriginal social work education in Canada: Decolonizing pedagogy for the seventh generation. *First Peoples Child & Family Review*, 1(1):49–61.

Sokol, J. 2009. Identity development throughout the lifetime: An examination of Eriksonian theory. *Graduate Journal of Counseling Psychology*, 1(2):139–148.

Yamagishi, R & Houtekamer, T. 2005. Assessment and goal setting with the Circle of Courage. *Reclaiming Children and Youth*, 14(3):160–163.

Annotated websites and activities

https://youtu.be/dclMi2Luq0o
This video is called *Facets and applications of the CoC: Discussions with two experts, Circle of Courage Institute president Larry Brendtro, Ph.D., and paediatrician Paula Duncan.* These experts discuss facets and applications of the Circle of Courage that form the basis of the Developmental Audit, a strength-based approach to assessing the emotional development of children.

https://youtu.be/MoOXcFZgzhI
The title of this video is *Solution tree: Reclaiming youth at risk* by Martin Brokenleg and Larry Brendtro. It explores the four needs every child has by using the Circle of Courage to summarise the approach to reclaiming youth at risk.

https://youtu.be/qj4CIL3LkBY
This video shows how the Edmonton Native Basketball Association (ENBA) used the game of basketball and the Circle of Courage programme to help young people to become more involved, engaged and resilient. The video showcases each component to illustrate how basketball can impact positively on the lives of youth.

https://youtu.be/6ieipo8-tpg
Youth at Lakeview Elementary School discover the Circle of Courage by making this cartoon using acting, animation and documentary.

Annotated websites and activities are also available on Learning Zone.

oxford.co.za/learningzone

Mapping the way forward in decolonising social work theory in South Africa

CHAPTER 15

Johannah Sekudu

15.1 Introduction

The chapters in this book have been developed by different authors with the aim of providing a new perspective on social work theory in South Africa. The authors used existing social work theories to show their application in the South African contexts, at the different levels of intervention. This is the first attempt by South African academics to apply their minds to developing local literature focused on social work theory, for students to be able to see how social work theories can be applied to local contexts.

The clarion call for the decolonisation of the curriculum by students and institutions of higher education challenges all social work practitioners and educators to get involved in developing indigenous literature that is relevant for the South African context. For years, social work has been taught and practised based on Western and Northern theories, as you have already learnt in Chapter 1. As a result, there is a need to focus on developing local theory that will be responsive to the needs of local clients. This process will still take some time, since we are still at the beginning of such a process. But, it would be beneficial to the profession and to indigenous communities if all practitioners could commit to this call.

15.2 Aspects to consider in mapping the way forward

There are several aspects that should be taken into consideration in mapping the way forward with developing indigenous social work theories that can contribute towards decolonial social work practice.

15.2.1 Decentring Global North theory

One of the key choices social workers can make is to decentre the theories that emerge from the Global North. This is not to say that these theories should be thrown away, but rather that these theories should not occupy the central and privileged space that they currently occupy. Ngũgĩ wa Thiong'o (1993) refers to this as 'moving the centre'. When we allow Global North theory (together with literature, skills, values, etc.) to be in the centre, we are, in effect, saying that the ideas that come from the North are truer, more valid and more important than ideas that come from the Global South. This is a continuation of colonialism. It is the subordination and inferiorisation of Global South ideas.

One way to decentre the Global North is to think of Northern knowledge as situated in its context, and in this way as 'indigenous' to the North (Brydon, 2011). Chakrabarty (2000), Mbembe (2011) and Ndlovu-Gatsheni (2018) refer to this as the 'provincialisation' of the Global North, that is, to think of the North as just a province of the globe. The challenge the world faces with Global North ideas is the assumption (often unconscious) that ideas (literature and theory) from the North are somehow 'true' – that they reflect what is universally true of the whole world. Thus, we treat them as 'world' knowledge. But, in fact, they emerged in particular times and places, in contexts, that are not universal. Provincialisation reminds us that Global North theory is just as much situated or context-bound or indigenous as theory from Africa, Latin America or Asia.

Thinking of Northern knowledge as provincial or indigenous can help us loosen the sense that Global North knowledge has priority or is more important or true than knowledge from elsewhere in the world. It places a question mark over that body of theory and frees us up to question, critique, change and even discard it. This process of being freed from Northern knowledge is a process of decoloniality.

The partner to the notion of provincialising the Global North is the notion of 'deprovincial-izing Africa' (Ndlovu-Gatsheni, 2018:3) or, as Mabin (2013:6) expresses it, the 'worlding' of the South. A decolonial project thus involves embracing the idea 'that the north-south axis of power can be inverted – that northern hegemonies intellectually may be challenged – that Europe may be provincialised (Chakrabarty), Africa may be worlded (Mbembe)' (Mabin, 2013:6).

Thinking of Africa (and the Global South) as (part of) the world, rather than as a province, enables our own knowledge to take on a new level of stature and truthfulness. And this, in turn, enables us to embrace that knowledge as of at least equal importance to the Global North knowledge. Indeed, we would argue that African knowledge is truer and more important than Northern knowledge, since it is knowledge that emerged in our own contexts. Ndlovu-Gatsheni (2018:2) writes:

> Africans always had their own valid, legitimate and useful knowledge systems and education systems. This is the decolonial tale at the centre of this book.

Thus, African knowledge takes centre place, and knowledge from the Global North takes a subordinate or peripheral position.

In formal terms, Ndlovu-Gatsheni (2018:4) explains the project as follows:

> The process of ... 'deprovincializing Africa' [is] an intellectual and academic process of centring of Africa as a legitimate historical unit of analysis and epistemic site from which to interpret the world while at the same time globalizing knowledge from Africa. Such a move constitutes epistemic freedom as that essential prerequisite for political, cultural, economic and other freedoms.

Ndlovu-Gatsheni (2018:3) terms this 'epistemic freedom [which] is fundamentally about the right to think, theorize, interpret the world, develop own methodologies and write from where one is located and unencumbered by Eurocentrism'.

15.2.2 Doing research on indigenous African practices

As we have been and still are using social work theories from the Global North, the social work fraternity is now faced with the challenge of ensuring that its practice is based on the realities of their clients. Social work educators and practitioners must make an effort to engage in research on indigenous practices with the aim of using their findings to develop social work theories that are relevant to the local context. By engaging in research, social work practitioners and educators should use their knowledge and skills to engage communities to explore indigenous practices and knowledge. It is important to always bear in mind that indigenous people have always been able to address the challenges that they were facing in their lives. This challenges the social work researchers to explore these practices so that intervention methods and theories used are responsive to the actual needs of indigenous peoples. Communities have rich narratives to share with researchers, and this information can enrich the process of developing indigenous social work theories. Theories based on indigenous knowledge and practices will be more acceptable to communities in Africa and more responsive to their indigenous needs.

Prior to colonisation, people were living productive lives, based on traditional practices that were not recorded in writing. As a result, we know little about these practices. This challenges social work educators and practitioners to engage in research projects that will uncover these original practices that were used to maintain the collectiveness of the communities. It will be particularly useful to identify traditional practices that are still in use today. Having found out what these practices were and are, it will be possible to develop local theories that are responsive to the current needs of local people. It is common knowledge that South Africa is currently faced with numerous social ills that social workers are expected to address. I believe that these social ills cannot be understood and addressed using a foreign knowledge base and foreign social work theories. We need to engage seriously in research that would empower us to address these social ills appropriately.

Partnerships and teamwork among social work educators, social work practitioners and communities are needed to identify researchable topics that are geared towards discovering indigenous practices amongst communities. After determining these topics, there is a need to engage in participatory action research, where community members take a lead in directing the research process based on the scientific knowledge from social work educators and practitioners. For example, traditionally, when a child with disabilities was born into a family, there were some practices that the family/clan implemented to deal effectively with the challenges accompanying the child's disability. It is these kinds of practices that need to be unearthed through research, so that theories can be developed that talk to the needs of local communities, without disregarding what they have always used and found to be effective in their lives.

15.2.3 Developing African values and techniques

Social work is a profession that is based on professional values developed in the Global North. African social workers have, for the most part, uncritically adopted these principles and values as they are. It has been evident throughout the years that not all the social work values from the Global North are directly applicable to indigenous cultural situations in Africa.

The worldview of African people needs to be taken into consideration. Social workers need to learn why things are done the way they are done in local communities, as well as the meanings or values that are attached to those practices. As you have already learned in Chapter 6 of this book, *Ubuntu* is a value of African origin that seems to have been eroded by colonisation. The fact that this value has been abandoned is evidenced in many of the social ills that we see in our country such as violence against women and children, crime, and family fragmentation. In a society where a value like *Ubuntu* is upheld, these social ills would not be heard of, because people would be living in harmony and mutual respect, sharing their belongings to ensure that every community member is well cared for. Poverty has been part of community existence, but community members were able and prepared to always care for one another, because the value of *Ubuntu* was cherished by all community members.

This challenges social work educators and practitioners to make efforts to uncover the indigenous values that have been used by indigenous communities to keep the members together as one. Uncovering these values by using scientific methods could lead to the development of local professional values that could be applicable and acceptable to the local communities. Unpacking *Ubuntu* as a value, and examining how it used to enhance cohesion amongst community members, could assist social work practitioners and educators to develop more values that could be used to deal with current social ills. By developing respect for one another as a value based on *Ubuntu*, where each community member interacts with others in a manner of mutual existence, social ills that are breaking the society into pieces could be addressed effectively.

Some of the techniques used in social work do not resonate well with indigenous practices. For example, maintaining eye contact with another person is seen as a sign of disrespect in most African cultures, whereas from a Global North perspective this is seen as a technique that helps the social worker to communicate her or his interest in the client. We have a task to uncover why eye contact came to be seen as a sign of disrespect amongst indigenous African communities, and then work together with the communities as a whole to develop techniques that will not be offensive to members of these communities.

15.2.4 Theorising change processes

It cannot be denied that we are living in an ever-changing society. Within as few as 10 years, things can change significantly. This requires social workers to be conscious of these developments and how they impact the lives of people. Again, it must be taken into consideration that as much as colonisation has disturbed many processes in the lives of indigenous African people, it has also led to technological changes that can make life easier. As much as we should embrace such change as an inevitable reality, we also have to take control of how these changes affect our service delivery to clients in order to help people adapt to these societal changes.

We need to engage our clients to learn from them what has been working for them and use these positive aspects to develop theories that are relevant to the changes that we do not have control over, for the benefit of our clients and the profession at large.

For instance, amongst African indigenous communities there were old ladies who played the role of midwives, as there were no health facilities within reach. These midwives were trusted and respected by all community members. Generally, people adhered to whatever instructions they gave without question, and this contributed to the harmony that existed within communities. They also took responsibility for keeping the family together while the mother was still recuperating from the trauma of childbirth. With technological changes that brought about health-care facilities in these communities, we see the fibre that made communities to live in harmony being disturbed. Insofar as these technological changes brought about hope and improved maternal and infant health outcomes, they have also brought about disturbance in families. When a woman gives birth, she has to go to the nearest clinic or hospital, and sometimes has to leave her family without any adult person to take care of them. The older midwives no longer have a place within the communities, resulting in them not enjoying the same respect that they used to enjoy. All these aspects must be taken into consideration when interacting with families in such a situation. Exploring how family life has been disturbed by new developments is important to social workers in order for them to understand and assist families to adjust to these unavoidable changes.

15.2.5 Developing African approaches to macro change

Community development is one of the cornerstones of decolonial social work practice, aimed at ensuring that communities are empowered to deal with their challenges in an acceptable manner. Since the success of community development is determined by the way the practitioner negotiates entry into such a community, this phase of community practice should be done carefully. The community developer must ensure that she or he learns about the community, so that acceptable ways are employed in gaining entry and co-operation from community leaders and members. For us to ultimately decolonise community development practices, we need to learn from community leaders and members how they have tackled issues in the past and use this knowledge to develop relevant approaches that are based on local practices.

We have seen community projects that were implemented without the engagement of community members. For example, the government would decide to develop a food garden in a community that is poverty-stricken, without engaging the community. As a result, it was difficult for the community to own the project and put their energy into making it a success, and such projects died before anybody could benefit from them. Engaging community members in exploring and thinking about the challenges that they are facing, in giving them an opportunity to prioritise the challenges and deciding which one to tackle first, is the approach that could ensure that challenges are effectively addressed. Community projects that are owned by the community members go a long way and are in most cases successful, because when the time comes for the community developer to withdraw, community members can continue to sustain the project. This becomes possible when, during the community work process, the community developer shares her or his professional knowledge and skills with community members, empowering them to continue with the project. This way of approaching community development enables the community members to address future challenges without the intervention of the community developer because they have learnt knowledge and skills.

It would also be important for social workers to explore the income-generating schemes that indigenous community members have employed over generations to ensure that their families survive. For example, indigenous people used to establish 'stokvels' as a means of helping one another financially. With this scheme, several people would club together, and with their meagre income, they would agree to put an amount of money together and give it to one of the 'stokvel' members. This would continue until all the members have obtained their chance to get the money. This could be monthly or fortnightly, depending on the availability of their income. This way of operating kept the members of the community together, sharing what they had and ensuring that they all enjoy life together in harmony. Social workers could use some of the practices that are compatible with the ever-changing technology to learn from the communities what would work best for them. We should always remember that community needs in the Global North are very different from the needs of communities in Africa. This challenges community developers to learn and develop approaches that will be relevant to local contexts.

15.2.6 Developing skills of researchers, theorists and authors

You have seen in Chapter 1 of this book that South Africa, compared to the Global North, has not done well in developing social work literature. This could be because of a lack of knowledge and skills in research and writing, due to the past ways of doing things, where there was an unequal distribution of resources amongst the racial groups in the country. In general, white people had opportunities to access quality education, while black people did not. This led to many white people advancing in research and writing skills while black people were left behind. Most of the social work literature of South African origin is produced by white people, leading to the continued marginalisation of black voices.

This can and must now change, as we (as black people) now have opportunities, though not yet equal, to gain access to knowledge and skills. Focus must be put on inculcating the inner hunger in young academics to strive to excel in research and to develop local literature. The past must be used to accelerate the process of engaging everyone in developing local literature. As you use this book to learn about social work theories, challenge yourself as well to contribute to the development of local social work theory and other literature.

Institutions of higher learning have programmes that support emerging academics to enhance their research and writing skills. If these opportunities could be fully utilised, we would have a considerable number of authors and researchers, leading to an expanded body of local social work literature that is relevant to South African clients.

The responsibility of producing local literature does not fall only on social work educators and researchers. Social work practitioners also have a responsibility in this regard, specifically because they are the foot soldiers who interact daily with communities. This gives them the advantage of learning more from communities at grassroots level and then using the indigenous information learnt from such communities to develop local literature. Social work practitioners could use this opportunity to engage in research projects in partnership with academics or in pursuing their postgraduate qualifications. Such findings could then be used to produce local literature that is authentic and responsive to the actual needs of indigenous communities.

15.3 Conclusion

This chapter gave you some pointers on how social work educators and practitioners, together with local communities, could form partnerships to develop local social work theories that are responsive to the indigenous needs of communities in South Africa. It is a challenge to all social workers not to rely on the Global North community to develop social work theories for us, but to actively engage in the development of local theories. Empowering emerging and aspiring social work academics could yield better results in developing indigenous theories.

References

Brydon, K. 2011. Promoting diversity or confirming hegemony? In search of new insights for social work. *International Social Work*, 55(2):155–167.

Chakrabarty, D. 2000. *Provincializing Europe: Postcolonial thought and historical difference.* Princeton, NJ: Princeton University Press.

Mabin, A. 2013. *Debating 'southern theory' and cities of the south (and the north) of the world: Conception problems, issues of method and empirical research.* Wits Institute for Social and Economic Research (WISER). Johannesburg, RSA: WISER, University of the Witwatersrand.

Mbembe, AJ. 2011. Provincializing France? *Public Culture,* 23(1):85–119.

Ndlovu-Gatsheni, SJ. 2018. *Epistemic freedom in Africa: Deprovincialization and decolonization.* London: Routledge.

Ngũgĩ wa Thiong'o. 1993. *Moving the centre: The struggle for cultural freedoms.* London: James Currey.

Index

Page numbers in *italics* indicate diagrams

A

adaptation 92
advanced communication skills 213–217
advanced empathy 214–215
African feminisms 162–163
Africana womanisms 163–164
anxious-ambivalent attachment 145–146
appreciative inquiry, 4D methodology 249
asset-based community development
    appreciative inquiry 248–250
    decolonial social work practice, contribution 252–253
    methods 246–248
    sustainable livelihoods 250–251
    see also narrative therapy; strengths-based practices
attachment in the making 143
attachment theory
    application in social work practice 149–154
    for decolonial practice 147–149
    introduction 141
    macro level intervention 154
    micro level intervention 150–154
    overview 142–147
    role of attachment 143–144
    stages of attachment 142–143
    styles of attachment 144–147

B

basic communication skills 213
belonging 266–267, 274
biopsychosocial-spiritual approach 233–235
boundaries 93
building a caring community 276

C

case studies
    Circle of Courage 262, 274

connecting experiences to the self 215
cultural mindsets 37
decolonising the her-story of feminism 159
deconstructing psychoanalysis 9
disrupted attachments 140
domestic violence 157
experience of disrupted attachments 140
family systems theory 4–5
feminist theory 4
how words construct reality 67
humanity of all peoples 39–40
identifying how self is threatened 214
indigenous theory, constructing 13
link between experiences and perception 205
listening for themes in a person's narrative 215
narrative therapy used to reclaim cultural identity 257–258
nonverbal distortions, exploring 216
orphans and vulnerable children 120
parenting, constructionist approach 80–81
person-centred approach 198
promoting humanness 40
religious beliefs 222
resilience 47, 120
social environments of Maluta 86
sustainable livelihoods and community 178
theory needed to inform social work practice 1
thinking about oppression 34
thinking about theory 77–78
traditional knowledge, reclaiming 38
Ubuntu 5–6, 105
underlying assumptions of theories 10
using AI with community groups 250

using AI with community organisations 250
verbal distortions, exploring 216
working from a deficit perspective 243
change through dialogue, participation and collective action 41
Circle of Courage
    in decolonial practice 270
    embedded theoretical frameworks 265–266
    and Erikson's psychosocial theory 265
    four quadrants 266–269
    introduction 263
    macro practice 275–276
    micro and mezzo practice 272–275
    origins and foundations 263–266
    philosophical base 264–265
    and resilience theory 265–266
    social work use 271–276
    the South African child: Status and care 270–271
    in the South African context 269–271
    and systems theory 266
coloniality 24–25
    and social work 31–34
colonisation 24
    of Africa 27–28
    historical background 26–28
    of the person, process 29–30
    of the rest of the world 28
colony 23
community economic development 248
confidentiality 210–211
congruency 207
coping 92
core conditions for facilitation of person-centred approach 206–208
critical consciousness and conscientisation 34–36

D

decolonial person-centred
practice 218–219
decolonial social work practice
feminisms 165
narrative therapy 256–257
relevance of *Ubuntu* 113–117
sustainable livelihoods
193–194
decoloniality
change through dialogue,
participation and collective
action 41
critical consciousness and
conscientisation 34–36
facilitating as an action-reflection process 41–42
knowledge, reconstructing 38
power and hierarchies,
reconstructing 36–37
as process of creating a
humanity 39–41
reconstructing the self 38–39
summary of premises 34–42
wholeness thinking requirement 41
decoloniality in social work
definitions of terms 23–26
historical background to
colonisation 26–28
introduction 21–23
decolonisation 26
historical process 30–31
decolonising, and theory of social
work 10–11
decolonising social work theory in
SA, mapping the way forward
African values and techniques,
developing 282–283
change processes, theorising
283–284
developing skills of
researchers, theorists and
authors 285
Global North theory,
decentring 280–281
indigenous African practices,
doing research on 281–282
introduction 280–285
macro change, developing
African approaches 284
Ubuntu 282–283
Department for International
Development (DFID) 179–195
developmental social work 13–14

context for 48–50
definitions 50–52
features of 56–60
human rights and human
development, promotion
56–57
introduction 48
micro and macro practice,
integration 58–59
partnerships, collaborating in
59–60
people participation,
facilitation 59
relevance for decolonial social
work 60–62
social and economic
development, integration
57–58
and sustainable development
53–56
differentiation 94
disorganised or disordered type of
attachment 146–147
distortions or discrepancies,
exploring 215–217
domestic violence 157

E

ecological system levels 95–97
ecosystems theory
for decolonial social work
practice 100–101
historical background and
overview 88–90
introduction 87–88
key concepts 90–93
in social work practice 98–99
embedded theoretical frameworks
265–266
empathy 208
empowering citizens for
democracy 276
ending the facilitation process 213
energy 91
entropy 94
equifinality 95
exosystems 97

F

facilitating as an action-reflection
process 41–42
family systems theory 4–5
feminisms
African 162–163
Africana womanisms 163–164

commonalities among feminist
strands 171–173
decolonial social work practice
165
introduction 158
liberal 165–166
Nego-feminism 164
pre-, post-, anti- and de-colonial feminisms 161–165
radical 169–171
socialist and Marxist 167–169
strands of 159–160
feminist strands, commonalities
171–173
feminist theory 4
financial capital 190
frameworks for sustainable
livelihoods 187–193

G

general systems theory, key
concepts 93–95
generosity 269, 275
genuineness 207
grounded theory 12

H

historical background to
colonisation 26–28
homeostasis 94
human capital 188–189
human rights and human
development, promotion
56–57

I

immediacy 217
independence 268–269, 274–275
indigenous theory, constructing
11–14, 13
individualisation 209
insecure attachment 145–146
interdependence 92–93
interface 92

K

knowledge, reconstructing 38

L

liberal feminism 165–166
livelihood assets 188–190
livelihood outcomes 192–193
livelihood strategies 191–192

M

macro assessment and intervention 235–236

macro level intervention 154

macro practice, Circle of Courage 275–276

macrosystems 97

Marxist and socialist feminisms 167–169

mastery 267–268, 274

mesosystems 96–97

micro and macro practice, integration 58–59

micro level intervention 150–154

microsystems 96

N

narrative practice 253–255

narrative therapy
   for decolonial social work practice 256–257
   narrative practice 253–255
   solution-focused brief therapy 255–256

natural capital 189

negative entropy 95

Nego-feminism 164

O

overview of this book 14–16

P

participatory approaches 248

people participation, facilitation 59

person-centred approach
   communication skills 213–218
   core conditions for facilitation 206–208
   decolonial practice 218–219
   facilitation 211–213
   historical background 199–200
   introduction 199
   Rogers' 19 propositions 201–206
   values inherent 208–211

physical capital 189–190

poverty, development and sustainable livelihoods 180–182

power and hierarchies, reconstructing 36–37

principles and values that guide *Ubuntu* 110–113

professional identity and self-awareness in spirituality and religion 236–237

psychoanalysis, deconstructing 9

R

radical feminisms 169–171

reciprocal relationship 143

reconstructing the self 38–39, 212

religion
   defining 225–227
   sectarian origins 227–228
   secularisation and professionalism 228–229

resilience theory
   adversity 125
   conceptual building blocks 124–127
   definitions 127–130
   ecological approach 132–134
   individualised approach 130–131
   introduction 121
   outcomes 126
   pathogenic approach 121–122
   person-in-environment framework *134*
   protective factors 126–127
   relevance for decolonial social work 134–136
   salutogenic approach 122–124

respect 209

Rogers' 19 propositions 201–206

role modelling 275

S

safe place for facilitation, creating 211–212

sectarian origins and religion 227–228

secularisation and professionalism 228–229

securely attached infants 145

self-awareness and professional identity 236–237

self-determination 209–210

social and economic development, integration 57–58

social capital 189, 247–248

social constructionism
   applying 78–81
   assumptions about people 76–78
   constructivism and social constructionism 71–72

dialogue 79–80

epistemology 68–72

examples 74–75

ideas about the self 76

importance of the relationship 79

introduction 68

language and meaning making 77–78

people or the system closed to information 76–77

positivistic thinking 70–71

realities constructed collectively 77

relevance for decolonised social work 81

religious beliefs as examples 74

trauma as example 75

view of change 78

waste pickers example 74

what it is 72–73

social environment 91

social work with communities, using *Ubuntu* 116

social work with individuals, using *Ubuntu* 114–116

socialist and Marxist feminisms 167–169

solution-focused brief therapy 255–256

spirituality, defining 224–225

spirituality and religion
   biopsychosocial-spiritual approach 233–235
   and decoloniality 230–231
   defining 223–227
   helping process, starting 231–233
   history in social work 227–230
   introduction 223
   macro assessment and intervention 235–236
   resurgence of interest in social work 230
   self-awareness and professional identity 236–237
   spiritual assessment and intervention 231–233

stages of attachment 142–143

storytelling 275

strands of feminisms 159–160

strengths perspective 244–246

strengths-based practices
   introduction 244
   strengths perspective 244–246

290

see also asset-based community development
styles of attachment 144–147
subsystems 93–94
sustainable development, and developmental social work 53–56
sustainable livelihoods
asset-based community development 250–251
definitions 182–186
frameworks 187–193
introduction 179–180
livelihood assets 188–190
livelihood outcomes 192–193
livelihood strategies 191–192
poverty and development 180–182
relevance for decolonial social practice 193–194
structures and processes, transforming 191
vulnerability context 191

T
teaching and sharing circles 275
theory of social work
decolonising 10–11
deconstructing 8–10
definition of terms 7–8
developmental social work 13–14
eclectic use of 6–7
grounded theory 12
indigenous theory, constructing 11–14
introduction 2–3
needed to inform social work practice 1
relevance for social work 3–6
Ubuntu-based practice 14
traditional knowledge, reclaiming 38
transactions 91
true attachment 143

U
Ubuntu 282–283
as foundation for practical mutual existence 109–110
introduction 106
meaning 107–113
origin 106–107
principles and values 110–113

relevance for decolonial social work practice 113–117
using in social work with communities 116
using in social work with individuals 114–116
Ubuntu-based practice, and theory of social work 14
unconditional positive regard 207
underlying assumptions of theories 10
unsymbolised experiences 212

V
values inherent in person-centred approach 208–211
vulnerability context of sustainable livelihoods 191

W
wholeness thinking requirement 41